SLEEPY PRINCESS IN THE DEMON CASTLE

1

Story & Art by
KAGIJI KUMANOMATA

NIGHTS

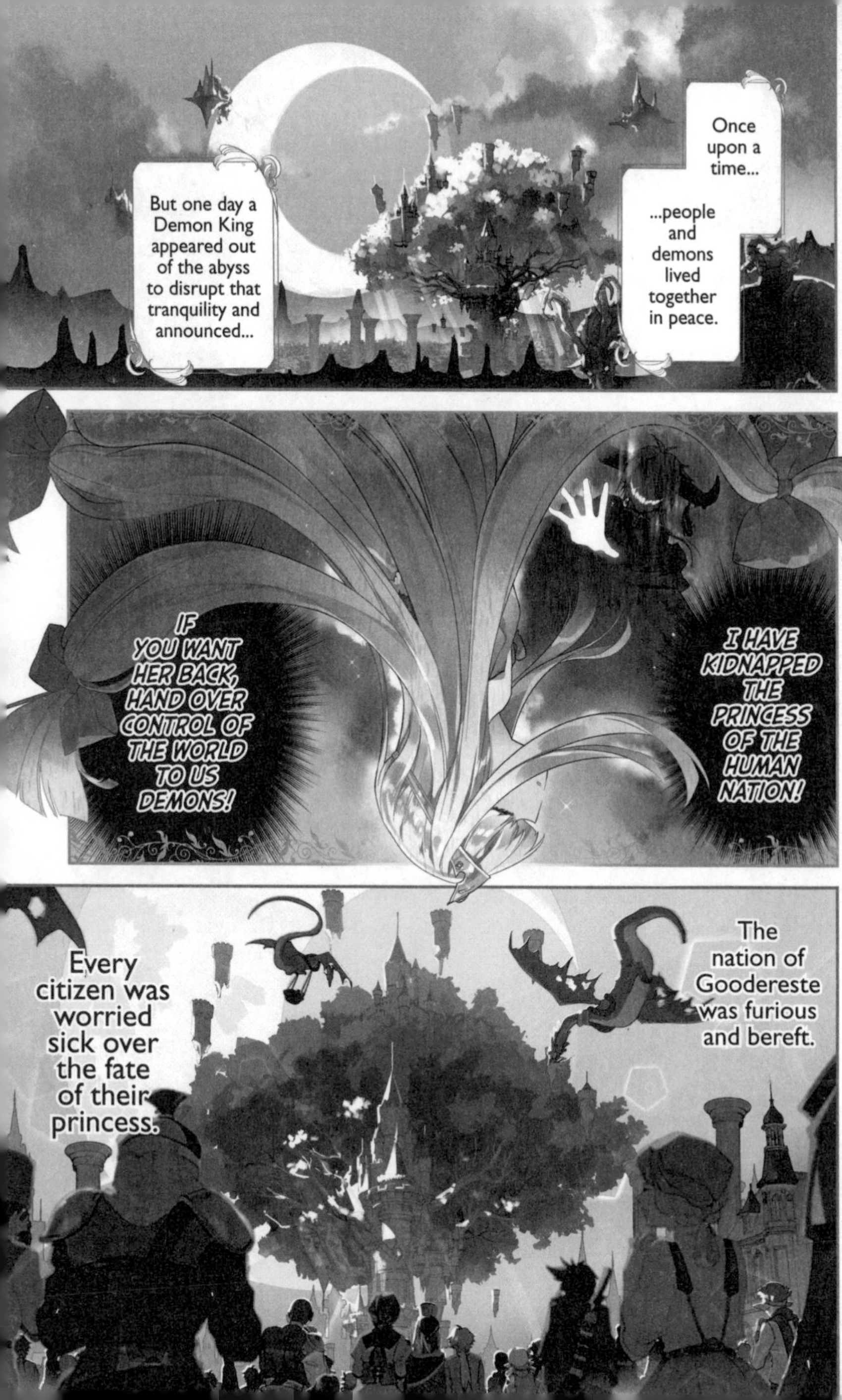
Once upon a time...
...people and demons lived together in peace.
But one day a Demon King appeared out of the abyss to disrupt that tranquility and announced...
I HAVE KIDNAPPED THE PRINCESS OF THE HUMAN NATION!
IF YOU WANT HER BACK, HAND OVER CONTROL OF THE WORLD TO US DEMONS!
The nation of Goodereste was furious and bereft.
Every citizen was worried sick over the fate of their princess.

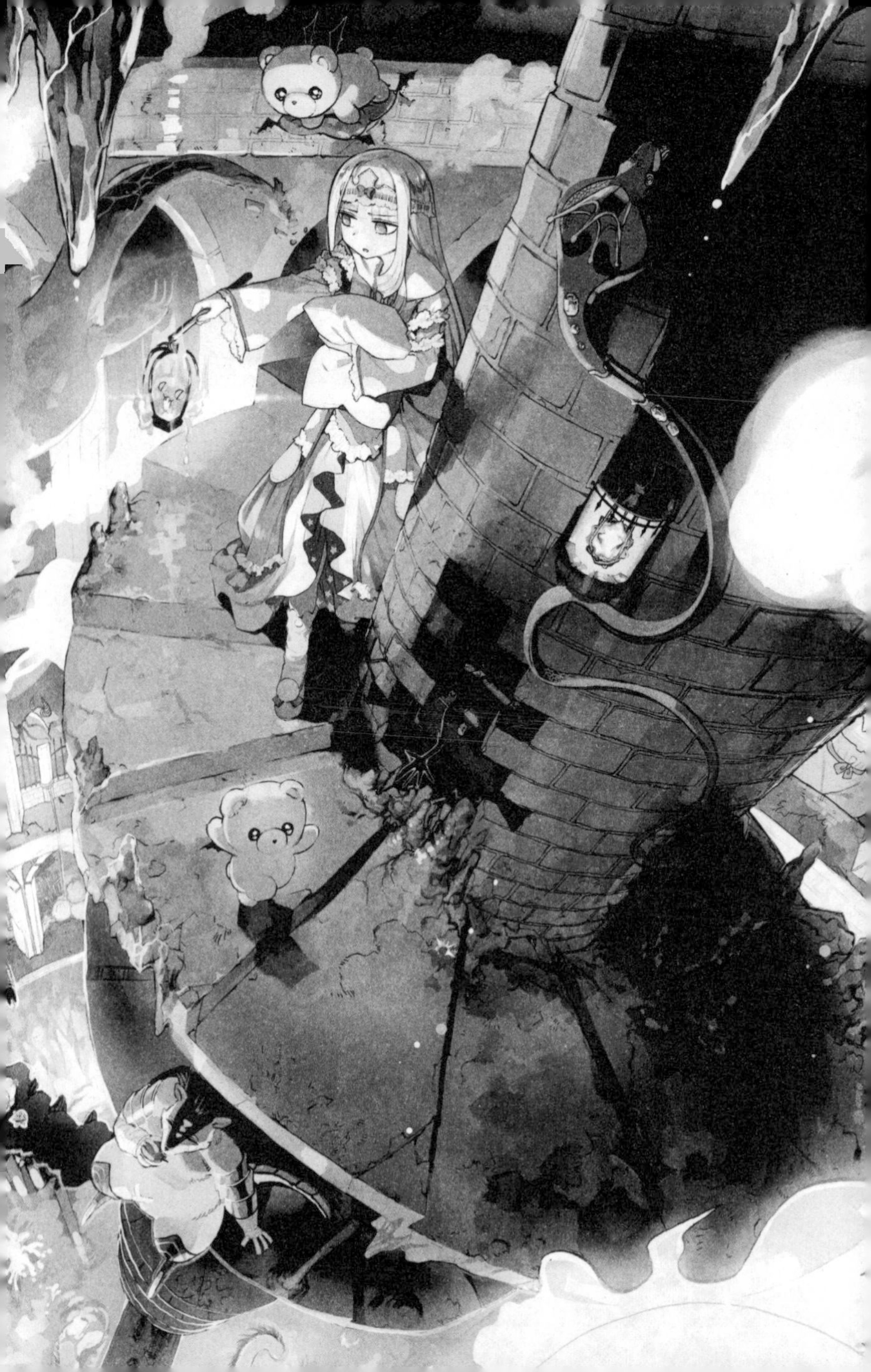

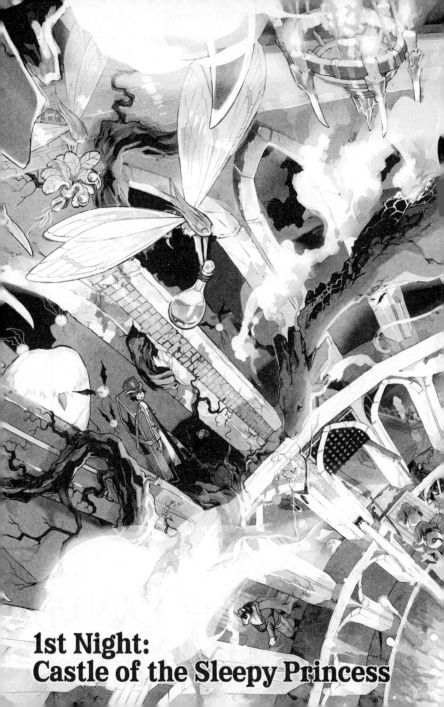

1st Night:
Castle of the Sleepy Princess

SLEEPY PRINCESS IN THE DEMON CASTLE

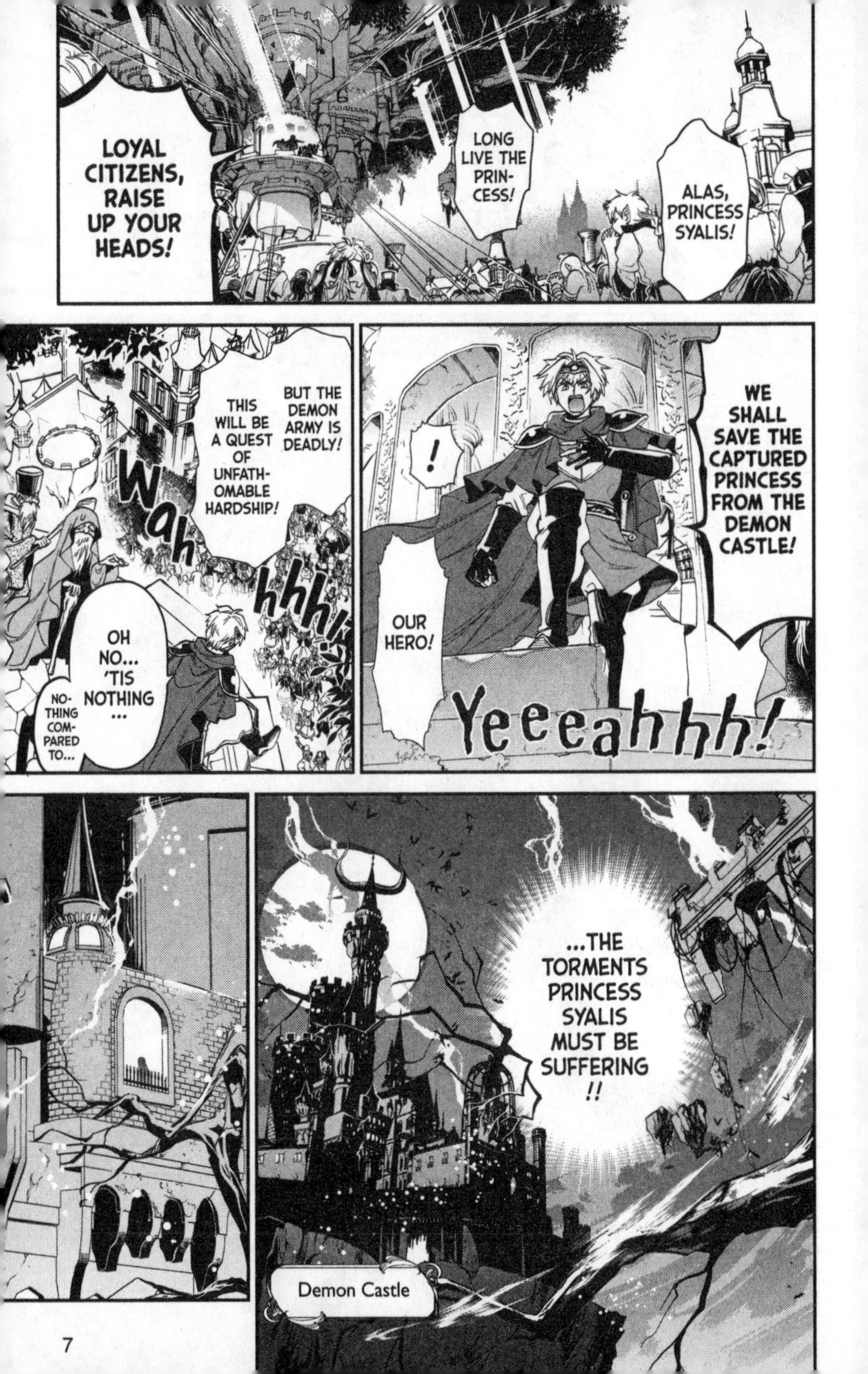
ALAS, PRINCESS SYALIS!
LONG LIVE THE PRINCESS!
LOYAL CITIZENS, RAISE UP YOUR HEADS!
WE SHALL SAVE THE CAPTURED PRINCESS FROM THE DEMON CASTLE!
!
OUR HERO!
Yeeeahhh!
BUT THE DEMON ARMY IS DEADLY!
THIS WILL BE A QUEST OF UNFATHOMABLE HARDSHIP!
Wahhhh!
OH NO... 'TIS NOTHING...
NOTHING COMPARED TO...
...THE TORMENTS PRINCESS SYALIS MUST BE SUFFERING!!
Demon Castle

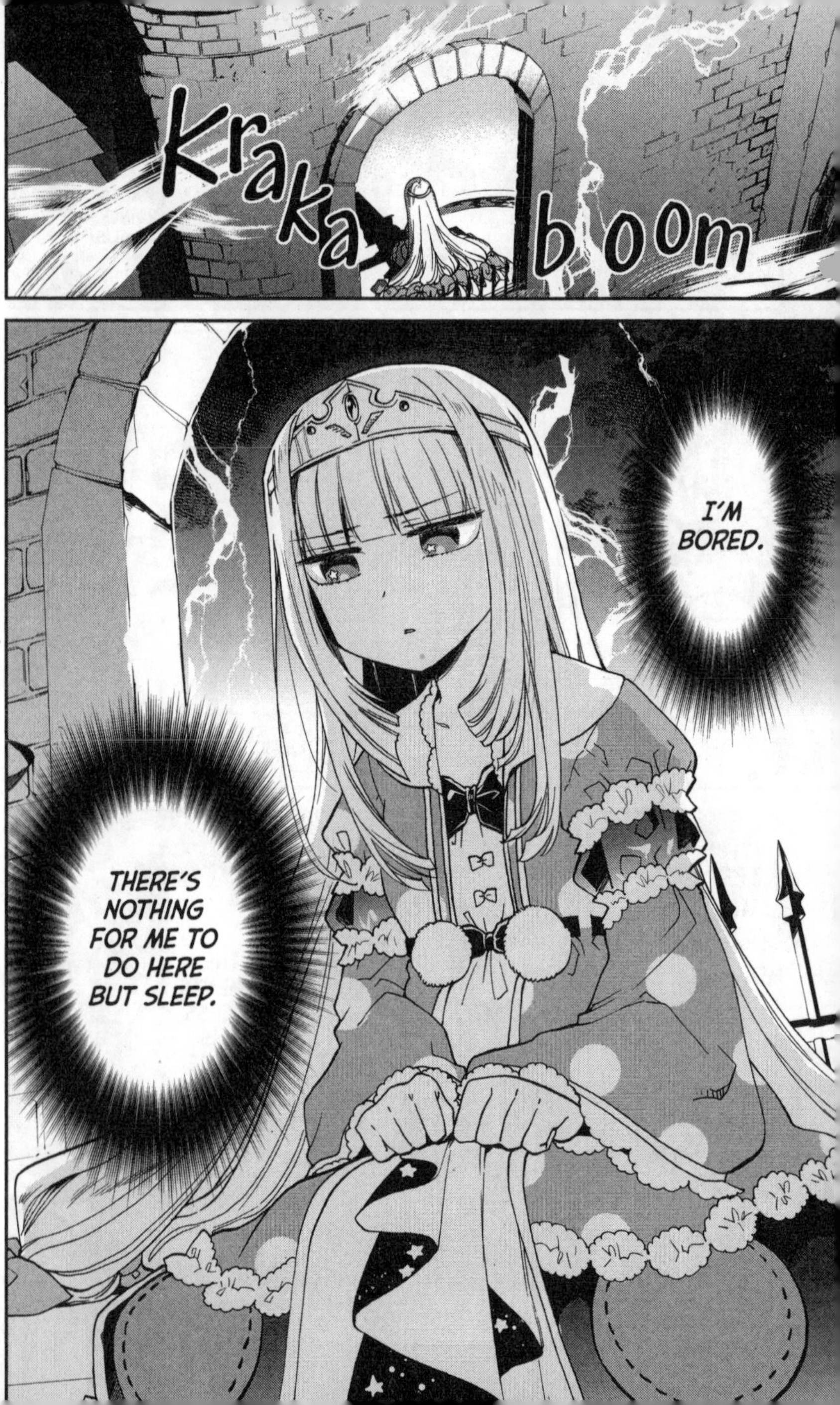
Krakaboom
I'M BORED.
THERE'S NOTHING FOR ME TO DO HERE BUT SLEEP.

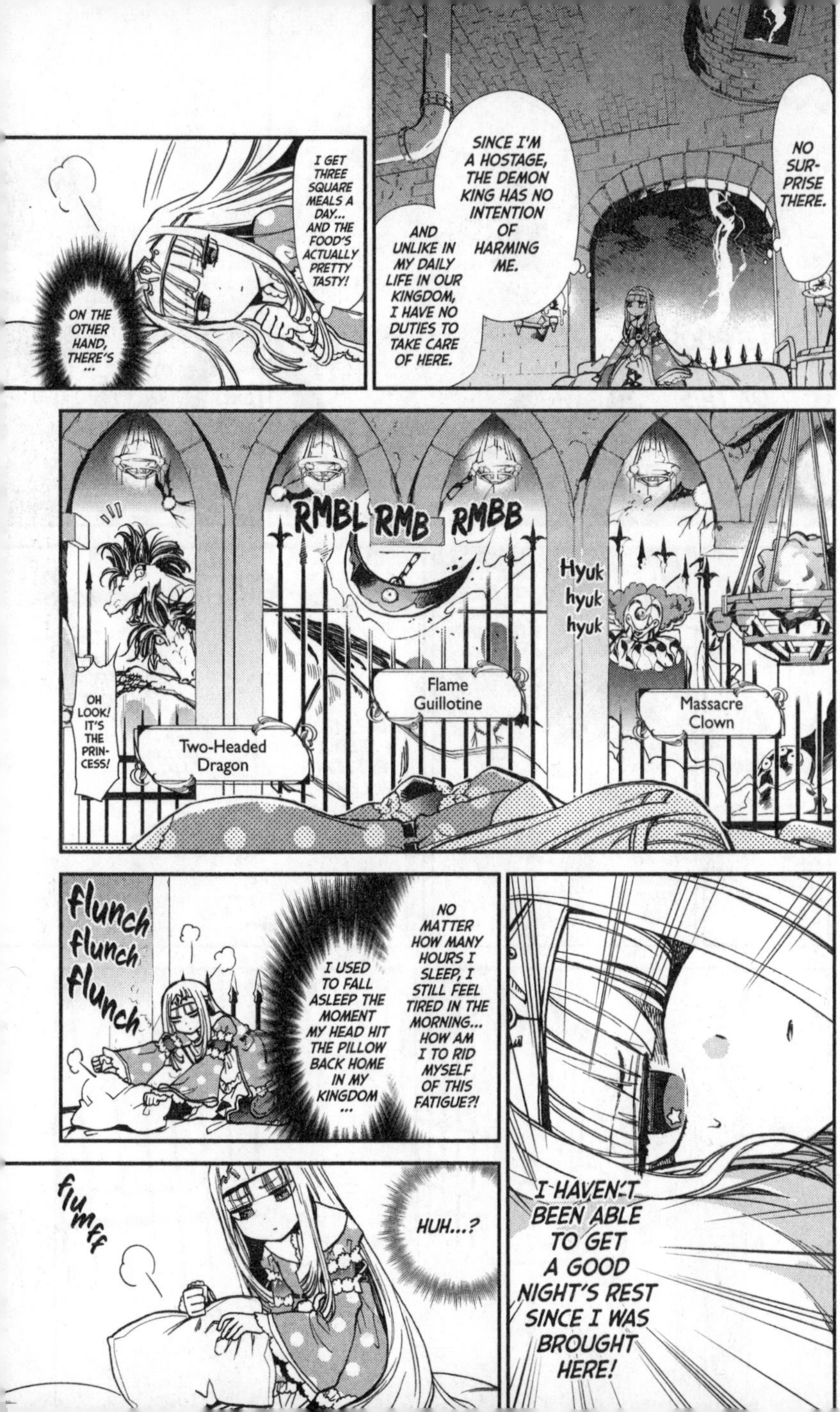
NO SURPRISE THERE.
SINCE I'M A HOSTAGE, THE DEMON KING HAS NO INTENTION OF HARMING ME.
AND UNLIKE IN MY DAILY LIFE IN OUR KINGDOM, I HAVE NO DUTIES TO TAKE CARE OF HERE.
I GET THREE SQUARE MEALS A DAY... AND THE FOOD'S ACTUALLY PRETTY TASTY!
ON THE OTHER HAND, THERE'S ...
RMBL RMB RMBB
Hyuk hyuk hyuk
Massacre Clown
Flame Guillotine
Two-Headed Dragon
OH LOOK! IT'S THE PRINCESS!
I HAVEN'T BEEN ABLE TO GET A GOOD NIGHT'S REST SINCE I WAS BROUGHT HERE!
NO MATTER HOW MANY HOURS I SLEEP, I STILL FEEL TIRED IN THE MORNING... HOW AM I TO RID MYSELF OF THIS FATIGUE?!
I USED TO FALL ASLEEP THE MOMENT MY HEAD HIT THE PILLOW BACK HOME IN MY KINGDOM ...
flunch flunch flunch
HUH...?
flumff

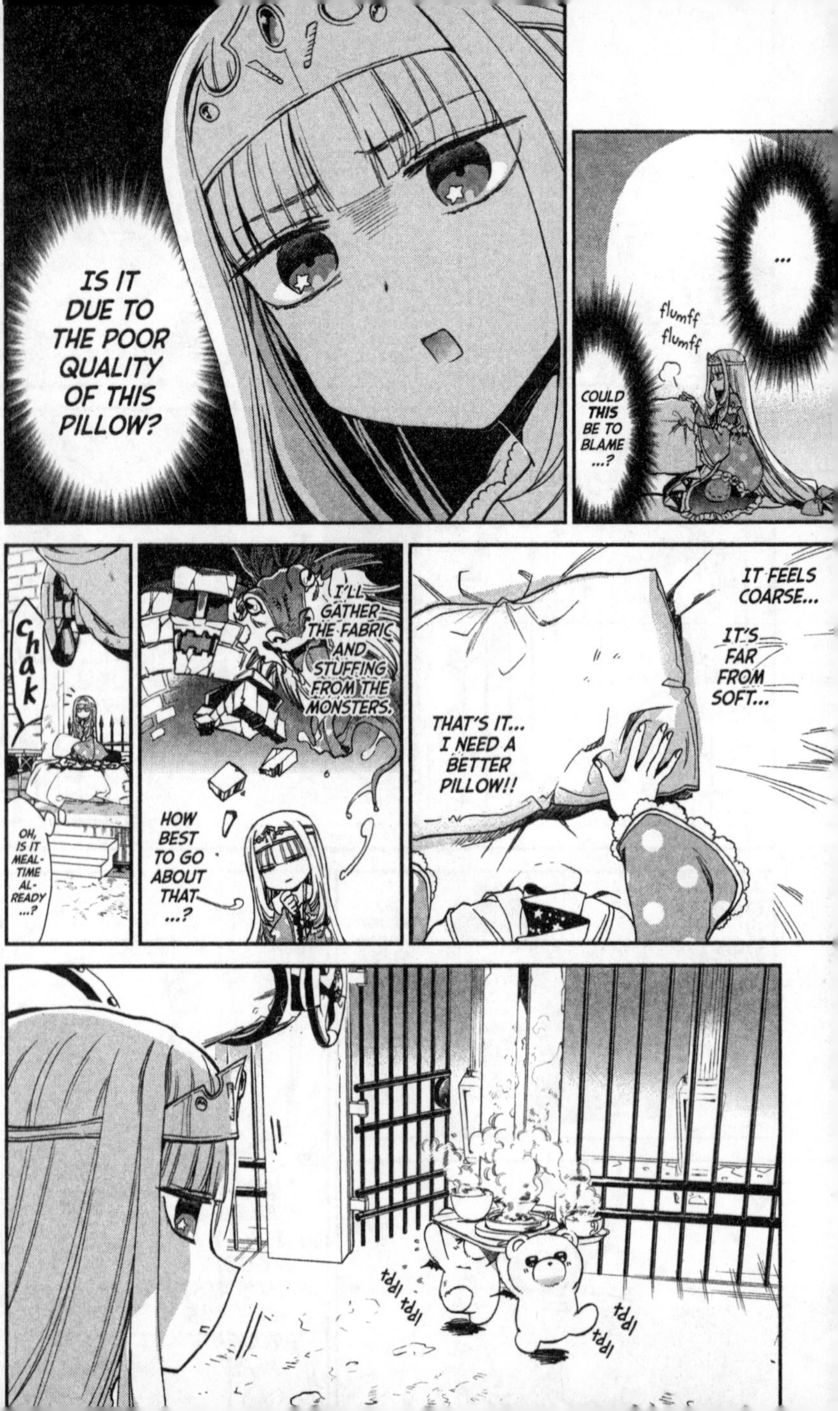
...
flumff
flumff
COULD THIS BE TO BLAME ...?
IS IT DUE TO THE POOR QUALITY OF THIS PILLOW?
IT FEELS COARSE...
IT'S FAR FROM SOFT...
THAT'S IT... I NEED A BETTER PILLOW!!
I'LL GATHER THE FABRIC AND STUFFING FROM THE MONSTERS.
HOW BEST TO GO ABOUT THAT ...?
Chak
OH, IS IT MEAL-TIME AL-READY ...?

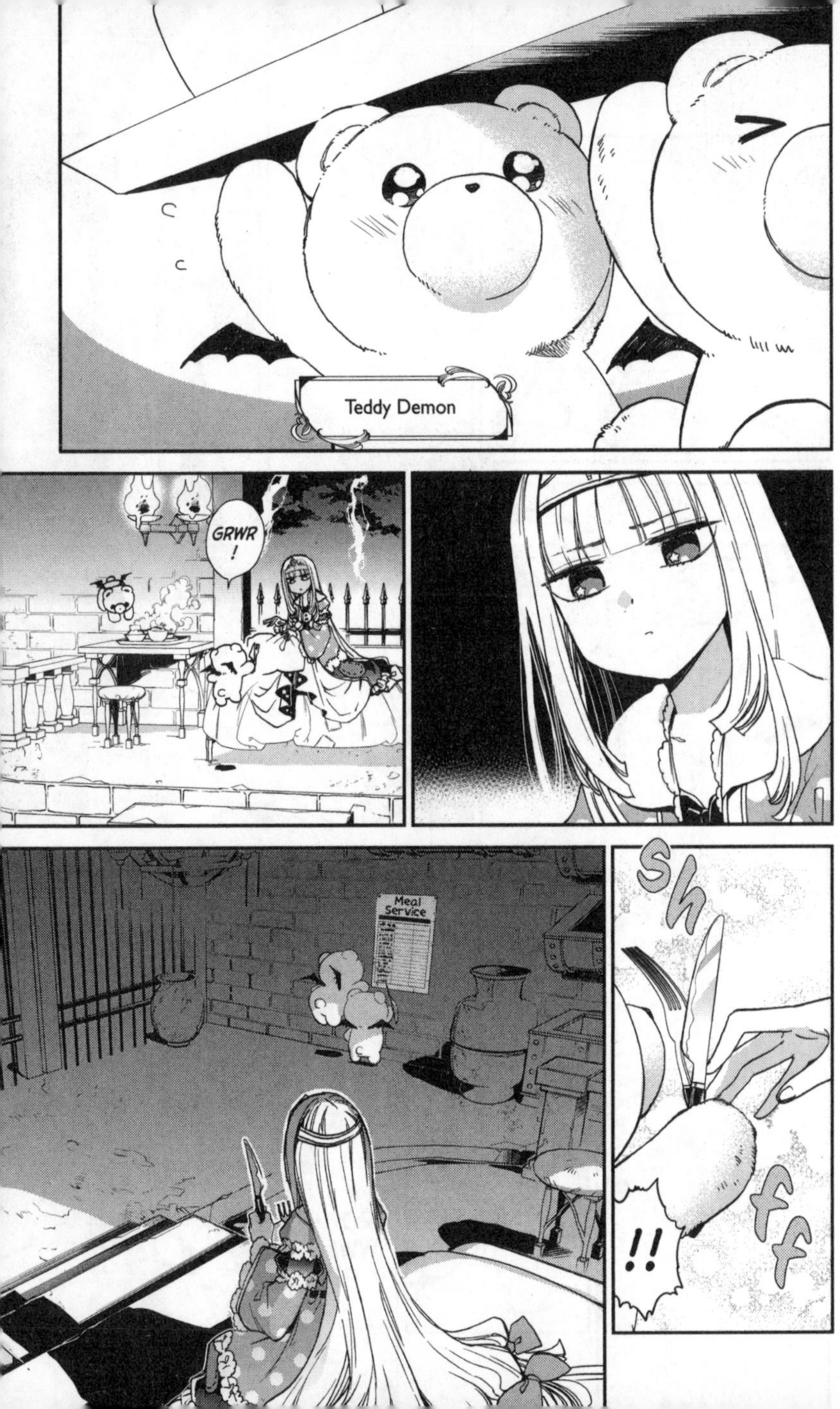
Teddy Demon
GRWR!
Shff
!!
Meal Service

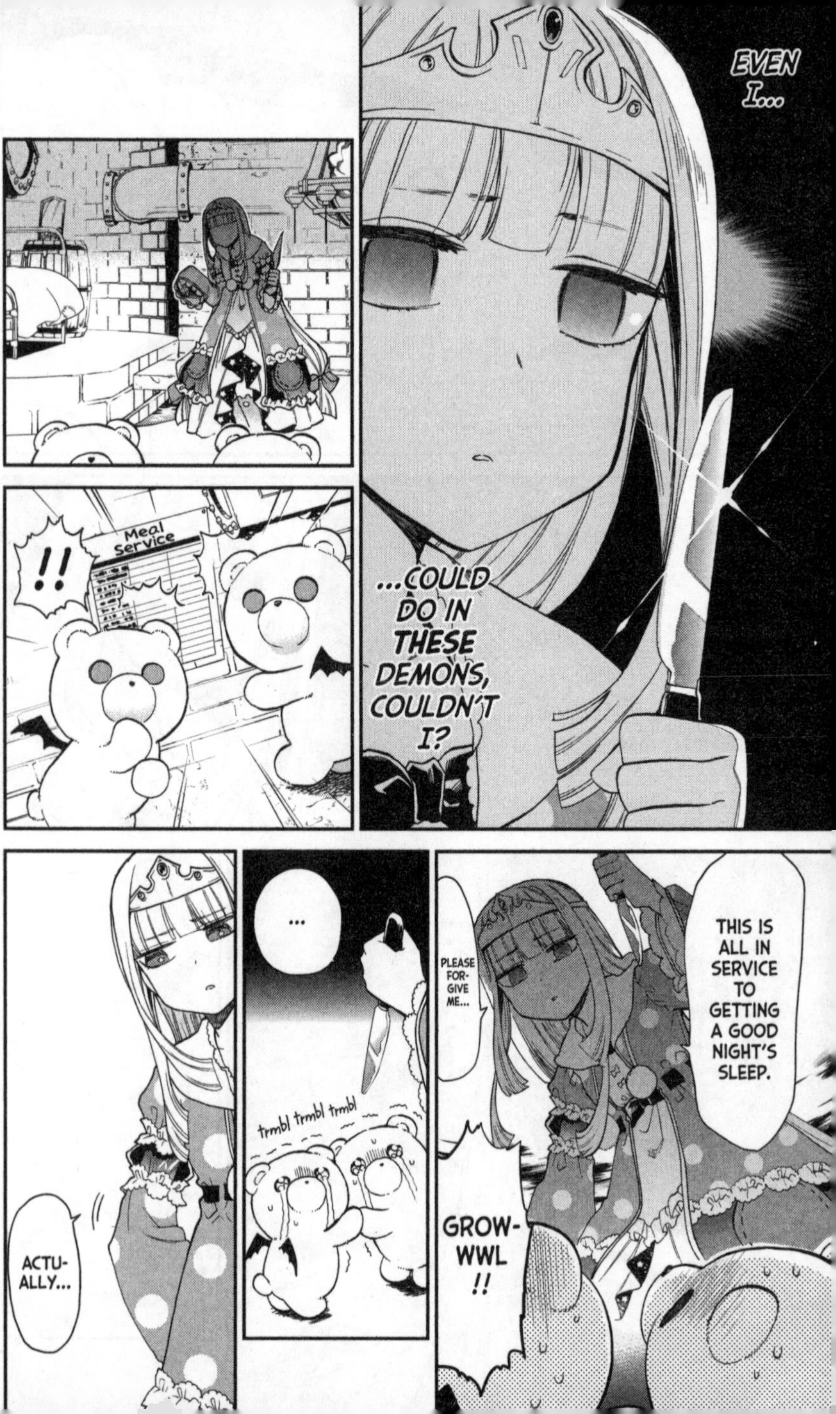
EVEN I...
...COULD DO IN THESE DEMONS, COULDN'T I?
Meal Service
!!
THIS IS ALL IN SERVICE TO GETTING A GOOD NIGHT'S SLEEP.
PLEASE FOR-GIVE ME...
GROW-WWL !!
...
trmbl trmbl trmbl
ACTU-ALLY...

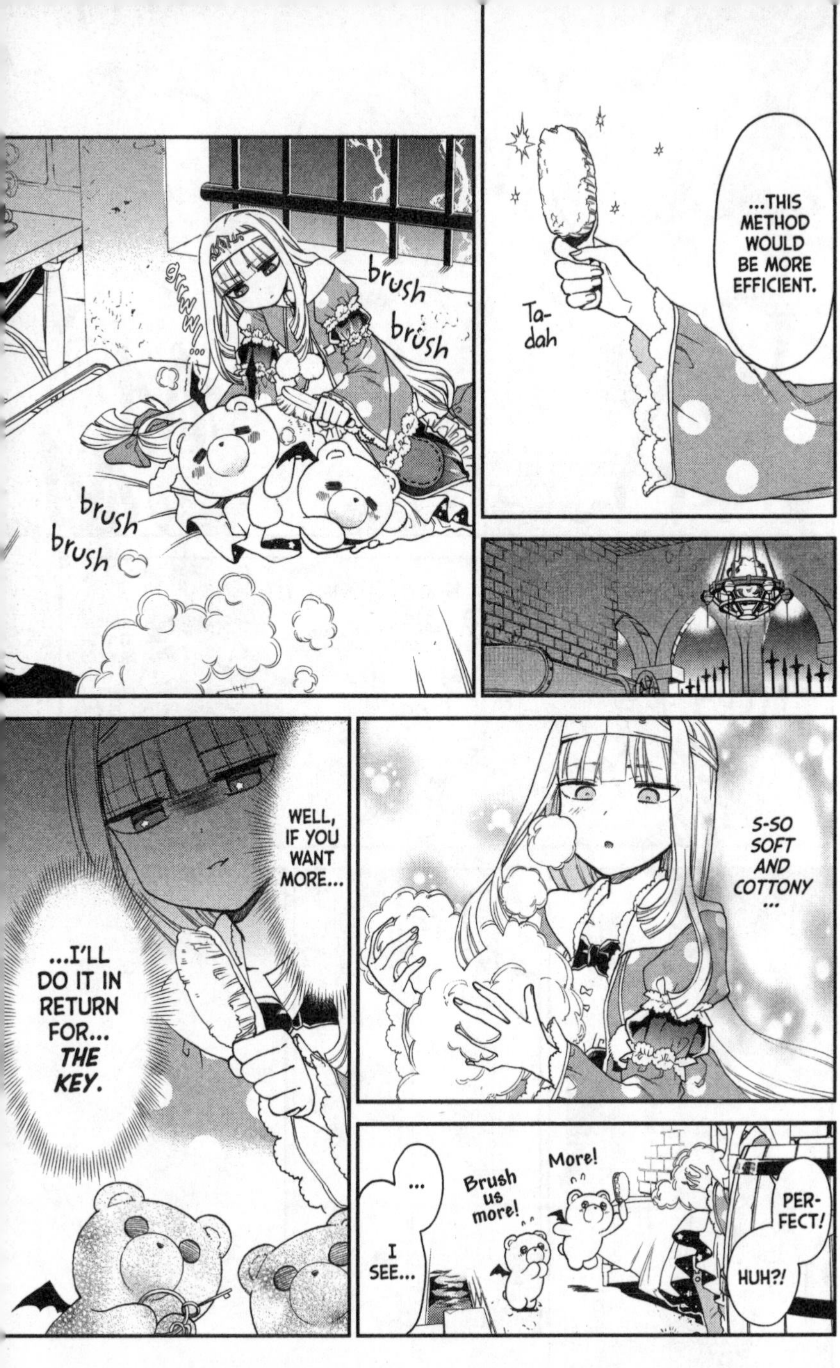
...THIS METHOD WOULD BE MORE EFFICIENT.
Ta-dah
brush
brush
grrwl...
brush
brush
S-SO SOFT AND COTTONY ...
PER-FECT!
HUH?!
More!
Brush us more!
...
I SEE...
WELL, IF YOU WANT MORE...
...I'LL DO IT IN RETURN FOR... THE KEY.

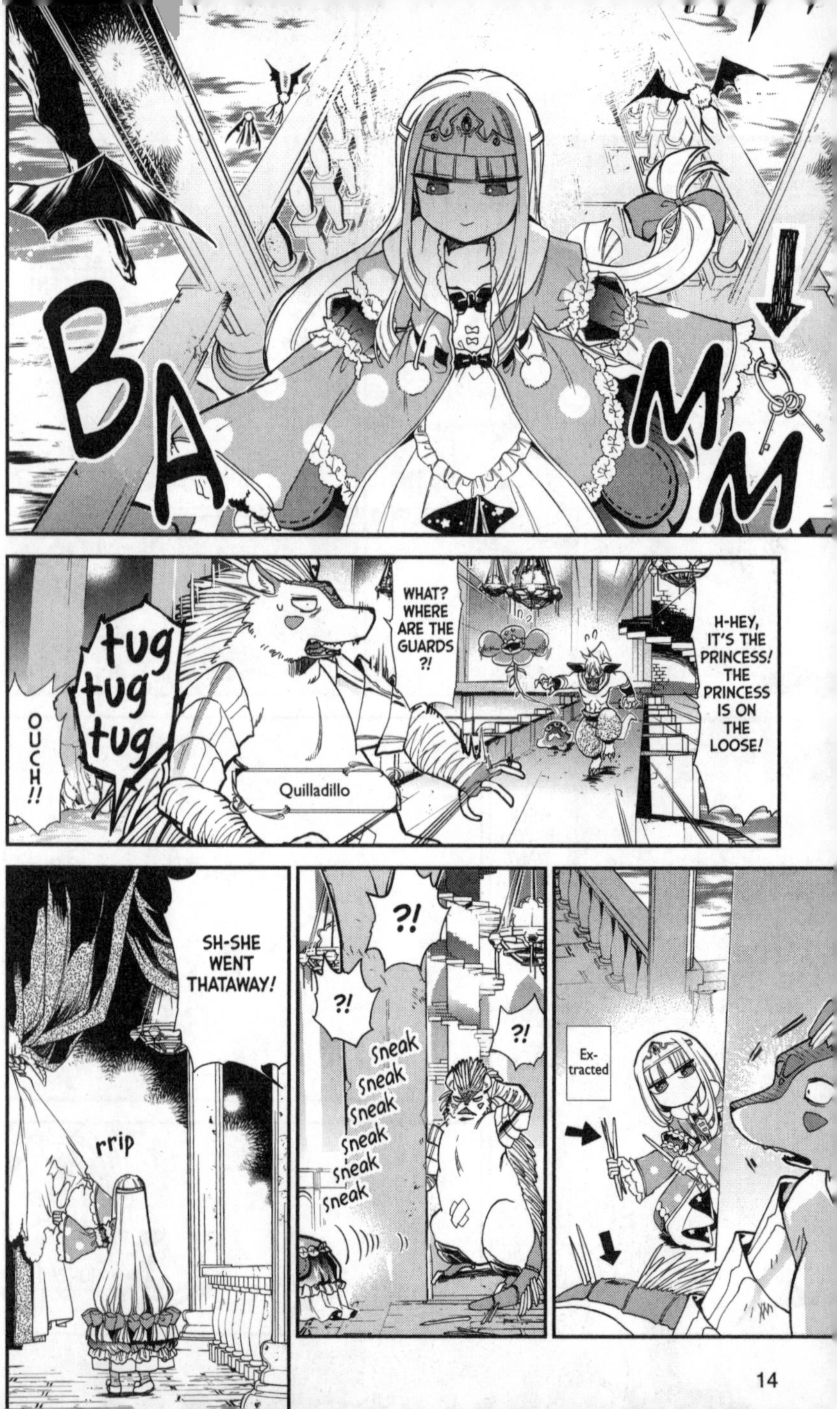
BAMMM
H-HEY, IT'S THE PRINCESS! THE PRINCESS IS ON THE LOOSE!
WHAT? WHERE ARE THE GUARDS ?!
tug tug tug
Quilladillo
OUCH!!
Ex-tracted
?!
?!
?!
sneak sneak sneak sneak sneak sneak
SH-SHE WENT THATAWAY!
rrip

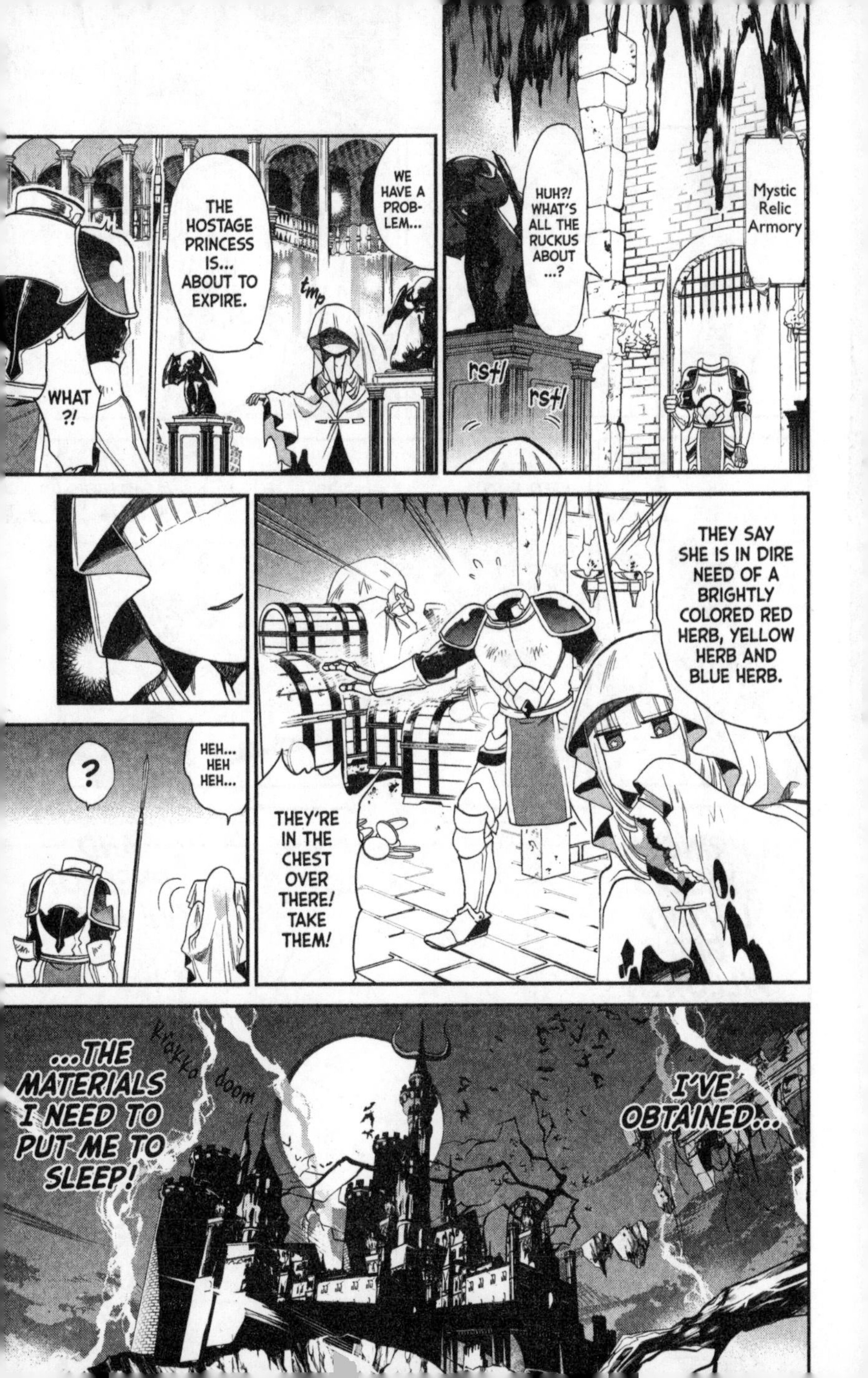
Mystic Relic Armory
HUH?! WHAT'S ALL THE RUCKUS ABOUT ...?
rst! rst!
WE HAVE A PROB-LEM...
THE HOSTAGE PRINCESS IS... ABOUT TO EXPIRE.
tmp
WHAT?!
THEY SAY SHE IS IN DIRE NEED OF A BRIGHTLY COLORED RED HERB, YELLOW HERB AND BLUE HERB.
THEY'RE IN THE CHEST OVER THERE! TAKE THEM!
HEH... HEH HEH...
?
I'VE OBTAINED...
krakka doom
...THE MATERIALS I NEED TO PUT ME TO SLEEP!

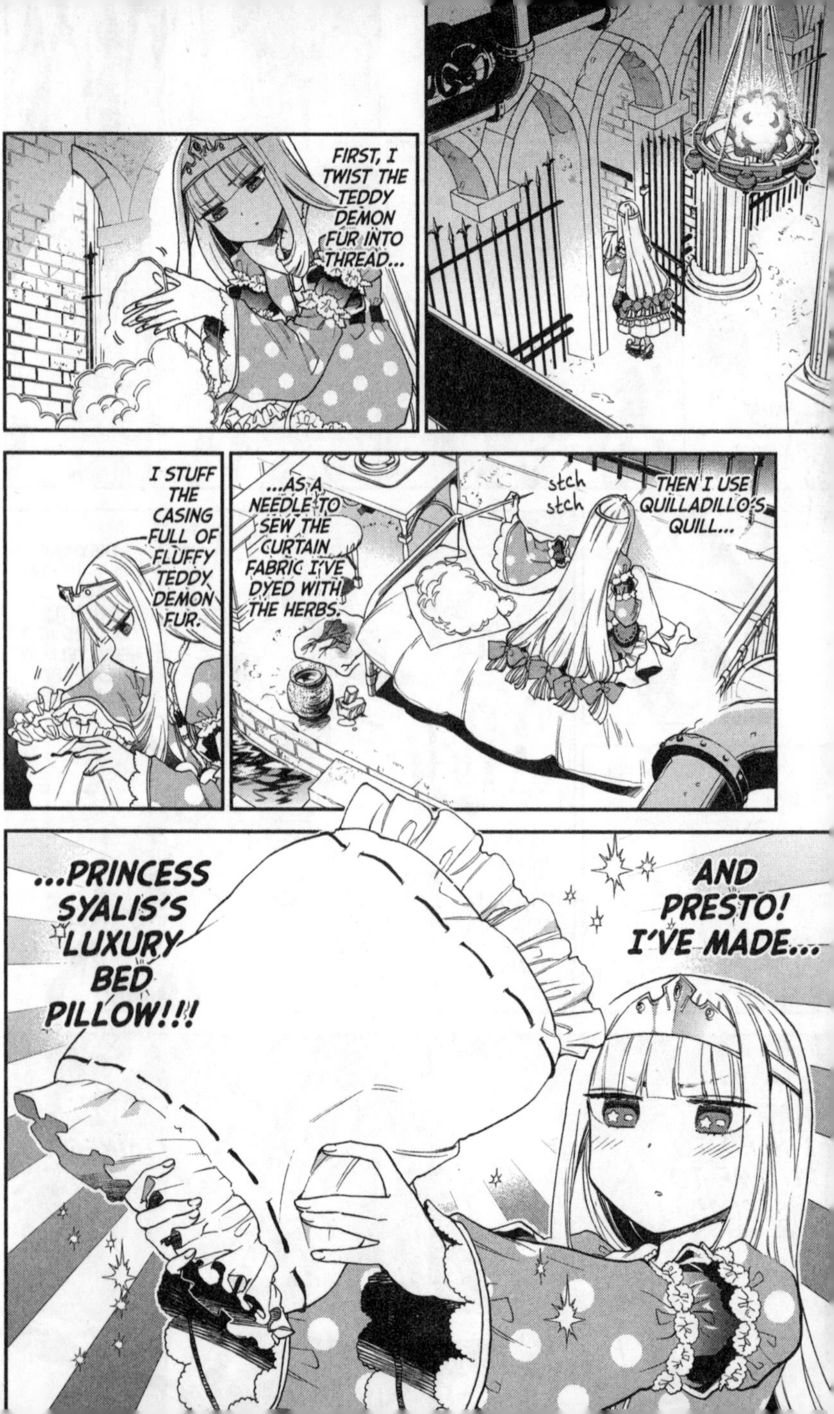
FIRST, I TWIST THE TEDDY DEMON FUR INTO THREAD...
THEN I USE QUILLADILLO'S QUILL...
stch stch
...AS A NEEDLE TO SEW THE CURTAIN FABRIC I'VE DYED WITH THE HERBS.
I STUFF THE CASING FULL OF FLUFFY TEDDY DEMON FUR.
AND PRESTO! I'VE MADE...
...PRINCESS SYALIS'S LUXURY BED PILLOW!!!

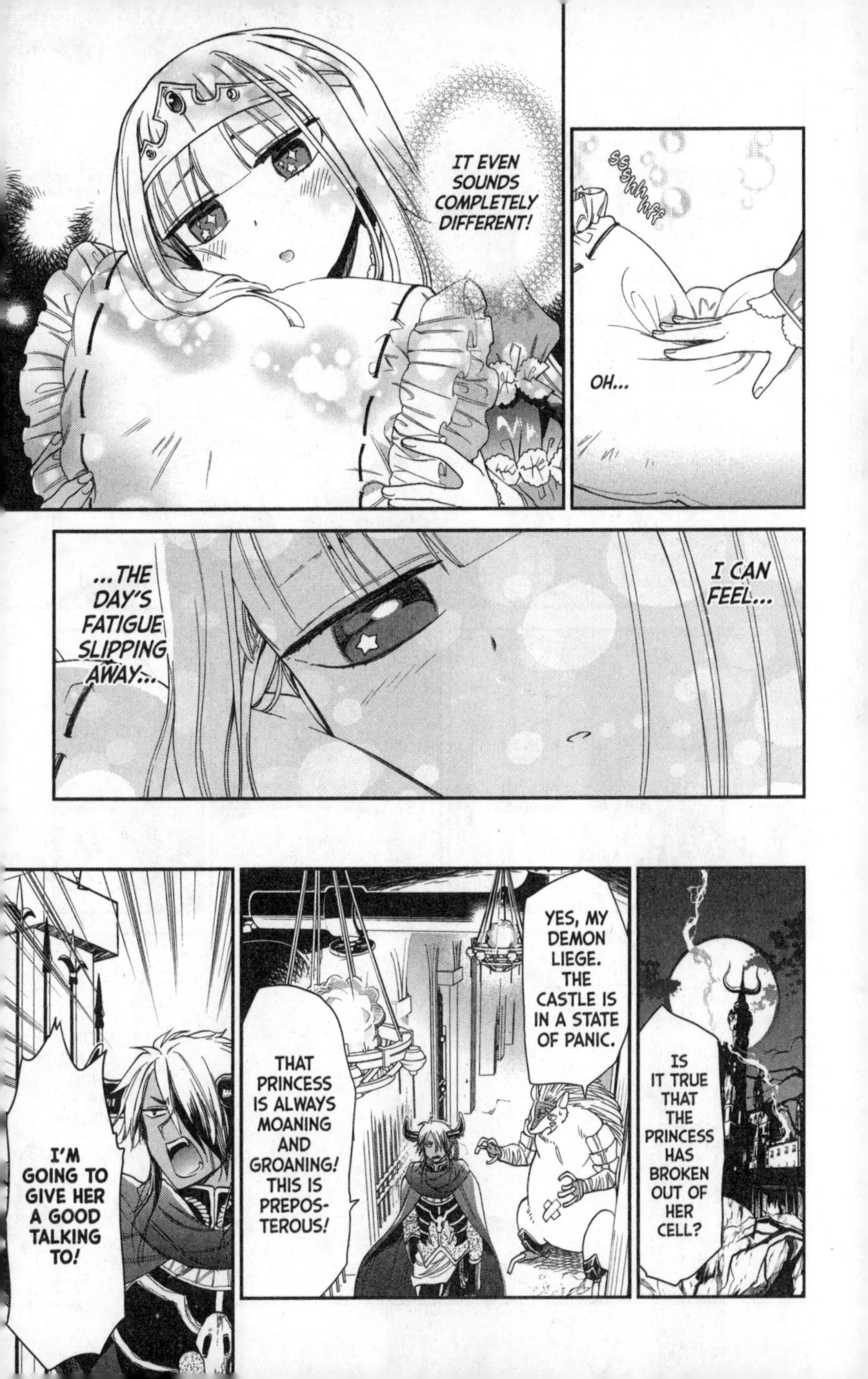
SSShhhff
OH...
IT EVEN SOUNDS COMPLETELY DIFFERENT!
I CAN FEEL...
...THE DAY'S FATIGUE SLIPPING AWAY...
IS IT TRUE THAT THE PRINCESS HAS BROKEN OUT OF HER CELL?
YES, MY DEMON LIEGE. THE CASTLE IS IN A STATE OF PANIC.
THAT PRINCESS IS ALWAYS MOANING AND GROANING! THIS IS PREPOS-TEROUS!
I'M GOING TO GIVE HER A GOOD TALKING TO!

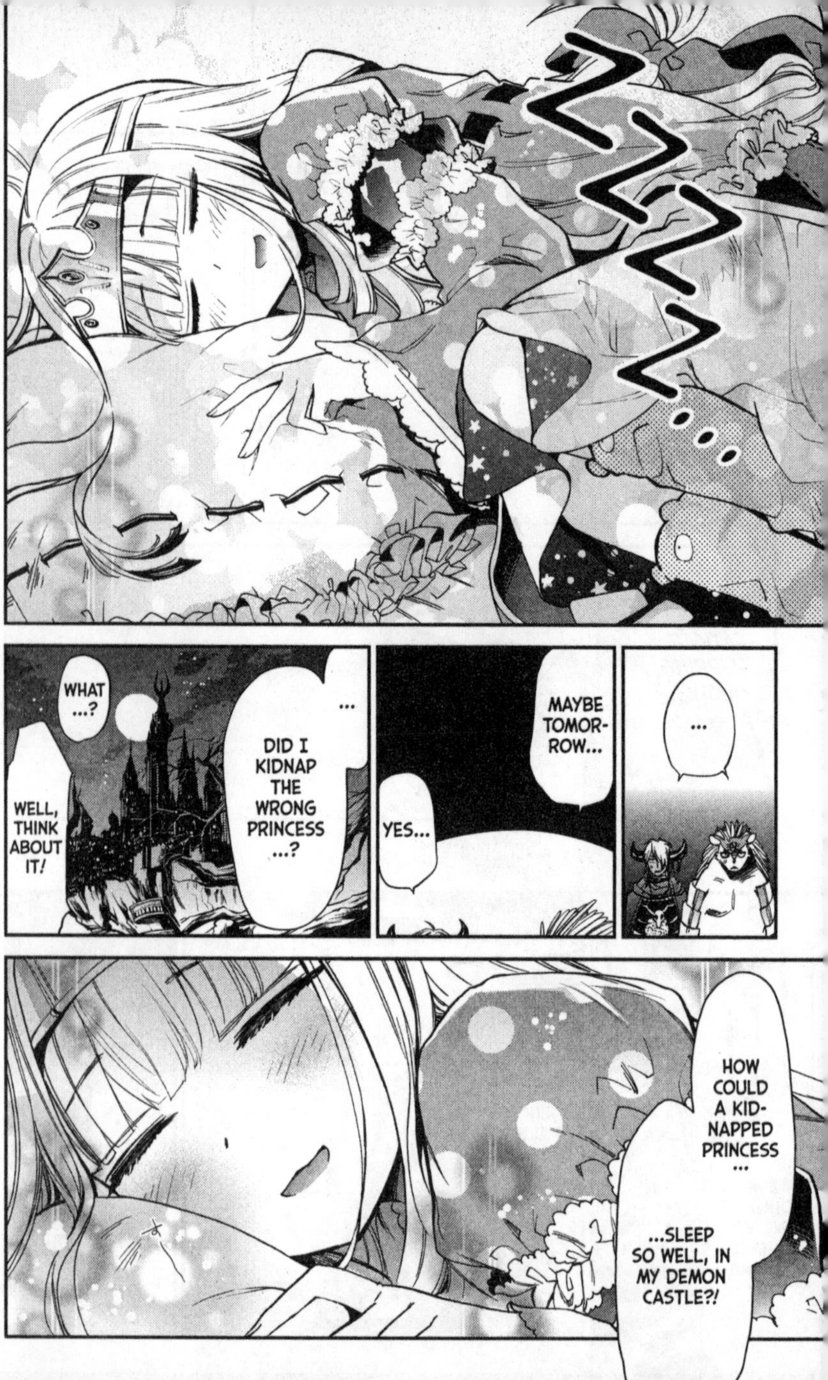
...
MAYBE TOMORROW...
YES...
... DID I KIDNAP THE WRONG PRINCESS ...?
WHAT ...?
WELL, THINK ABOUT IT!
HOW COULD A KIDNAPPED PRINCESS ...
...SLEEP SO WELL, IN MY DEMON CASTLE?!

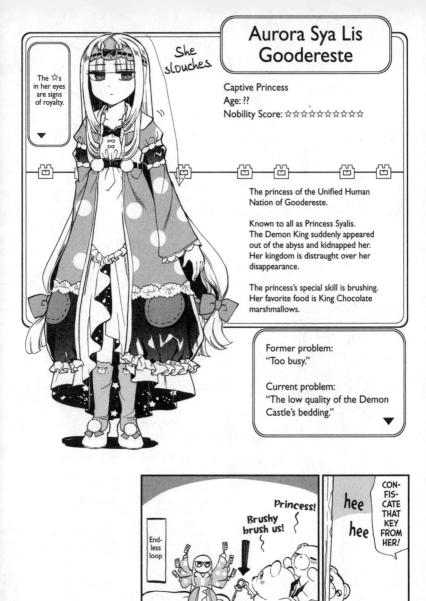

Aurora Sya Lis Goodereste

The ☆s in her eyes are signs of royalty.
She slouches.

Captive Princess
Age: ??
Nobility Score: ☆☆☆☆☆☆☆☆☆☆☆

The princess of the Unified Human Nation of Goodereste.

Known to all as Princess Syalis. The Demon King suddenly appeared out of the abyss and kidnapped her. Her kingdom is distraught over her disappearance.

The princess's special skill is brushing. Her favorite food is King Chocolate marshmallows.

Former problem:
"Too busy."

Current problem:
"The low quality of the Demon Castle's bedding."

CON-FIS-CATE THAT KEY FROM HER!
hee hee
Princess!
Brushy brush us!
End-less loop

Teddy Demon

Cuddliness: ☆☆☆☆☆☆☆☆☆
Willpower: ☆☆

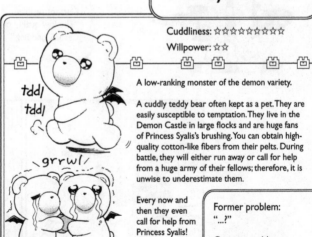

tddl
tddl

grrwl

A low-ranking monster of the demon variety.

A cuddly teddy bear often kept as a pet. They are easily susceptible to temptation. They live in the Demon Castle in large flocks and are huge fans of Princess Syalis's brushing. You can obtain high-quality cotton-like fibers from their pelts. During battle, they will either run away or call for help from a huge army of their fellows; therefore, it is unwise to underestimate them.

Every now and then they even call for help from Princess Syalis!

Former problem:
"...!"

Current problem:
"...??"

▼

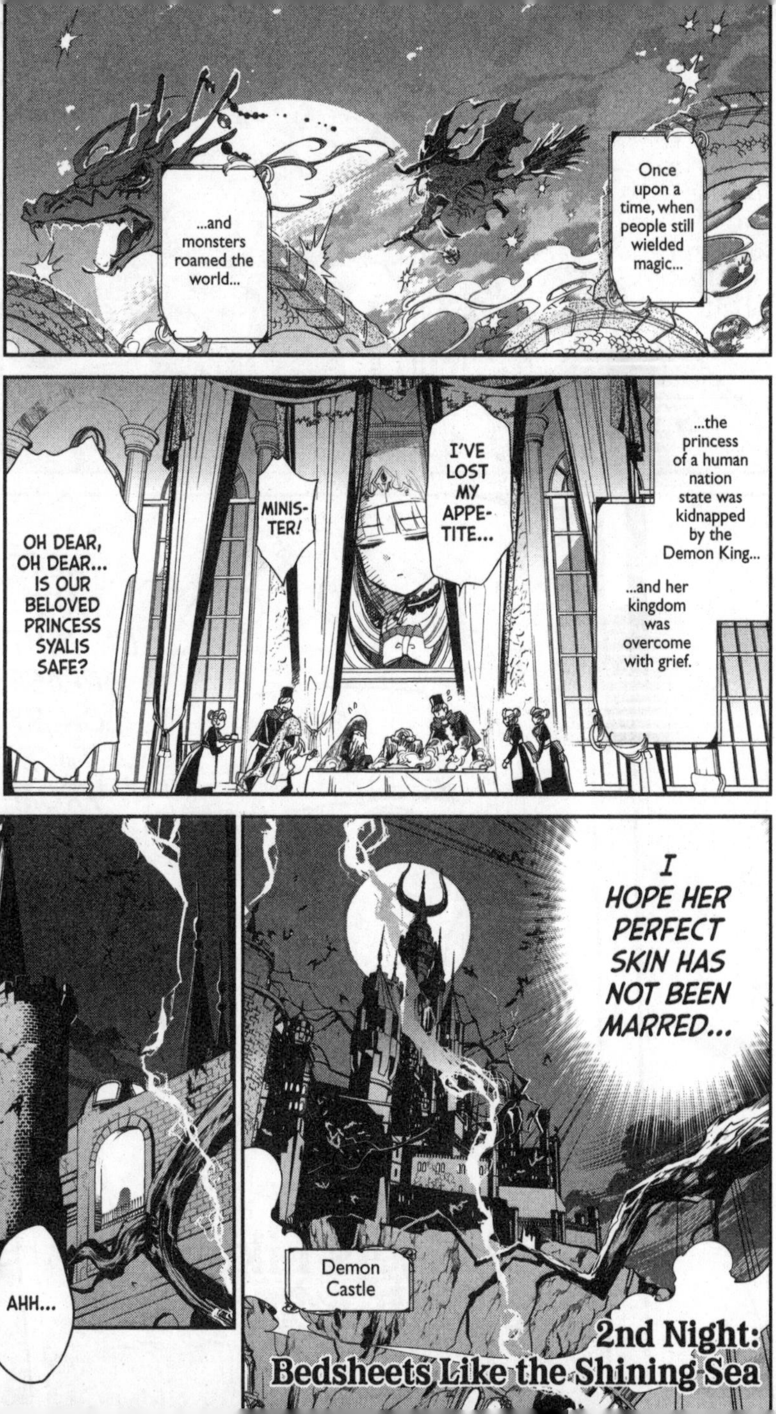
Once upon a time, when people still wielded magic...
...and monsters roamed the world...
...the princess of a human nation state was kidnapped by the Demon King...
...and her kingdom was overcome with grief.
I'VE LOST MY APPE-TITE...
MINIS-TER!
OH DEAR, OH DEAR... IS OUR BELOVED PRINCESS SYALIS SAFE?
I HOPE HER PERFECT SKIN HAS NOT BEEN MARRED...
Demon Castle
2nd Night: Bedsheets Like the Shining Sea
AHH...

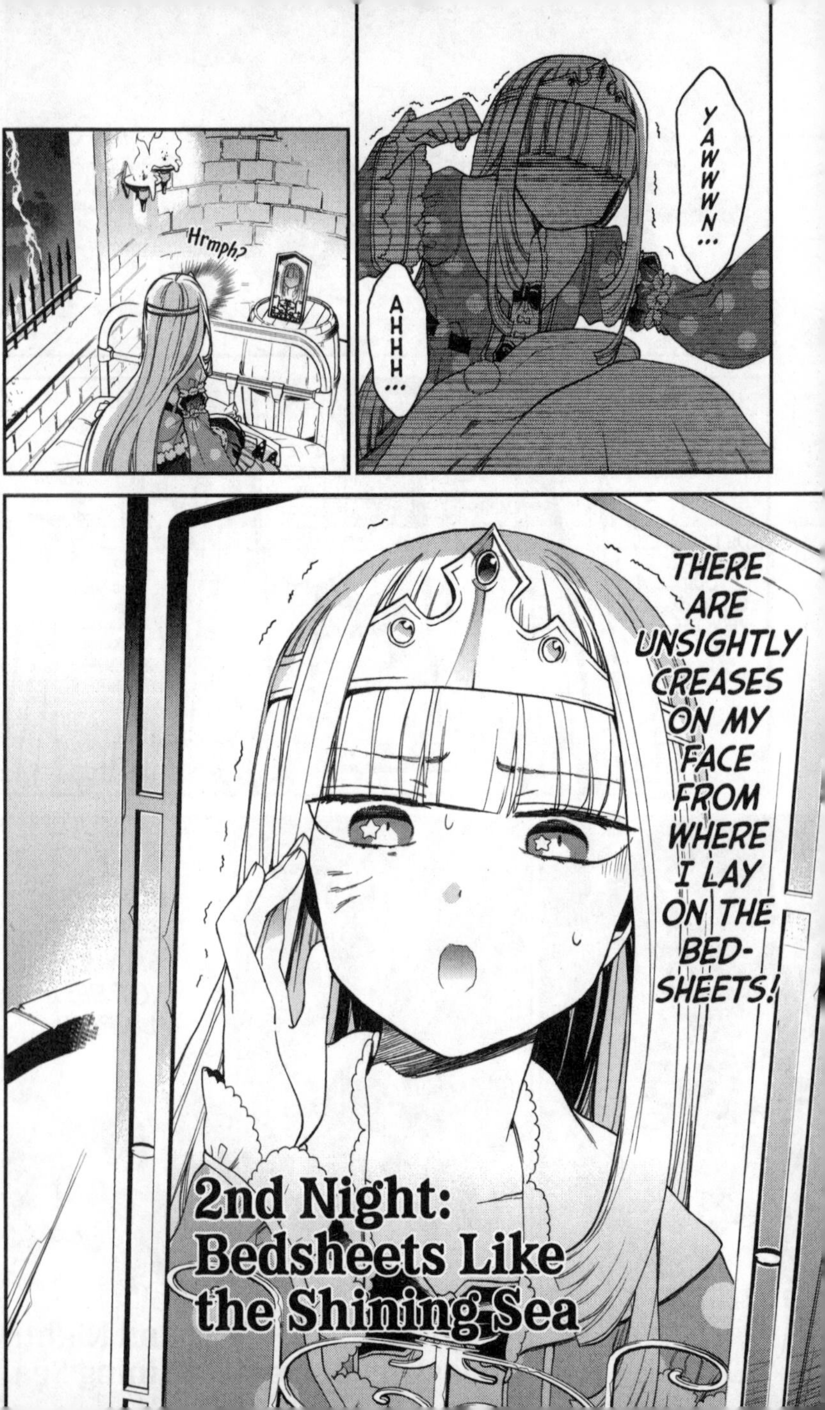
YAWWWN...
AHHH...
Hrmph?
THERE ARE UNSIGHTLY CREASES ON MY FACE FROM WHERE I LAY ON THE BED-SHEETS!
2nd Night: Bedsheets Like the Shining Sea

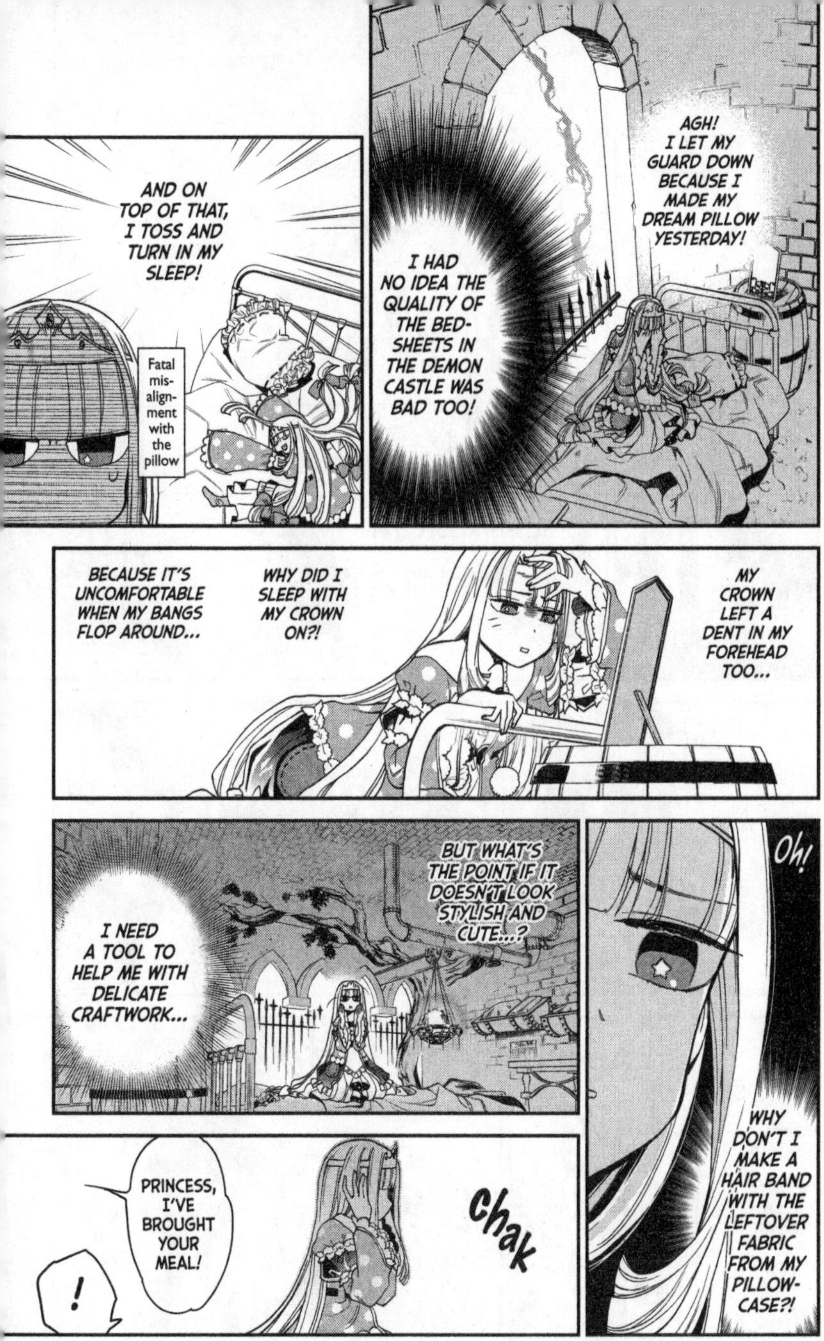
AGH! I LET MY GUARD DOWN BECAUSE I MADE MY DREAM PILLOW YESTERDAY!
I HAD NO IDEA THE QUALITY OF THE BED-SHEETS IN THE DEMON CASTLE WAS BAD TOO!
AND ON TOP OF THAT, I TOSS AND TURN IN MY SLEEP!
Fatal misalignment with the pillow
MY CROWN LEFT A DENT IN MY FOREHEAD TOO...
WHY DID I SLEEP WITH MY CROWN ON?!
BECAUSE IT'S UNCOMFORTABLE WHEN MY BANGS FLOP AROUND...
Oh!
WHY DON'T I MAKE A HAIR BAND WITH THE LEFTOVER FABRIC FROM MY PILLOW-CASE?!
BUT WHAT'S THE POINT IF IT DOESN'T LOOK STYLISH AND CUTE...?
I NEED A TOOL TO HELP ME WITH DELICATE CRAFTWORK...
chak
PRINCESS, I'VE BROUGHT YOUR MEAL!
!

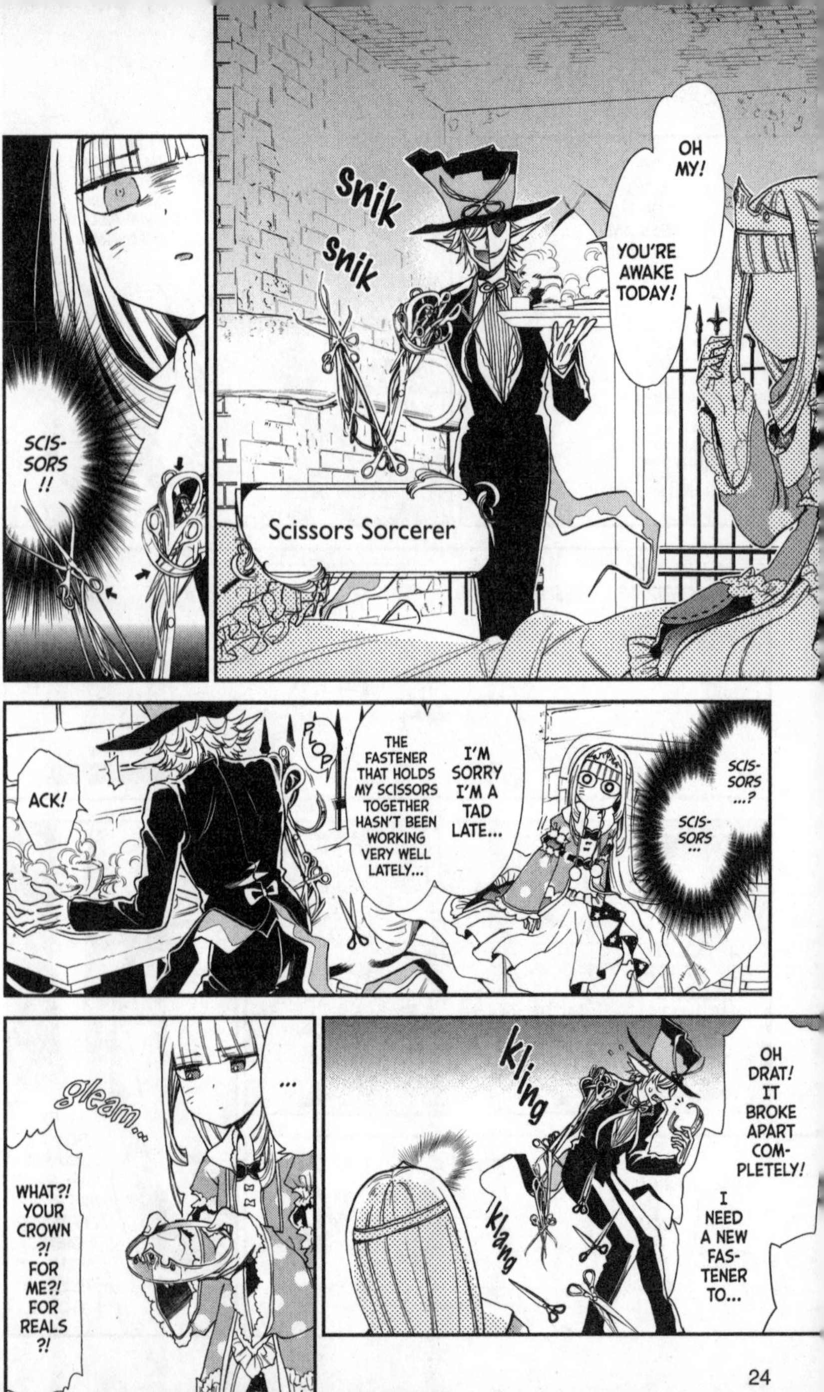
OH MY!
YOU'RE AWAKE TODAY!
Snik
snik
Scissors Sorcerer
SCIS-SORS!!
SCIS-SORS...?
SCIS-SORS...
I'M SORRY I'M A TAD LATE...
THE FASTENER THAT HOLDS MY SCISSORS TOGETHER HASN'T BEEN WORKING VERY WELL LATELY...
PLOP
ACK!
OH DRAT! IT BROKE APART COMPLETELY!
I NEED A NEW FASTENER TO...
kling
klang
...
gleam...
WHAT?! YOUR CROWN?! FOR ME?! FOR REALS?!

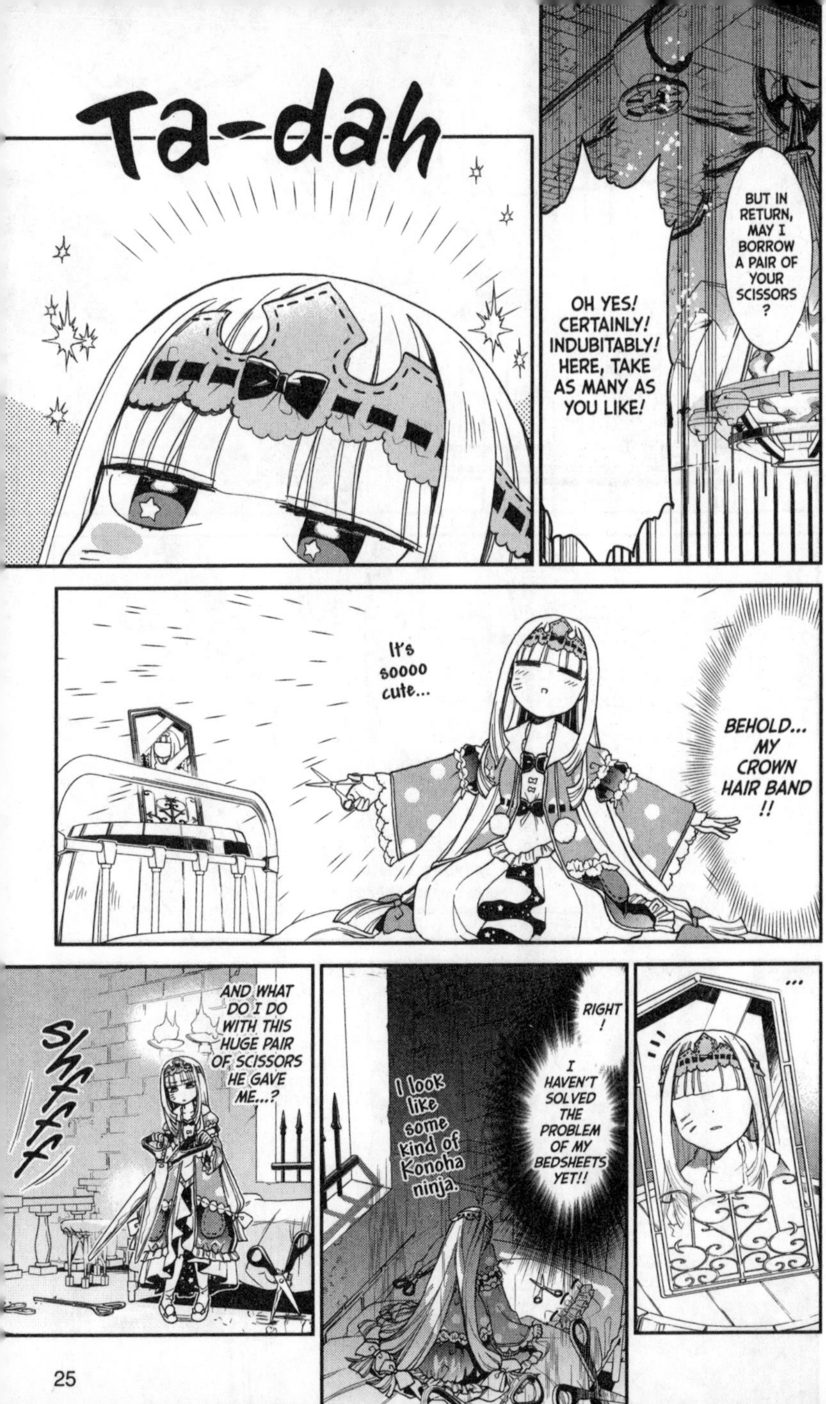
BUT IN RETURN, MAY I BORROW A PAIR OF YOUR SCISSORS?
OH YES! CERTAINLY! INDUBITABLY! HERE, TAKE AS MANY AS YOU LIKE!
Ta-dah
BEHOLD... MY CROWN HAIR BAND!!
It's soooo cute...
...
RIGHT!
I HAVEN'T SOLVED THE PROBLEM OF MY BEDSHEETS YET!!
I look like some kind of Konoha ninja.
AND WHAT DO I DO WITH THIS HUGE PAIR OF SCISSORS HE GAVE ME...?
SHFFFF

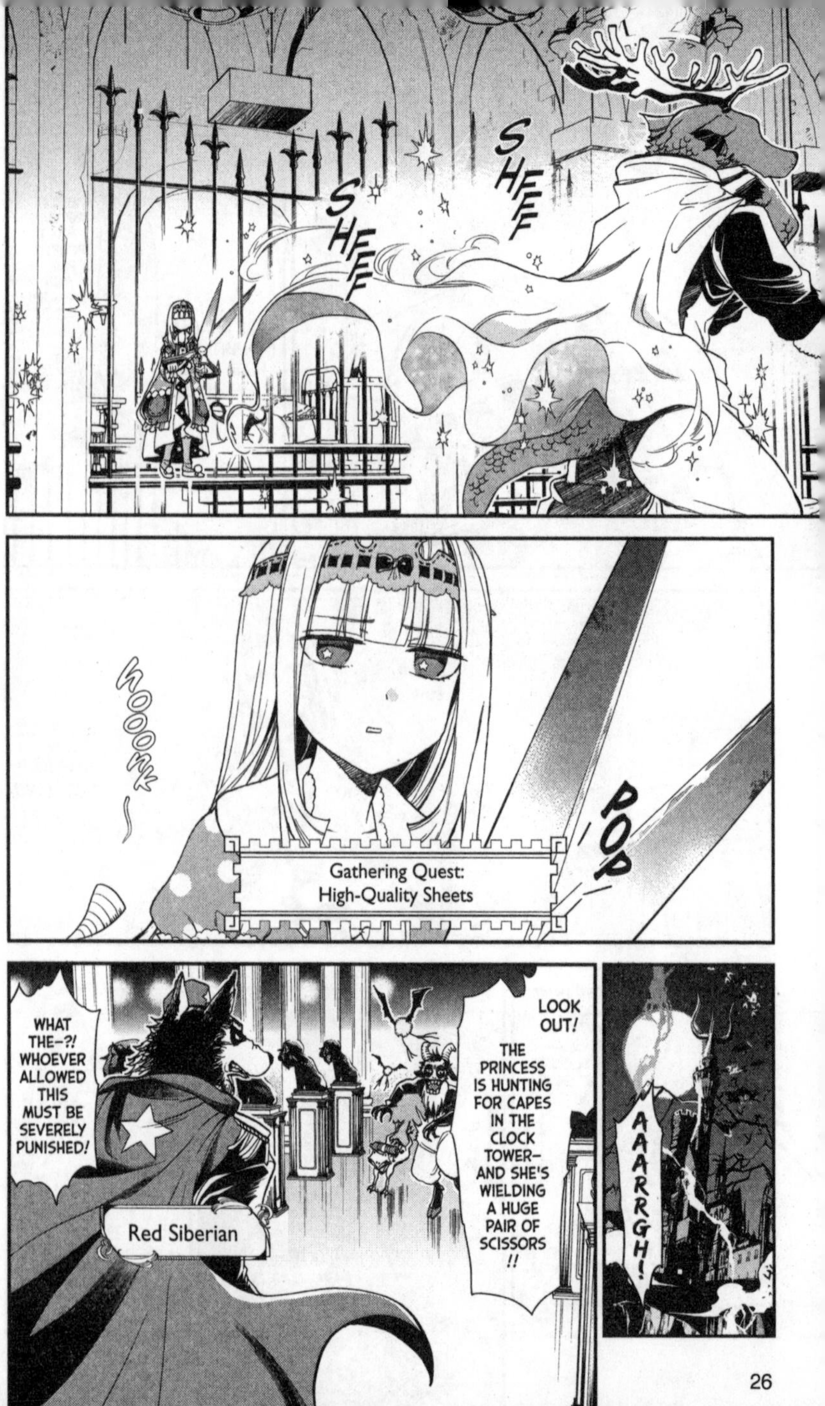
SHEFF
SHEFF
POP
Gathering Quest:
High-Quality Sheets
WOOONK~
AAAARGH!
LOOK OUT!
THE PRINCESS IS HUNTING FOR CAPES IN THE CLOCK TOWER— AND SHE'S WIELDING A HUGE PAIR OF SCISSORS!!
WHAT THE—?! WHOEVER ALLOWED THIS MUST BE SEVERELY PUNISHED!
Red Siberian

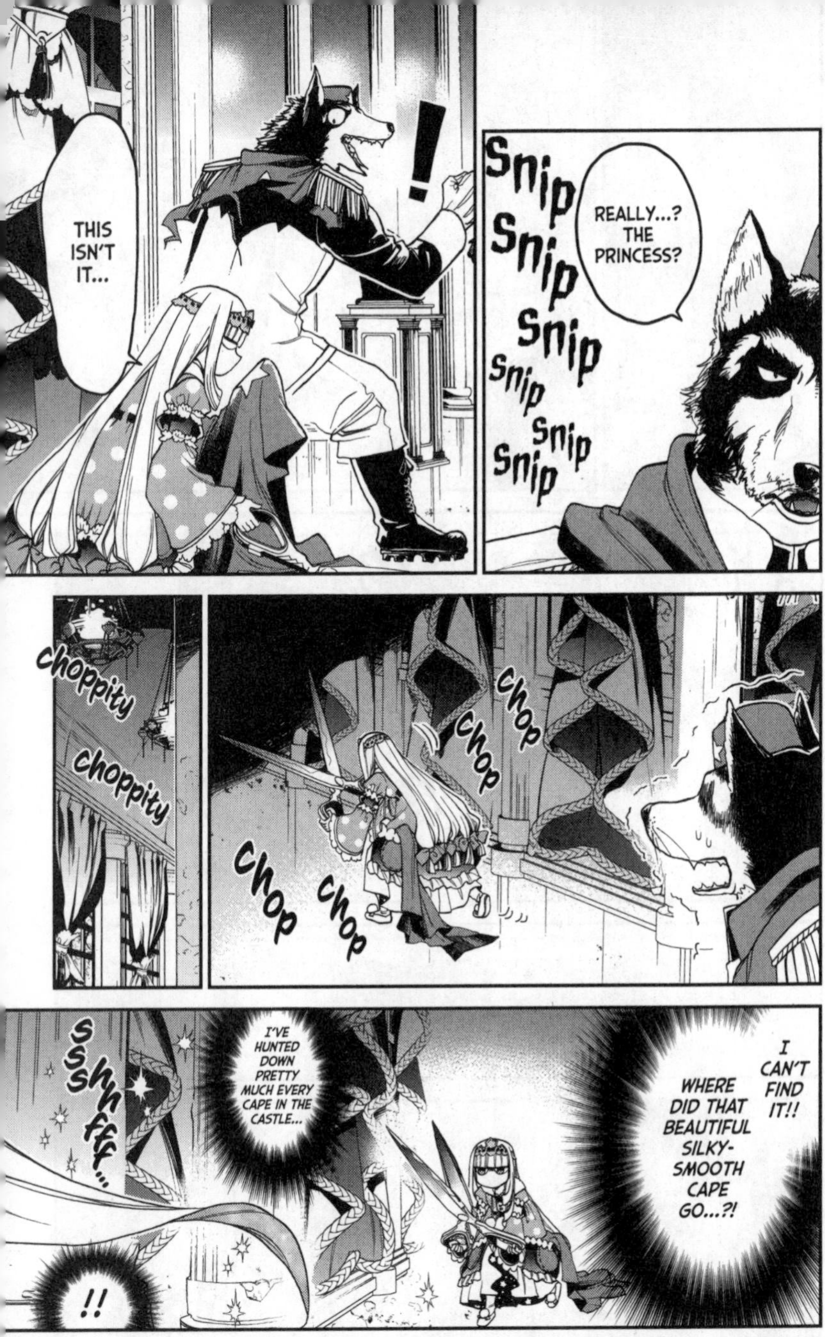
Snip Snip Snip Snip Snip Snip Snip
REALLY...? THE PRINCESS?
!
THIS ISN'T IT...
Chop Chop Chop Chop
choppity choppity
I CAN'T FIND IT!!
WHERE DID THAT BEAUTIFUL SILKY-SMOOTH CAPE GO...?!
I'VE HUNTED DOWN PRETTY MUCH EVERY CAPE IN THE CASTLE...
SSHFFF...
!!

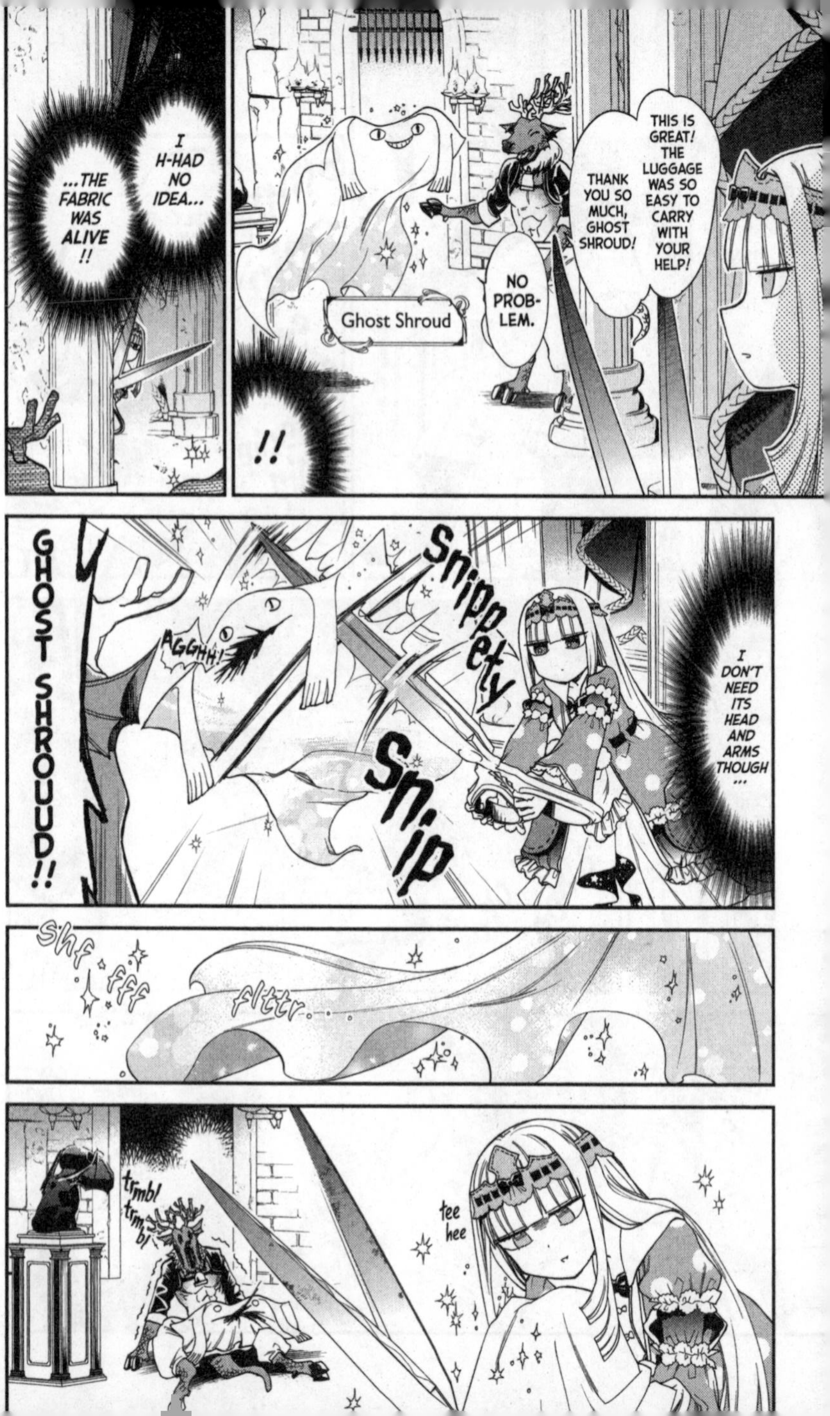
THIS IS GREAT! THE LUGGAGE WAS SO EASY TO CARRY WITH YOUR HELP!
THANK YOU SO MUCH, GHOST SHROUD!
NO PROB-LEM.
Ghost Shroud
!!
I H-HAD NO IDEA...
...THE FABRIC WAS ALIVE !!
I DON'T NEED ITS HEAD AND ARMS THOUGH...
Snippety
Snip
AGGHH!
GHOST SHROUUD!!
shf fff
flttr
tee hee
trmbl trmbl

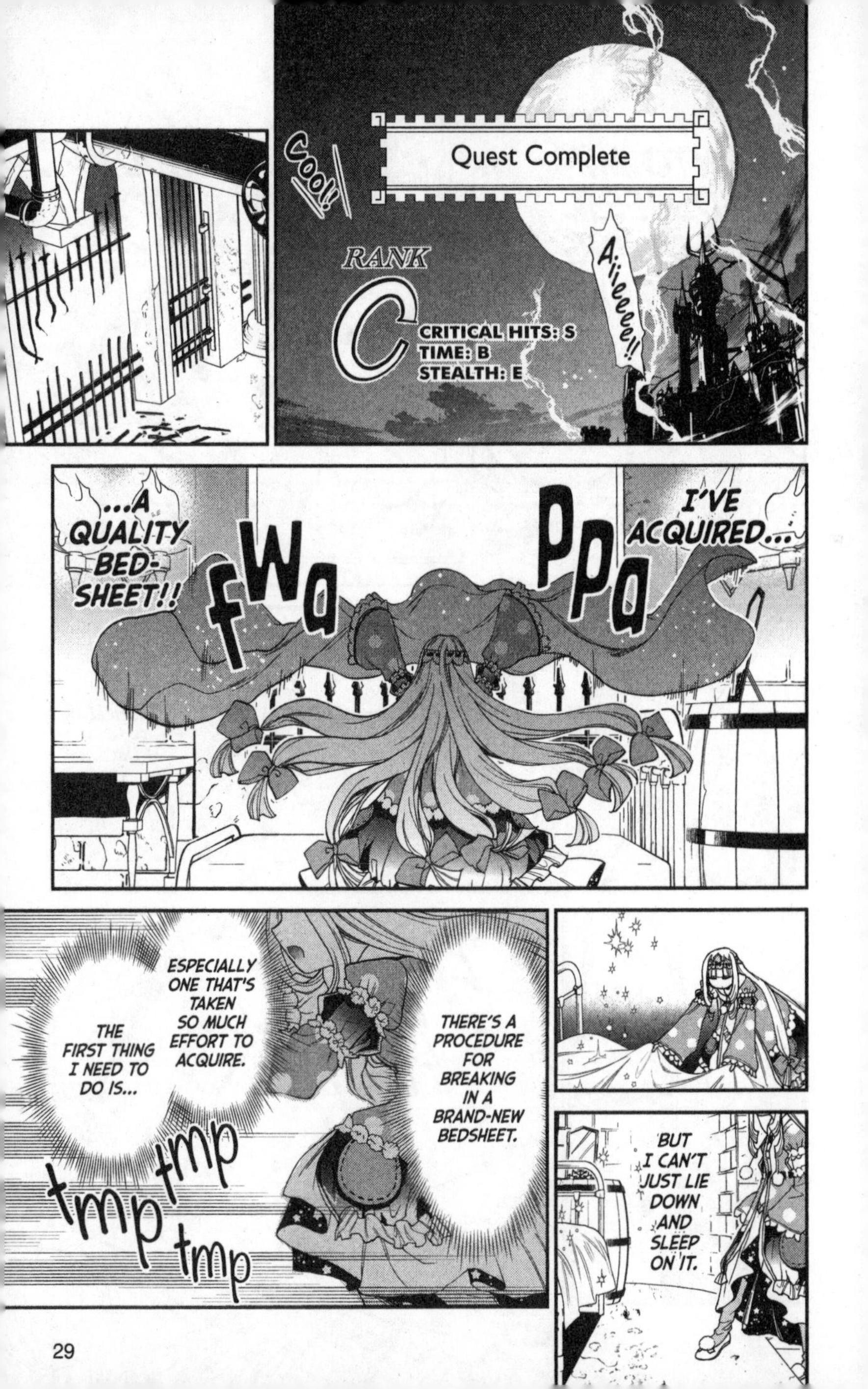
Quest Complete
Aiieeee!!
Cool!
RANK
C
CRITICAL HITS: S
TIME: B
STEALTH: E
I'VE ACQUIRED...
fWa PPa
...A QUALITY BED-SHEET!!
BUT I CAN'T JUST LIE DOWN AND SLEEP ON IT.
THERE'S A PROCEDURE FOR BREAKING IN A BRAND-NEW BEDSHEET.
ESPECIALLY ONE THAT'S TAKEN SO MUCH EFFORT TO ACQUIRE.
THE FIRST THING I NEED TO DO IS...
tmp tmp
tmp tmp

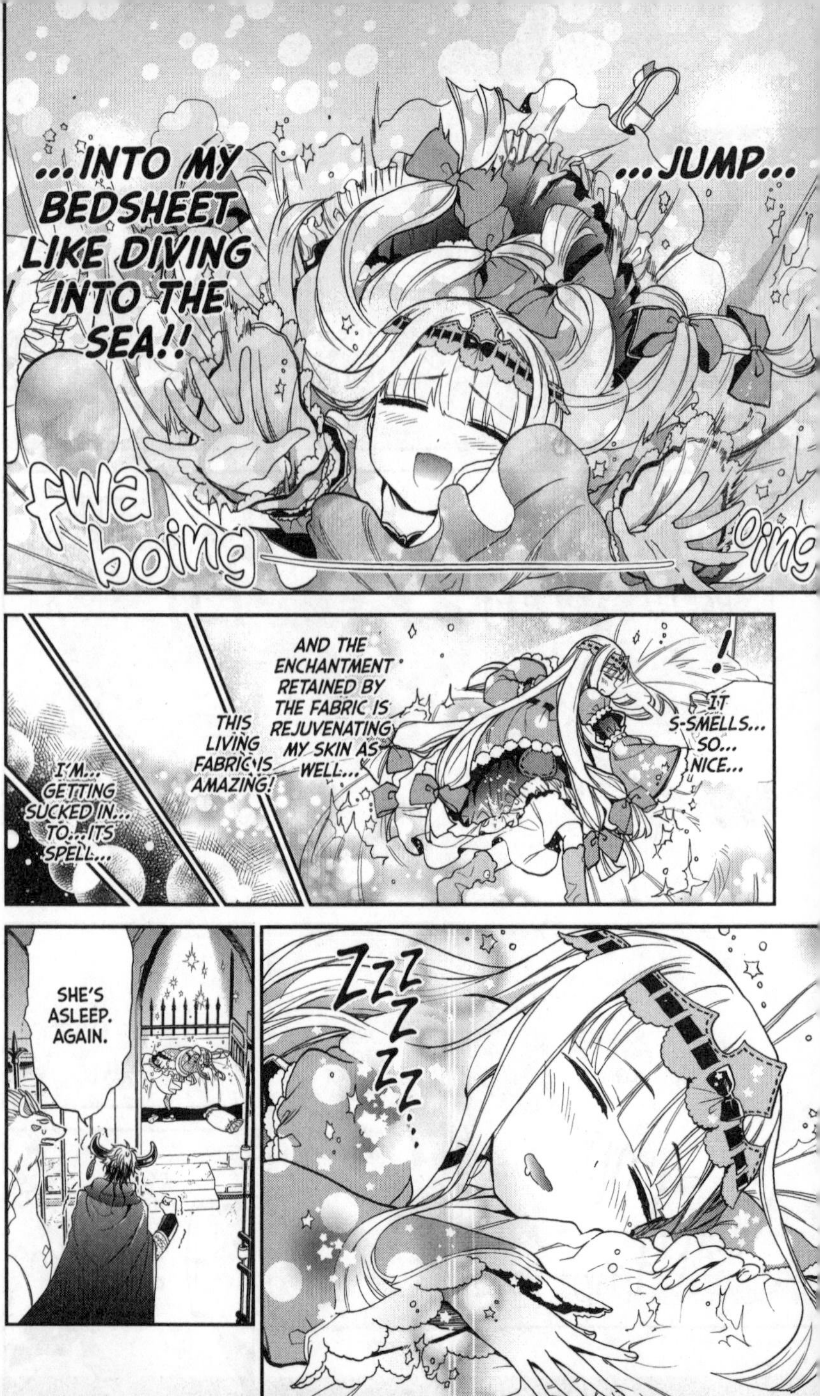

...JUMP...
...INTO MY BEDSHEET LIKE DIVING INTO THE SEA!!
fwa
boing
oing
!
IT S-SMELLS... SO... NICE...
AND THE ENCHANTMENT RETAINED BY THE FABRIC IS REJUVENATING MY SKIN AS WELL...
THIS LIVING FABRIC IS AMAZING!
I'M... GETTING SUCKED IN... TO... ITS SPELL...
ZZZZZZ...
SHE'S ASLEEP. AGAIN.

Ghost Shroud

Quality of Fabric: ☆☆☆☆☆☆☆

Luck: ☆☆

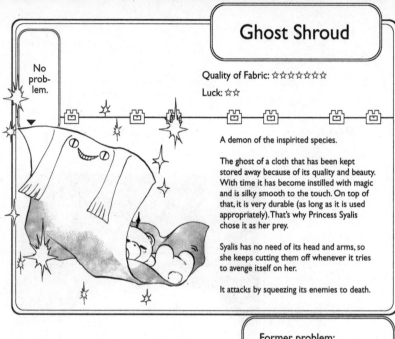

No prob-lem.

A demon of the inspirited species.

The ghost of a cloth that has been kept stored away because of its quality and beauty. With time it has become instilled with magic and is silky smooth to the touch. On top of that, it is very durable (as long as it is used appropriately). That's why Princess Syalis chose it as her prey.

Syalis has no need of its head and arms, so she keeps cutting them off whenever it tries to avenge itself on her.

It attacks by squeezing its enemies to death.

Former problem:
"Lack of presence."

Current problem:
"The princess."

OH MY!

Mr. Oh My

WHO?

MR. OH MY.

...

MR. OH MY!

PRINCESS... WHO DID YOU GET THOSE SCISSORS FROM...?

Would you like to change your class?
10 changes remaining
▶Yes
No▼
Slacker
The princess as herself.

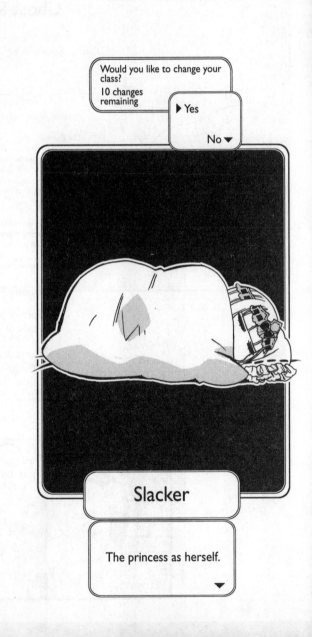

3rd Night: Sweet Sleep Like the Dead

Once upon a time, when swords and spells ruled the world...

...and people were threatened by dangerous monsters...

A NEW TYPE OF MONSTER...?

YES.

I ENCOUNTERED THEM NUMEROUS TIMES IN THE NEIGHBORING DESERT.

HMM... THAT MUST BE HARD ON A HERO LIKE YOU.

NO... MY SUFFERING IS INSIGNIFICANT...

tak tak

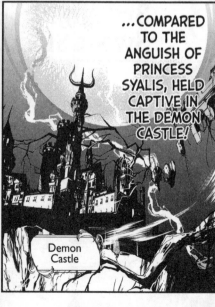

...COMPARED TO THE ANGUISH OF PRINCESS SYALIS, HELD CAPTIVE IN THE DEMON CASTLE!

Demon Castle

I'VE HAD IT UP TO HERE!

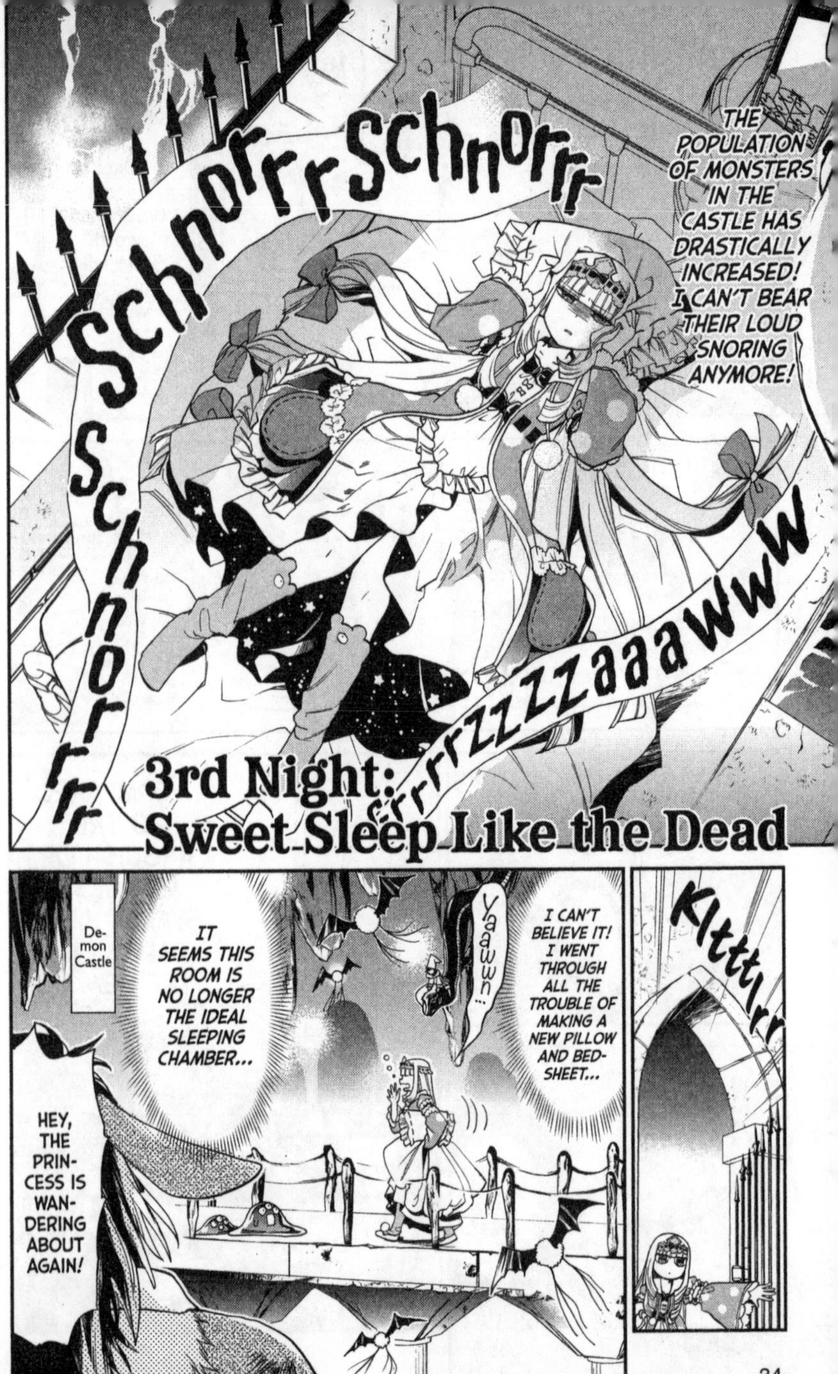
THE POPULATION OF MONSTERS IN THE CASTLE HAS DRASTICALLY INCREASED! I CAN'T BEAR THEIR LOUD SNORING ANYMORE!
Schnorrr Schnorrrr
Schnorrrr
rrrrrzzzzzaaawww
3rd Night: Sweet Sleep Like the Dead
Klttttlrrr
De-mon Castle
I CAN'T BELIEVE IT! I WENT THROUGH ALL THE TROUBLE OF MAKING A NEW PILLOW AND BED-SHEET...
Yaaawwn...
IT SEEMS THIS ROOM IS NO LONGER THE IDEAL SLEEPING CHAMBER...
HEY, THE PRIN-CESS IS WAN-DERING ABOUT AGAIN!

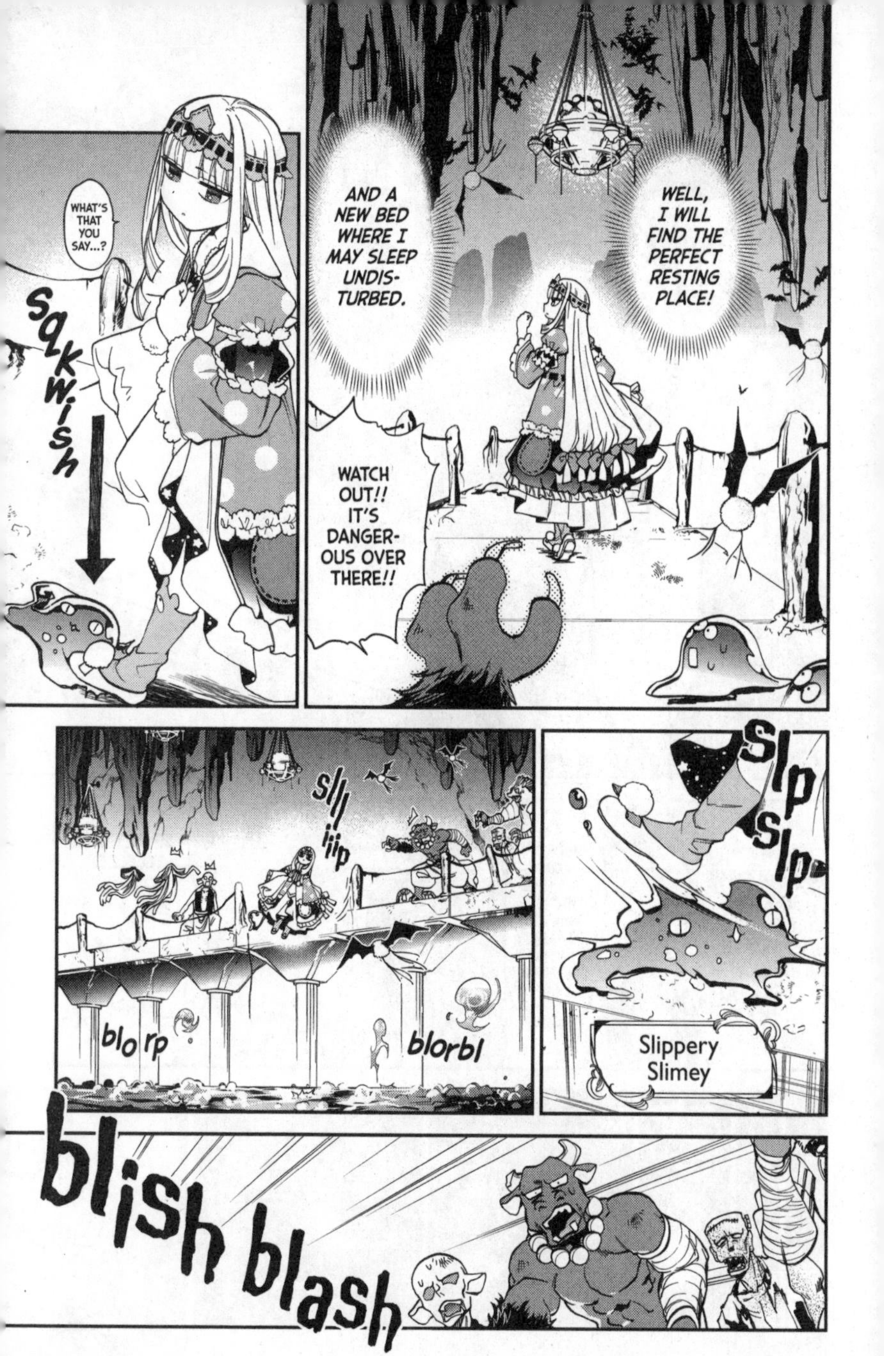
WELL, I WILL FIND THE PERFECT RESTING PLACE!
AND A NEW BED WHERE I MAY SLEEP UNDISTURBED.
WATCH OUT!! IT'S DANGEROUS OVER THERE!!
WHAT'S THAT YOU SAY...?
sqkwish
slp slp slp
Slippery Slimey
sllllllip
blorp
blorbl
blish blash

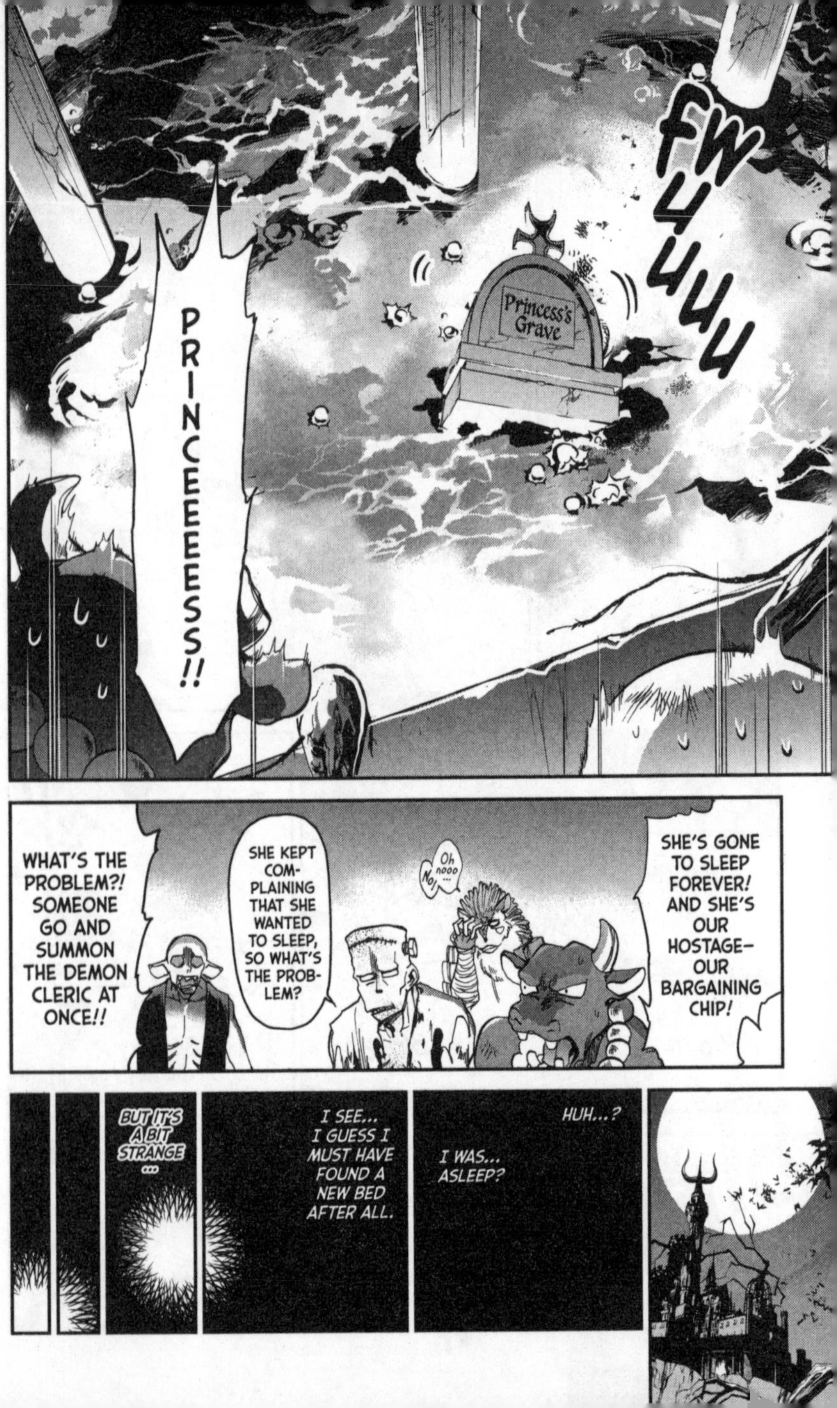
fwuuuu
Princess's Grave
PRINCEEEEESS!!
SHE'S GONE TO SLEEP FOREVER! AND SHE'S OUR HOSTAGE—OUR BARGAINING CHIP!
Oh nooo... No!
SHE KEPT COM-PLAINING THAT SHE WANTED TO SLEEP, SO WHAT'S THE PROB-LEM?
WHAT'S THE PROBLEM?! SOMEONE GO AND SUMMON THE DEMON CLERIC AT ONCE!!
HUH...?
I WAS... ASLEEP?
I SEE... I GUESS I MUST HAVE FOUND A NEW BED AFTER ALL.
BUT IT'S A BIT STRANGE...

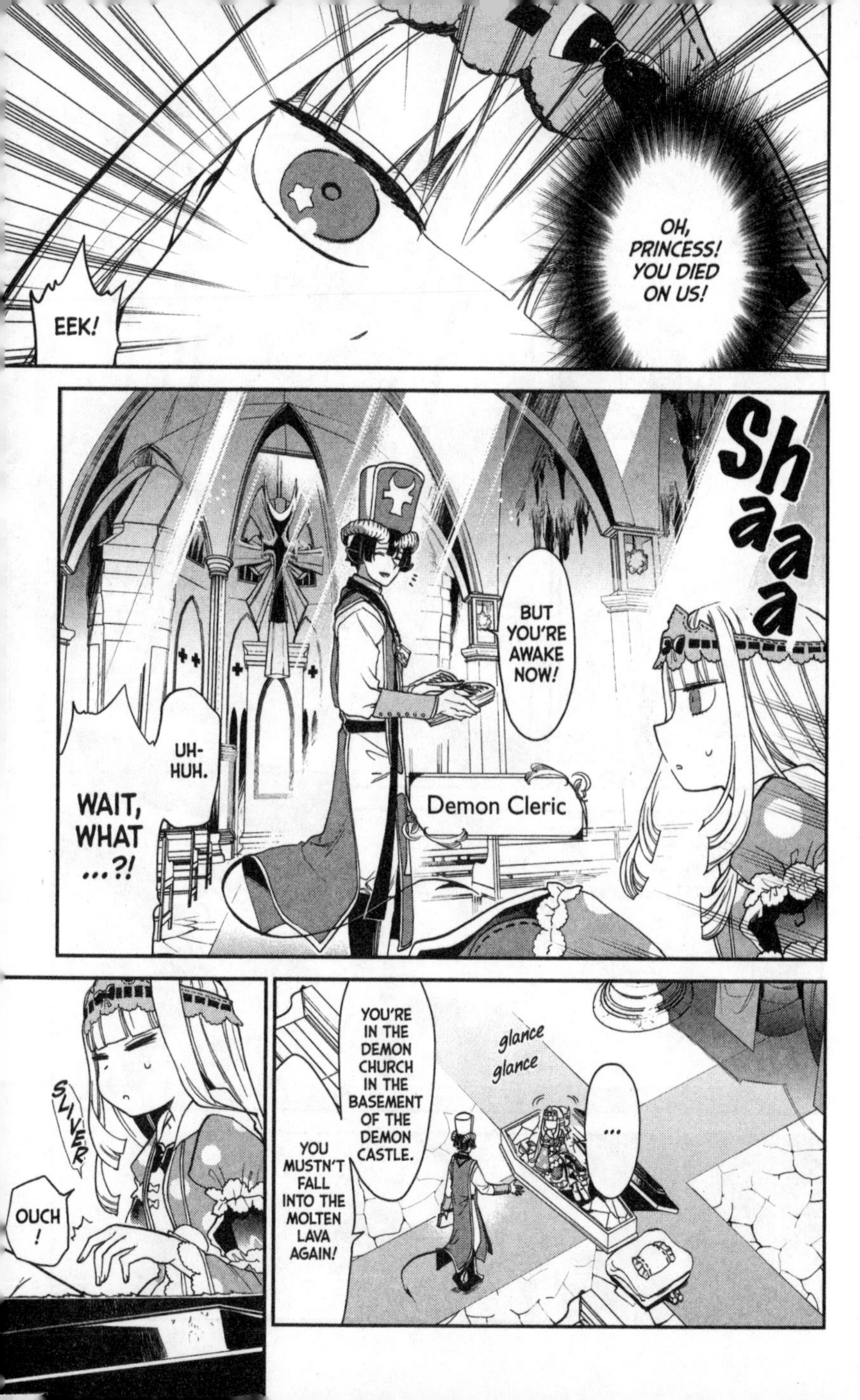
OH, PRINCESS! YOU DIED ON US!
EEK!
Shaaaa
BUT YOU'RE AWAKE NOW!
Demon Cleric
UH-HUH.
WAIT, WHAT ...?!
glance glance
...
YOU'RE IN THE DEMON CHURCH IN THE BASEMENT OF THE DEMON CASTLE.
YOU MUSTN'T FALL INTO THE MOLTEN LAVA AGAIN!
SLIVER
OUCH!

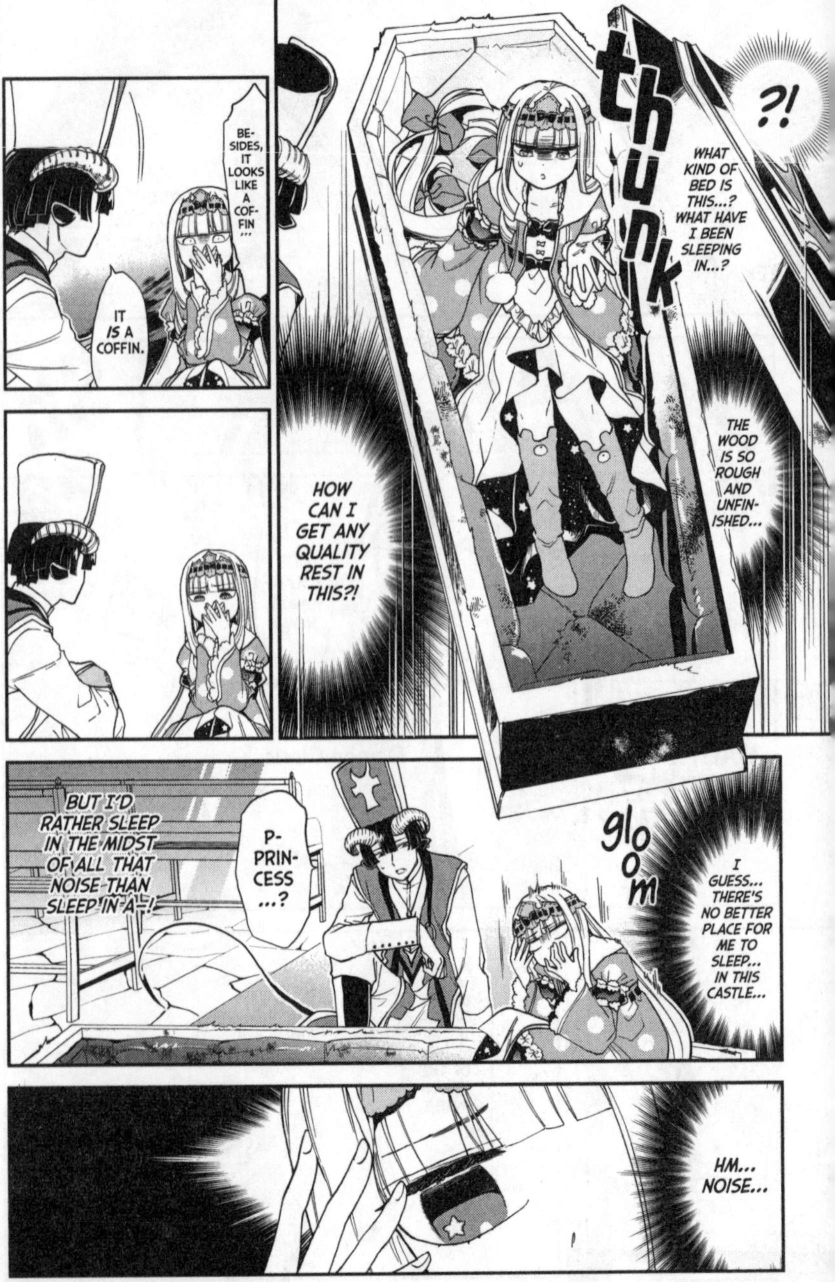
?!
WHAT KIND OF BED IS THIS...? WHAT HAVE I BEEN SLEEPING IN...?
thunk
THE WOOD IS SO ROUGH AND UNFINISHED...
HOW CAN I GET ANY QUALITY REST IN THIS?!
BESIDES, IT LOOKS LIKE A COFFIN...
IT IS A COFFIN.
I GUESS... THERE'S NO BETTER PLACE FOR ME TO SLEEP... IN THIS CASTLE...
gloom
P-PRINCESS...?
BUT I'D RATHER SLEEP IN THE MIDST OF ALL THAT NOISE THAN SLEEP IN A--!
HM... NOISE...

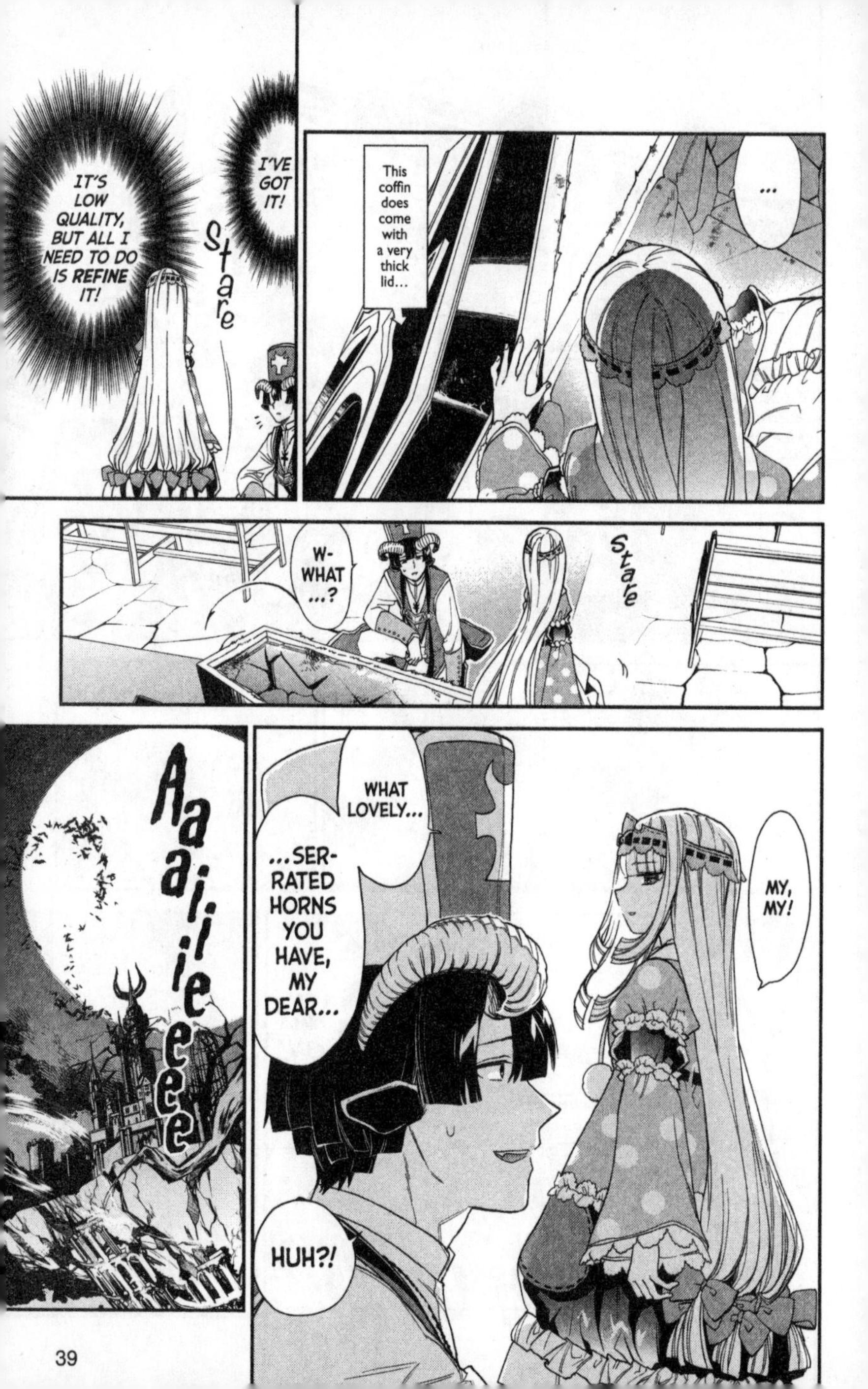
...
This coffin does come with a very thick lid...
I'VE GOT IT!
Stare
IT'S LOW QUALITY, BUT ALL I NEED TO DO IS REFINE IT!
Stare
W-WHAT...?
MY, MY!
WHAT LOVELY...
...SER-RATED HORNS YOU HAVE, MY DEAR...
HUH?!
Aaaiiieeee

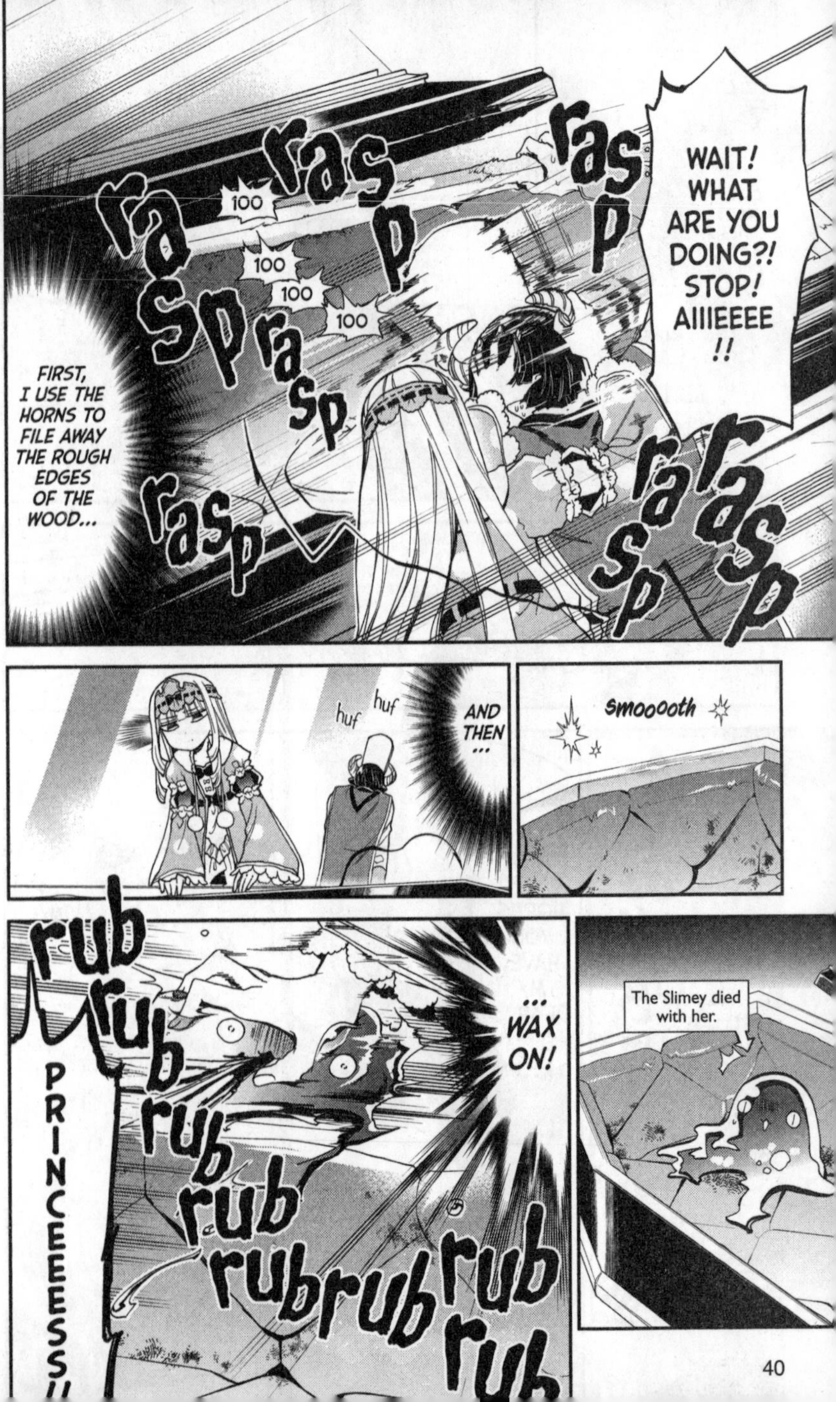
WAIT! WHAT ARE YOU DOING?! STOP! AIIIEEEE!!
rasp
rasp
100
100
100
100
rasp
rasp
rasp
FIRST, I USE THE HORNS TO FILE AWAY THE ROUGH EDGES OF THE WOOD...
rasp
rasp
smoooooth
AND THEN...
huf
huf
The Slimey died with her.
...WAX ON!
rub rub rub rub rub rub rubrubrubrub rub
PRINCEEEESS!!

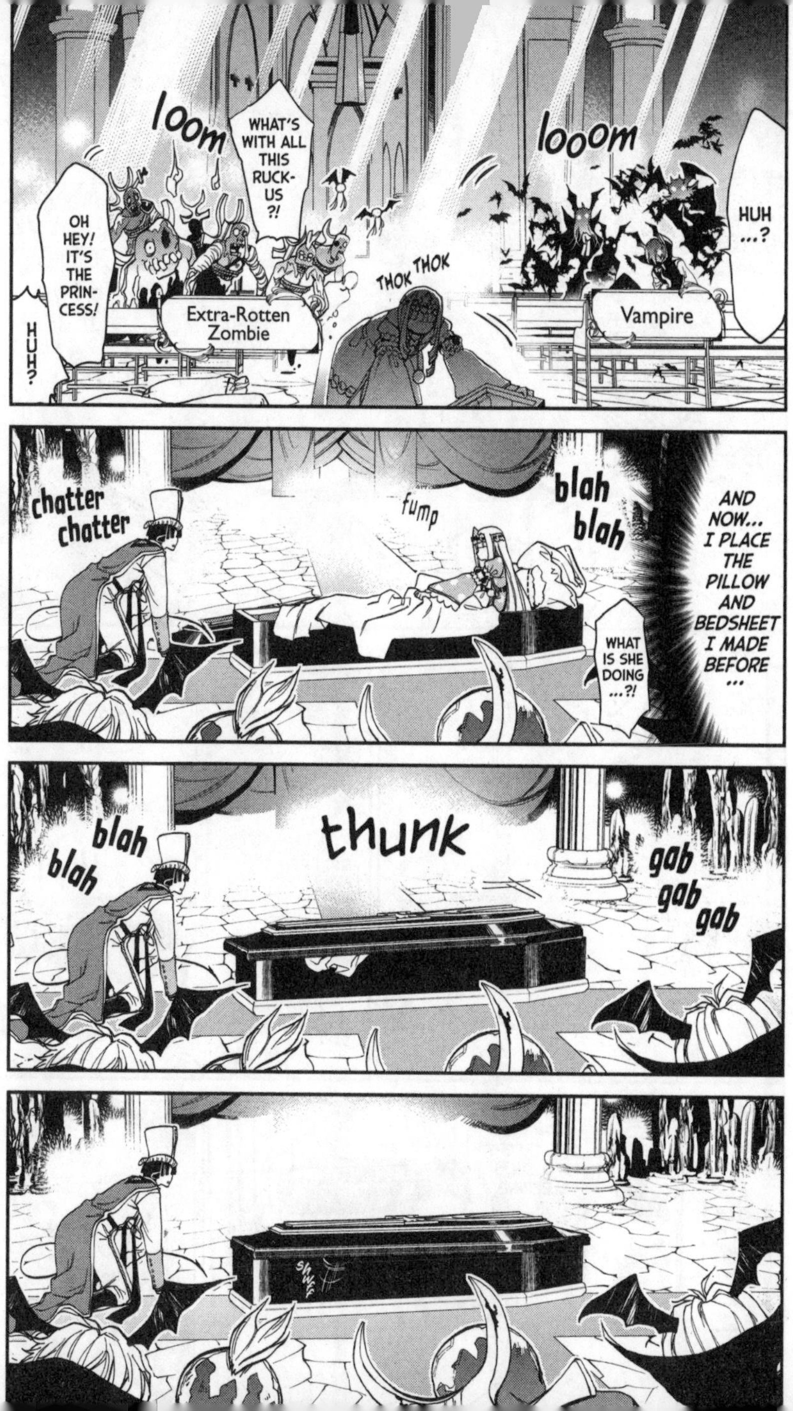
looom
HUH ...?
Vampire
THOK THOK
WHAT'S WITH ALL THIS RUCK-US ?!
loom
OH HEY! IT'S THE PRIN-CESS!
Extra-Rotten Zombie
HUH?
AND NOW... I PLACE THE PILLOW AND BEDSHEET I MADE BEFORE ...
blah blah
WHAT IS SHE DOING ...?!
fump
chatter chatter
gab gab gab
thunk
blah blah

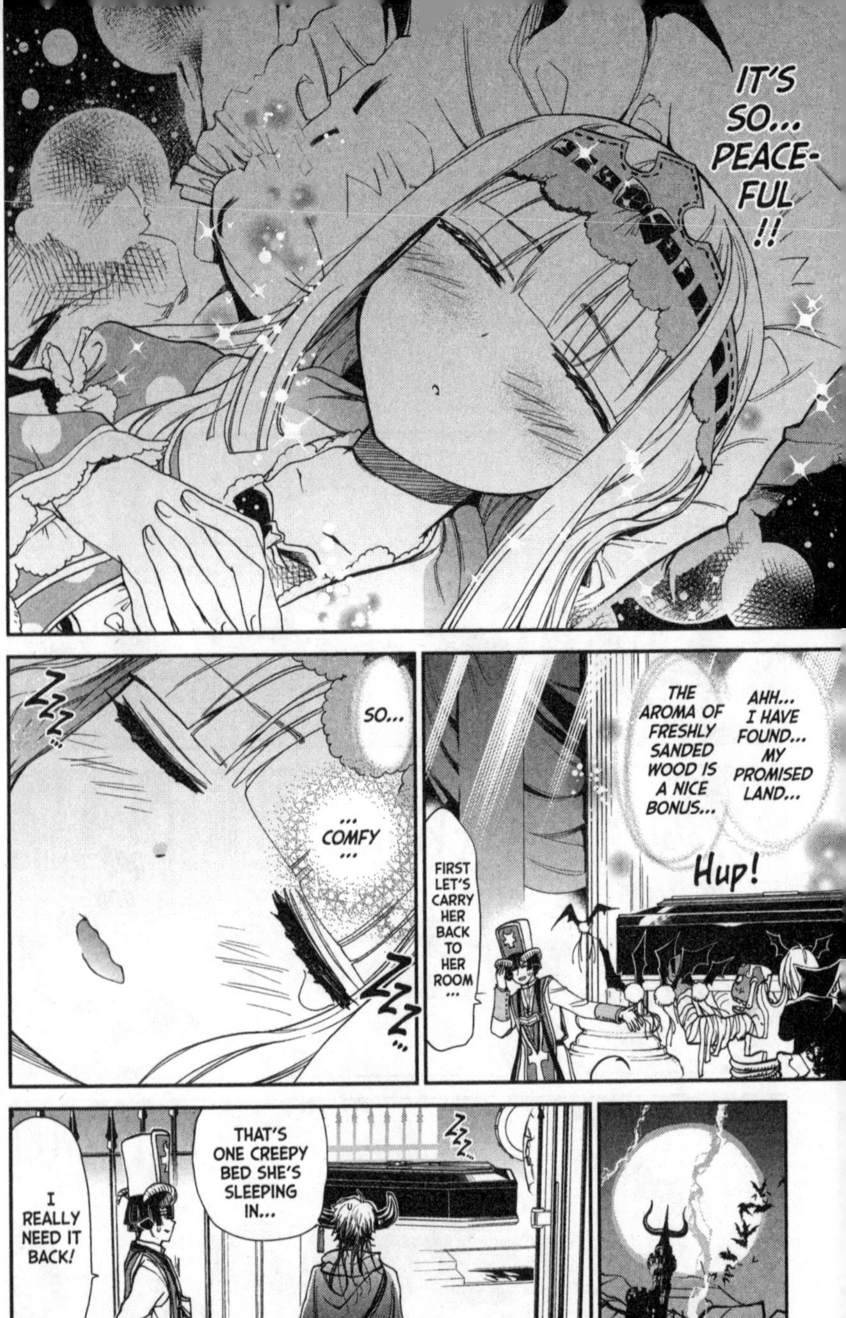
IT'S SO... PEACE-FUL !!
AHH... I HAVE FOUND... MY PROMISED LAND...
THE AROMA OF FRESHLY SANDED WOOD IS A NICE BONUS...
Hup!
FIRST LET'S CARRY HER BACK TO HER ROOM...
SO...
... COMFY ...
ZZZ...
ZZZ...
ZZZ...
THAT'S ONE CREEPY BED SHE'S SLEEPING IN...
I REALLY NEED IT BACK!

Demon Cleric

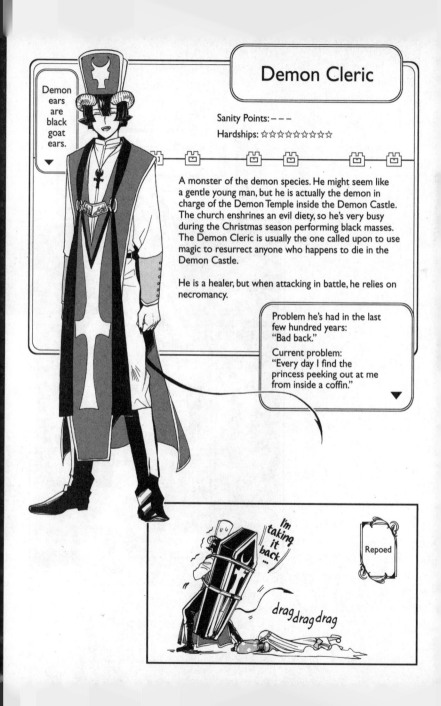

Demon ears are black goat ears.

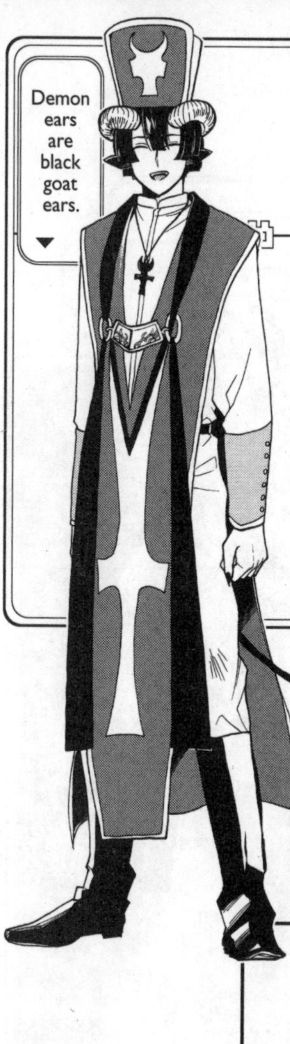

Sanity Points: – – –

Hardships: ☆☆☆☆☆☆☆☆☆☆

A monster of the demon species. He might seem like a gentle young man, but he is actually the demon in charge of the Demon Temple inside the Demon Castle. The church enshrines an evil diety, so he's very busy during the Christmas season performing black masses. The Demon Cleric is usually the one called upon to use magic to resurrect anyone who happens to die in the Demon Castle.

He is a healer, but when attacking in battle, he relies on necromancy.

Problem he's had in the last few hundred years:
"Bad back."

Current problem:
"Every day I find the princess peeking out at me from inside a coffin."

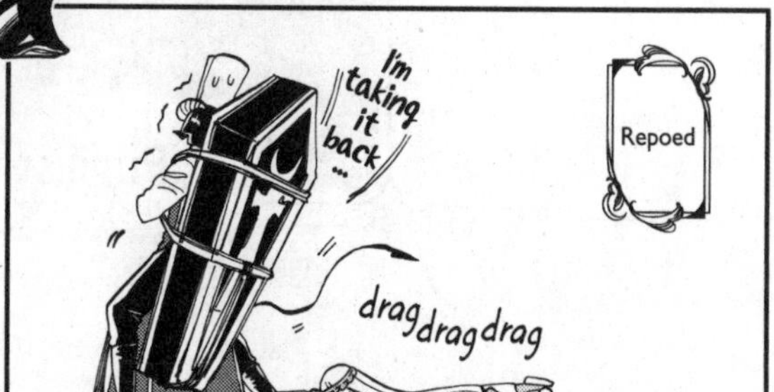
Repoed
I'm taking it back...
drag drag drag

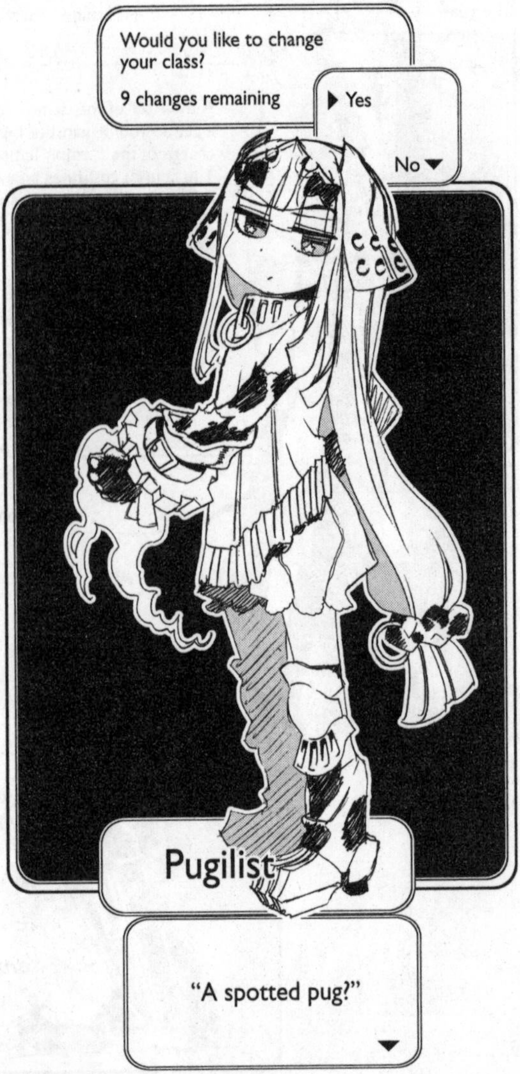
Would you like to change your class?
9 changes remaining
▶ Yes
No ▼
Pugilist
"A spotted pug?"

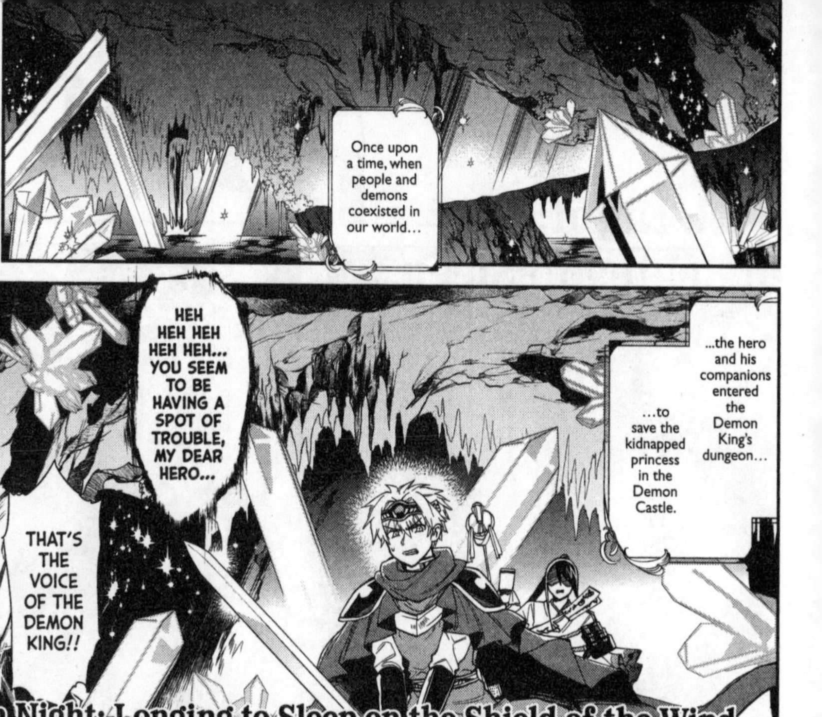
Once upon a time, when people and demons coexisted in our world…
…the hero and his companions entered the Demon King's dungeon…
…to save the kidnapped princess in the Demon Castle.
HEH HEH HEH HEH HEH… YOU SEEM TO BE HAVING A SPOT OF TROUBLE, MY DEAR HERO…
THAT'S THE VOICE OF THE DEMON KING!!

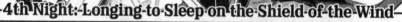

4th Night: Longing to Sleep on the Shield of the Wind

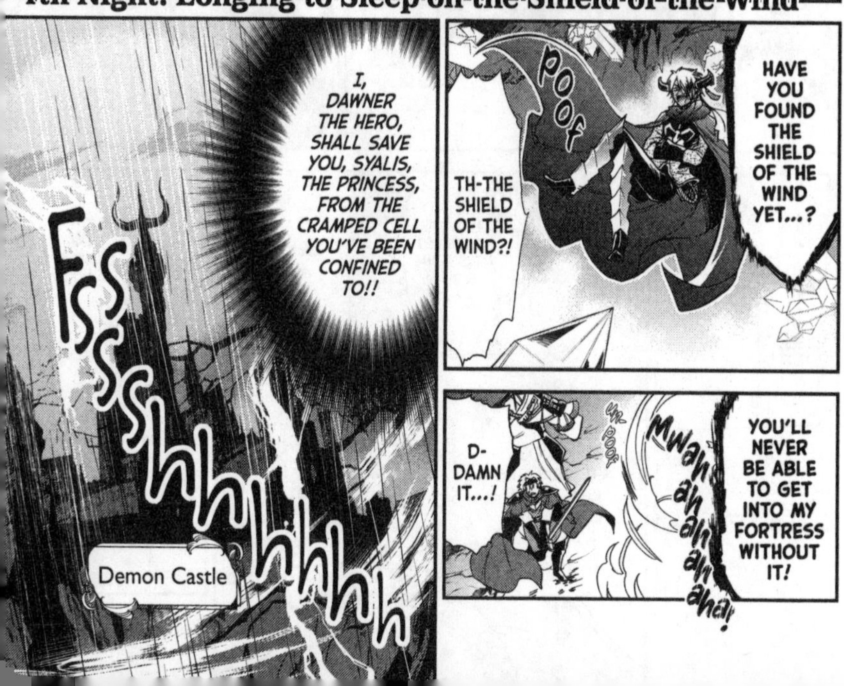
HAVE YOU FOUND THE SHIELD OF THE WIND YET…?
POOF
TH-THE SHIELD OF THE WIND?!
YOU'LL NEVER BE ABLE TO GET INTO MY FORTRESS WITHOUT IT!
Mwah ah ah ah ah aha!
D-DAMN IT…!
I, DAWNER THE HERO, SHALL SAVE YOU, SYALIS, THE PRINCESS, FROM THE CRAMPED CELL YOU'VE BEEN CONFINED TO!!
Fsssshhhhhhhh
Demon Castle

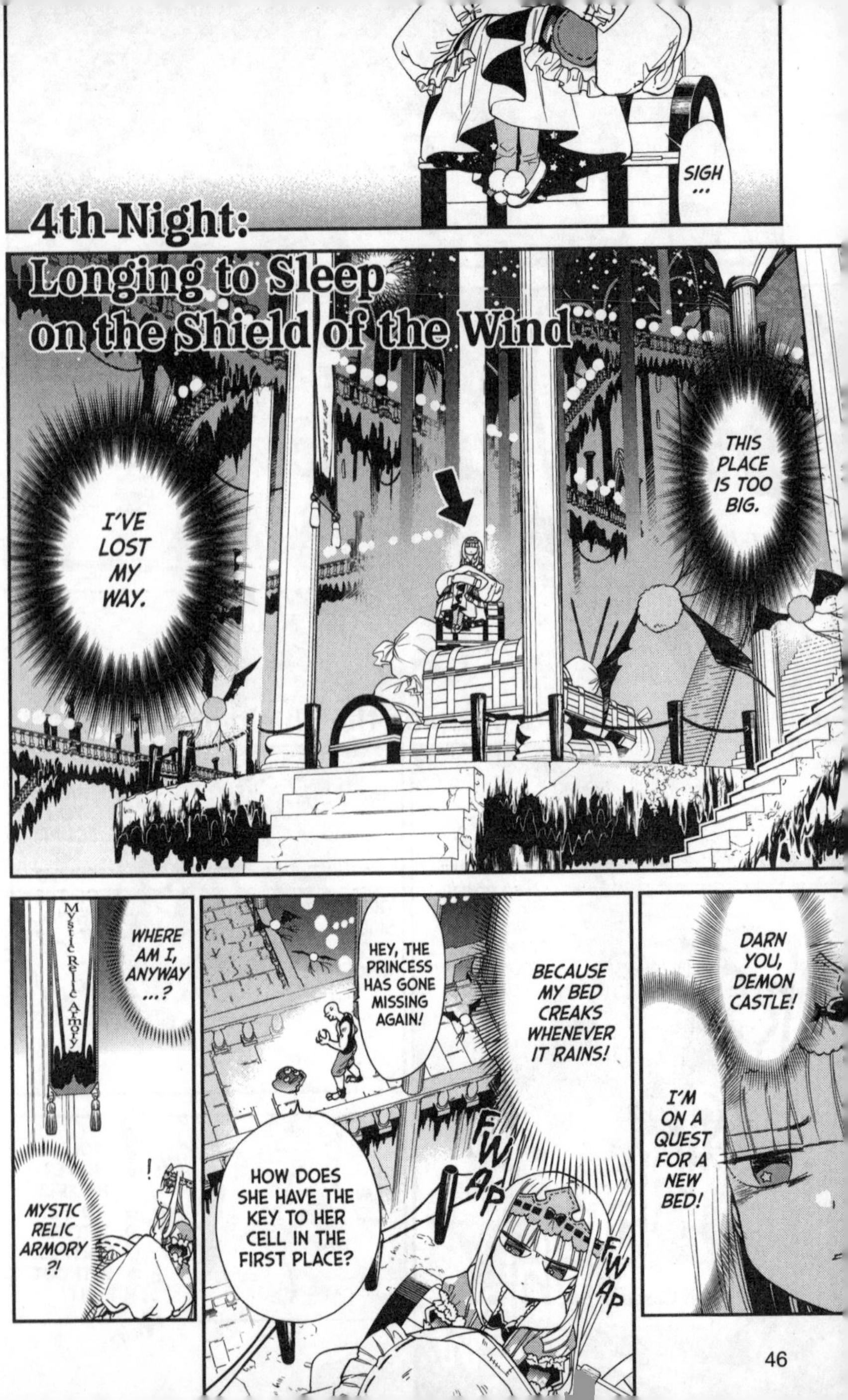
SIGH...
4th Night: Longing to Sleep on the Shield of the Wind
THIS PLACE IS TOO BIG.
I'VE LOST MY WAY.
DARN YOU, DEMON CASTLE!
I'M ON A QUEST FOR A NEW BED!
BECAUSE MY BED CREAKS WHENEVER IT RAINS!
HEY, THE PRINCESS HAS GONE MISSING AGAIN!
FWAP
FWAP
HOW DOES SHE HAVE THE KEY TO HER CELL IN THE FIRST PLACE?
WHERE AM I, ANYWAY...?
Mystic Relic Armory
!
MYSTIC RELIC ARMORY?!

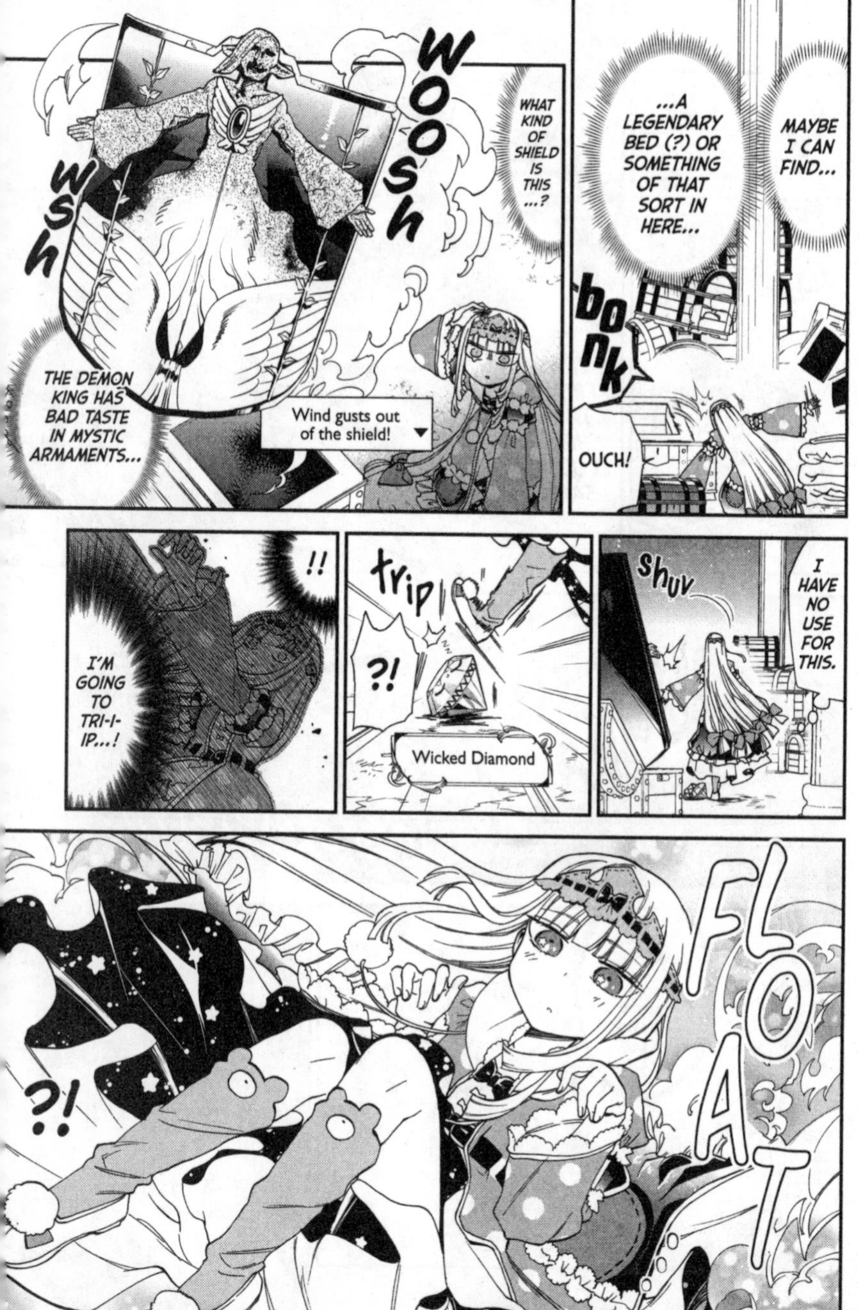
MAYBE I CAN FIND...
...A LEGENDARY BED (?) OR SOMETHING OF THAT SORT IN HERE...
bonk
OUCH!
WHAT KIND OF SHIELD IS THIS ...?
WOOSH
WSH
Wind gusts out of the shield!
THE DEMON KING HAS BAD TASTE IN MYSTIC ARMAMENTS...
I HAVE NO USE FOR THIS.
shuv
trip
?!
Wicked Diamond
!!
I'M GOING TO TRI-I-IP...!
FLOAT
?!

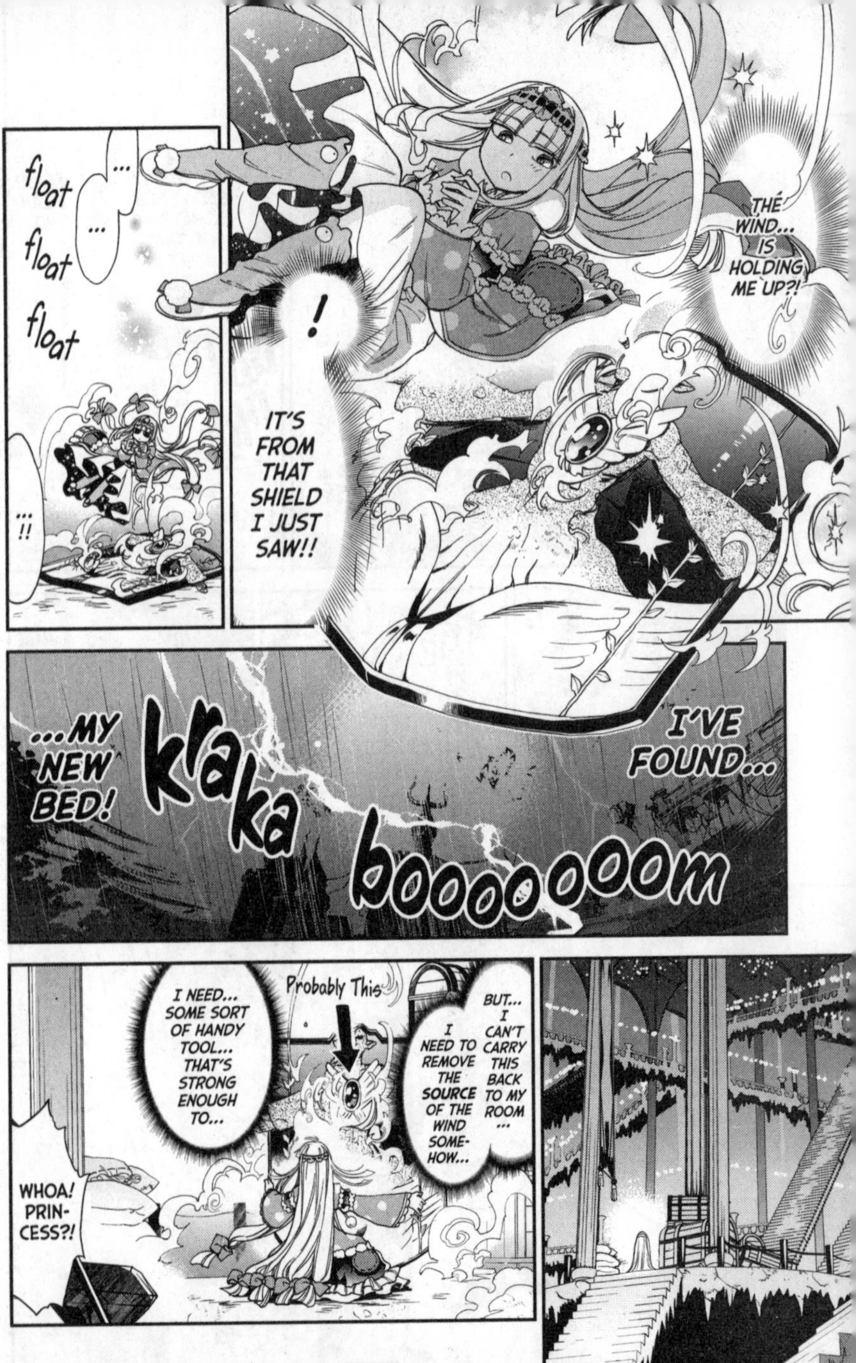
THE WIND... IS HOLDING ME UP?!
!
IT'S FROM THAT SHIELD I JUST SAW!!
float
float
float
...
...
...!!
I'VE FOUND...
kraka
booooooom
...MY NEW BED!
BUT... I CAN'T CARRY THIS BACK TO MY ROOM ...
I NEED TO REMOVE THE SOURCE OF THE WIND SOME-HOW...
Probably This
I NEED... SOME SORT OF HANDY TOOL... THAT'S STRONG ENOUGH TO...
WHOA! PRINCESS?!

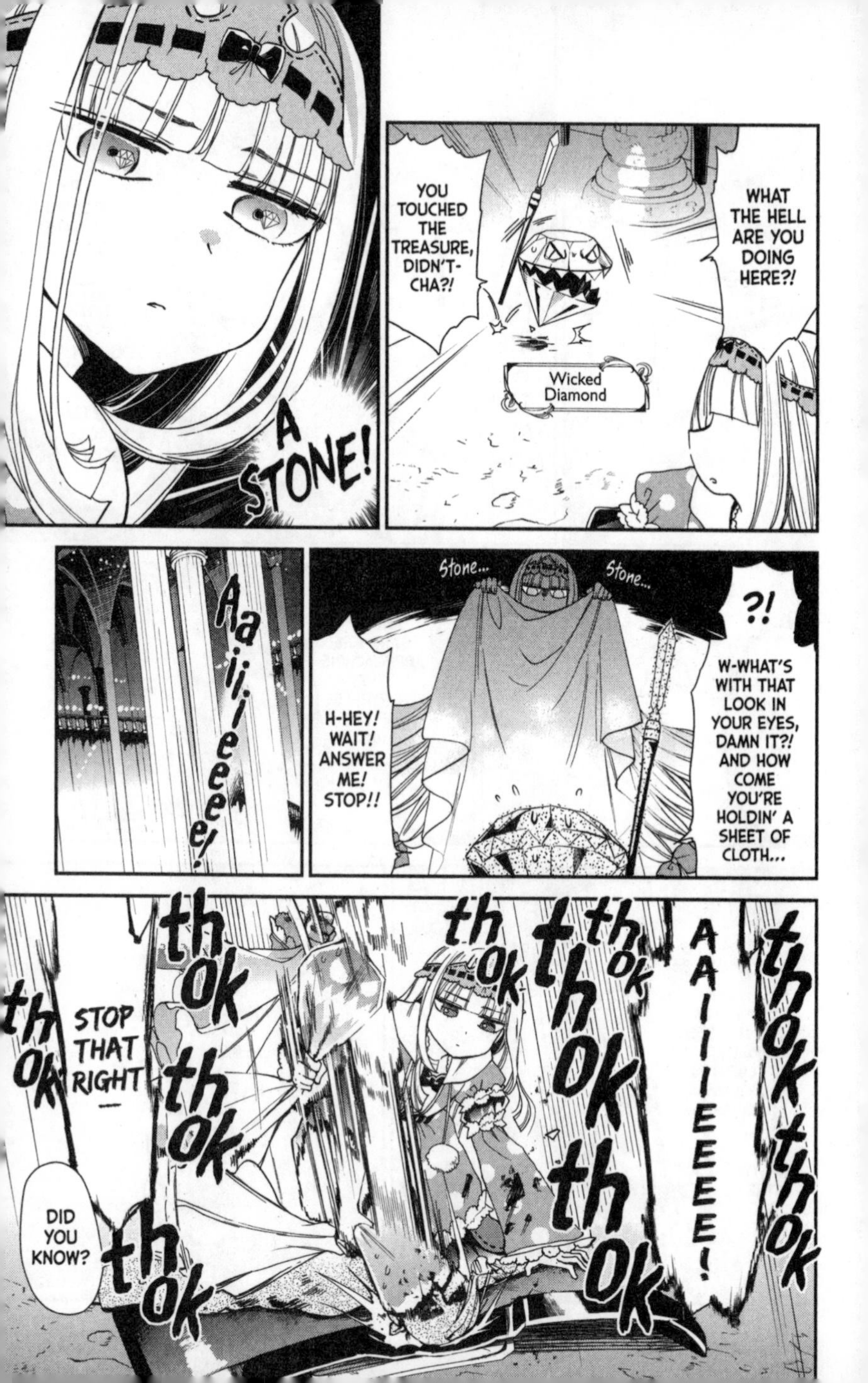
WHAT THE HELL ARE YOU DOING HERE?!
YOU TOUCHED THE TREASURE, DIDN'T-CHA?!
Wicked Diamond
A STONE!
?!
Stone...
Stone...
W-WHAT'S WITH THAT LOOK IN YOUR EYES, DAMN IT?! AND HOW COME YOU'RE HOLDIN' A SHEET OF CLOTH...
H-HEY! WAIT! ANSWER ME! STOP!!
Aaaiiieeeee!
thok
thok
AAIIIEEEE!
thok
STOP THAT RIGHT—
thok
DID YOU KNOW?

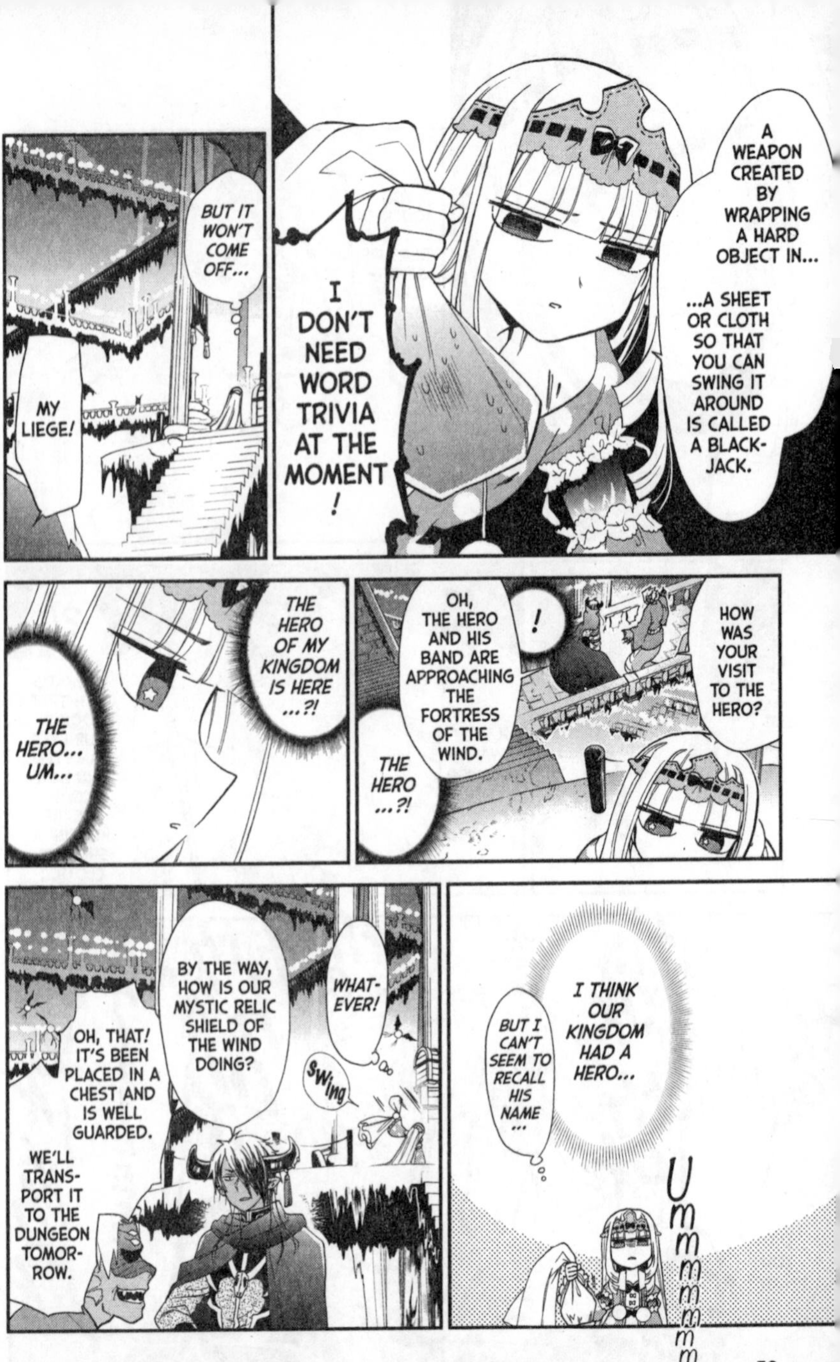

A WEAPON CREATED BY WRAPPING A HARD OBJECT IN...
...A SHEET OR CLOTH SO THAT YOU CAN SWING IT AROUND IS CALLED A BLACK-JACK.
I DON'T NEED WORD TRIVIA AT THE MOMENT!
BUT IT WON'T COME OFF...
MY LIEGE!
HOW WAS YOUR VISIT TO THE HERO?
!
OH, THE HERO AND HIS BAND ARE APPROACHING THE FORTRESS OF THE WIND.
THE HERO...?!
THE HERO OF MY KINGDOM IS HERE...?!
THE HERO... UM...
I THINK OUR KINGDOM HAD A HERO...
BUT I CAN'T SEEM TO RECALL HIS NAME...
Ummmmmmmm
BY THE WAY, HOW IS OUR MYSTIC RELIC SHIELD OF THE WIND DOING?
WHAT-EVER!
SWING
OH, THAT! IT'S BEEN PLACED IN A CHEST AND IS WELL GUARDED.
WE'LL TRANS-PORT IT TO THE DUNGEON TOMOR-ROW.

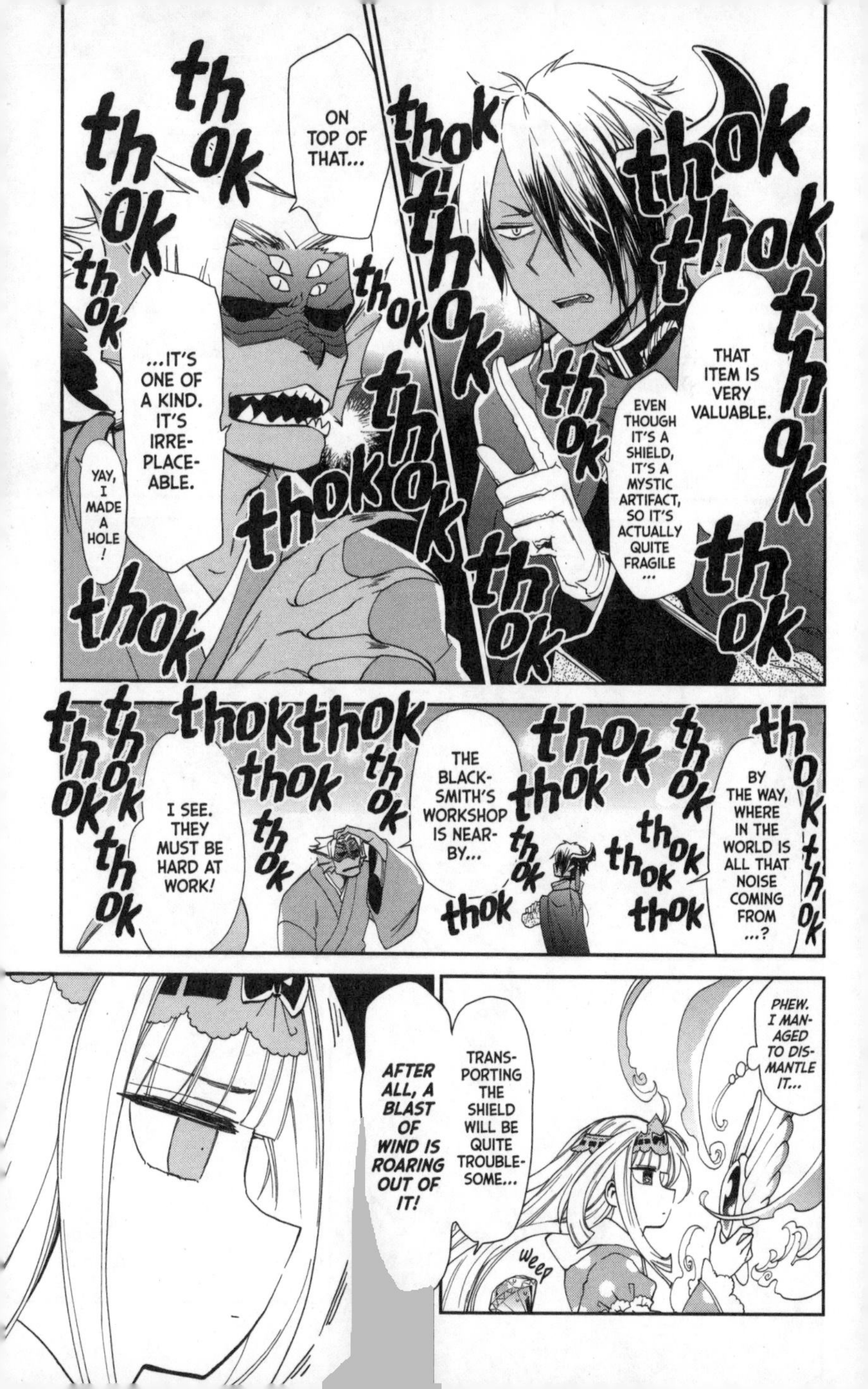
thok
THAT ITEM IS VERY VALUABLE.
EVEN THOUGH IT'S A SHIELD, IT'S A MYSTIC ARTIFACT, SO IT'S ACTUALLY QUITE FRAGILE...
ON TOP OF THAT...
...IT'S ONE OF A KIND. IT'S IRREPLACEABLE.
YAY, I MADE A HOLE!
thok
BY THE WAY, WHERE IN THE WORLD IS ALL THAT NOISE COMING FROM...?
THE BLACKSMITH'S WORKSHOP IS NEARBY...
I SEE. THEY MUST BE HARD AT WORK!
PHEW. I MANAGED TO DISMANTLE IT...
weep
TRANSPORTING THE SHIELD WILL BE QUITE TROUBLESOME...
AFTER ALL, A BLAST OF WIND IS ROARING OUT OF IT!

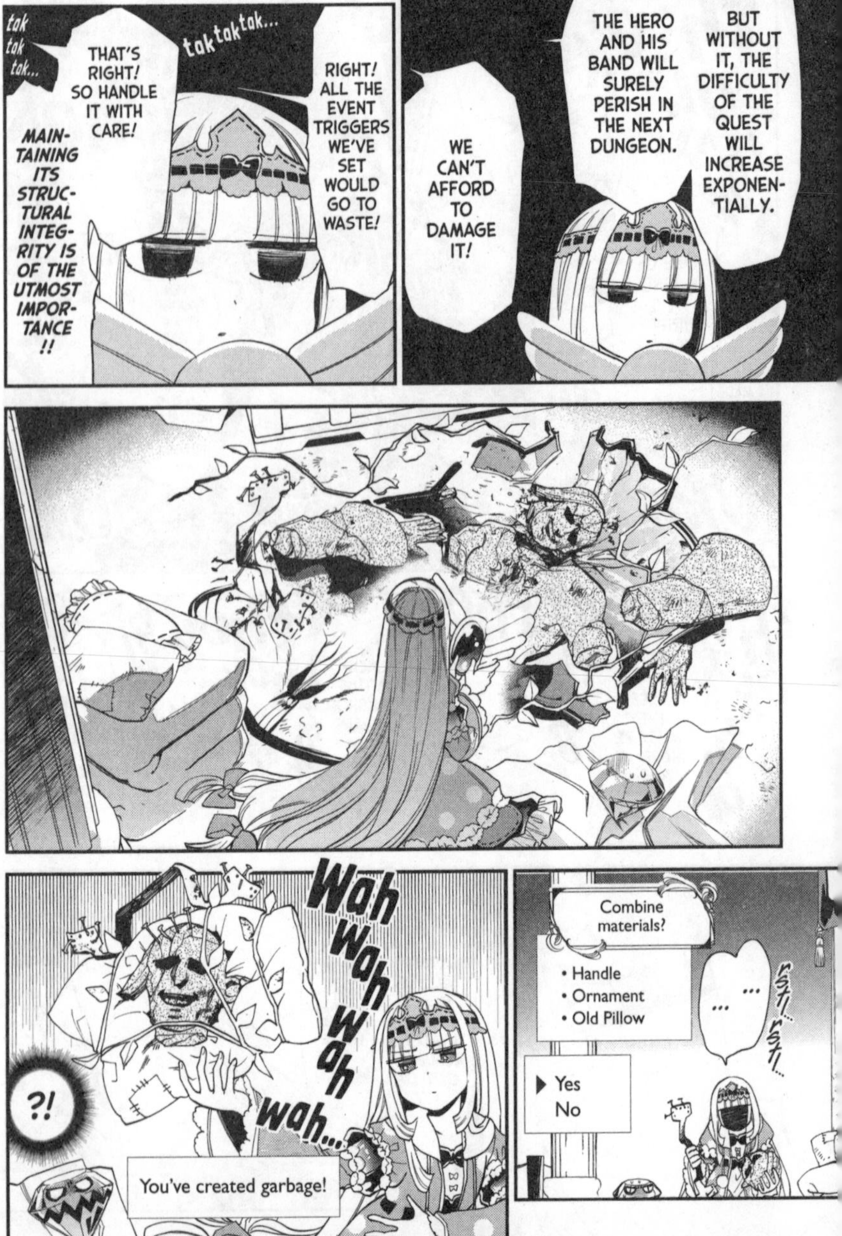
BUT WITHOUT IT, THE DIFFICULTY OF THE QUEST WILL INCREASE EXPONENTIALLY.
THE HERO AND HIS BAND WILL SURELY PERISH IN THE NEXT DUNGEON.
WE CAN'T AFFORD TO DAMAGE IT!
RIGHT! ALL THE EVENT TRIGGERS WE'VE SET WOULD GO TO WASTE!
tak tak tak...
THAT'S RIGHT! SO HANDLE IT WITH CARE!
tak tak tak...
MAINTAINING ITS STRUCTURAL INTEGRITY IS OF THE UTMOST IMPORTANCE!!
Combine materials?
• Handle
• Ornament
• Old Pillow
▸ Yes
No
rstl rstl...
... ...
Wah wah wah wah wah wah...
?!
You've created garbage!

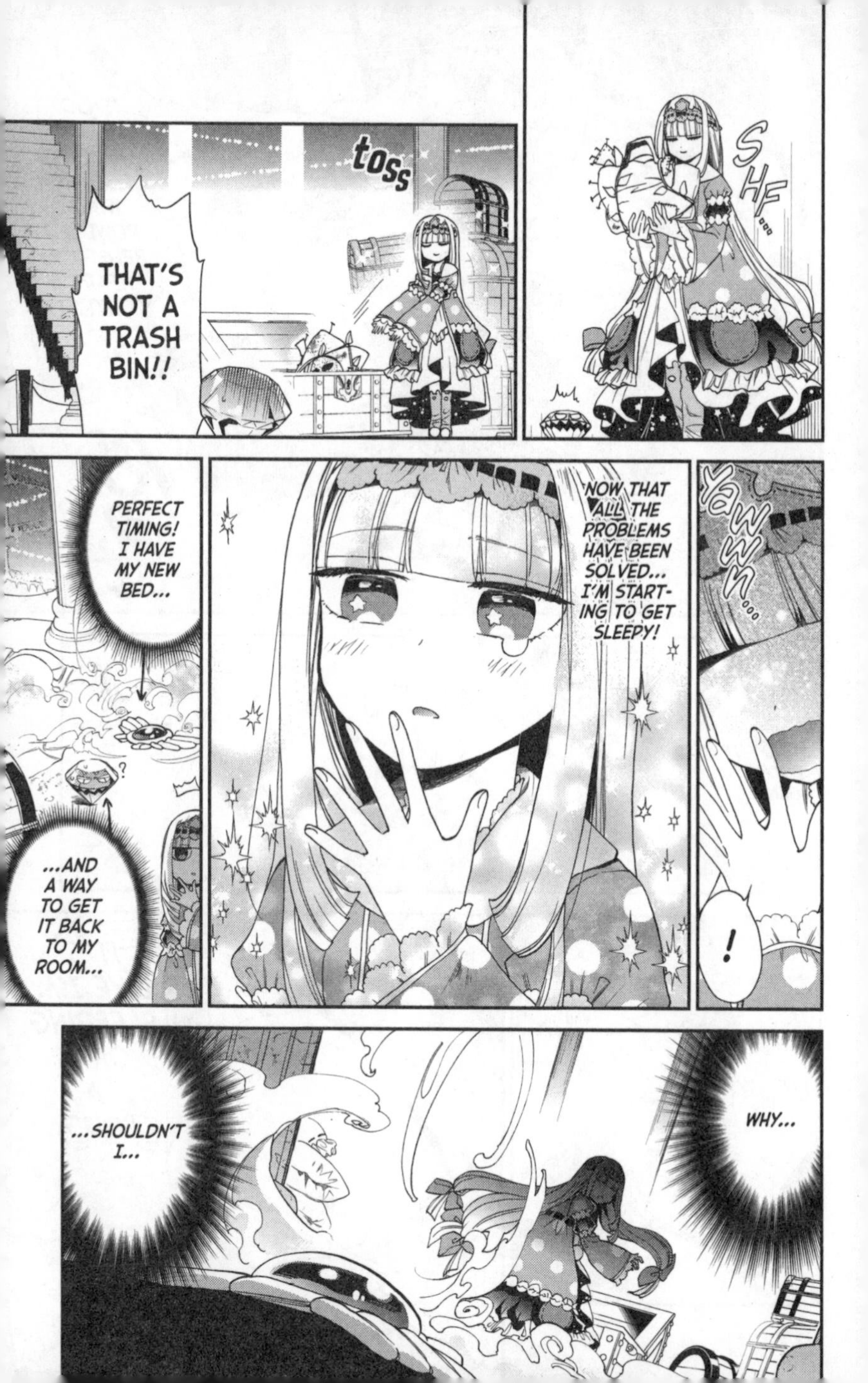
SHF...
toss
THAT'S NOT A TRASH BIN!!
YAWWN...
!
NOW THAT ALL THE PROBLEMS HAVE BEEN SOLVED... I'M STARTING TO GET SLEEPY!
PERFECT TIMING! I HAVE MY NEW BED...
...AND A WAY TO GET IT BACK TO MY ROOM...
?
WHY...
...SHOULDN'T I...

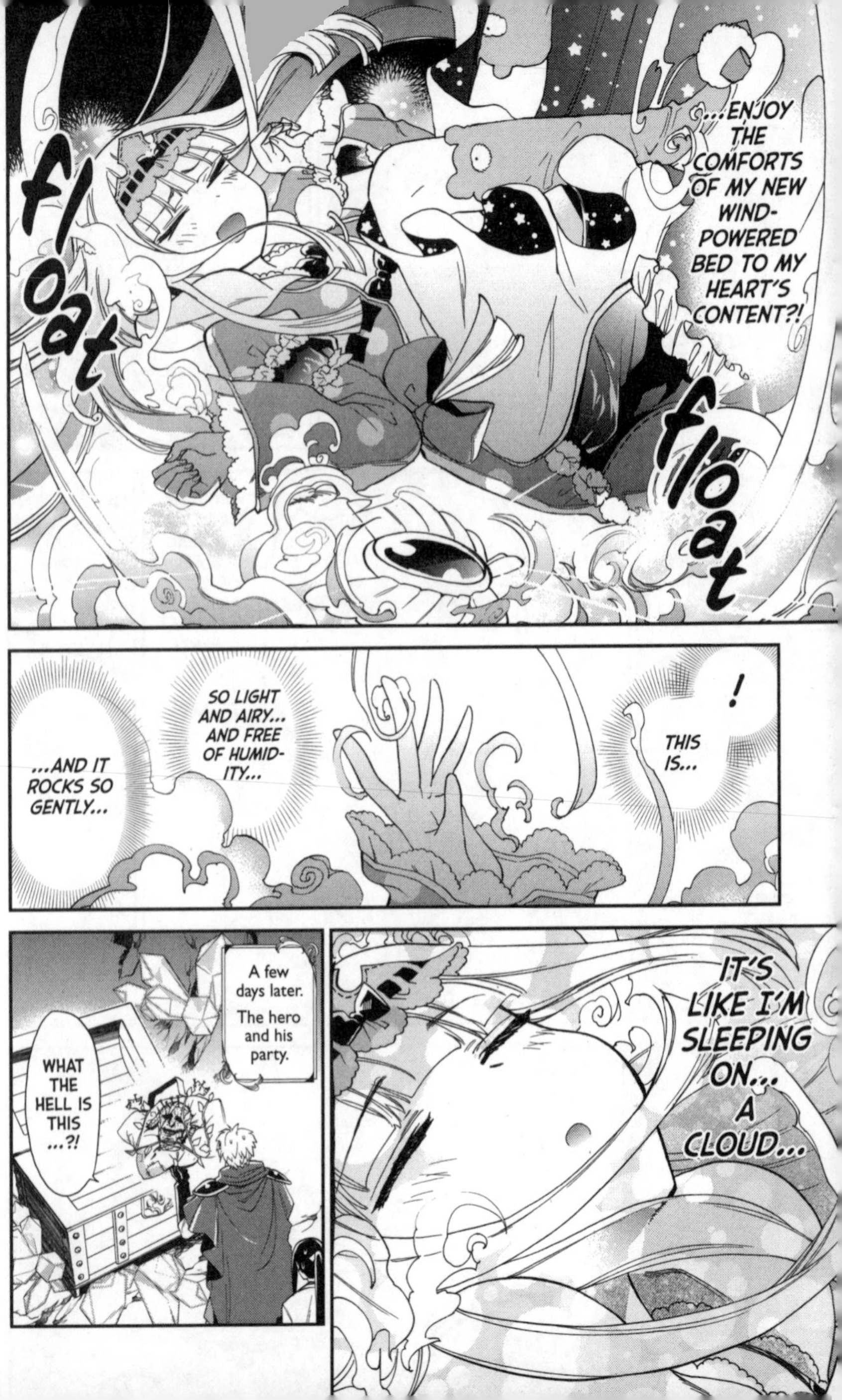
...ENJOY THE COMFORTS OF MY NEW WIND-POWERED BED TO MY HEART'S CONTENT?!
float
float
!
THIS IS...
SO LIGHT AND AIRY... AND FREE OF HUMID-ITY...
...AND IT ROCKS SO GENTLY...
IT'S LIKE I'M SLEEPING ON... A CLOUD...
A few days later.
The hero and his party.
WHAT THE HELL IS THIS ...?!

Dawner the Hero

Courage: ☆☆☆☆☆☆☆☆☆

Presence: ☆

The hero who has appeared to save the kidnapped princess. Human. As a hero, he lives to rescue princesses.

The Unified Human Nation of Goodereste has great faith in Dawner, and he has been credited with many noble deeds, so Princess Syalis has definitely met him before. But for some reason, he leaves no memorable impression on her.

Favorite food:
"Goodereste-style meat loaf."

Former problem:
"The princess doesn't remember who I am."

Current problem:
"I must rescue the princess!"

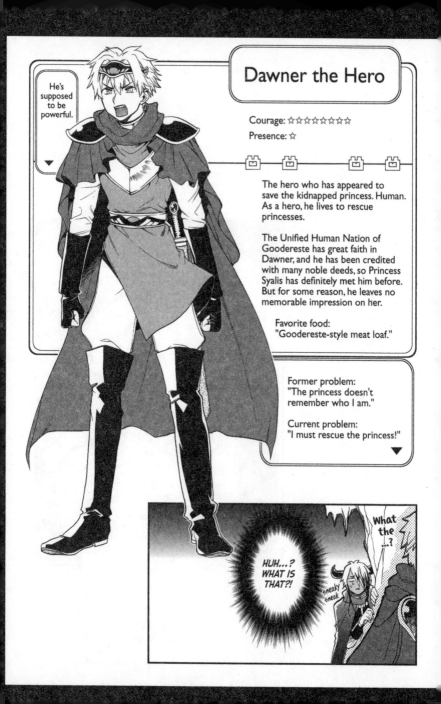

He's supposed to be powerful.

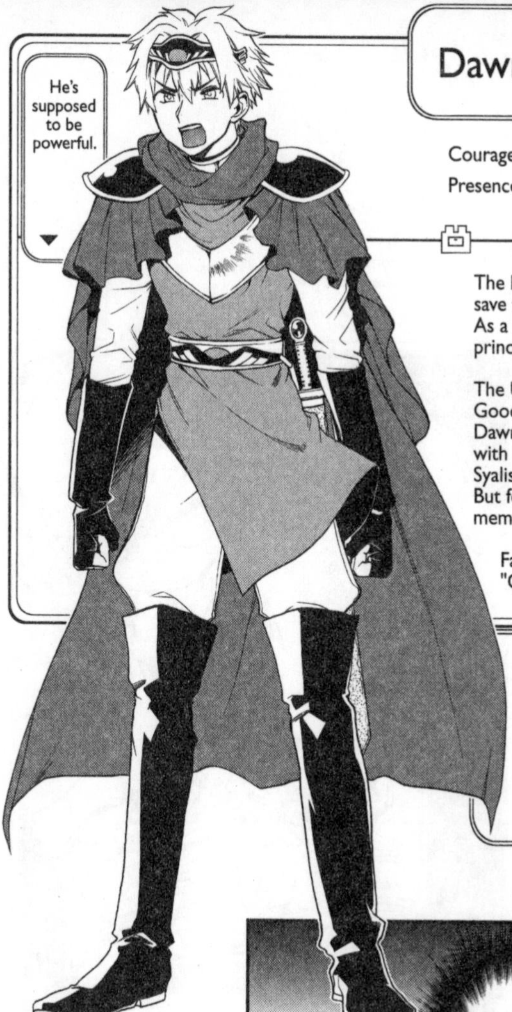

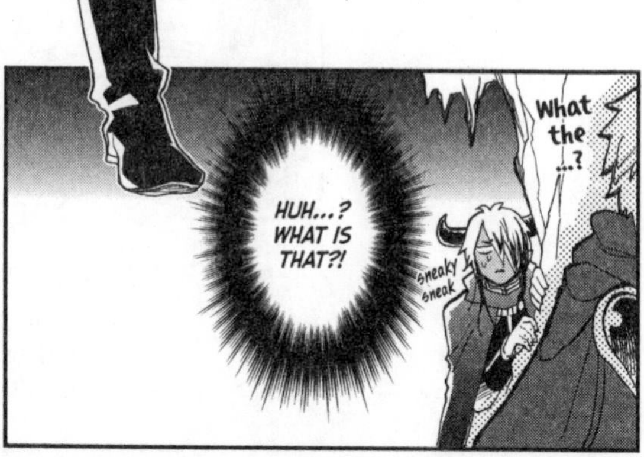
What the ...?
HUH...? WHAT IS THAT?!
sneaky sneak

Would you like to change
your class?

8 changes
remaining

▶ Yes

No ▼

Sage

You have obtained
sacrilegious
knowledge.

▼

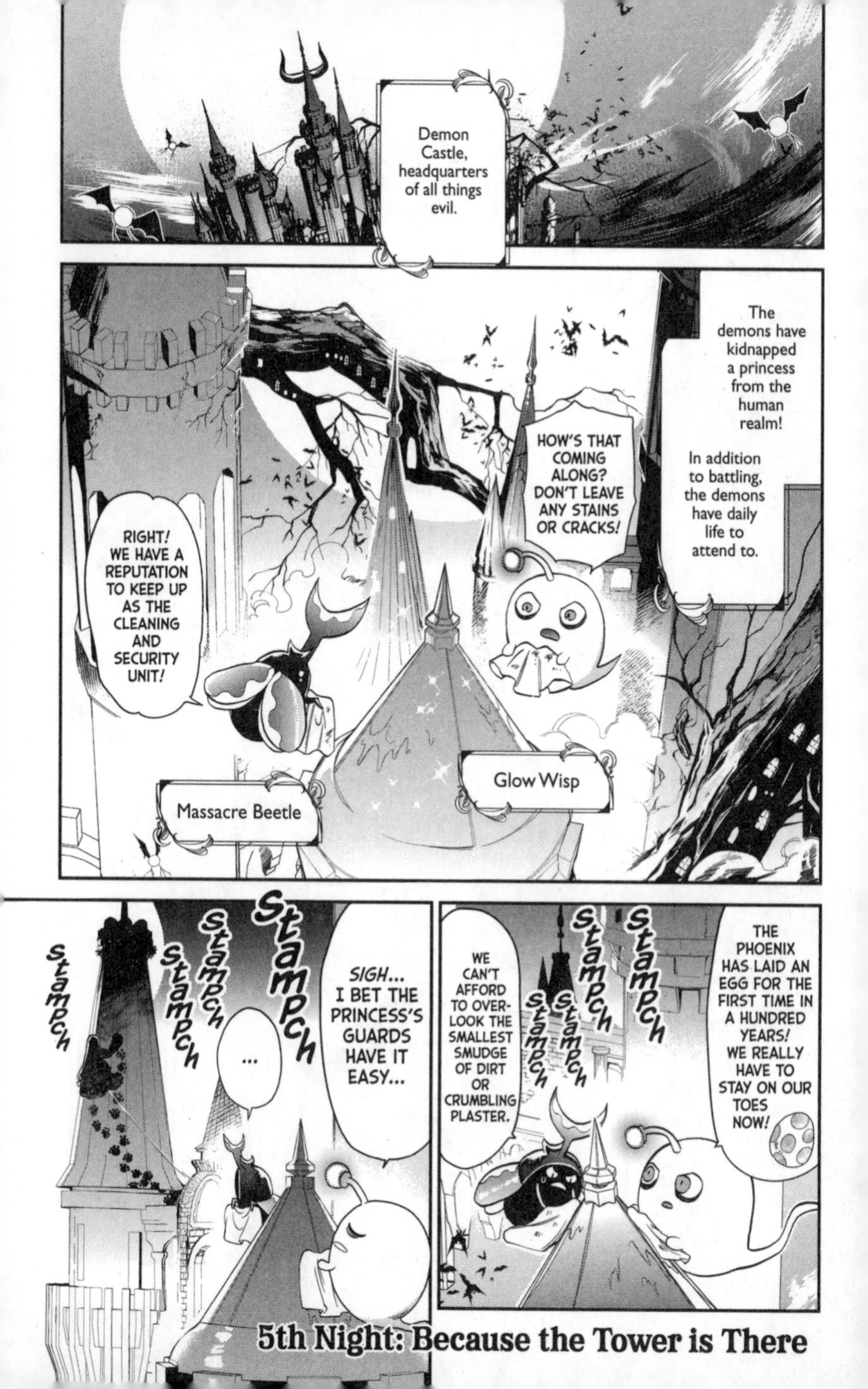
Demon Castle, headquarters of all things evil.
The demons have kidnapped a princess from the human realm!
In addition to battling, the demons have daily life to attend to.
HOW'S THAT COMING ALONG? DON'T LEAVE ANY STAINS OR CRACKS!
Glow Wisp
RIGHT! WE HAVE A REPUTATION TO KEEP UP AS THE CLEANING AND SECURITY UNIT!
Massacre Beetle
THE PHOENIX HAS LAID AN EGG FOR THE FIRST TIME IN A HUNDRED YEARS! WE REALLY HAVE TO STAY ON OUR TOES NOW!
Stampch stampch
Stampch stampch
WE CAN'T AFFORD TO OVER-LOOK THE SMALLEST SMUDGE OF DIRT OR CRUMBLING PLASTER.
SIGH... I BET THE PRINCESS'S GUARDS HAVE IT EASY...
...
Stampch stampch stampch
Stampch

5th Night: Because the Tower is There

HUH?

5th Night: Because the Tower is There

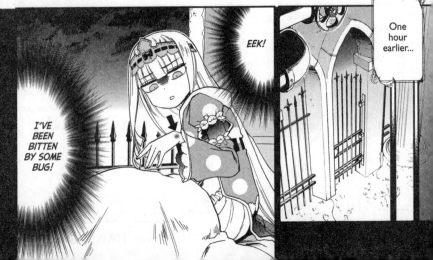

EEK!

One hour earlier...

I'VE BEEN BITTEN BY SOME BUG!

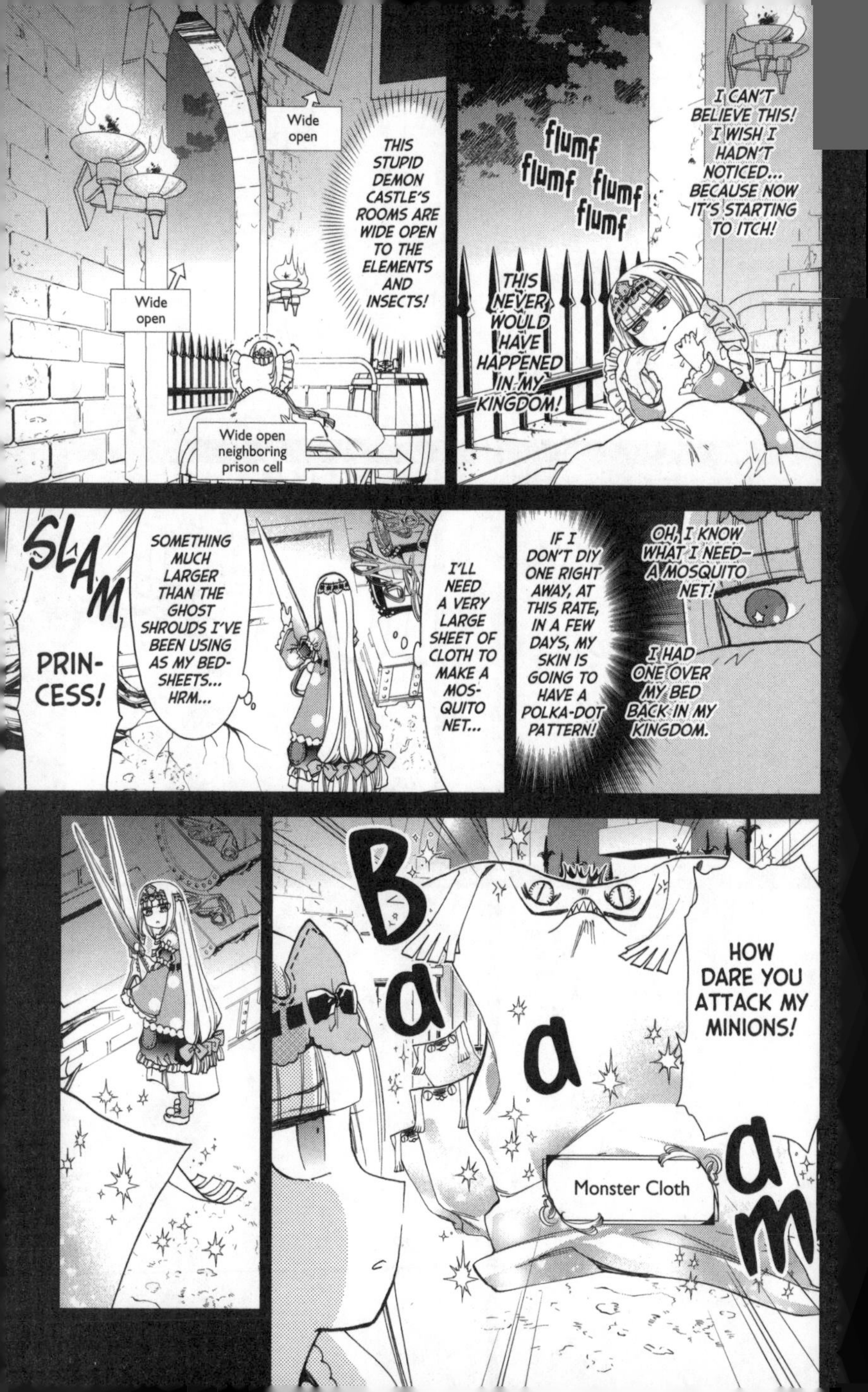
I CAN'T BELIEVE THIS! I WISH I HADN'T NOTICED... BECAUSE NOW IT'S STARTING TO ITCH!
flumf flumf flumf flumf
THIS NEVER WOULD HAVE HAPPENED IN MY KINGDOM!
THIS STUPID DEMON CASTLE'S ROOMS ARE WIDE OPEN TO THE ELEMENTS AND INSECTS!
Wide open
Wide open
Wide open neighboring prison cell
OH, I KNOW WHAT I NEED— A MOSQUITO NET!
I HAD ONE OVER MY BED BACK IN MY KINGDOM.
IF I DON'T DIY ONE RIGHT AWAY, AT THIS RATE, IN A FEW DAYS, MY SKIN IS GOING TO HAVE A POLKA-DOT PATTERN!
I'LL NEED A VERY LARGE SHEET OF CLOTH TO MAKE A MOS-QUITO NET...
SOMETHING MUCH LARGER THAN THE GHOST SHROUDS I'VE BEEN USING AS MY BED-SHEETS... HRM...
SLAM
PRIN-CESS!
HOW DARE YOU ATTACK MY MINIONS!
Baaam
Monster Cloth

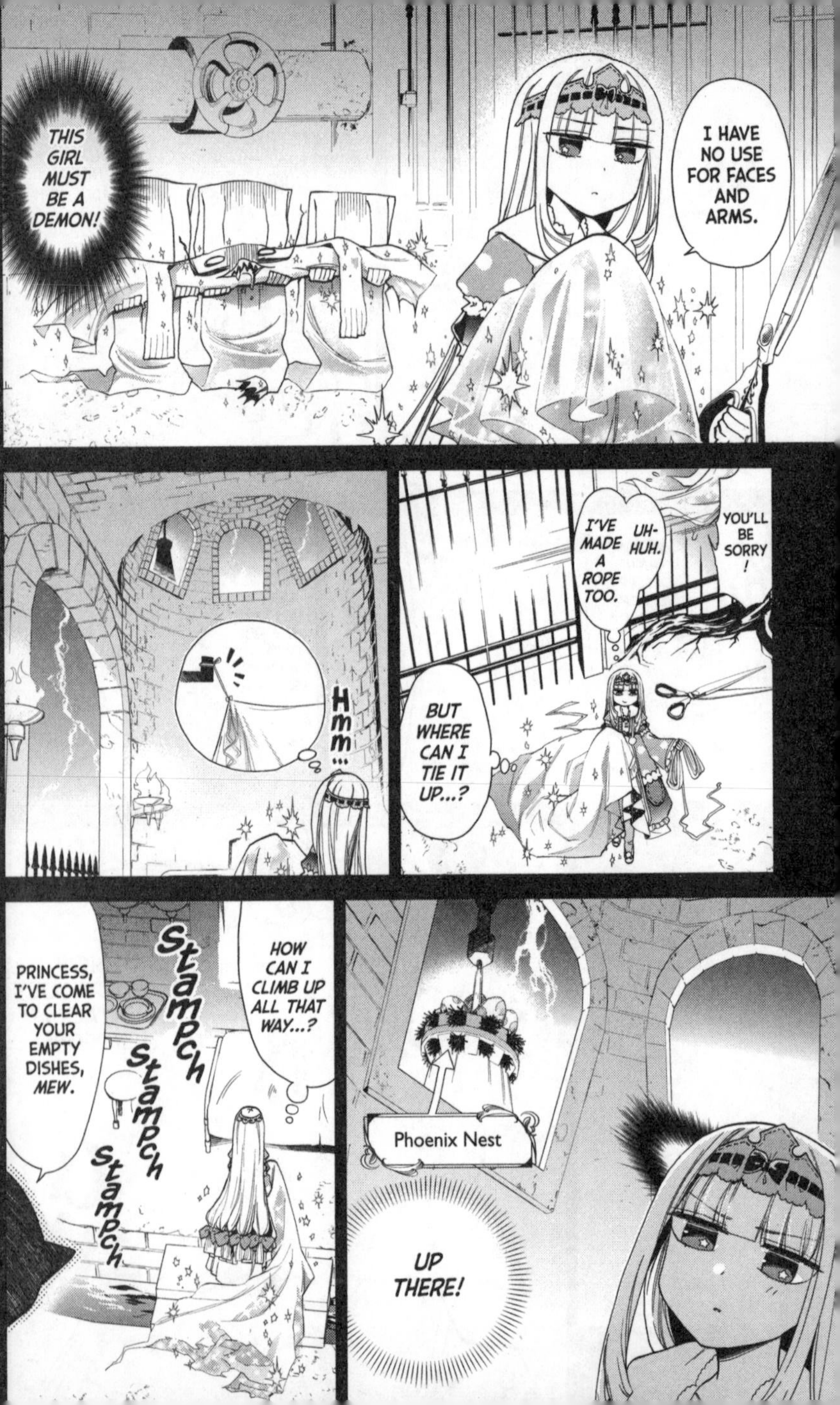
I HAVE NO USE FOR FACES AND ARMS.
THIS GIRL MUST BE A DEMON!
YOU'LL BE SORRY!
UH-HUH.
I'VE MADE A ROPE TOO.
BUT WHERE CAN I TIE IT UP...?
Hmm...
Phoenix Nest
UP THERE!
HOW CAN I CLIMB UP ALL THAT WAY...?
Stampch
Stampch
Stampch
PRINCESS, I'VE COME TO CLEAR YOUR EMPTY DISHES, MEW.

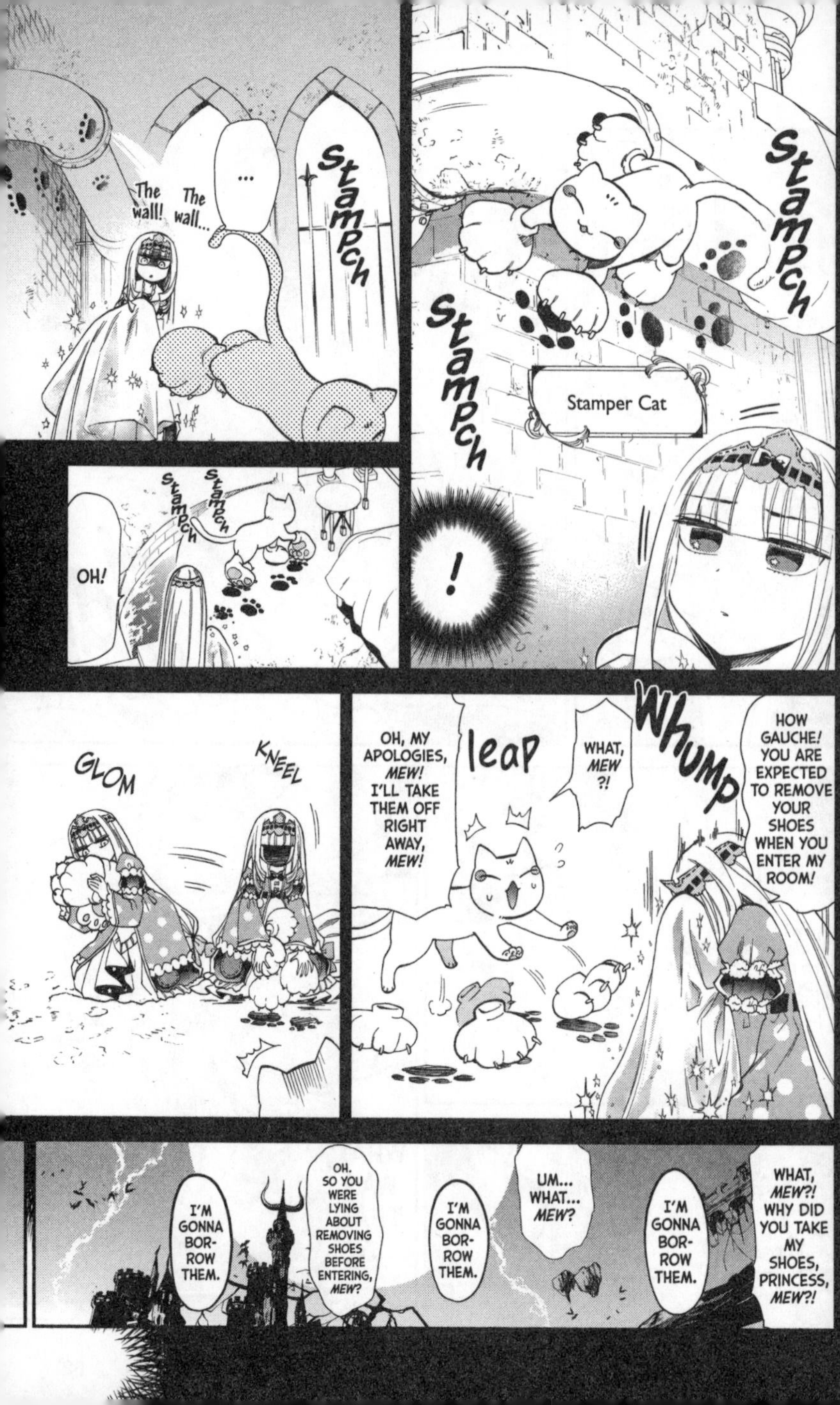
Stampch
Stampch
Stamper Cat
!
Stampch
...
The wall...
The wall!
Stampch
Stampch
OH!
HOW GAUCHE! YOU ARE EXPECTED TO REMOVE YOUR SHOES WHEN YOU ENTER MY ROOM!
WHUMP
WHAT, MEW?!
leap
OH, MY APOLOGIES, MEW! I'LL TAKE THEM OFF RIGHT AWAY, MEW!
KNEEL
GLOM
WHAT, MEW?! WHY DID YOU TAKE MY SHOES, PRINCESS, MEW?!
I'M GONNA BORROW THEM.
UM... WHAT... MEW?
I'M GONNA BORROW THEM.
OH. SO YOU WERE LYING ABOUT REMOVING SHOES BEFORE ENTERING, MEW?
I'M GONNA BORROW THEM.

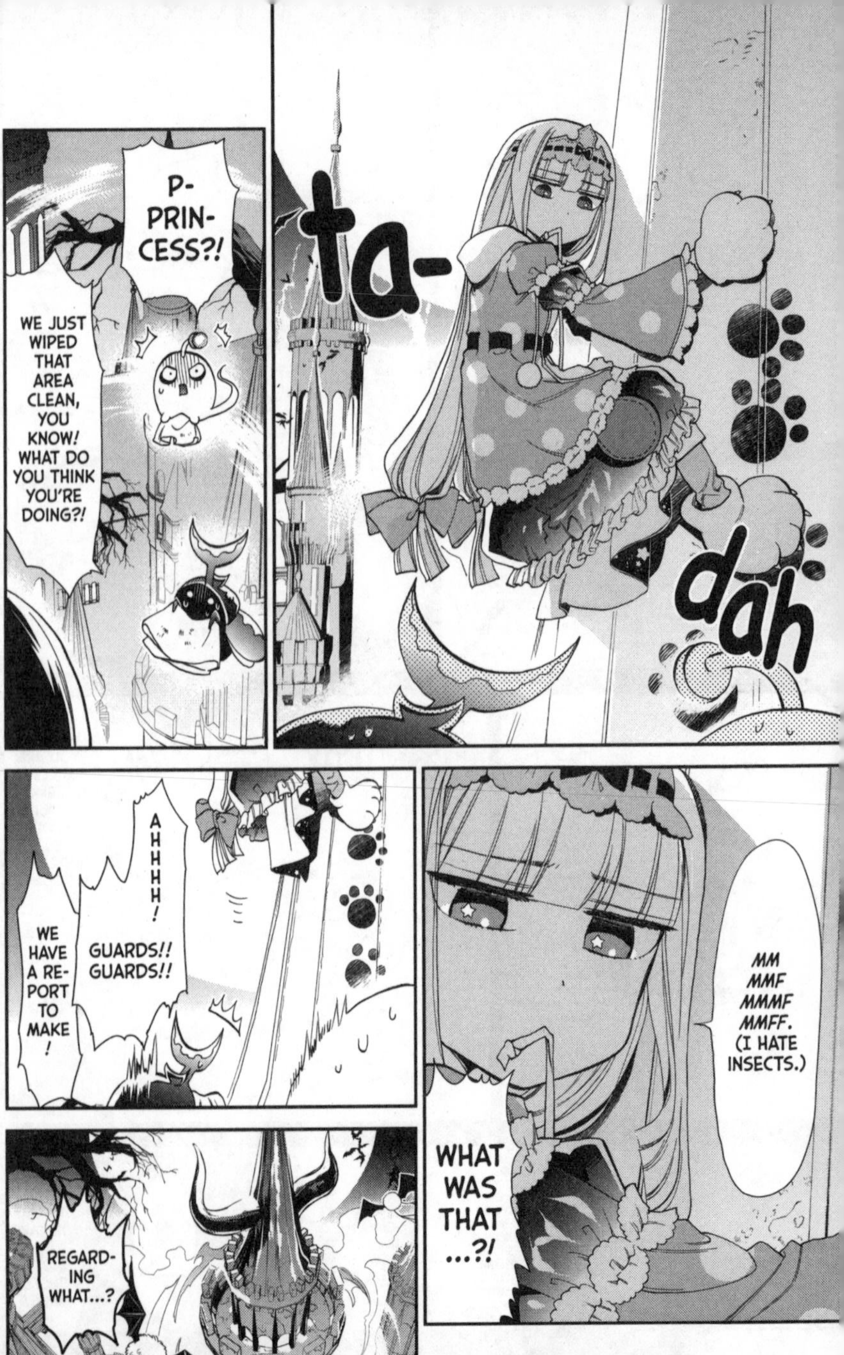
ta-
dah
P-PRINCESS?!
WE JUST WIPED THAT AREA CLEAN, YOU KNOW! WHAT DO YOU THINK YOU'RE DOING?!
MM MMF MMMF MMFF. (I HATE INSECTS.)
WHAT WAS THAT...?!
AHHHHH!
GUARDS!! GUARDS!!
WE HAVE A REPORT TO MAKE!
REGARDING WHAT...?

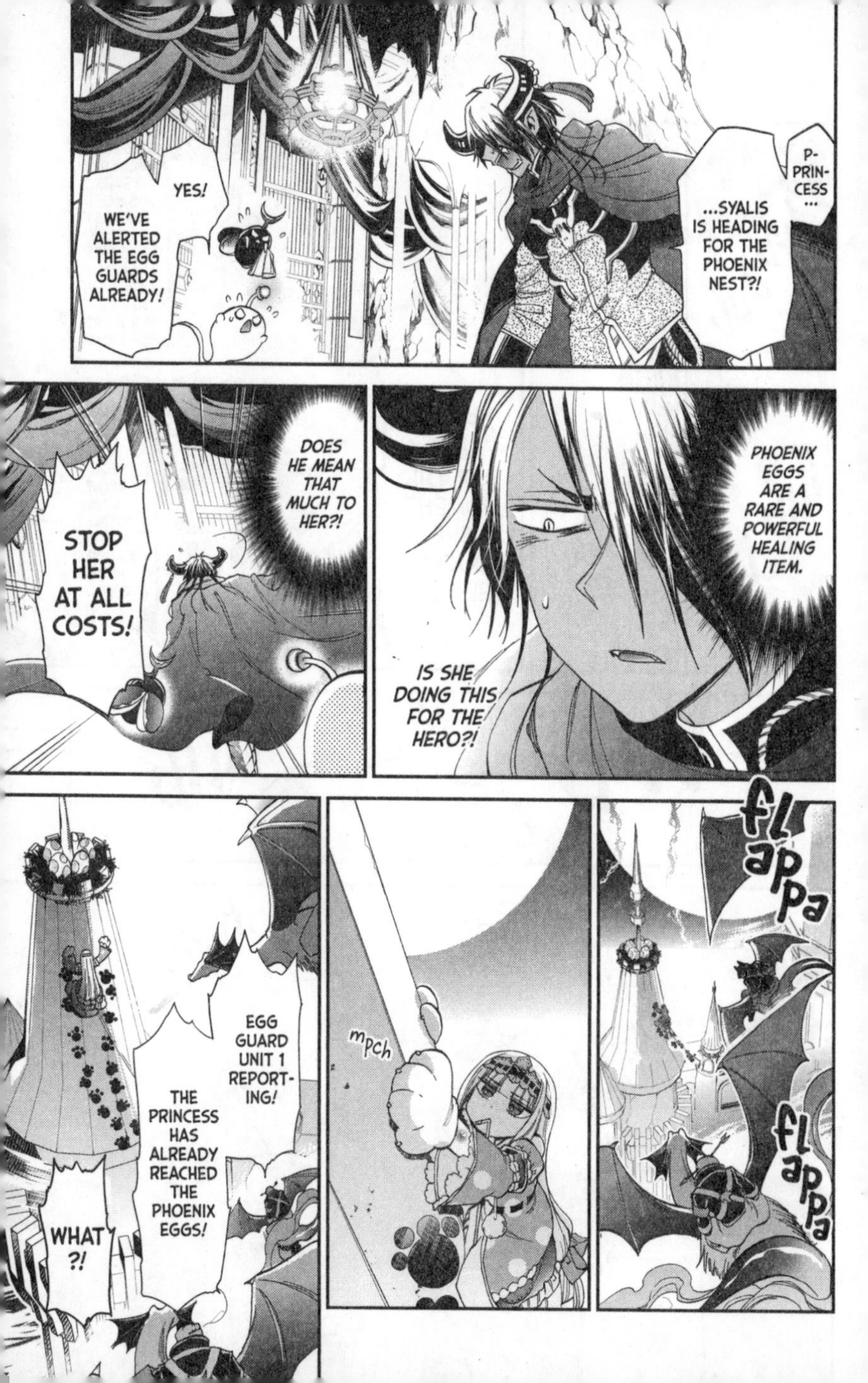
P-PRINCESS...
...SYALIS IS HEADING FOR THE PHOENIX NEST?!
YES!
WE'VE ALERTED THE EGG GUARDS ALREADY!
PHOENIX EGGS ARE A RARE AND POWERFUL HEALING ITEM.
IS SHE DOING THIS FOR THE HERO?!
DOES HE MEAN THAT MUCH TO HER?!
STOP HER AT ALL COSTS!
flappa
flappa
mpch
EGG GUARD UNIT 1 REPORTING!
THE PRINCESS HAS ALREADY REACHED THE PHOENIX EGGS!
WHAT?!

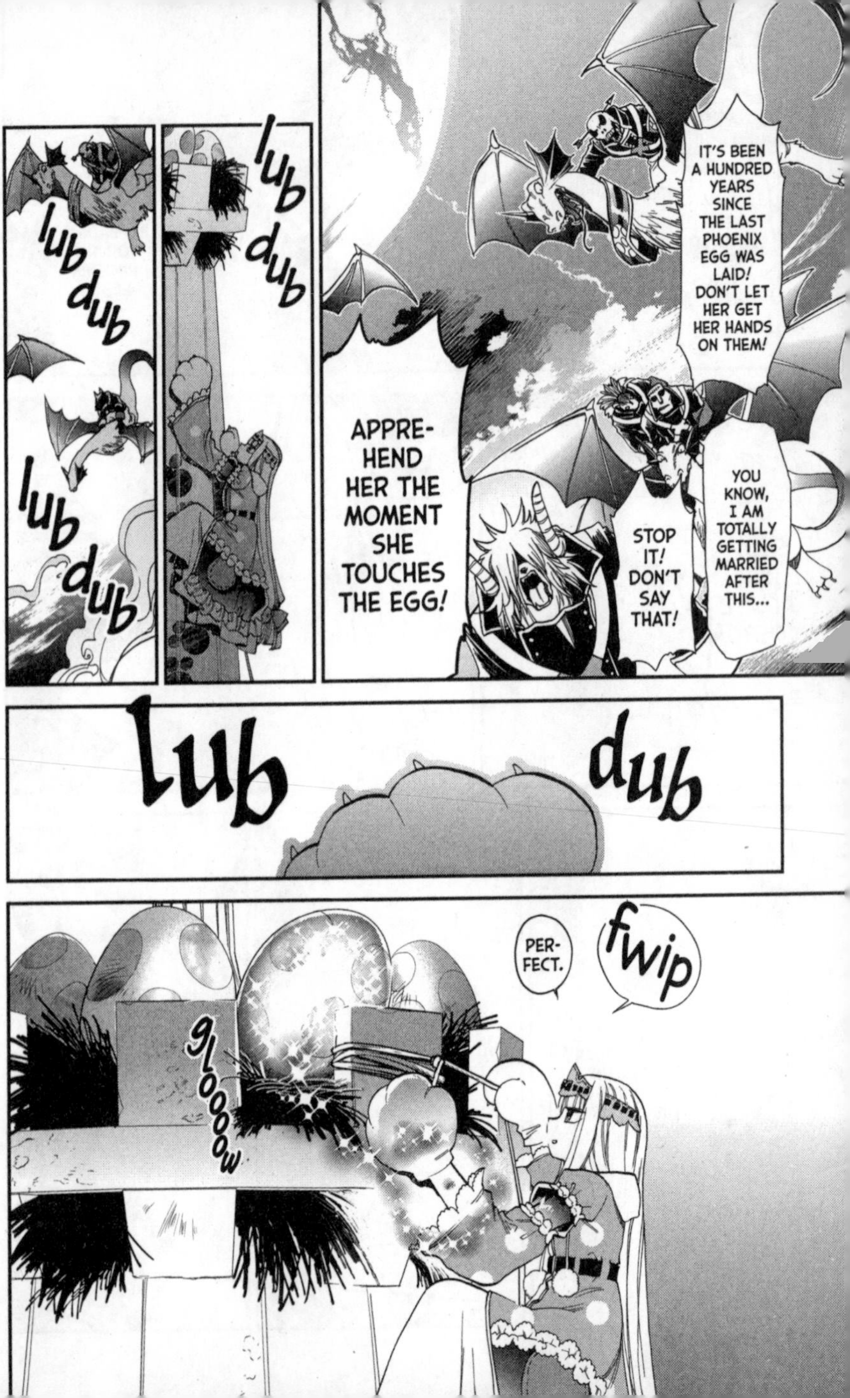
IT'S BEEN A HUNDRED YEARS SINCE THE LAST PHOENIX EGG WAS LAID! DON'T LET HER GET HER HANDS ON THEM!
YOU KNOW, I AM TOTALLY GETTING MARRIED AFTER THIS...
STOP IT! DON'T SAY THAT!
APPRE-HEND HER THE MOMENT SHE TOUCHES THE EGG!
lub dub
lub dub
lub dub
lub dub
fwip
PER-FECT.
glooooow

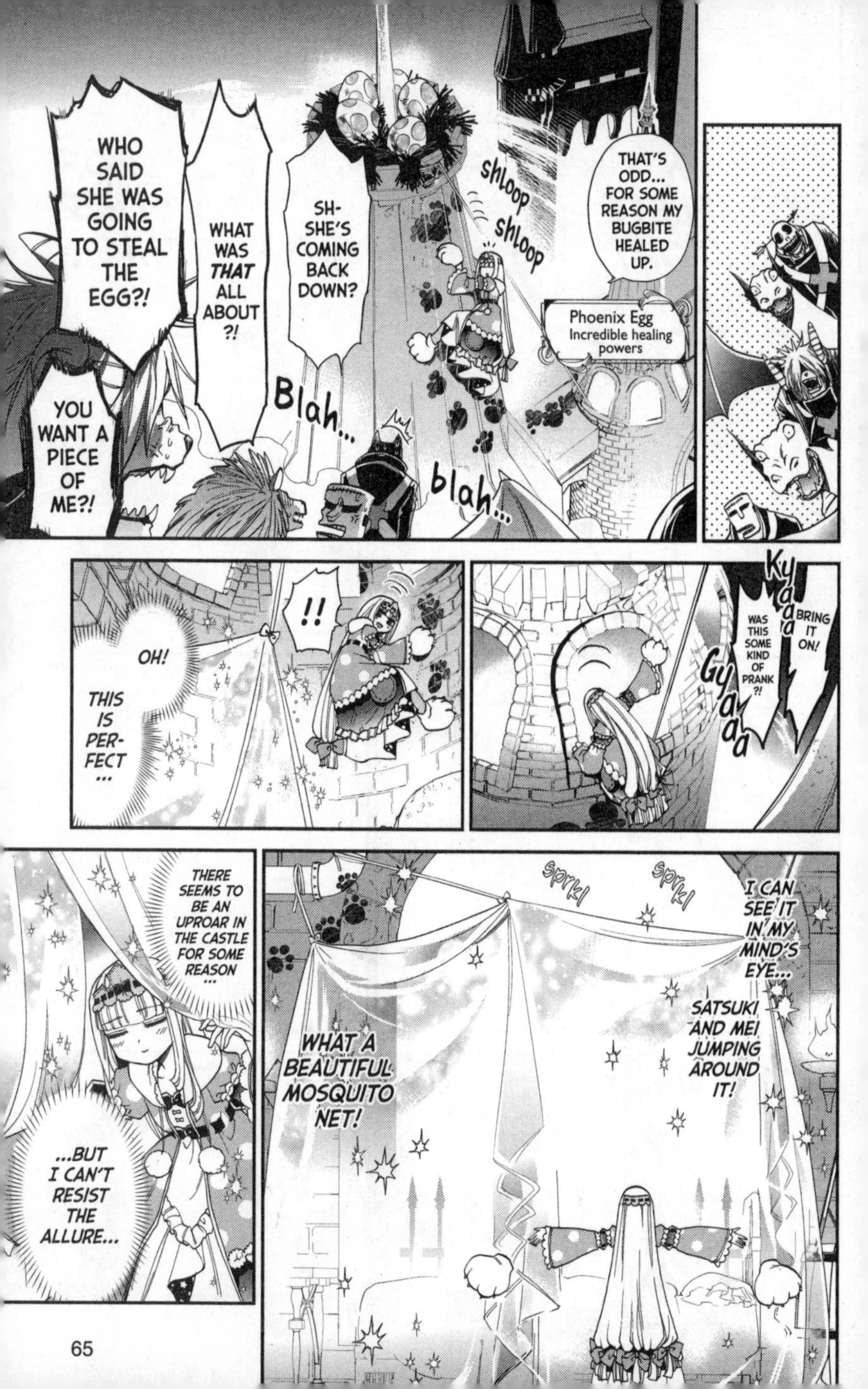
THAT'S ODD... FOR SOME REASON MY BUGBITE HEALED UP.
Phoenix Egg
Incredible healing powers
shloop
shloop
SH-SHE'S COMING BACK DOWN?
WHAT WAS THAT ALL ABOUT?!
WHO SAID SHE WAS GOING TO STEAL THE EGG?!
Blah...
blah...
YOU WANT A PIECE OF ME?!
Kyaaa
BRING IT ON!
WAS THIS SOME KIND OF PRANK?!
Gyaaaa
!!
OH!
THIS IS PERFECT...
sprkl
sprkl
I CAN SEE IT IN MY MIND'S EYE...
SATSUKI AND MEI JUMPING AROUND IT!
WHAT A BEAUTIFUL MOSQUITO NET!
THERE SEEMS TO BE AN UPROAR IN THE CASTLE FOR SOME REASON...
...BUT I CAN'T RESIST THE ALLURE...

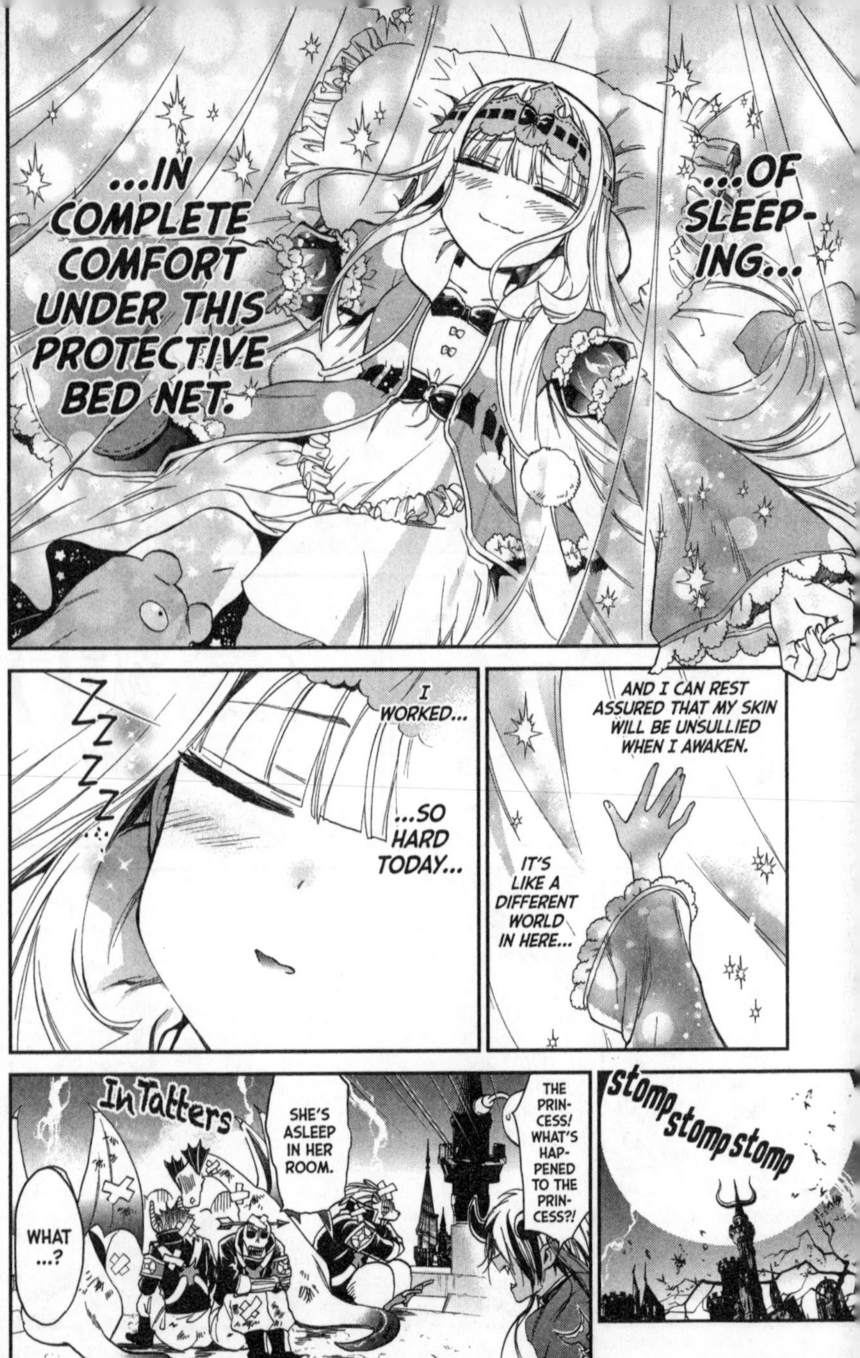
...OF SLEEP-ING...
...IN COMPLETE COMFORT UNDER THIS PROTECTIVE BED NET.
AND I CAN REST ASSURED THAT MY SKIN WILL BE UNSULLIED WHEN I AWAKEN.
IT'S LIKE A DIFFERENT WORLD IN HERE...
I WORKED...
...SO HARD TODAY...
ZZZZ
stomp stomp stomp
THE PRIN-CESS! WHAT'S HAP-PENED TO THE PRIN-CESS?!
SHE'S ASLEEP IN HER ROOM.
In Tatters
WHAT ...?

Quilladillo

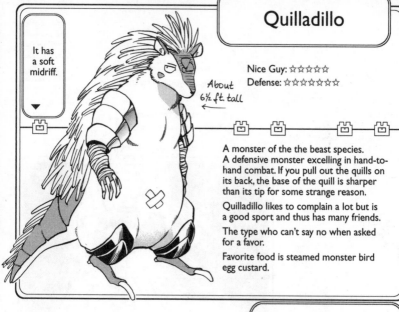

It has a soft midriff.

About 6½ ft. tall

Nice Guy: ☆☆☆☆☆
Defense: ☆☆☆☆☆☆☆☆

A monster of the the beast species.
A defensive monster excelling in hand-to-hand combat. If you pull out the quills on its back, the base of the quill is sharper than its tip for some strange reason.

Quilladillo likes to complain a lot but is a good sport and thus has many friends.

The type who can't say no when asked for a favor.

Favorite food is steamed monster bird egg custard.

Former problem:
"We monsters are better than this!"

Current problem:
"The princess keeps bumping into me whenever she passes by."

...
DOES IT EVEN MATTER IF SHE TOOK ONE OF THOSE EGGS...?
SHUSH!
SSHH!

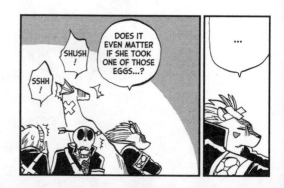

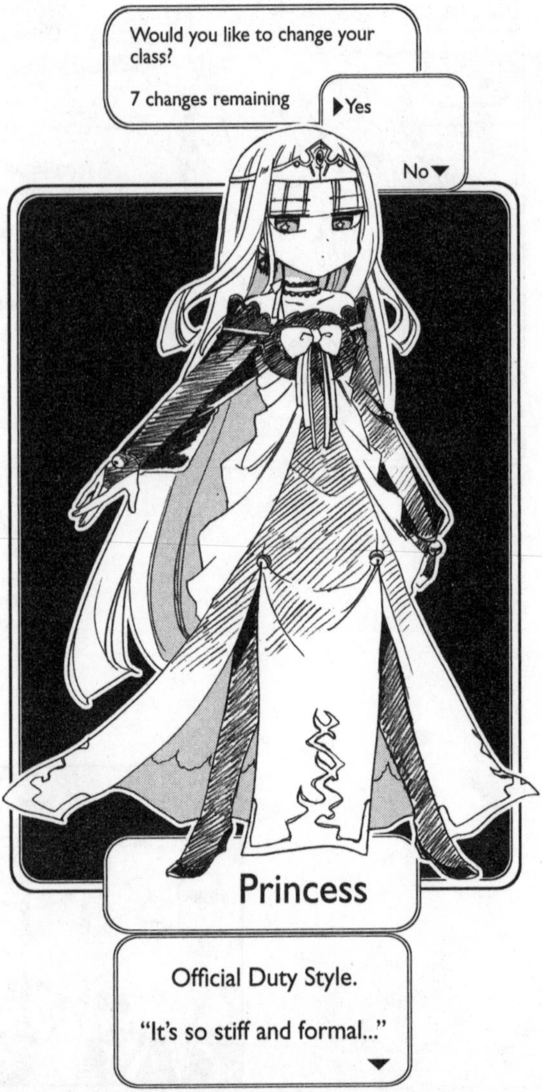
Would you like to change your class?
7 changes remaining
▶Yes
No▼
Princess
Official Duty Style.
"It's so stiff and formal..."

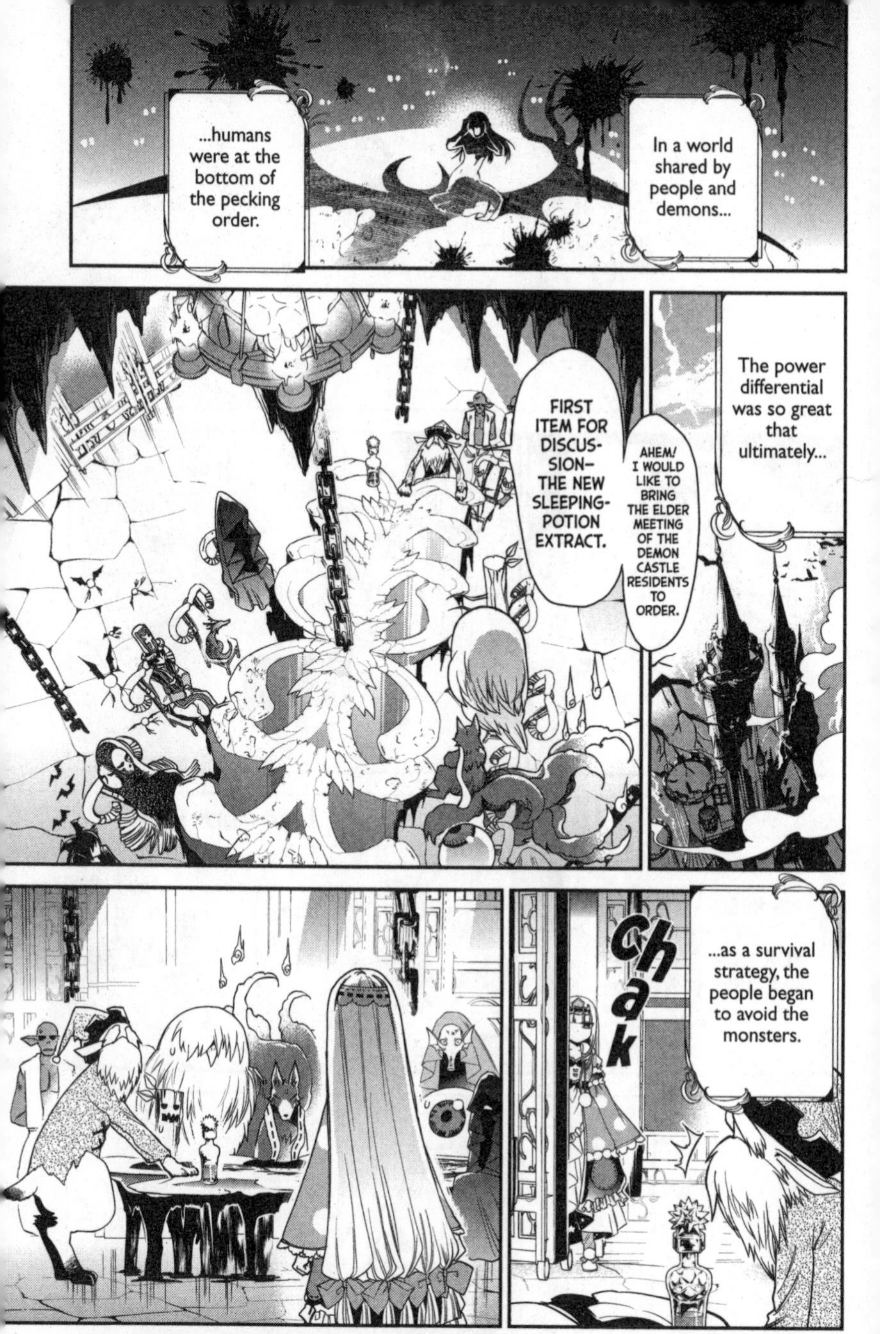
In a world shared by people and demons...
...humans were at the bottom of the pecking order.
The power differential was so great that ultimately...
AHEM! I WOULD LIKE TO BRING THE ELDER MEETING OF THE DEMON CASTLE RESIDENTS TO ORDER.
FIRST ITEM FOR DISCUSSION—THE NEW SLEEPING-POTION EXTRACT.
...as a survival strategy, the people began to avoid the monsters.
Chak

6th Night: Go Bark at the Moon

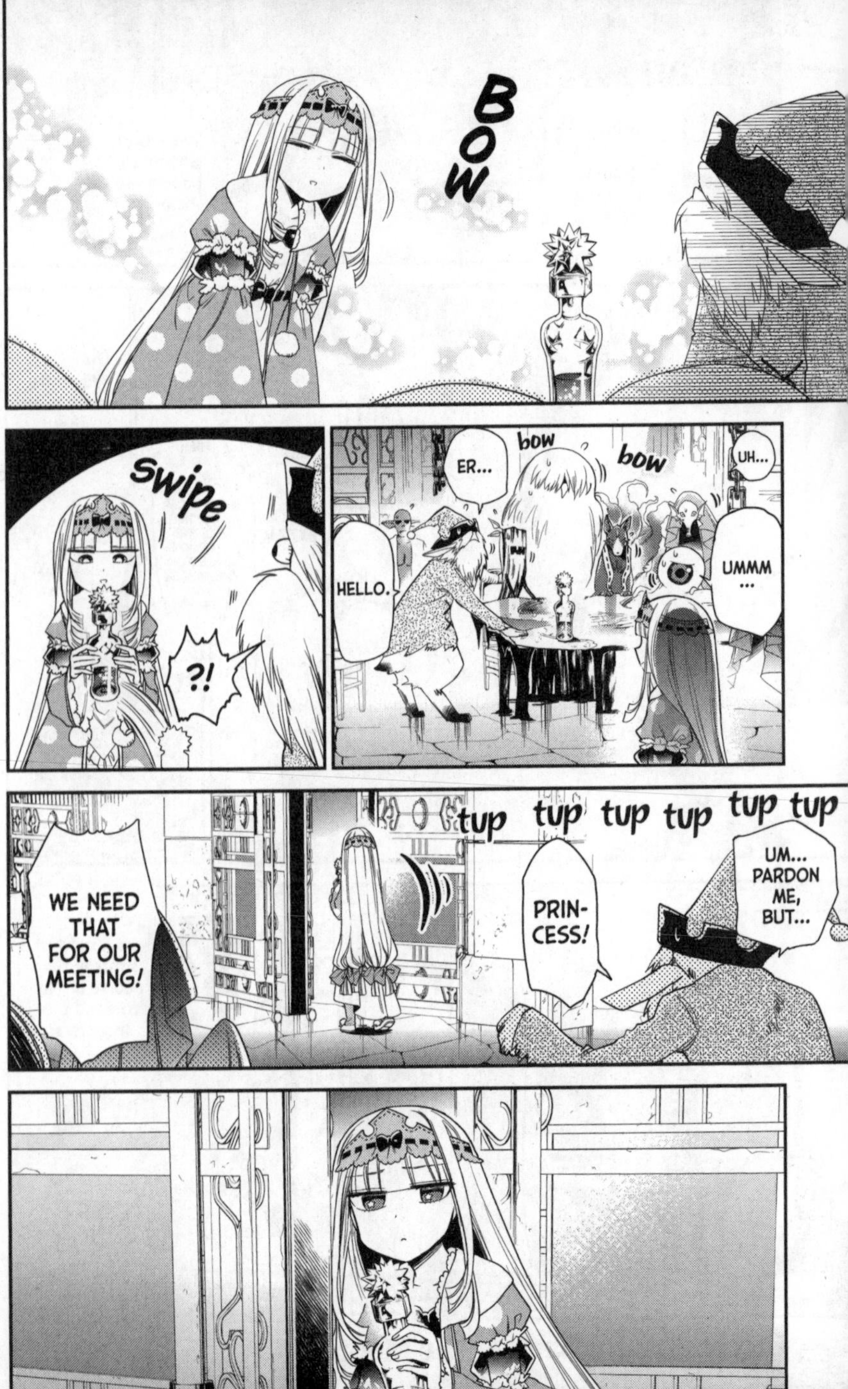
BOW
UH...
bow
UMMM...
bow
ER...
HELLO.
swipe
?!
tup tup tup tup tup tup
UM... PARDON ME, BUT...
PRIN-CESS!
WE NEED THAT FOR OUR MEETING!

6th Night: Go Bark at the Moon

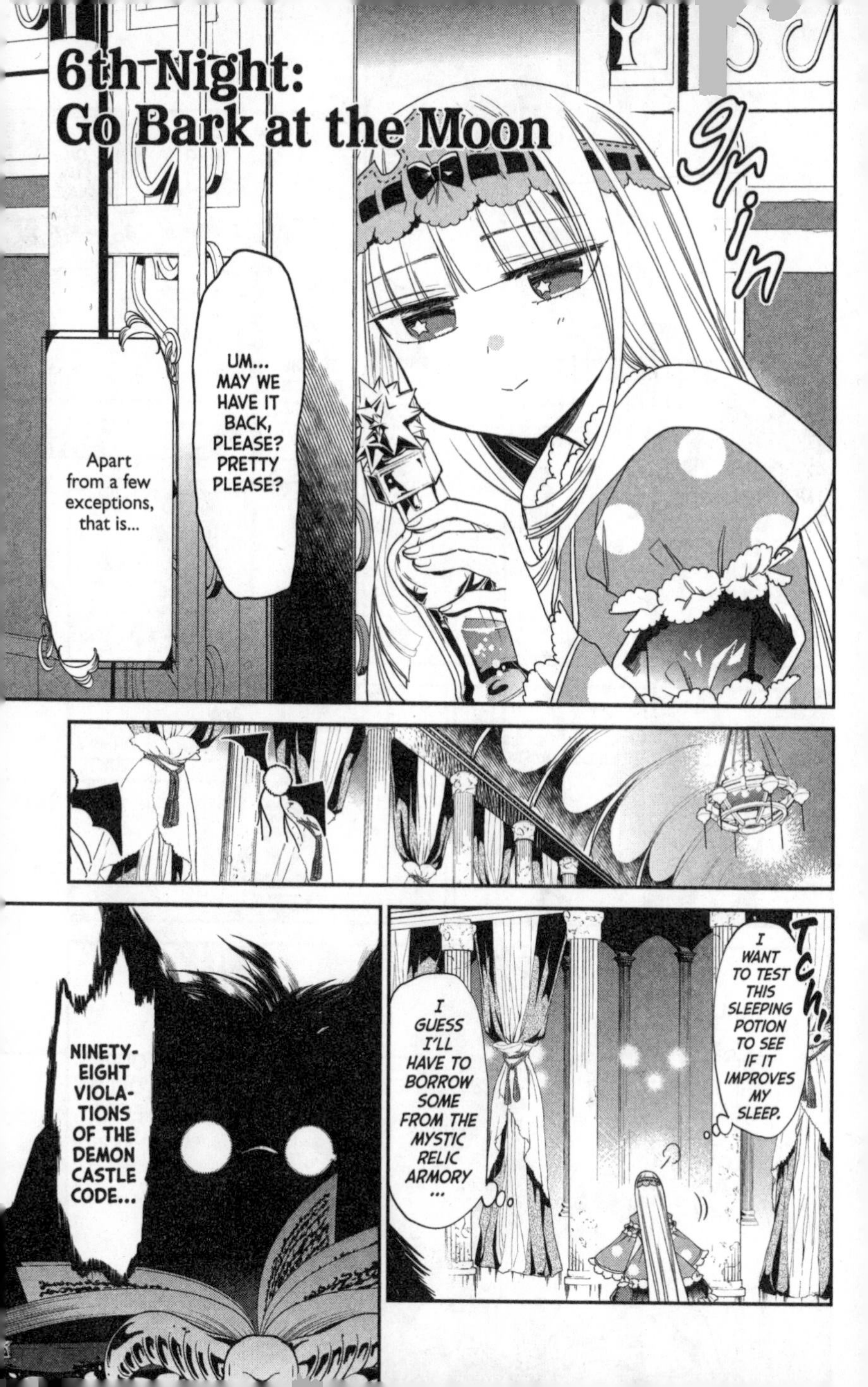
grin
UM... MAY WE HAVE IT BACK, PLEASE? PRETTY PLEASE?
Apart from a few exceptions, that is...
TCH!!
I WANT TO TEST THIS SLEEPING POTION TO SEE IF IT IMPROVES MY SLEEP.
I GUESS I'LL HAVE TO BORROW SOME FROM THE MYSTIC RELIC ARMORY...
NINETY-EIGHT VIOLATIONS OF THE DEMON CASTLE CODE...

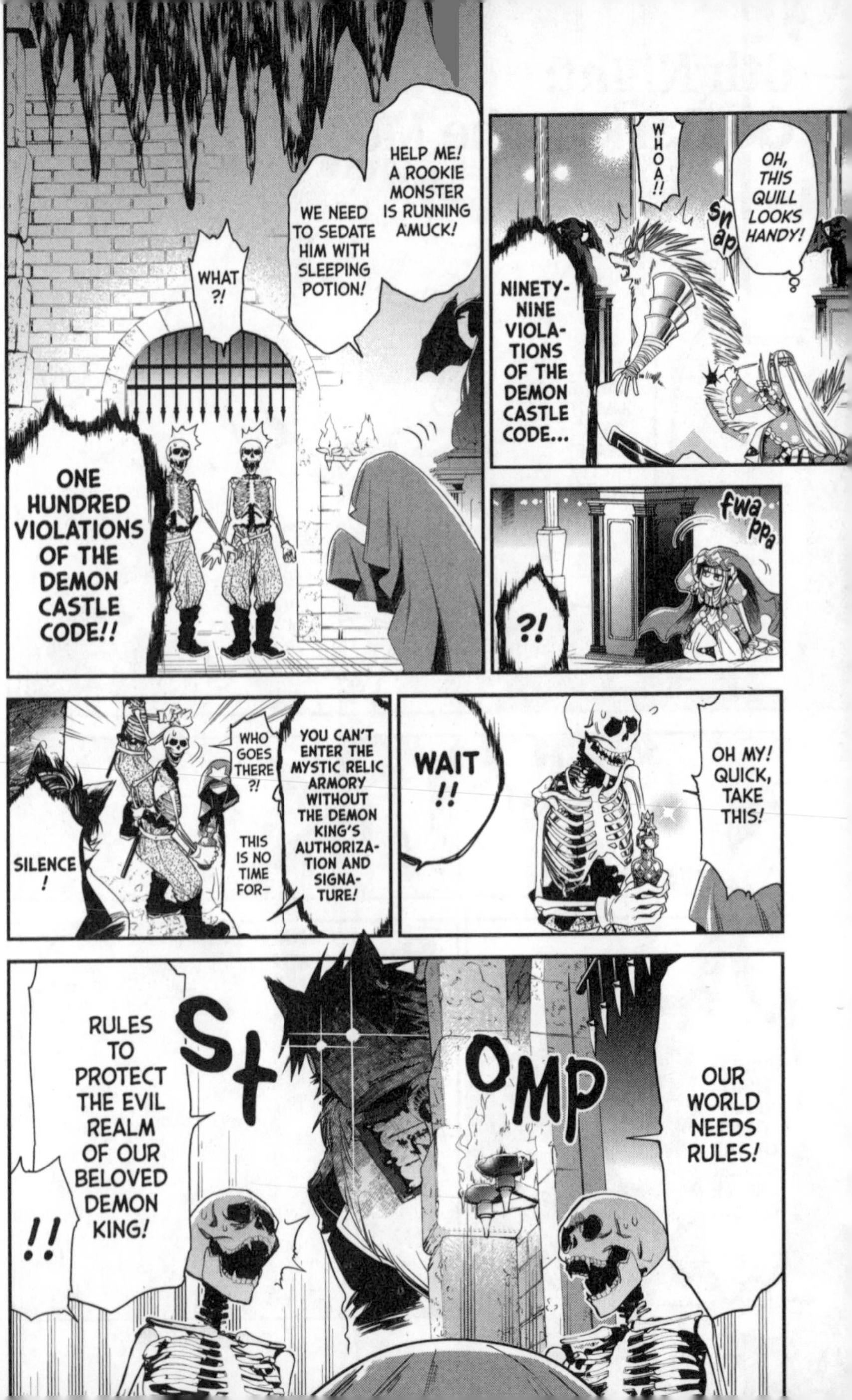

OH, THIS QUILL LOOKS HANDY!
snap
WHOA!!
NINETY-NINE VIOLATIONS OF THE DEMON CASTLE CODE...
fwappa
?!
HELP ME! A ROOKIE MONSTER IS RUNNING AMUCK!
WE NEED TO SEDATE HIM WITH SLEEPING POTION!
WHAT?!
ONE HUNDRED VIOLATIONS OF THE DEMON CASTLE CODE!!
OH MY! QUICK, TAKE THIS!
WAIT!!
YOU CAN'T ENTER THE MYSTIC RELIC ARMORY WITHOUT THE DEMON KING'S AUTHORIZATION AND SIGNATURE!
WHO GOES THERE?!
THIS IS NO TIME FOR–
SILENCE!
OUR WORLD NEEDS RULES!
StOMP
RULES TO PROTECT THE EVIL REALM OF OUR BELOVED DEMON KING!
!!

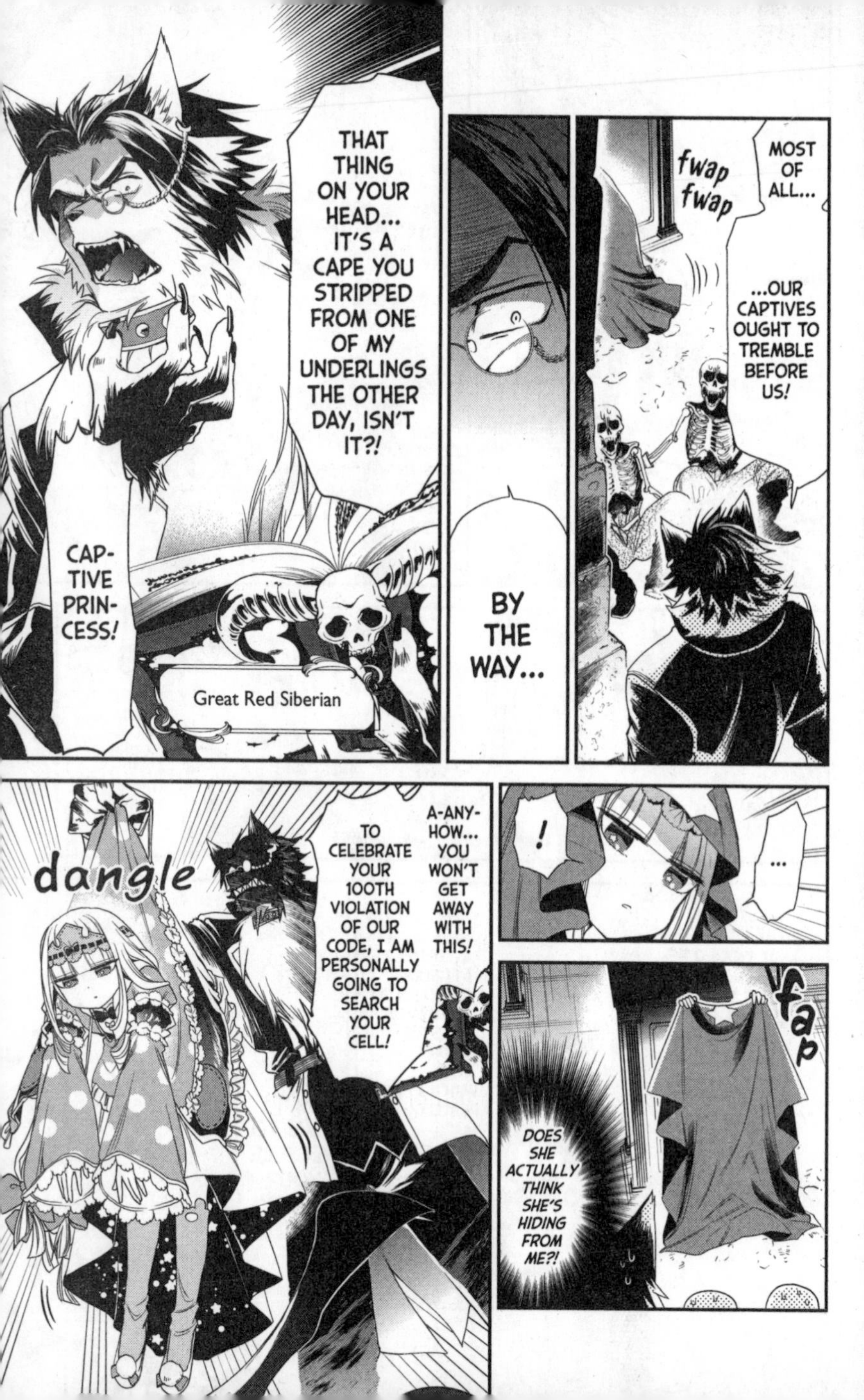
fwap fwap
MOST OF ALL...
...OUR CAPTIVES OUGHT TO TREMBLE BEFORE US!
BY THE WAY...
THAT THING ON YOUR HEAD... IT'S A CAPE YOU STRIPPED FROM ONE OF MY UNDERLINGS THE OTHER DAY, ISN'T IT?!
CAP-TIVE PRIN-CESS!
Great Red Siberian
...
!
fap
DOES SHE ACTUALLY THINK SHE'S HIDING FROM ME?!
A-ANY-HOW... YOU WON'T GET AWAY WITH THIS!
TO CELEBRATE YOUR 100TH VIOLATION OF OUR CODE, I AM PERSONALLY GOING TO SEARCH YOUR CELL!
dangle

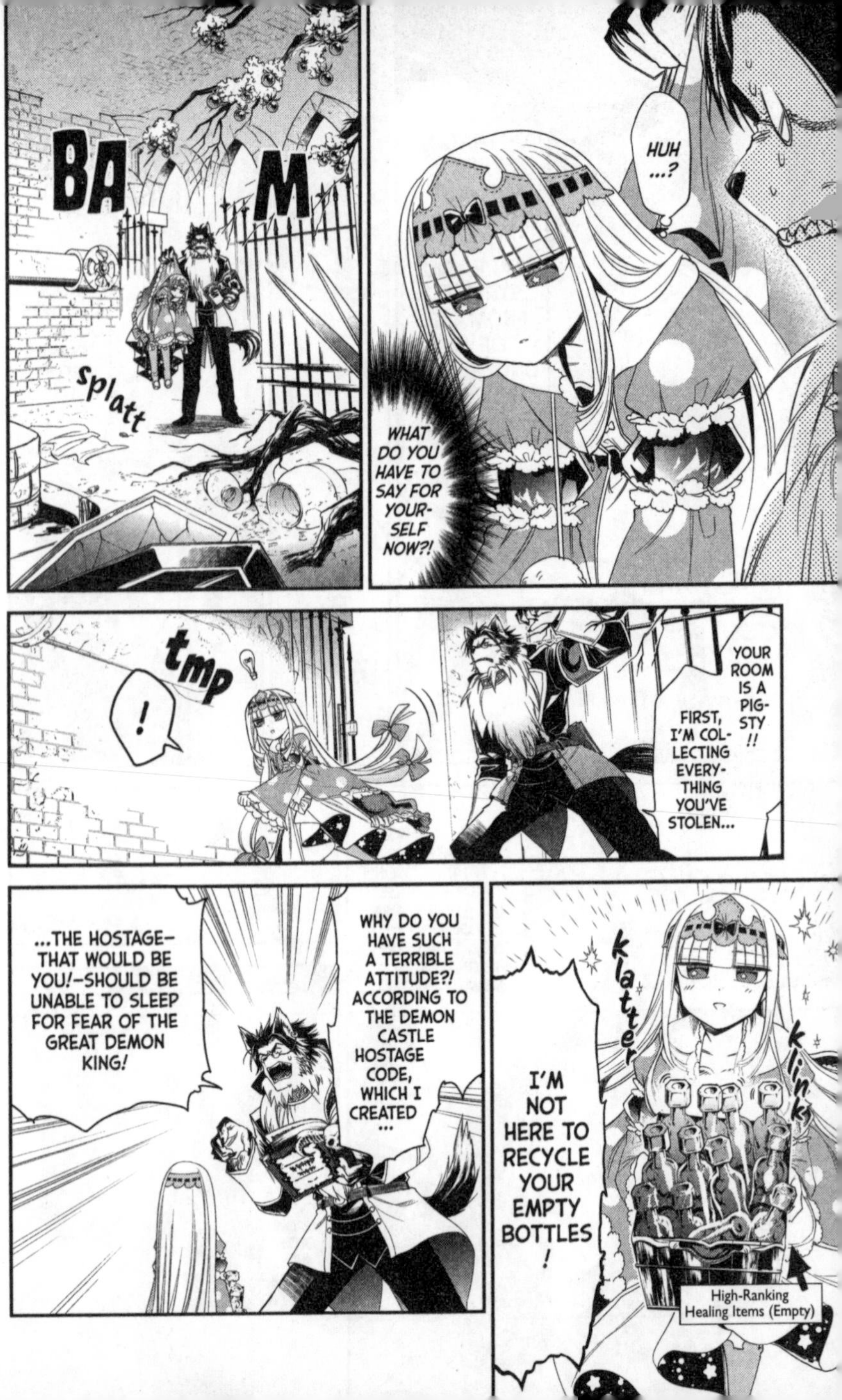
HUH ...?
WHAT DO YOU HAVE TO SAY FOR YOURSELF NOW?!
BAM
splatt
YOUR ROOM IS A PIGSTY!!
FIRST, I'M COLLECTING EVERYTHING YOU'VE STOLEN...
tmp
!
klatter
klink
I'M NOT HERE TO RECYCLE YOUR EMPTY BOTTLES!
High-Ranking Healing Items (Empty)
WHY DO YOU HAVE SUCH A TERRIBLE ATTITUDE?! ACCORDING TO THE DEMON CASTLE HOSTAGE CODE, WHICH I CREATED...
...THE HOSTAGE—THAT WOULD BE YOU!—SHOULD BE UNABLE TO SLEEP FOR FEAR OF THE GREAT DEMON KING!

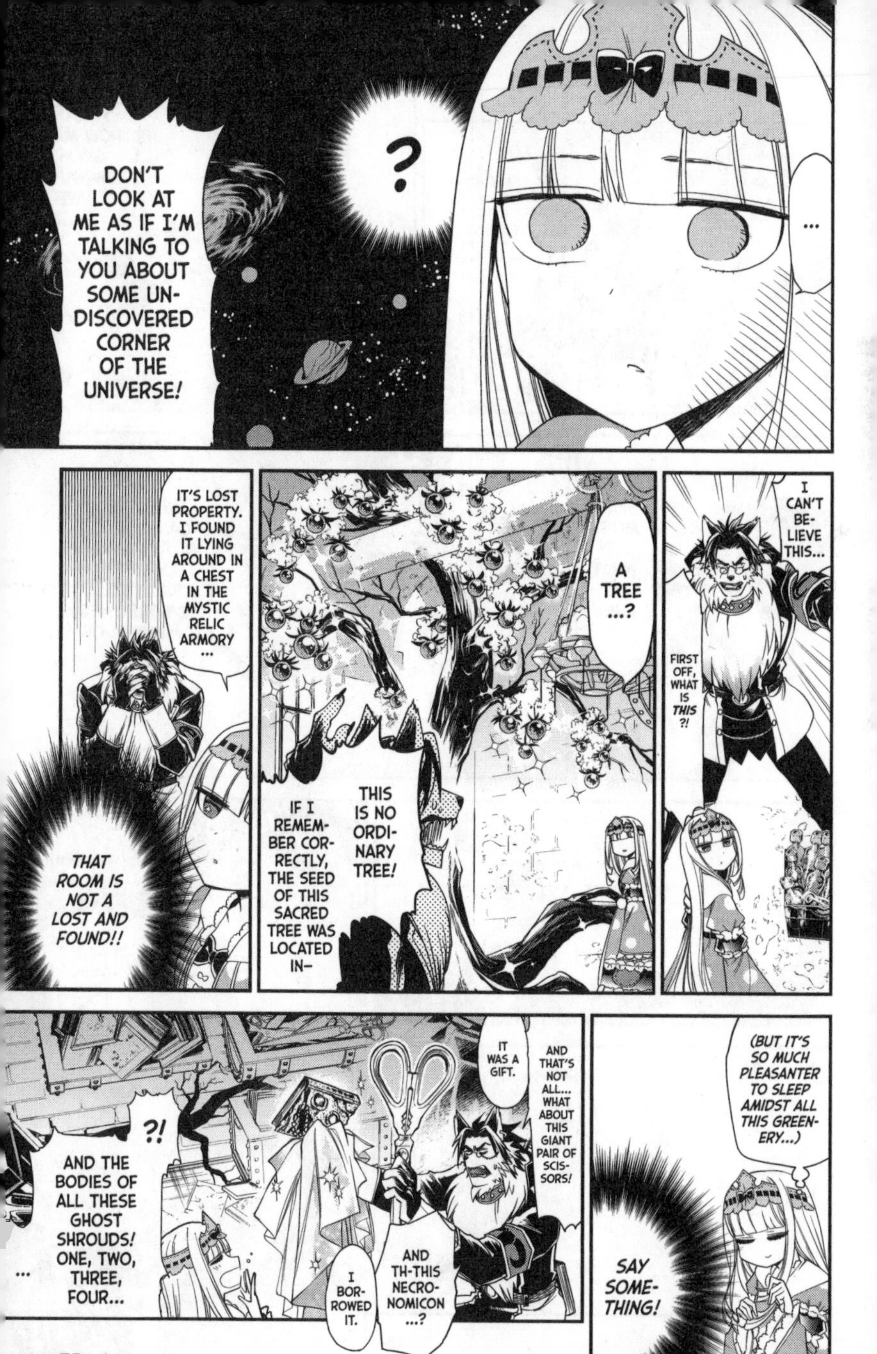
...
?
DON'T LOOK AT ME AS IF I'M TALKING TO YOU ABOUT SOME UN-DISCOVERED CORNER OF THE UNIVERSE!
I CAN'T BE-LIEVE THIS...
FIRST OFF, WHAT IS *THIS*?!
A TREE ...?
THIS IS NO ORDI-NARY TREE!
IF I REMEM-BER COR-RECTLY, THE SEED OF THIS SACRED TREE WAS LOCATED IN–
IT'S LOST PROPERTY. I FOUND IT LYING AROUND IN A CHEST IN THE MYSTIC RELIC ARMORY ...
THAT ROOM IS NOT A LOST AND FOUND!!
(BUT IT'S SO MUCH PLEASANTER TO SLEEP AMIDST ALL THIS GREEN-ERY...)
SAY SOME-THING!
AND THAT'S NOT ALL... WHAT ABOUT THIS GIANT PAIR OF SCIS-SORS!
IT WAS A GIFT.
AND TH-THIS NECRO-NOMICON ...?
I BOR-ROWED IT.
?!
AND THE BODIES OF ALL THESE GHOST SHROUDS! ONE, TWO, THREE, FOUR...
...

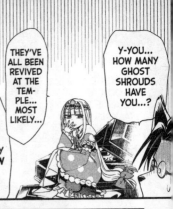

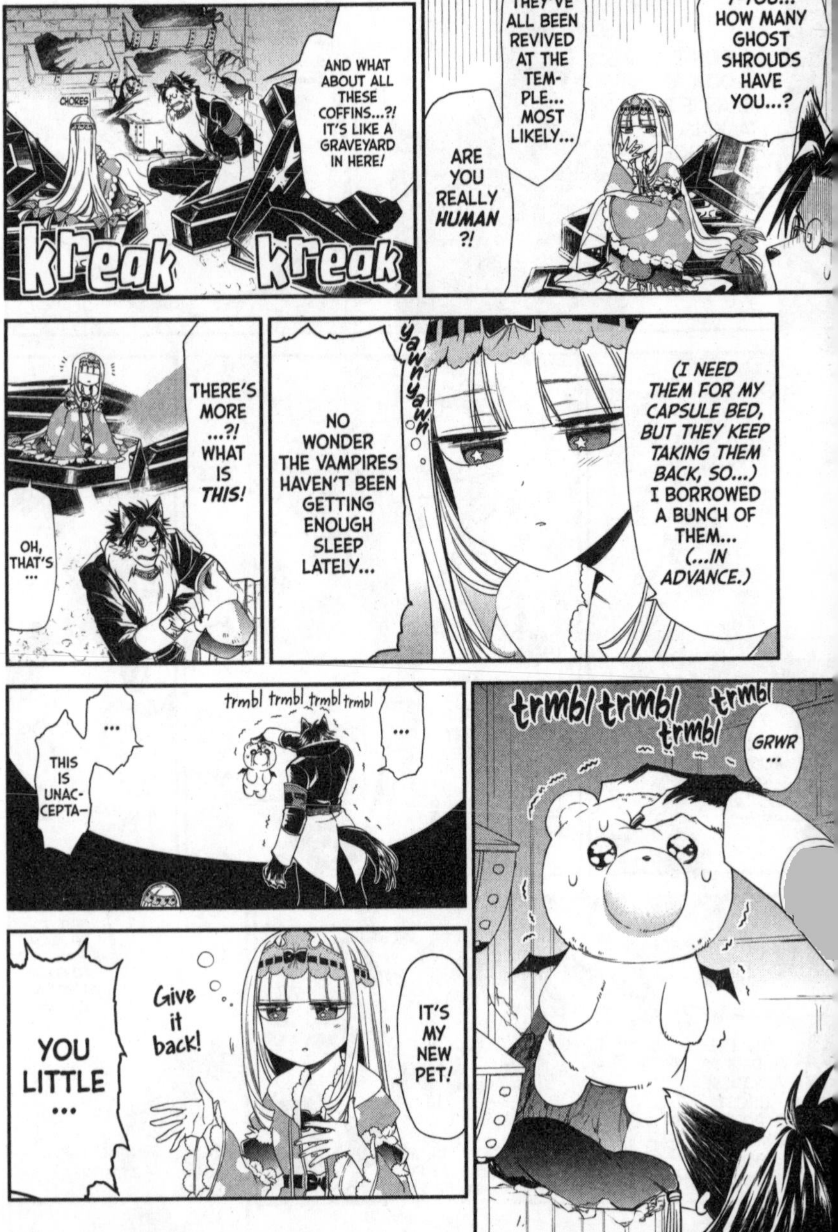
Y-YOU... HOW MANY GHOST SHROUDS HAVE YOU...?
THEY'VE ALL BEEN REVIVED AT THE TEM-PLE... MOST LIKELY...
ARE YOU REALLY HUMAN?!
AND WHAT ABOUT ALL THESE COFFINS...?! IT'S LIKE A GRAVEYARD IN HERE!
CHORES
kreak
kreak
(I NEED THEM FOR MY CAPSULE BED, BUT THEY KEEP TAKING THEM BACK, SO...) I BORROWED A BUNCH OF THEM... (...IN ADVANCE.)
yawn yawn
NO WONDER THE VAMPIRES HAVEN'T BEEN GETTING ENOUGH SLEEP LATELY...
THERE'S MORE ...?! WHAT IS THIS!
OH, THAT'S ...
trmbl trmbl trmbl trmbl
GRWR ...
...
trmbl trmbl trmbl trmbl
...
THIS IS UNAC-CEPTA-
IT'S MY NEW PET!
Give it back!
YOU LITTLE ...

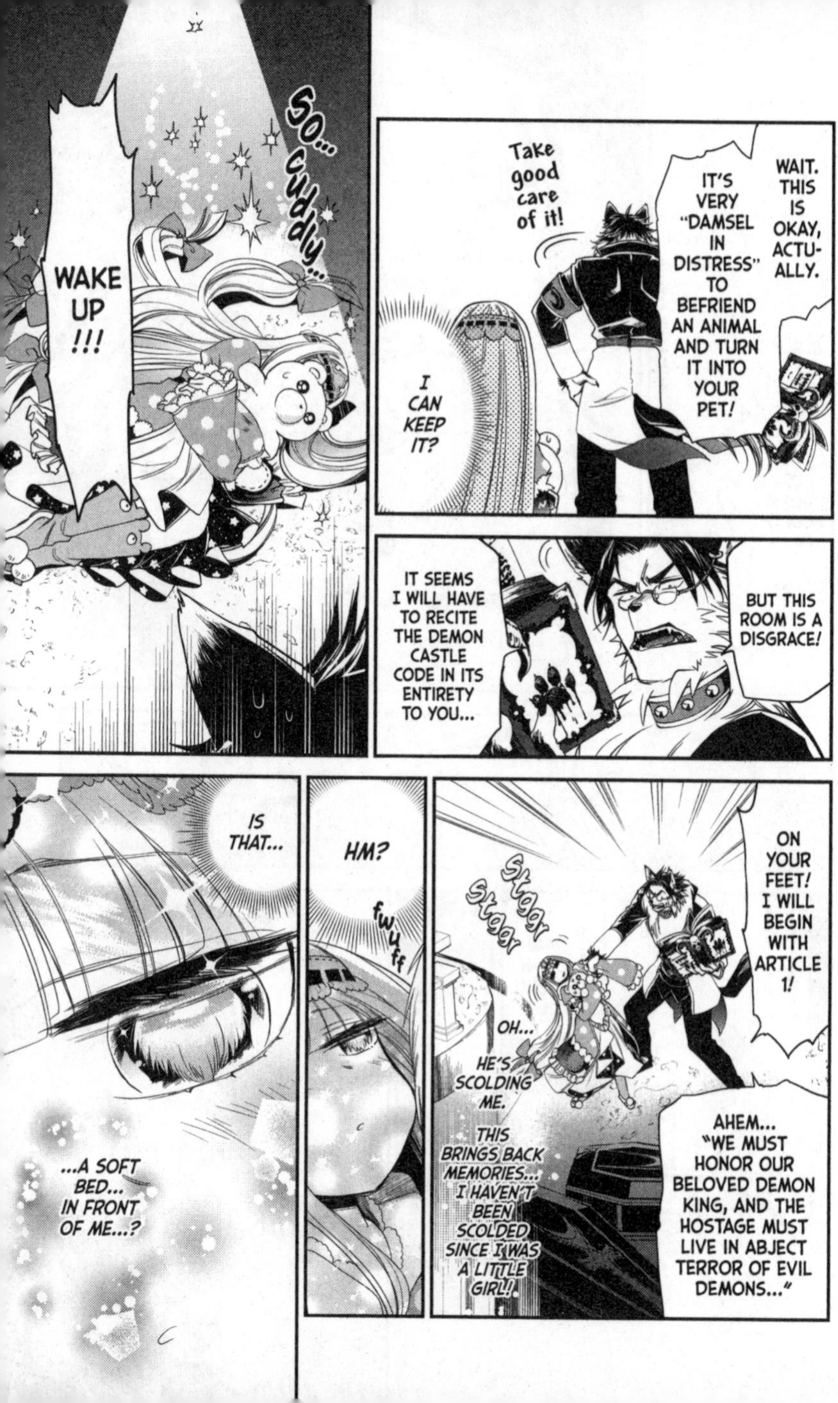
WAIT. THIS IS OKAY, ACTU-ALLY.
IT'S VERY "DAMSEL IN DISTRESS" TO BEFRIEND AN ANIMAL AND TURN IT INTO YOUR PET!
Take good care of it!
I CAN KEEP IT?
BUT THIS ROOM IS A DISGRACE!
IT SEEMS I WILL HAVE TO RECITE THE DEMON CASTLE CODE IN ITS ENTIRETY TO YOU...
SO... cuddly...
WAKE UP!!!
ON YOUR FEET! I WILL BEGIN WITH ARTICLE 1!
Stggr Stggr
OH... HE'S SCOLDING ME.
AHEM... "WE MUST HONOR OUR BELOVED DEMON KING, AND THE HOSTAGE MUST LIVE IN ABJECT TERROR OF EVIL DEMONS..."
THIS BRINGS BACK MEMORIES... I HAVEN'T BEEN SCOLDED SINCE I WAS A LITTLE GIRL!
HM?
fwuff
IS THAT...
...A SOFT BED... IN FRONT OF ME...?

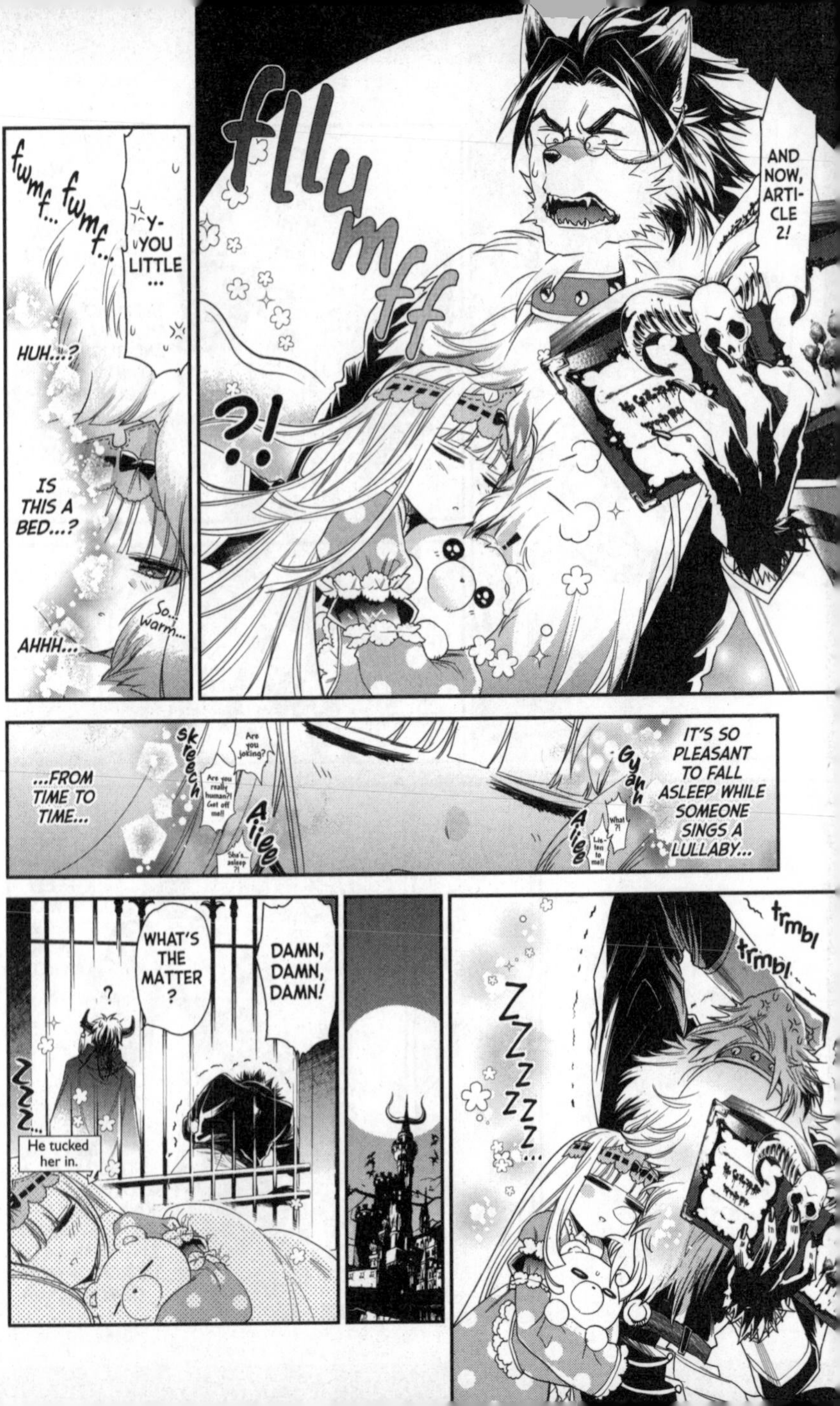
AND NOW, ARTICLE 2!
fllumff
?!
fwmf... fwmf...
Y-YOU LITTLE...
HUH...?
IS THIS A BED...?
So... warm...
AHHH...
IT'S SO PLEASANT TO FALL ASLEEP WHILE SOMEONE SINGS A LULLABY...
Gyahh
What?!
Listen to me!!
Aiiee
Are you joking?
Are you really human?! Get off me!!
She's... asleep?!
skreech
Aiiee
...FROM TIME TO TIME...
trmbl
trmbl
ZZZZZZ...
DAMN, DAMN, DAMN!
WHAT'S THE MATTER?
?
ZZZ...
He tucked her in.

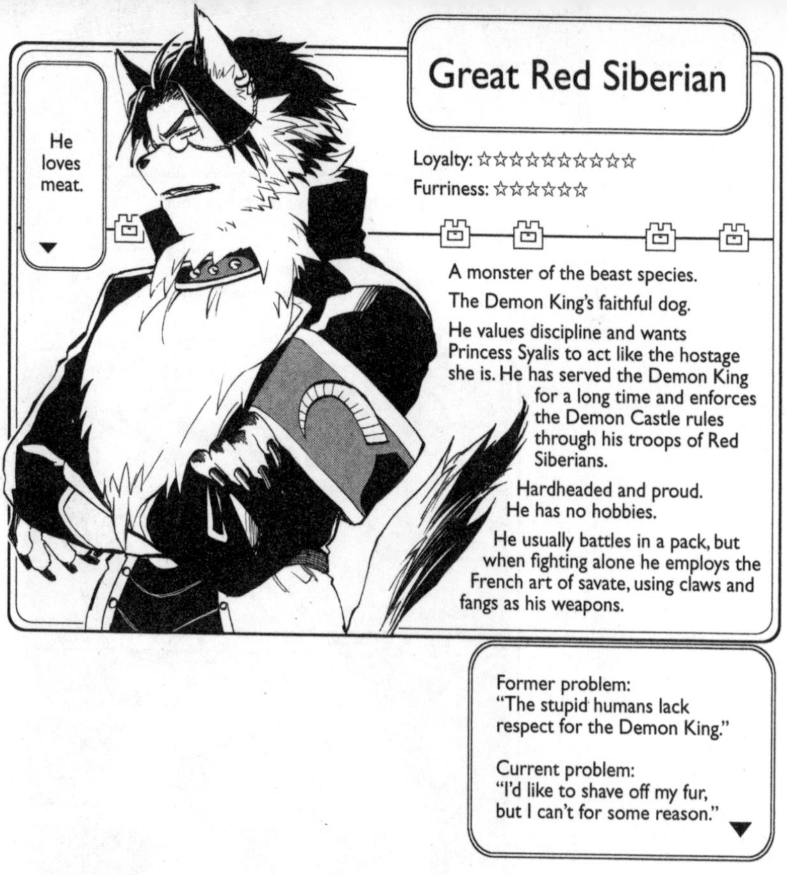

He loves meat.

Great Red Siberian

Loyalty: ☆☆☆☆☆☆☆☆☆☆☆

Furriness: ☆☆☆☆☆☆

A monster of the beast species.

The Demon King's faithful dog.

He values discipline and wants Princess Syalis to act like the hostage she is. He has served the Demon King for a long time and enforces the Demon Castle rules through his troops of Red Siberians.

Hardheaded and proud. He has no hobbies.

He usually battles in a pack, but when fighting alone he employs the French art of savate, using claws and fangs as his weapons.

Former problem:
"The stupid humans lack respect for the Demon King."

Current problem:
"I'd like to shave off my fur, but I can't for some reason."

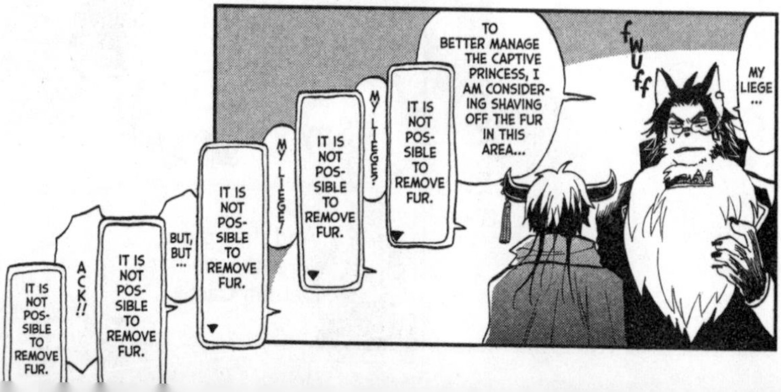
MY LIEGE...
FWUFF
TO BETTER MANAGE THE CAPTIVE PRINCESS, I AM CONSIDERING SHAVING OFF THE FUR IN THIS AREA...
IT IS NOT POSSIBLE TO REMOVE FUR.
MY LIEGE?!
IT IS NOT POSSIBLE TO REMOVE FUR.
MY LIEGE?!
IT IS NOT POSSIBLE TO REMOVE FUR.
BUT, BUT...
IT IS NOT POSSIBLE TO REMOVE FUR.
ACK!!
IT IS NOT POSSIBLE TO REMOVE FUR.

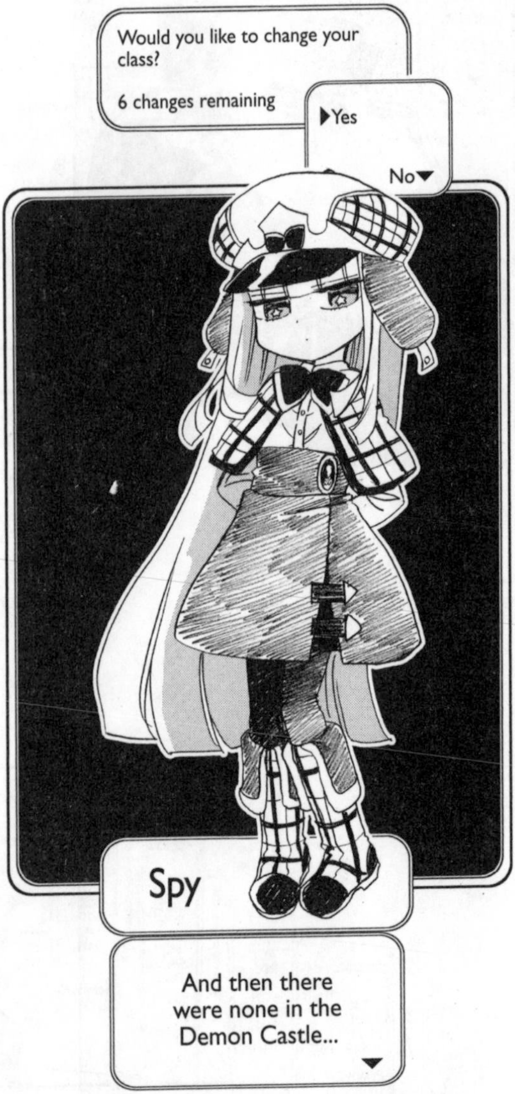
Would you like to change your class?
6 changes remaining
Yes
No
Spy
And then there were none in the Demon Castle...

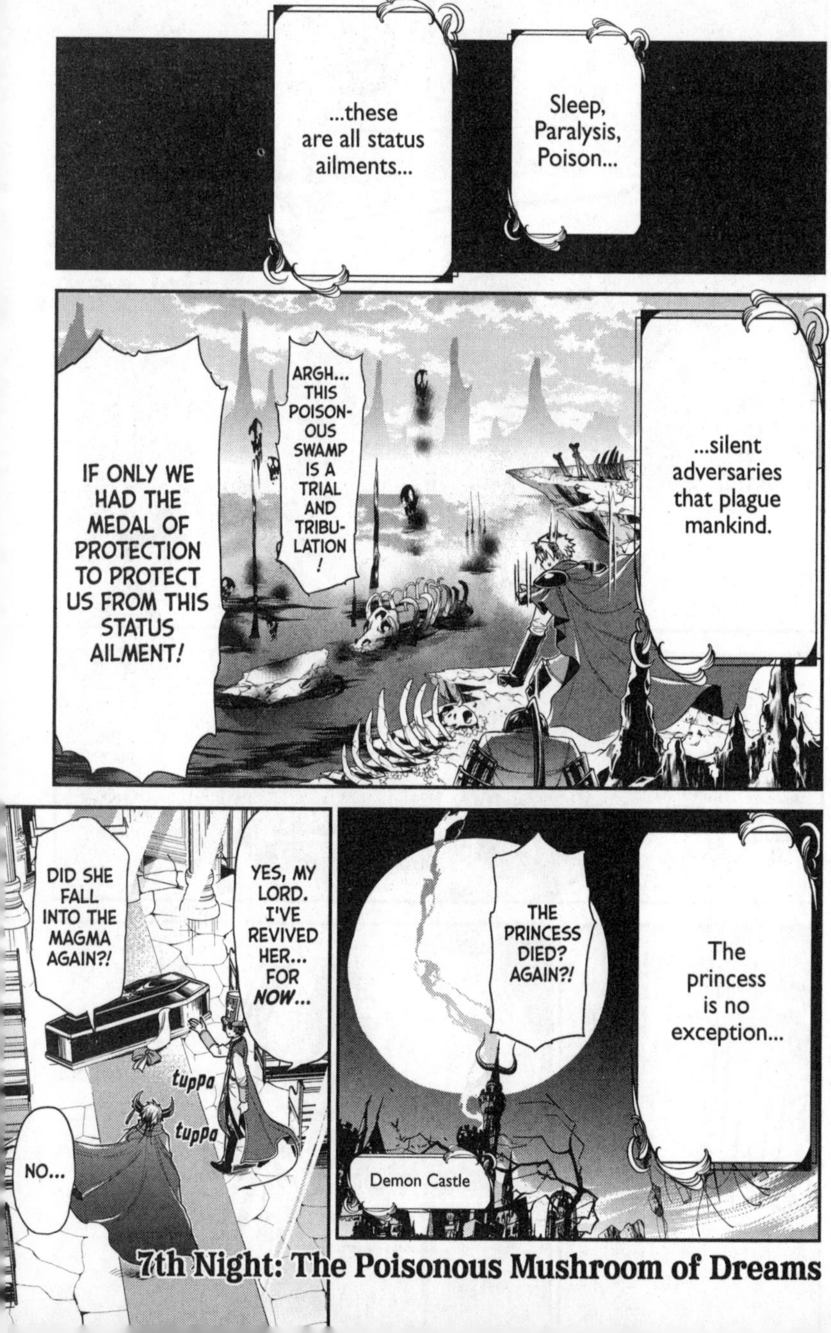
Sleep, Paralysis, Poison...
...these are all status ailments...
...silent adversaries that plague mankind.
ARGH... THIS POISON-OUS SWAMP IS A TRIAL AND TRIBU-LATION!
IF ONLY WE HAD THE MEDAL OF PROTECTION TO PROTECT US FROM THIS STATUS AILMENT!
The princess is no exception...
THE PRINCESS DIED? AGAIN?!
Demon Castle
YES, MY LORD. I'VE REVIVED HER... FOR *NOW*...
DID SHE FALL INTO THE MAGMA AGAIN?!
tuppa
tuppa
NO...

7th Night: The Poisonous Mushroom of Dreams

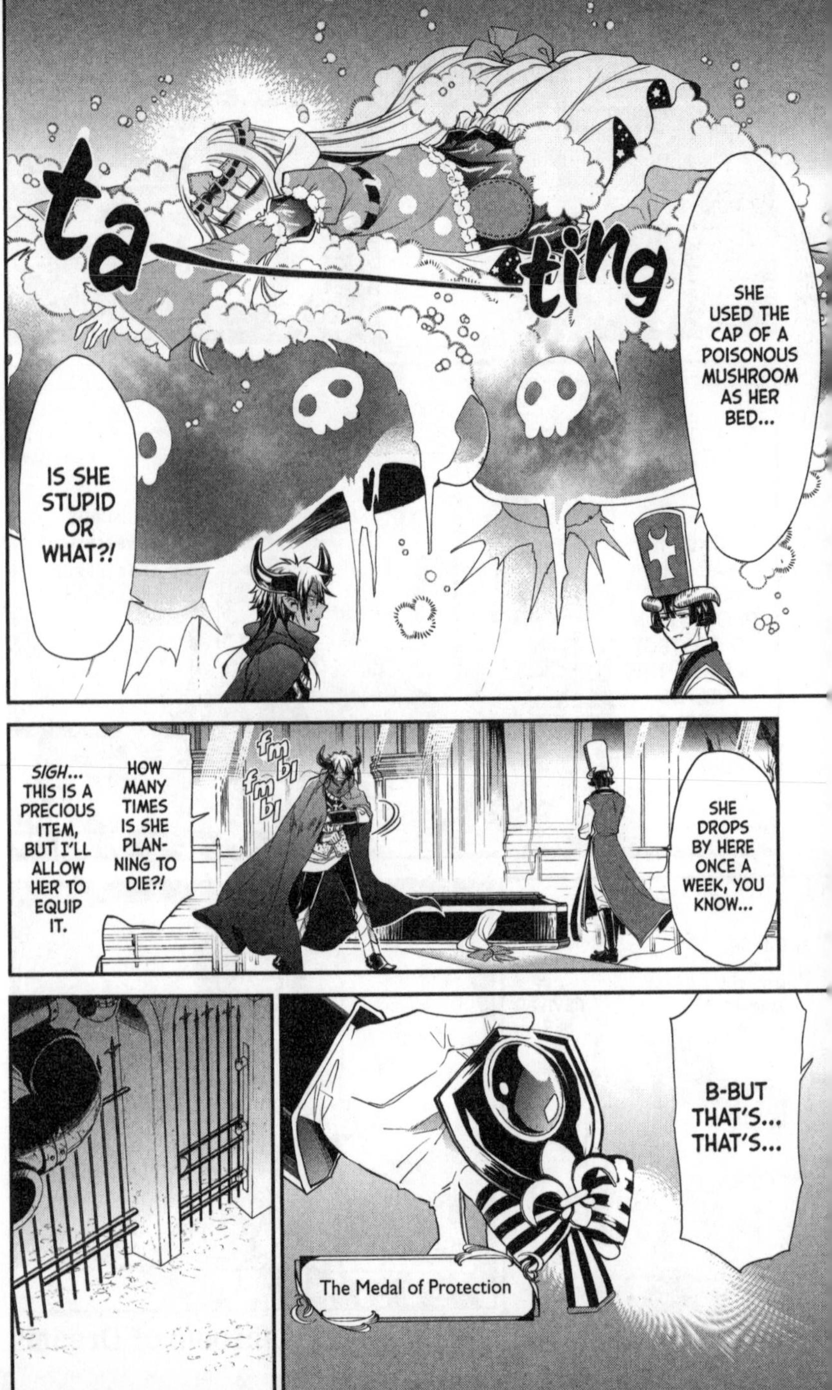
SHE USED THE CAP OF A POISONOUS MUSHROOM AS HER BED...
ta—ting
IS SHE STUPID OR WHAT?!
SHE DROPS BY HERE ONCE A WEEK, YOU KNOW...
fmbl fmbl
HOW MANY TIMES IS SHE PLAN-NING TO DIE?!
SIGH... THIS IS A PRECIOUS ITEM, BUT I'LL ALLOW HER TO EQUIP IT.
B-BUT THAT'S... THAT'S...
The Medal of Protection

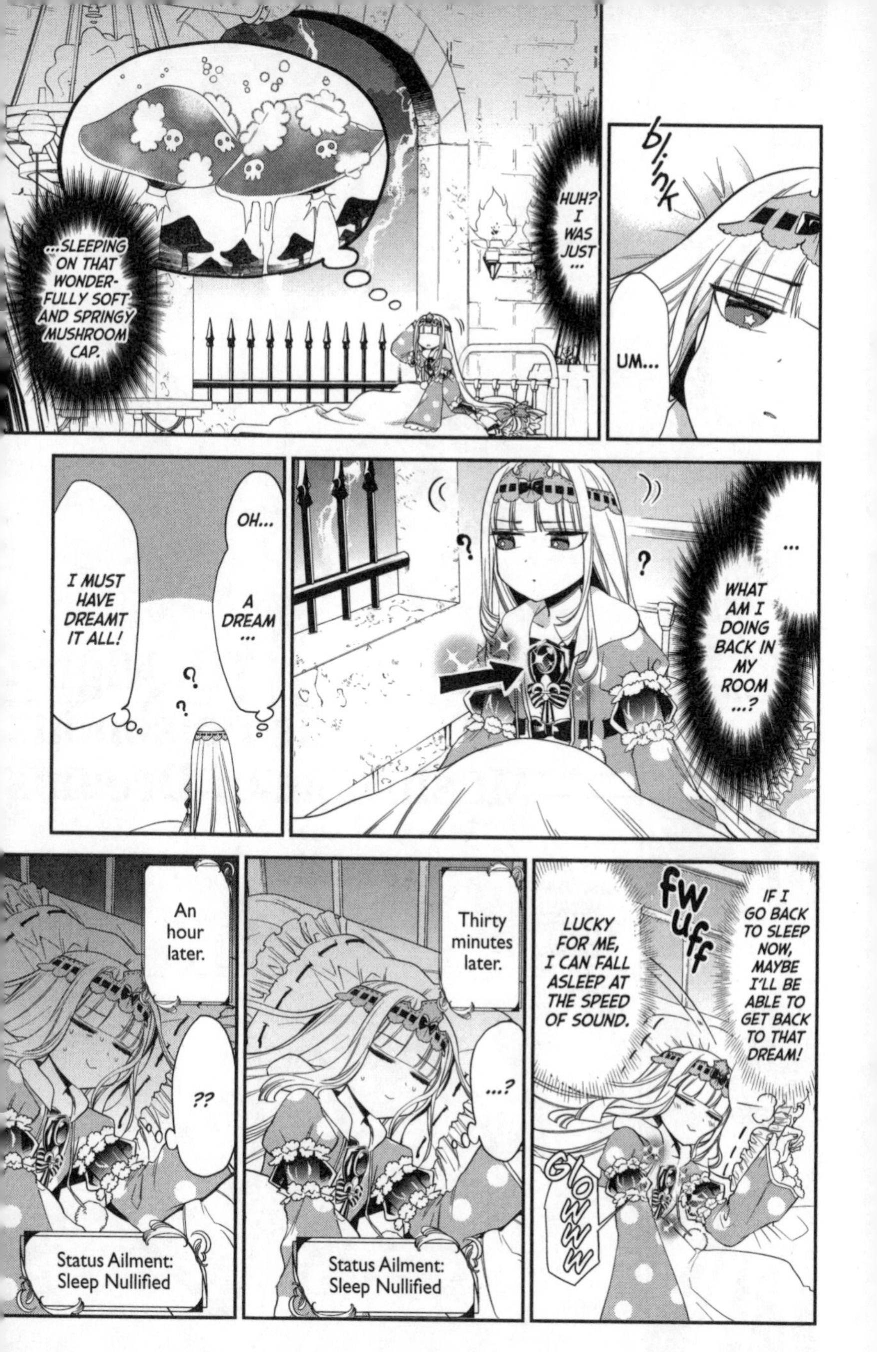
blink
HUH? I WAS JUST ...
UM...
...SLEEPING ON THAT WONDERFULLY SOFT AND SPRINGY MUSHROOM CAP.
...
WHAT AM I DOING BACK IN MY ROOM ...?
?
?
OH... A DREAM ...
I MUST HAVE DREAMT IT ALL!
?
?
IF I GO BACK TO SLEEP NOW, MAYBE I'LL BE ABLE TO GET BACK TO THAT DREAM!
fwuff
LUCKY FOR ME, I CAN FALL ASLEEP AT THE SPEED OF SOUND.
GLOWWW
Thirty minutes later.
...?
Status Ailment: Sleep Nullified
An hour later.
??
Status Ailment: Sleep Nullified

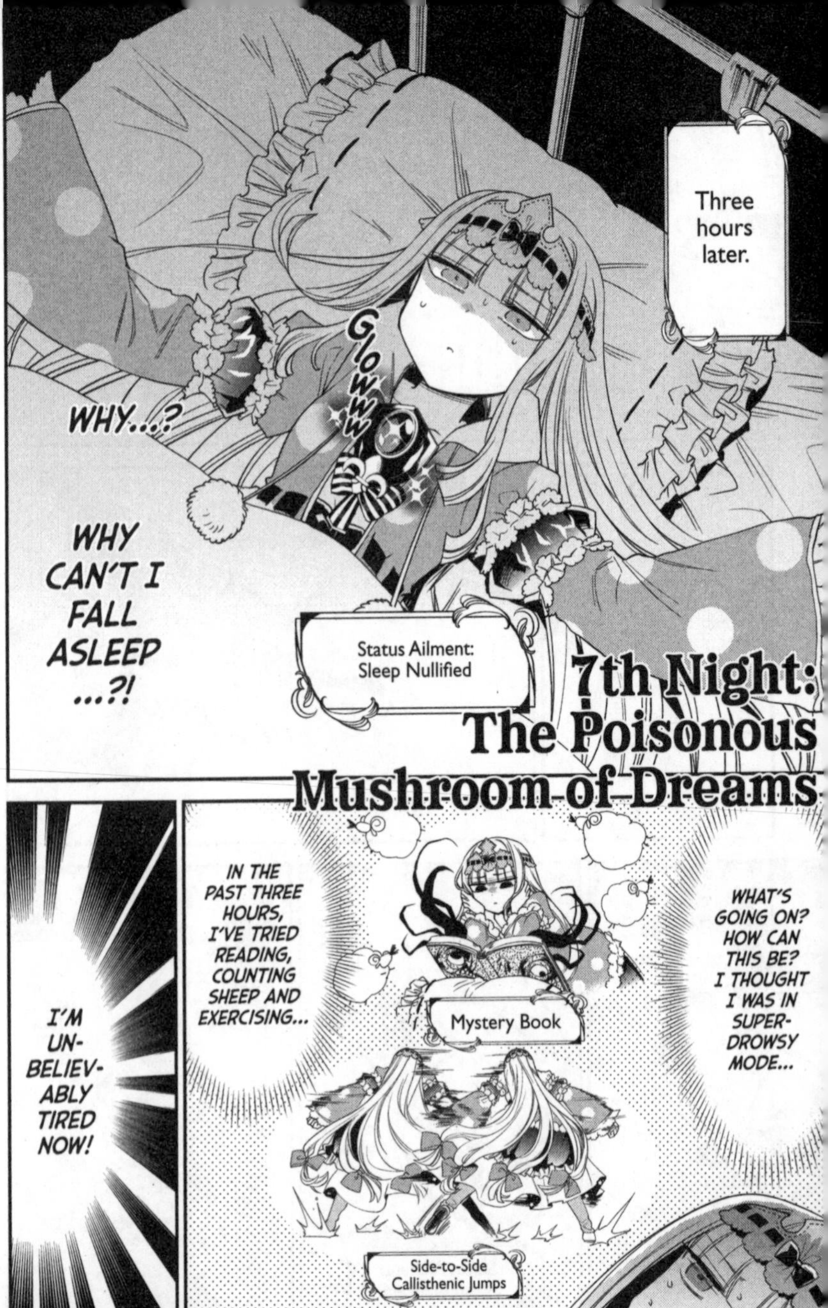
Three hours later.
GLOWWW
WHY...?
WHY CAN'T I FALL ASLEEP ...?!
Status Ailment: Sleep Nullified
7th Night: The Poisonous Mushroom of Dreams
WHAT'S GOING ON? HOW CAN THIS BE? I THOUGHT I WAS IN SUPER-DROWSY MODE...
IN THE PAST THREE HOURS, I'VE TRIED READING, COUNTING SHEEP AND EXERCISING...
Mystery Book
Side-to-Side Callisthenic Jumps
I'M UN-BELIEV-ABLY TIRED NOW!

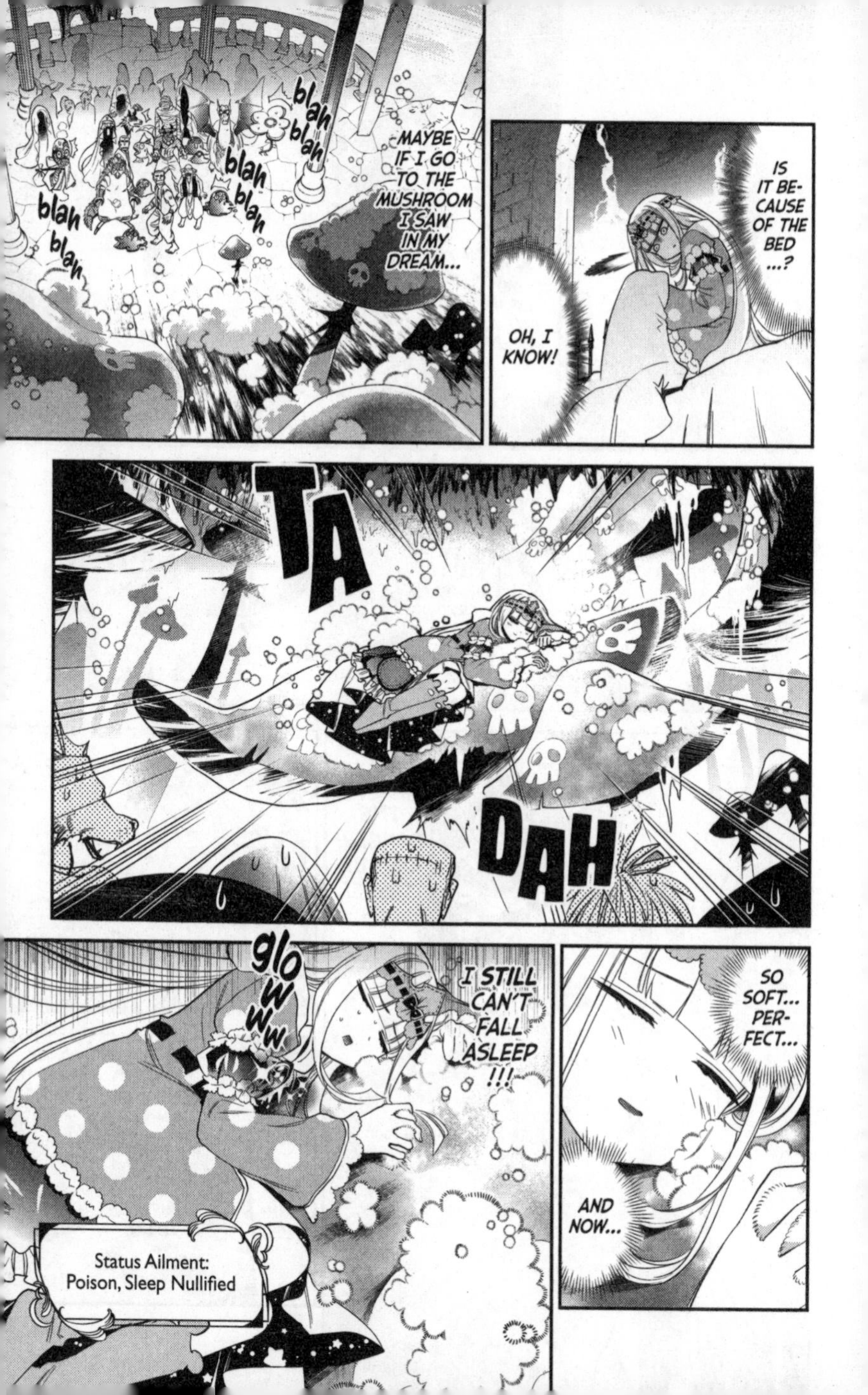
IS IT BE-CAUSE OF THE BED ...?
OH, I KNOW!
MAYBE IF I GO TO THE MUSHROOM I SAW IN MY DREAM...
blah blah
blah blah
blah blah
TA DAH
SO SOFT... PER-FECT...
AND NOW...
I STILL CAN'T FALL ASLEEP !!!
glowwww
Status Ailment: Poison, Sleep Nullified

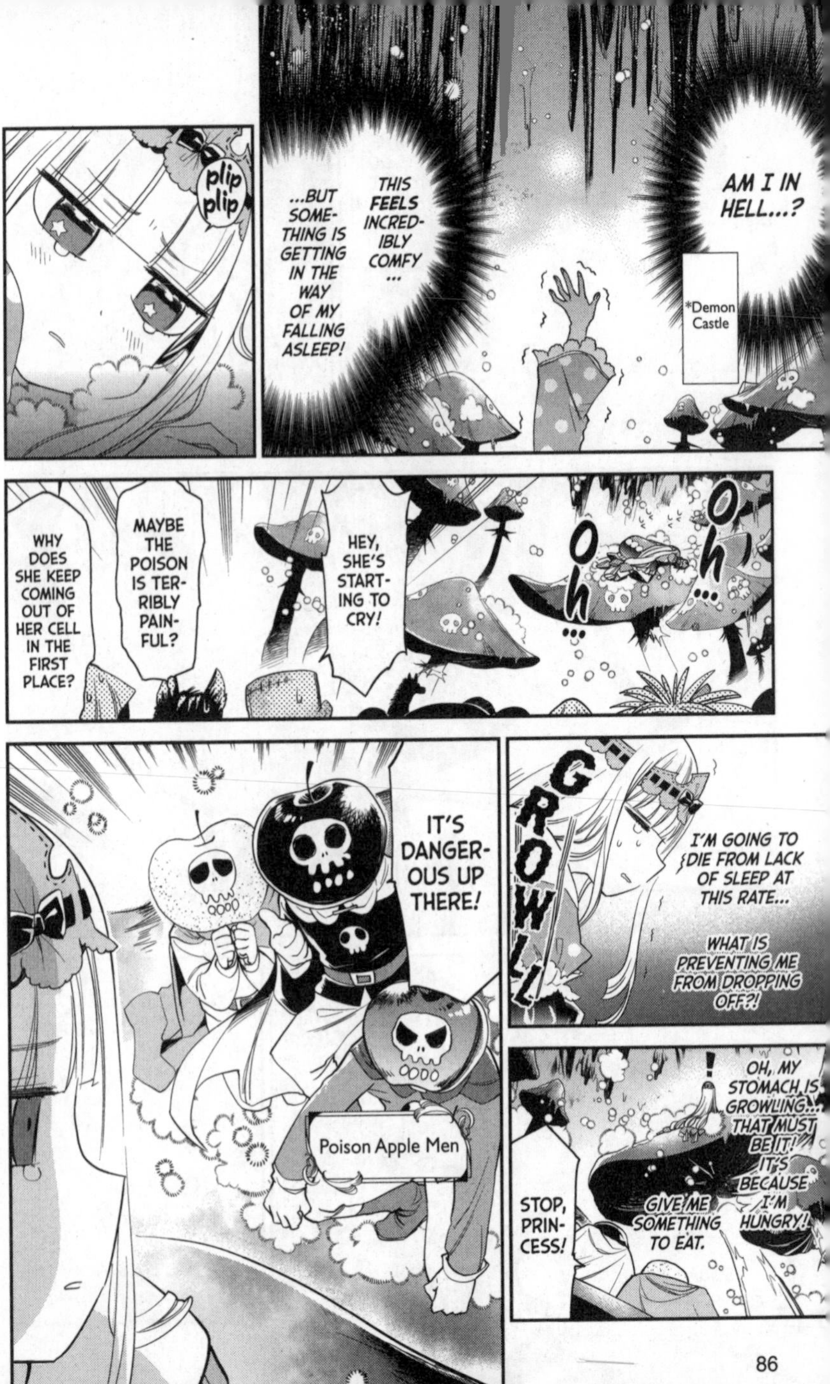
AM I IN HELL...?
*Demon Castle
THIS FEELS INCREDIBLY COMFY...
...BUT SOMETHING IS GETTING IN THE WAY OF MY FALLING ASLEEP!
plip plip
Oh... oh...
HEY, SHE'S STARTING TO CRY!
MAYBE THE POISON IS TERRIBLY PAINFUL?
WHY DOES SHE KEEP COMING OUT OF HER CELL IN THE FIRST PLACE?
I'M GOING TO DIE FROM LACK OF SLEEP AT THIS RATE...
WHAT IS PREVENTING ME FROM DROPPING OFF?!
GROWL
OH, MY STOMACH IS GROWLING... THAT MUST BE IT! IT'S BECAUSE I'M HUNGRY!
GIVE ME SOMETHING TO EAT.
STOP, PRINCESS!
IT'S DANGEROUS UP THERE!
Poison Apple Men

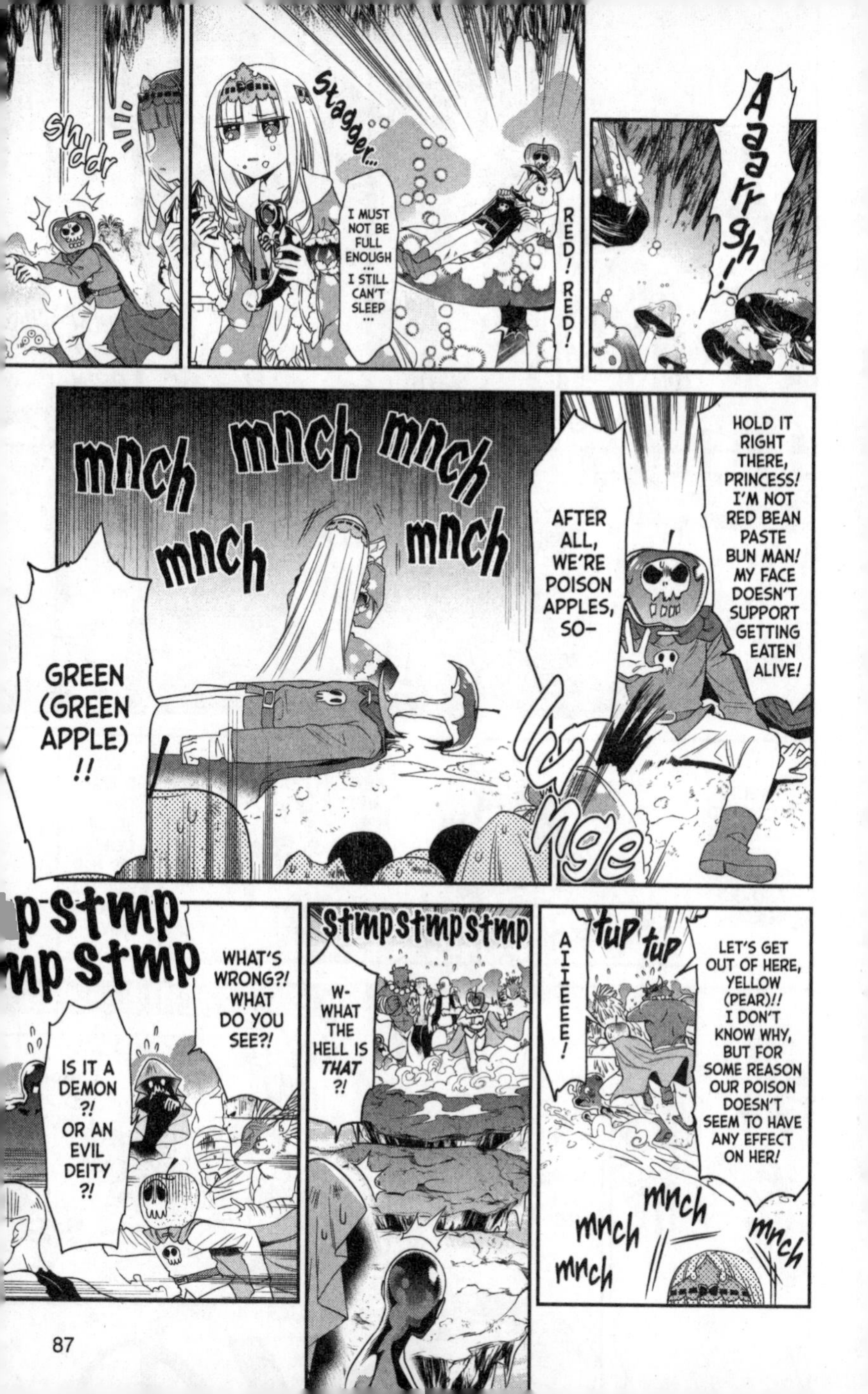
Aaarrgh!
RED! RED!
Stagger...
I MUST NOT BE FULL ENOUGH... I STILL CAN'T SLEEP...
shddr
HOLD IT RIGHT THERE, PRINCESS! I'M NOT RED BEAN PASTE BUN MAN! MY FACE DOESN'T SUPPORT GETTING EATEN ALIVE!
AFTER ALL, WE'RE POISON APPLES, SO—
lunge
mnch mnch mnch mnch mnch
GREEN (GREEN APPLE)!!
LET'S GET OUT OF HERE, YELLOW (PEAR)!! I DON'T KNOW WHY, BUT FOR SOME REASON OUR POISON DOESN'T SEEM TO HAVE ANY EFFECT ON HER!
tup tup
AIIEEEE!
mnch mnch mnch mnch
stmpstmpstmp
W-WHAT THE HELL IS THAT?!
p-stmp
mp stmp
WHAT'S WRONG?! WHAT DO YOU SEE?!
IS IT A DEMON?! OR AN EVIL DEITY?!

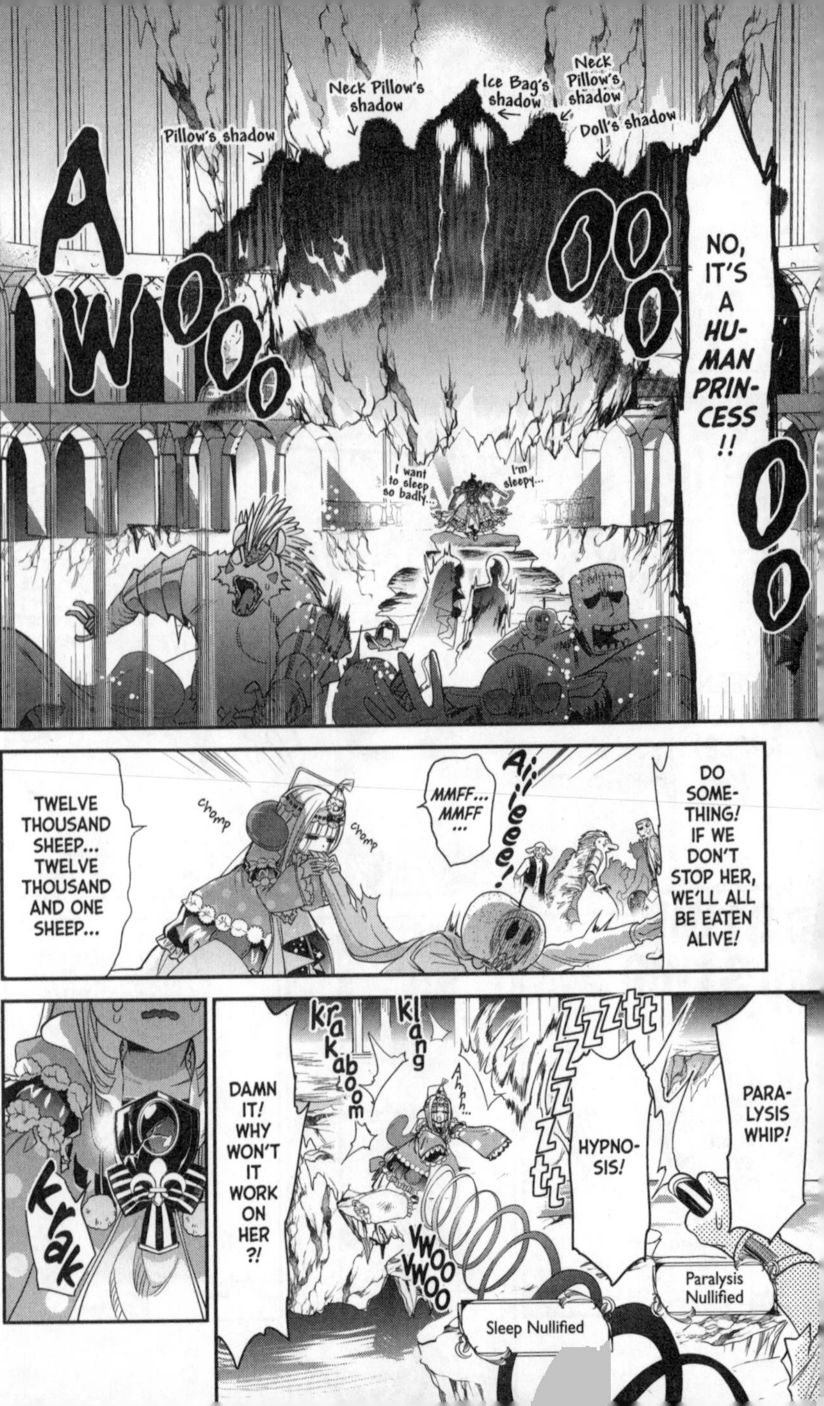
Neck Pillow's shadow
Ice Bag's shadow
Neck Pillow's shadow
Doll's shadow
Pillow's shadow
NO, IT'S A HUMAN PRINCESS!!
AWOOOOOOOOOO
I'm sleepy...
I want to sleep so badly...
DO SOMETHING! IF WE DON'T STOP HER, WE'LL ALL BE EATEN ALIVE!
Aiiieeee!
MMFF... MMFF...
chomp
chomp
TWELVE THOUSAND SHEEP... TWELVE THOUSAND AND ONE SHEEP...
PARALYSIS WHIP!
Paralysis Nullified
HYPNOSIS!
ZZZZTT
ZZZZTT
Sleep Nullified
klang
krakaboom
Ahhh...
VWOO VWOO
DAMN IT! WHY WON'T IT WORK ON HER?!
krak

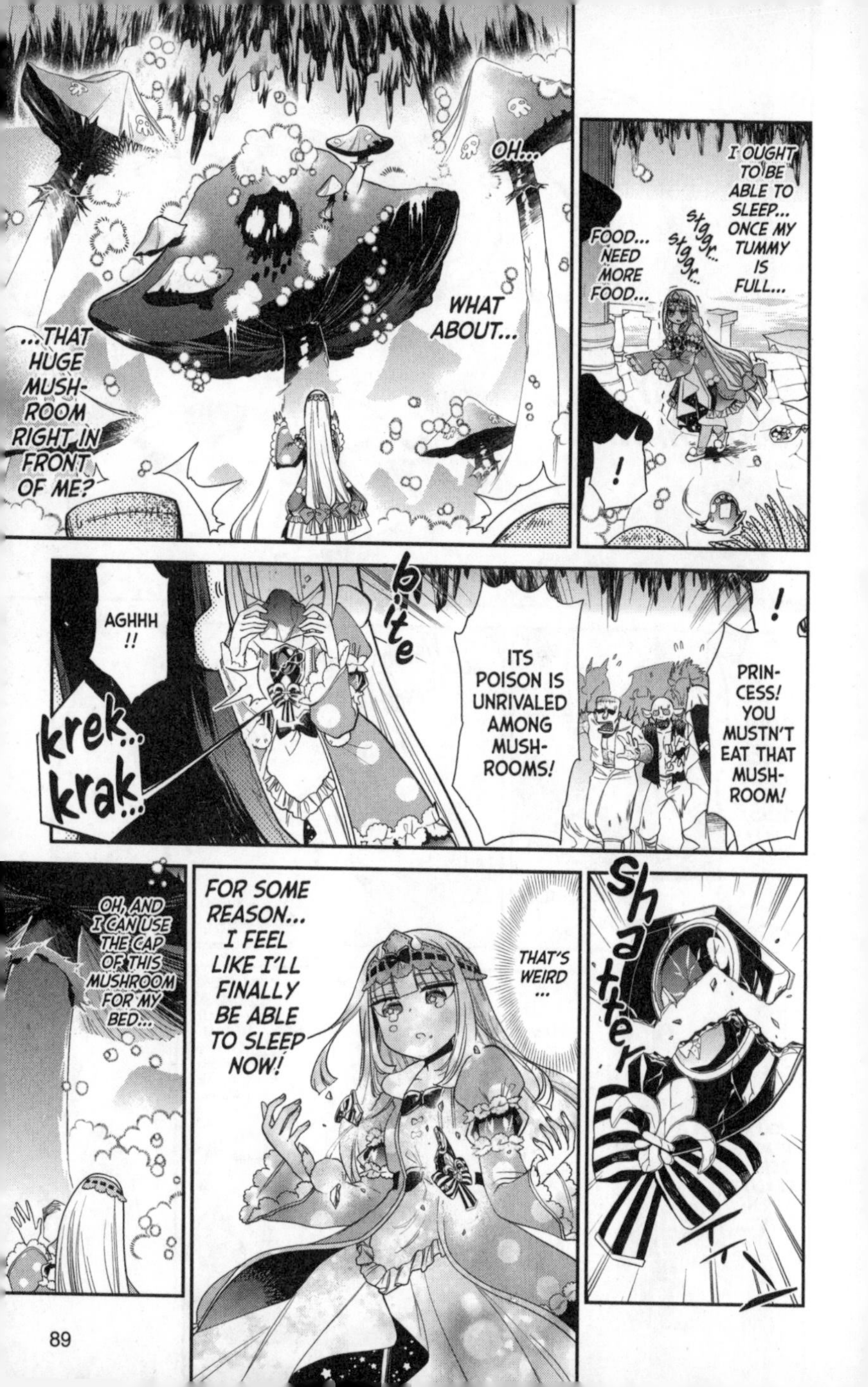
I OUGHT TO BE ABLE TO SLEEP... ONCE MY TUMMY IS FULL...
stggr... stggr...
FOOD... NEED MORE FOOD...
!
OH...
WHAT ABOUT...
...THAT HUGE MUSH-ROOM RIGHT IN FRONT OF ME?
!
PRIN-CESS! YOU MUSTN'T EAT THAT MUSH-ROOM!
ITS POISON IS UNRIVALED AMONG MUSH-ROOMS!
bite
AGHHH !!
krek... krak...
Shatter
THAT'S WEIRD ...
FOR SOME REASON... I FEEL LIKE I'LL FINALLY BE ABLE TO SLEEP NOW!
OH, AND I CAN USE THE CAP OF THIS MUSHROOM FOR MY BED...

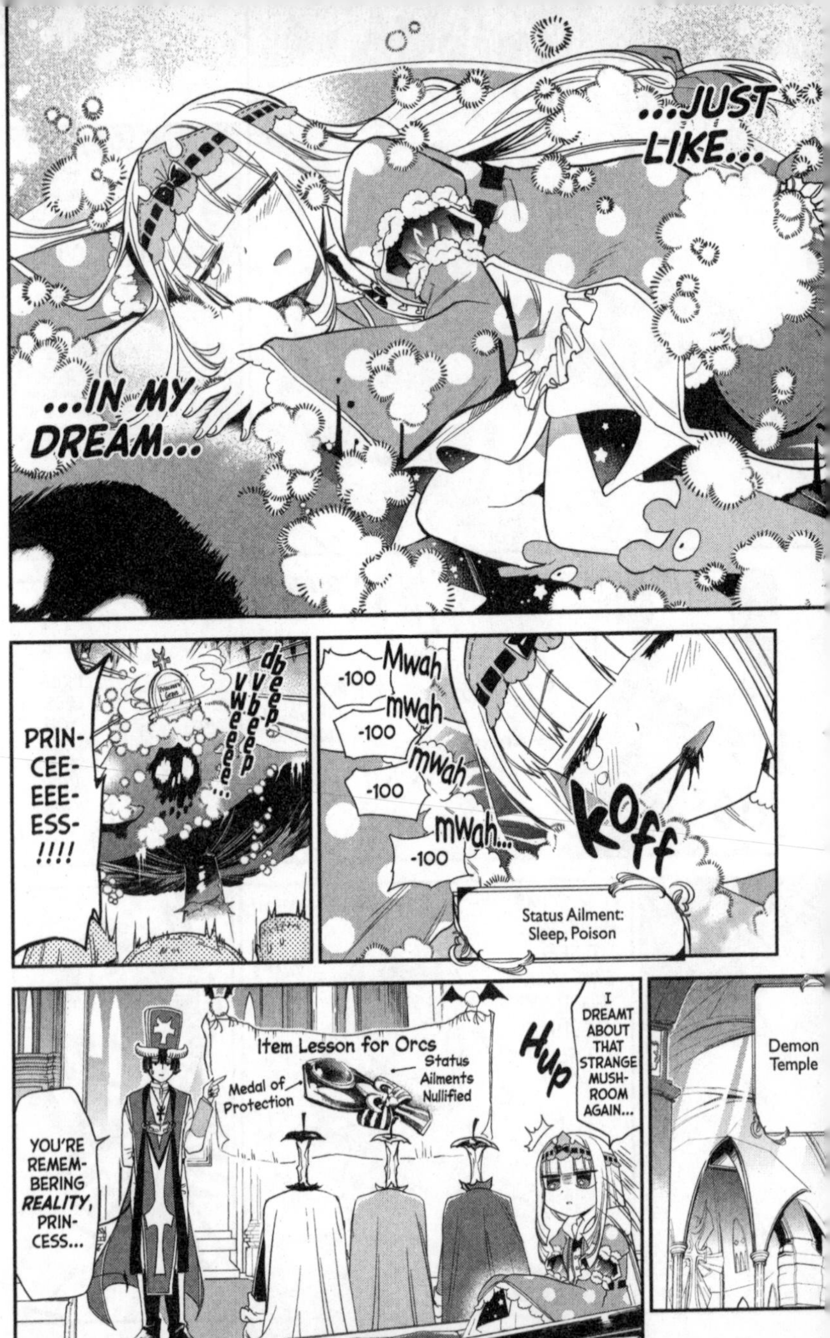
...JUST LIKE...
...IN MY DREAM...
Mwah
-100
mwah
-100
mwah
-100
mwah...
-100
koff
Status Ailment: Sleep, Poison
dbeep vbeep vweeeee...
PRIN-CEE-EEE-ESS-!!!!
Demon Temple
I DREAMT ABOUT THAT STRANGE MUSH-ROOM AGAIN...
Hup
Item Lesson for Orcs
Status Ailments Nullified
Medal of Protection
YOU'RE REMEM-BERING *REALITY*, PRIN-CESS...

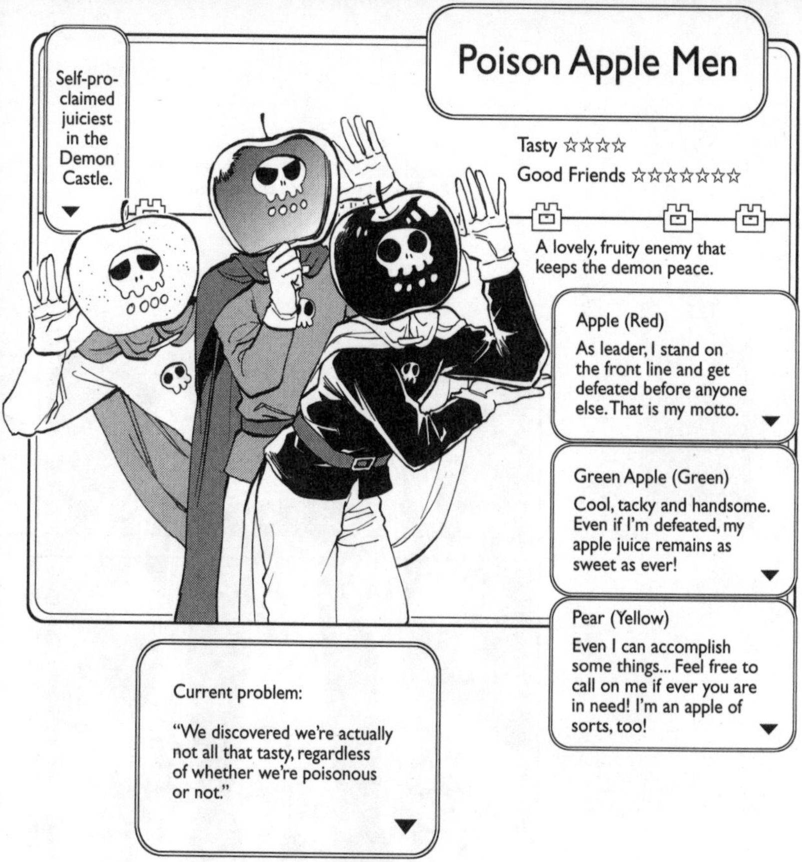
Poison Apple Men
Tasty ☆☆☆☆
Good Friends ☆☆☆☆☆☆☆☆
A lovely, fruity enemy that keeps the demon peace.
Self-proclaimed juiciest in the Demon Castle.
Apple (Red)
As leader, I stand on the front line and get defeated before anyone else. That is my motto.
Green Apple (Green)
Cool, tacky and handsome. Even if I'm defeated, my apple juice remains as sweet as ever!
Pear (Yellow)
Even I can accomplish some things... Feel free to call on me if ever you are in need! I'm an apple of sorts, too!
Current problem:
"We discovered we're actually not all that tasty, regardless of whether we're poisonous or not."

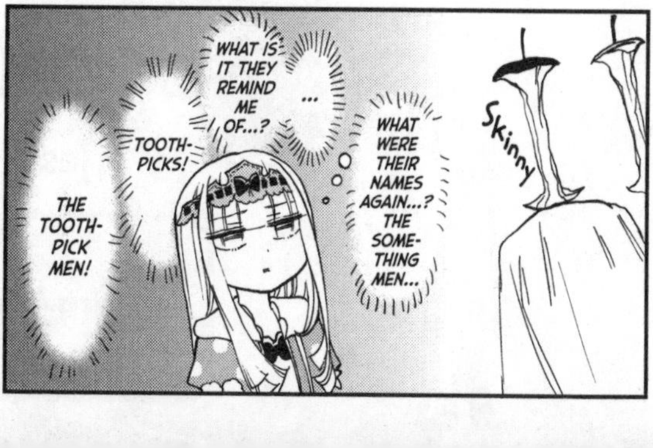
Skinny
WHAT WERE THEIR NAMES AGAIN...? THE SOMETHING MEN...
...
WHAT IS IT THEY REMIND ME OF...?
TOOTHPICKS!
THE TOOTHPICK MEN!

Would you like to change your class?
5 changes remaining
▶ Yes
No ▼
Jester
"This isn't funny..."

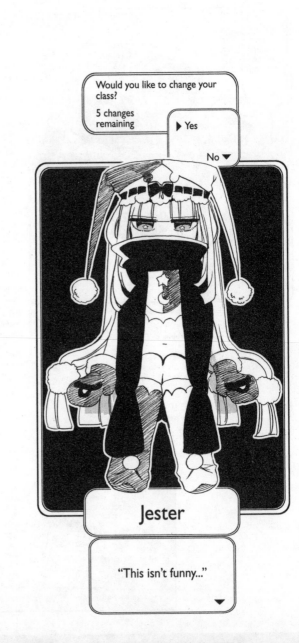

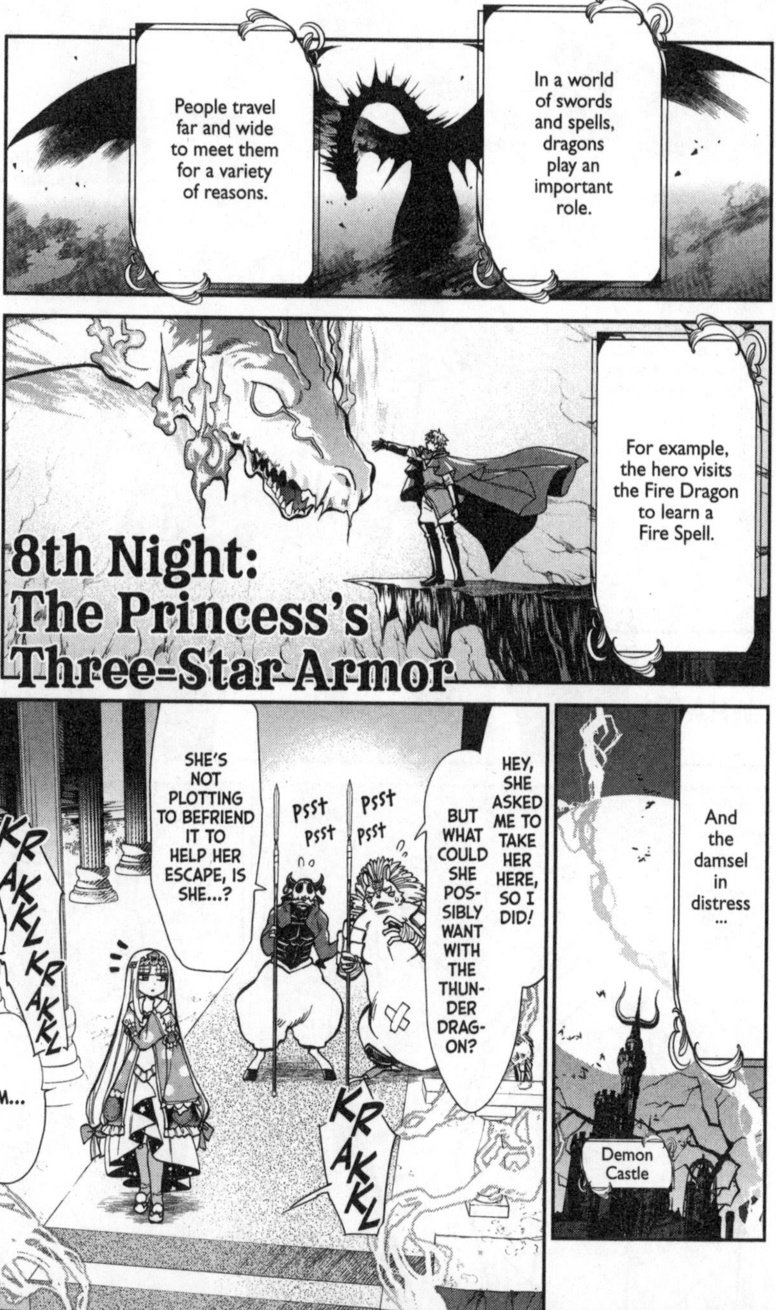
In a world of swords and spells, dragons play an important role.
People travel far and wide to meet them for a variety of reasons.
For example, the hero visits the Fire Dragon to learn a Fire Spell.
8th Night: The Princess's Three-Star Armor
And the damsel in distress...
Demon Castle
HEY, SHE ASKED ME TO TAKE HER HERE, SO I DID!
BUT WHAT COULD SHE POSSIBLY WANT WITH THE THUNDER DRAGON?
psst psst
psst psst
SHE'S NOT PLOTTING TO BEFRIEND IT TO HELP HER ESCAPE, IS SHE...?
KRAKKL
KRAKKL KRAKKL
UM...

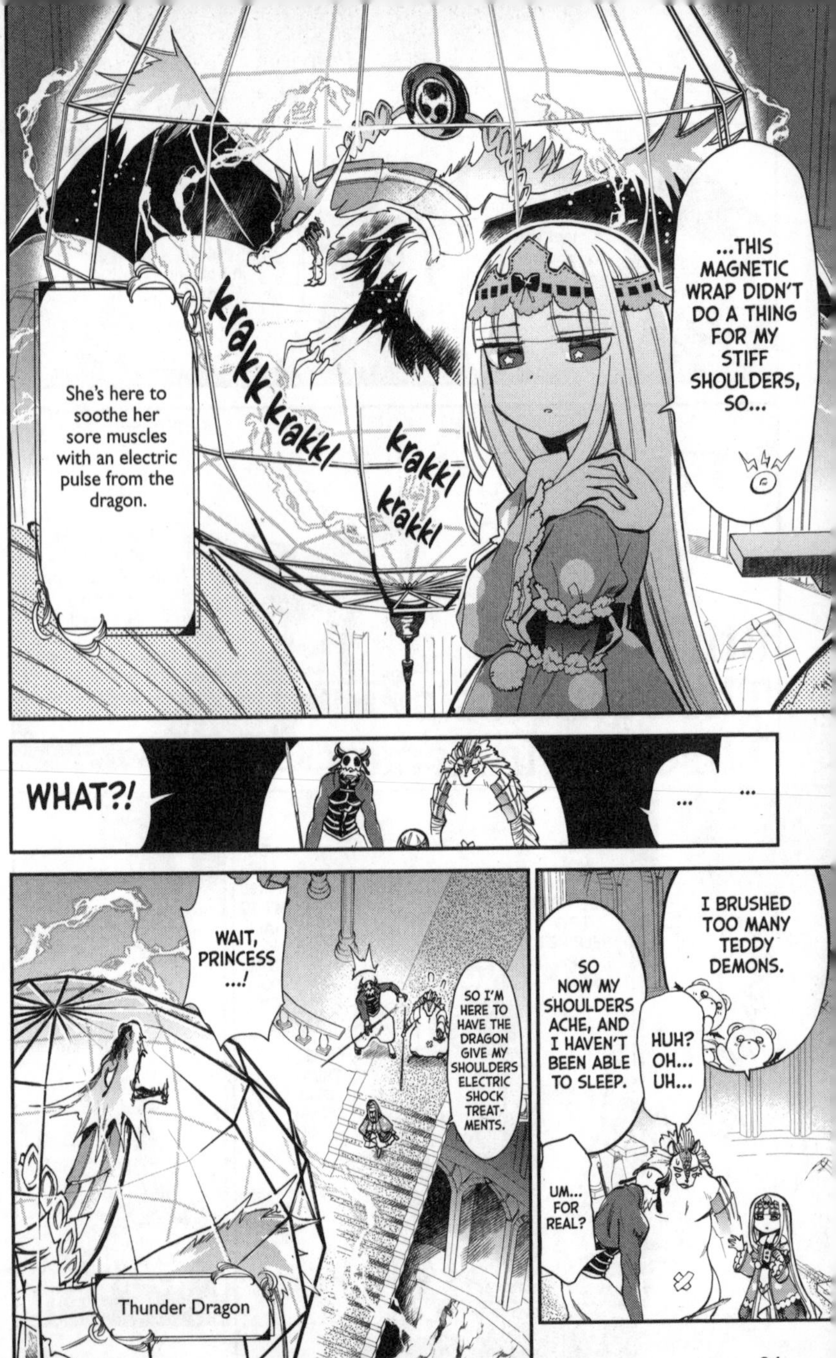
...THIS MAGNETIC WRAP DIDN'T DO A THING FOR MY STIFF SHOULDERS, SO...
krakkl krakkl
krakkl krakkl
krakk krakkl
She's here to soothe her sore muscles with an electric pulse from the dragon.
... ...
WHAT?!
I BRUSHED TOO MANY TEDDY DEMONS.
HUH? OH... UH...
SO NOW MY SHOULDERS ACHE, AND I HAVEN'T BEEN ABLE TO SLEEP.
UM... FOR REAL?
SO I'M HERE TO HAVE THE DRAGON GIVE MY SHOULDERS ELECTRIC SHOCK TREATMENTS.
WAIT, PRINCESS ...!
Thunder Dragon

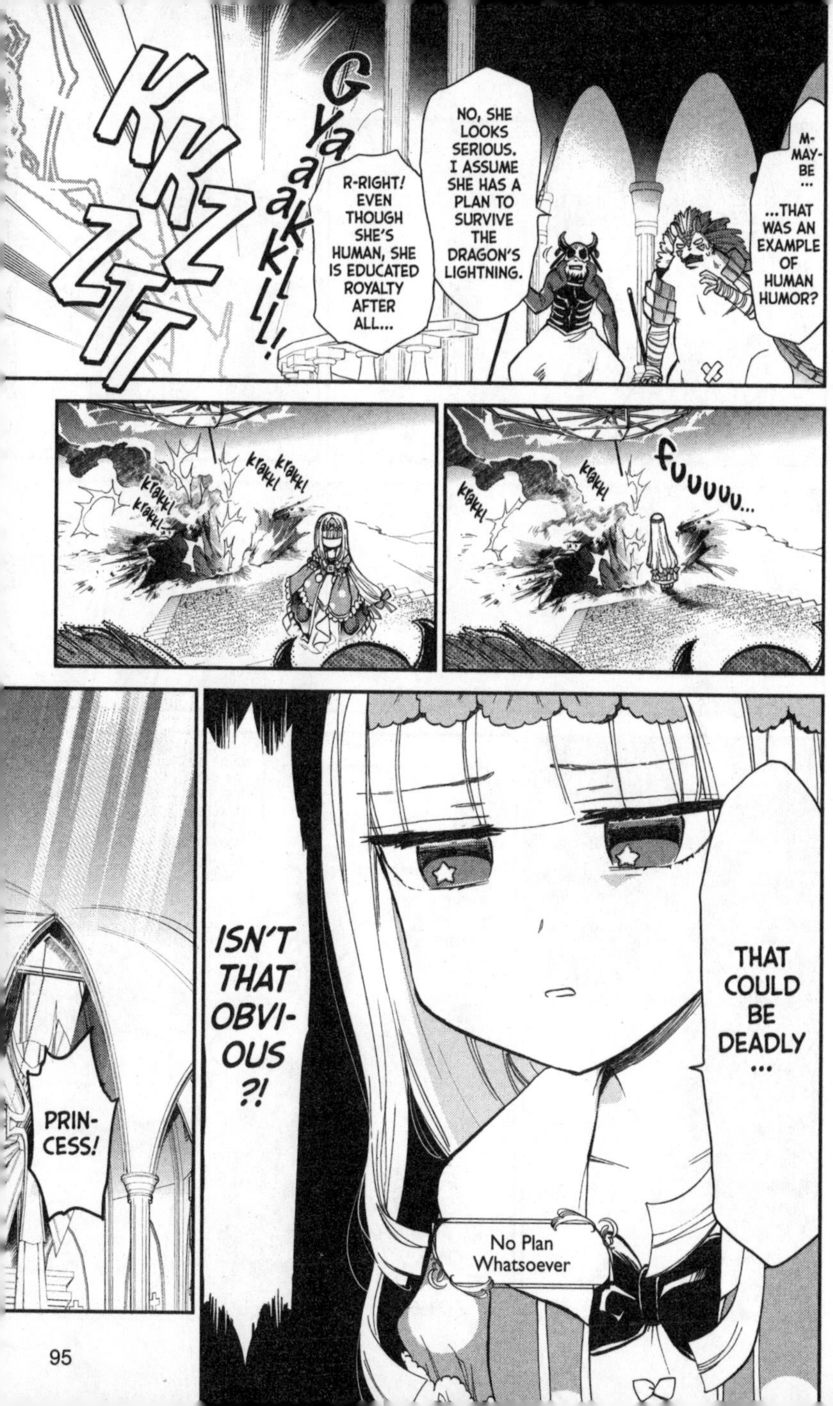
M-MAYBE... ...THAT WAS AN EXAMPLE OF HUMAN HUMOR?
NO, SHE LOOKS SERIOUS. I ASSUME SHE HAS A PLAN TO SURVIVE THE DRAGON'S LIGHTNING.
R-RIGHT! EVEN THOUGH SHE'S HUMAN, SHE IS EDUCATED ROYALTY AFTER ALL...
GYaaakkllll!
KKZZTT
fuuuuu...
krakkl
krakkl
krakkl
krakkl
krakkl
krakkl
THAT COULD BE DEADLY...
ISN'T THAT OBVIOUS?!
No Plan Whatsoever
PRINCESS!

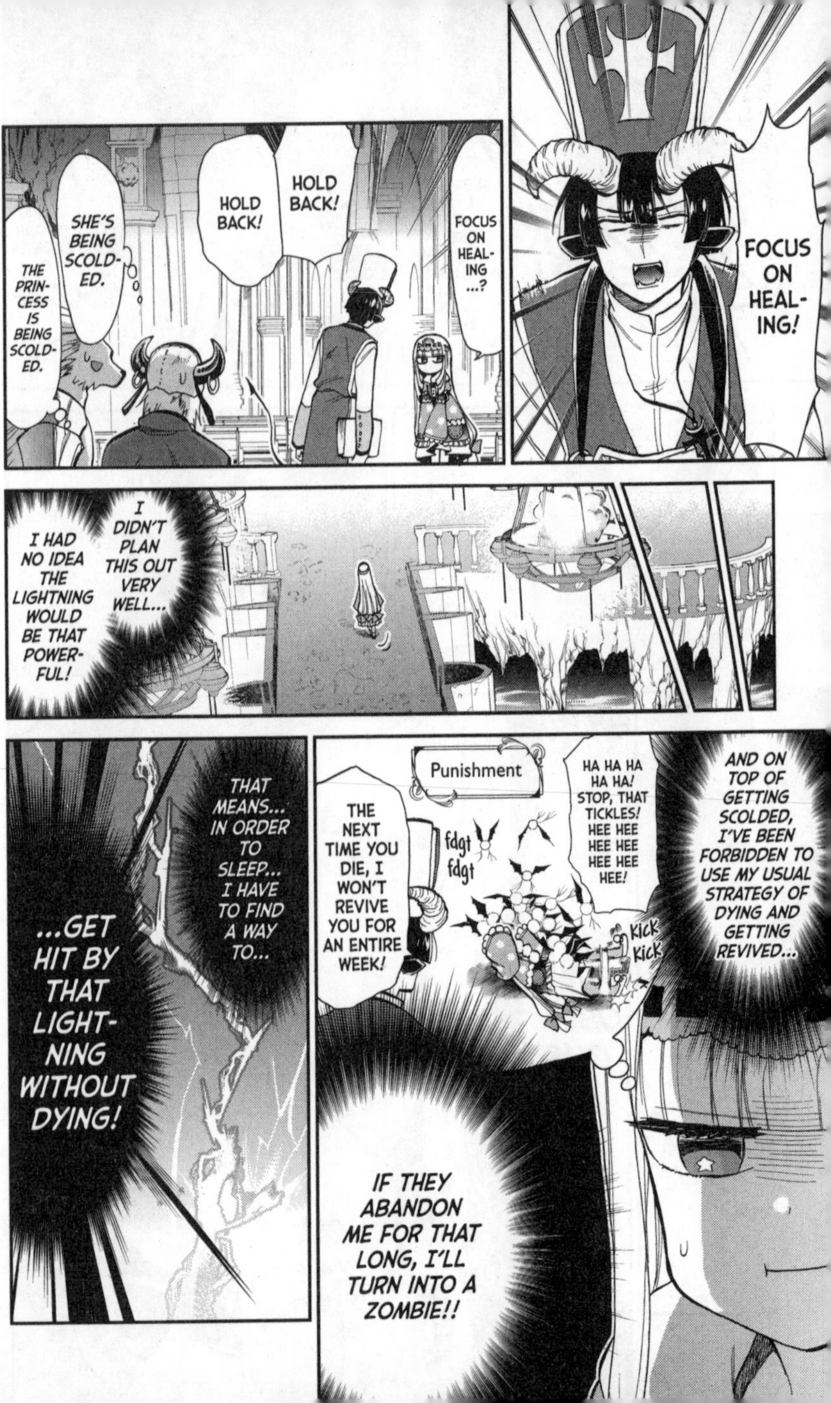
FOCUS ON HEALING!
FOCUS ON HEALING...?
HOLD BACK!
HOLD BACK!
SHE'S BEING SCOLDED.
THE PRINCESS IS BEING SCOLDED.
I DIDN'T PLAN THIS OUT VERY WELL...
I HAD NO IDEA THE LIGHTNING WOULD BE THAT POWERFUL!
AND ON TOP OF GETTING SCOLDED, I'VE BEEN FORBIDDEN TO USE MY USUAL STRATEGY OF DYING AND GETTING REVIVED...
HA HA HA HA HA! STOP, THAT TICKLES! HEE HEE HEE HEE HEE HEE HEE!
Punishment
THE NEXT TIME YOU DIE, I WON'T REVIVE YOU FOR AN ENTIRE WEEK!
fdgt fdgt
Kick Kick
IF THEY ABANDON ME FOR THAT LONG, I'LL TURN INTO A ZOMBIE!!
THAT MEANS... IN ORDER TO SLEEP... I HAVE TO FIND A WAY TO...
...GET HIT BY THAT LIGHTNING WITHOUT DYING!

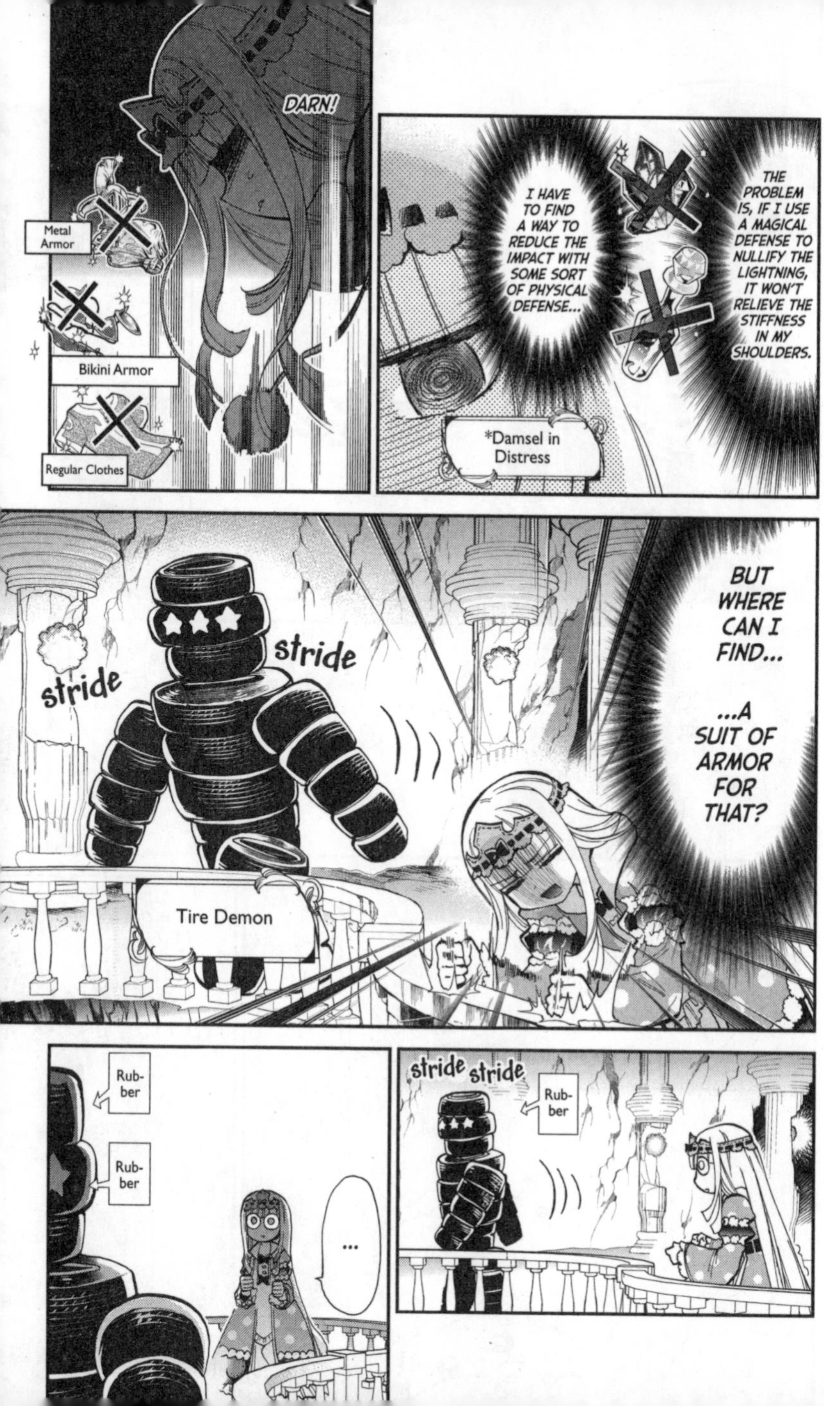

THE PROBLEM IS, IF I USE A MAGICAL DEFENSE TO NULLIFY THE LIGHTNING, IT WON'T RELIEVE THE STIFFNESS IN MY SHOULDERS.
I HAVE TO FIND A WAY TO REDUCE THE IMPACT WITH SOME SORT OF PHYSICAL DEFENSE...
*Damsel in Distress
DARN!
Metal Armor
Bikini Armor
Regular Clothes
BUT WHERE CAN I FIND...
...A SUIT OF ARMOR FOR THAT?
stride
stride
Tire Demon
stride stride
Rub-ber
Rub-ber
Rub-ber
...

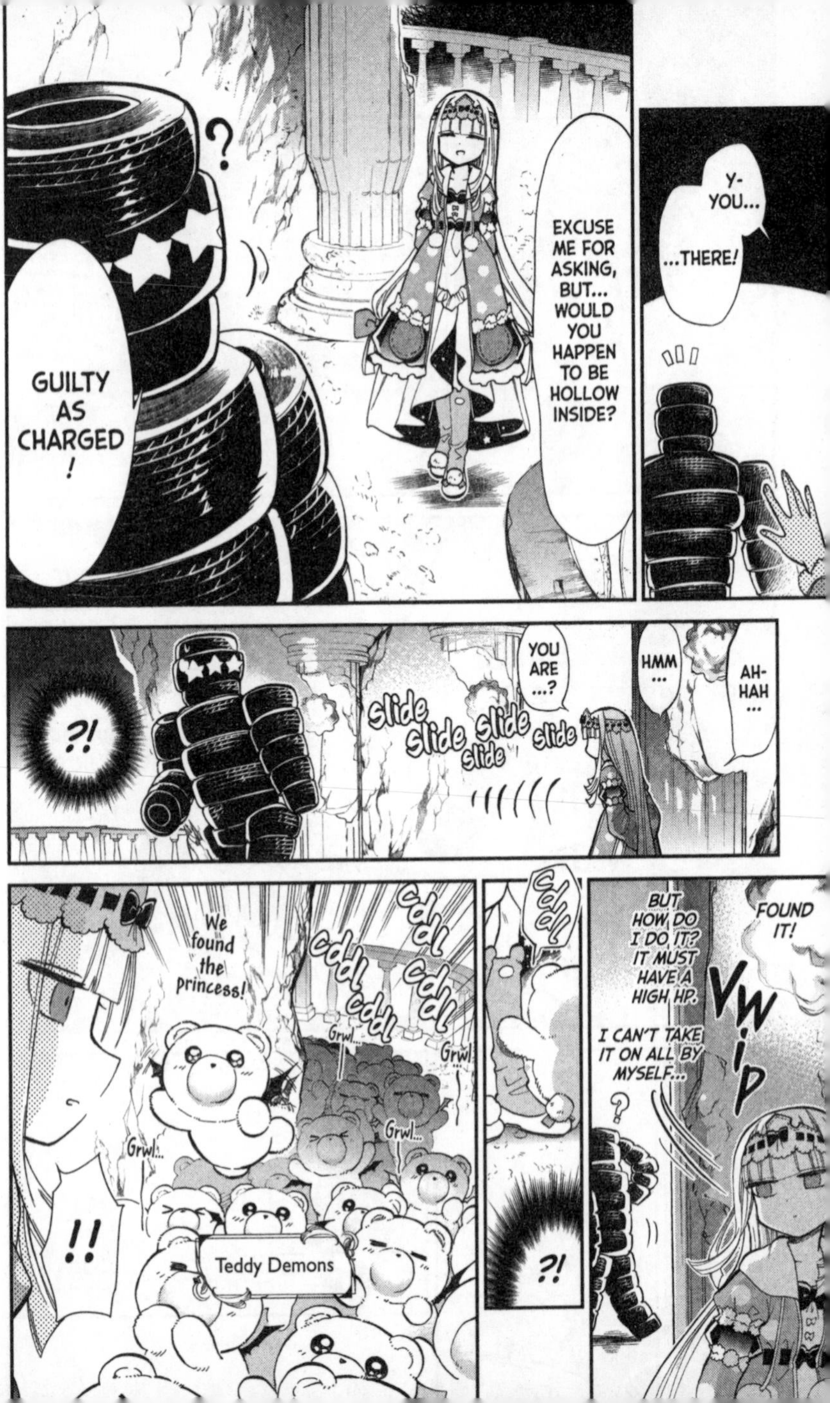

Y-YOU...
...THERE!
EXCUSE ME FOR ASKING, BUT... WOULD YOU HAPPEN TO BE HOLLOW INSIDE?
?
GUILTY AS CHARGED!
AH-HAH...
HMM...
YOU ARE...?
slide slide slide slide slide
?!
FOUND IT!
VWIP
BUT HOW DO I DO IT? IT MUST HAVE A HIGH HP.
I CAN'T TAKE IT ON ALL BY MYSELF...
?
?!
cddl
cddl cddl cddl cddl
We found the princess!
Grwl...
Grwl...
Grwl...
Grwl...
!!
Teddy Demons

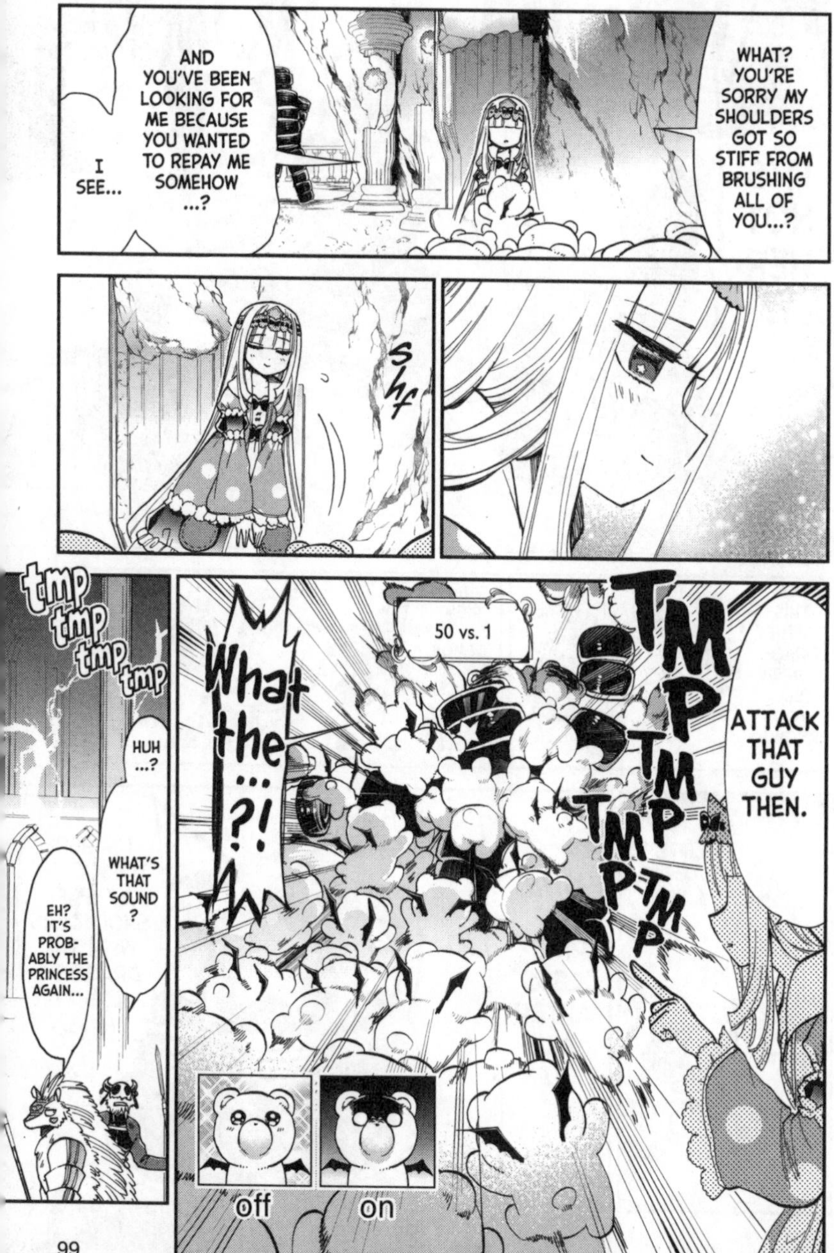

WHAT? YOU'RE SORRY MY SHOULDERS GOT SO STIFF FROM BRUSHING ALL OF YOU...?
AND YOU'VE BEEN LOOKING FOR ME BECAUSE YOU WANTED TO REPAY ME SOMEHOW ...?
I SEE...
shf
ATTACK THAT GUY THEN.
TMP TMP TMP TMP TMP
50 vs. 1
What the...?!
off
on
tmp tmp tmp tmp
HUH ...?
WHAT'S THAT SOUND?
EH? IT'S PROBABLY THE PRINCESS AGAIN...

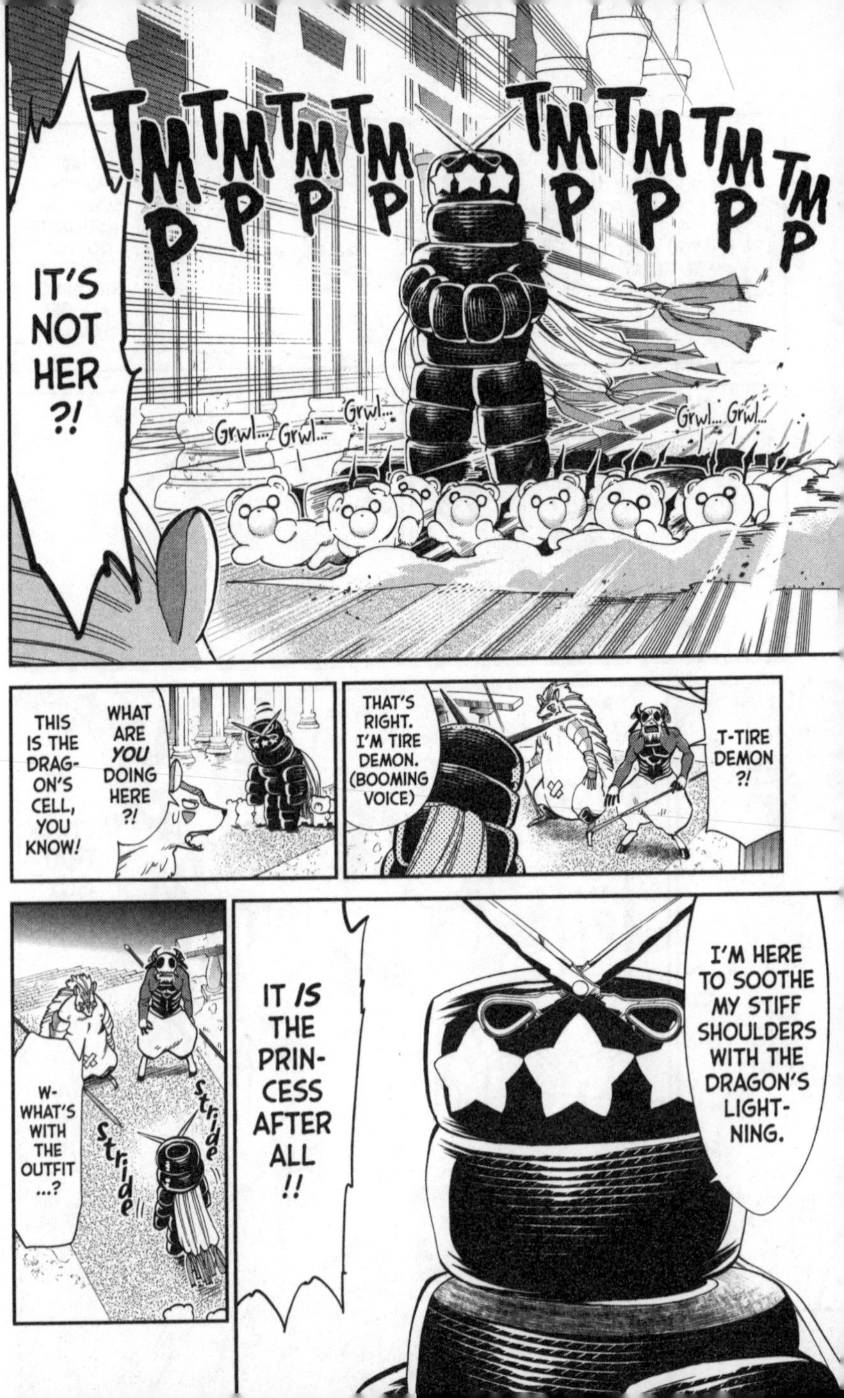
TMTMTMTMTMP TMTMTMTMP
Grwl... Grwl...
Grwl...
Grwl... Grwl...
IT'S NOT HER ?!
T-TIRE DEMON ?!
THAT'S RIGHT. I'M TIRE DEMON. (BOOMING VOICE)
WHAT ARE *YOU* DOING HERE ?!
THIS IS THE DRAG-ON'S CELL, YOU KNOW!
I'M HERE TO SOOTHE MY STIFF SHOULDERS WITH THE DRAGON'S LIGHT-NING.
IT *IS* THE PRIN-CESS AFTER ALL !!
stride
stride
W-WHAT'S WITH THE OUTFIT ...?

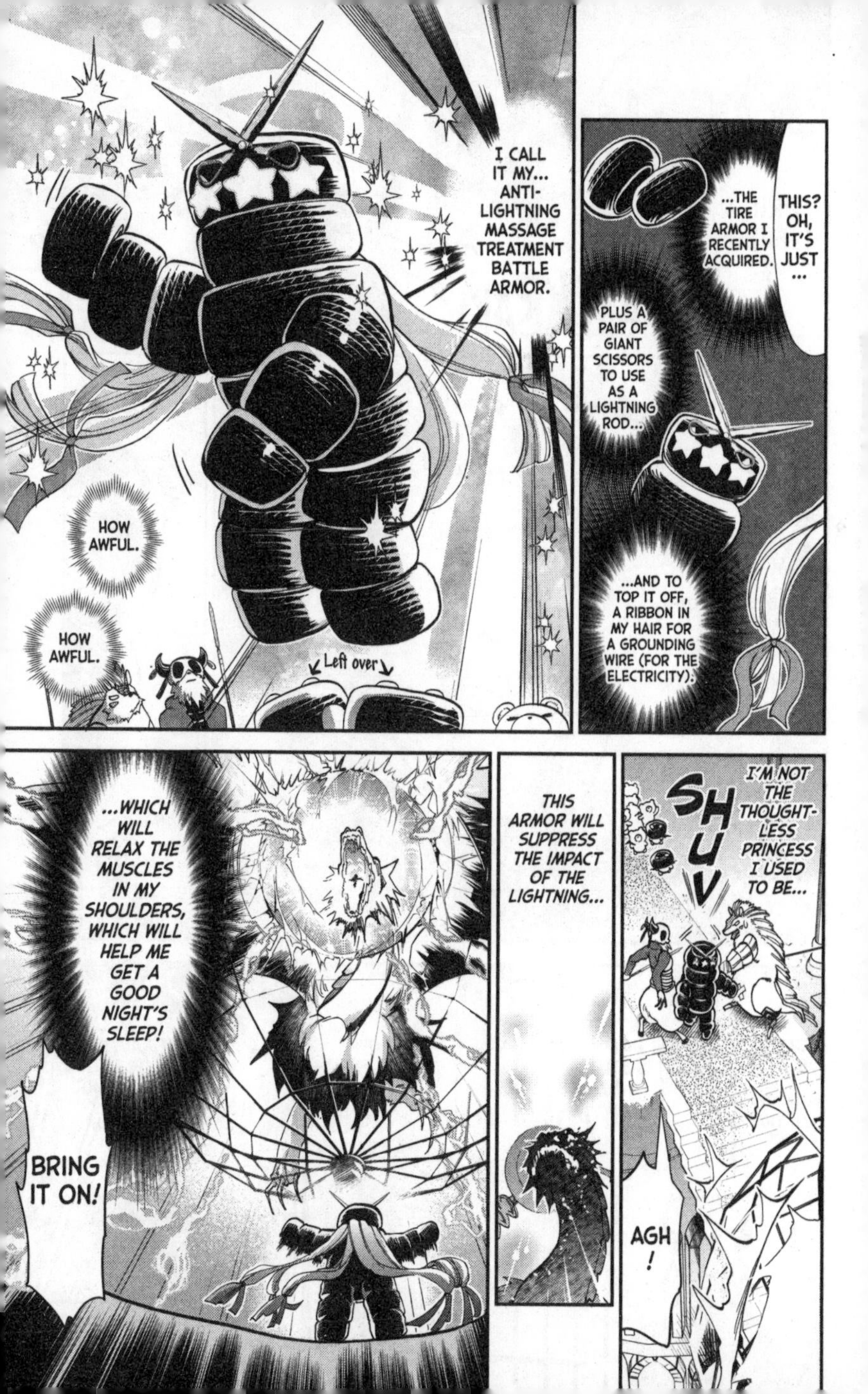
THIS? OH, IT'S JUST ...
...THE TIRE ARMOR I RECENTLY ACQUIRED.
PLUS A PAIR OF GIANT SCISSORS TO USE AS A LIGHTNING ROD...
...AND TO TOP IT OFF, A RIBBON IN MY HAIR FOR A GROUNDING WIRE (FOR THE ELECTRICITY).
I CALL IT MY... ANTI-LIGHTNING MASSAGE TREATMENT BATTLE ARMOR.
HOW AWFUL.
HOW AWFUL.
Left over
I'M NOT THE THOUGHT-LESS PRINCESS I USED TO BE...
SHUV
AGH!
THIS ARMOR WILL SUPPRESS THE IMPACT OF THE LIGHTNING...
...WHICH WILL RELAX THE MUSCLES IN MY SHOULDERS, WHICH WILL HELP ME GET A GOOD NIGHT'S SLEEP!
BRING IT ON!

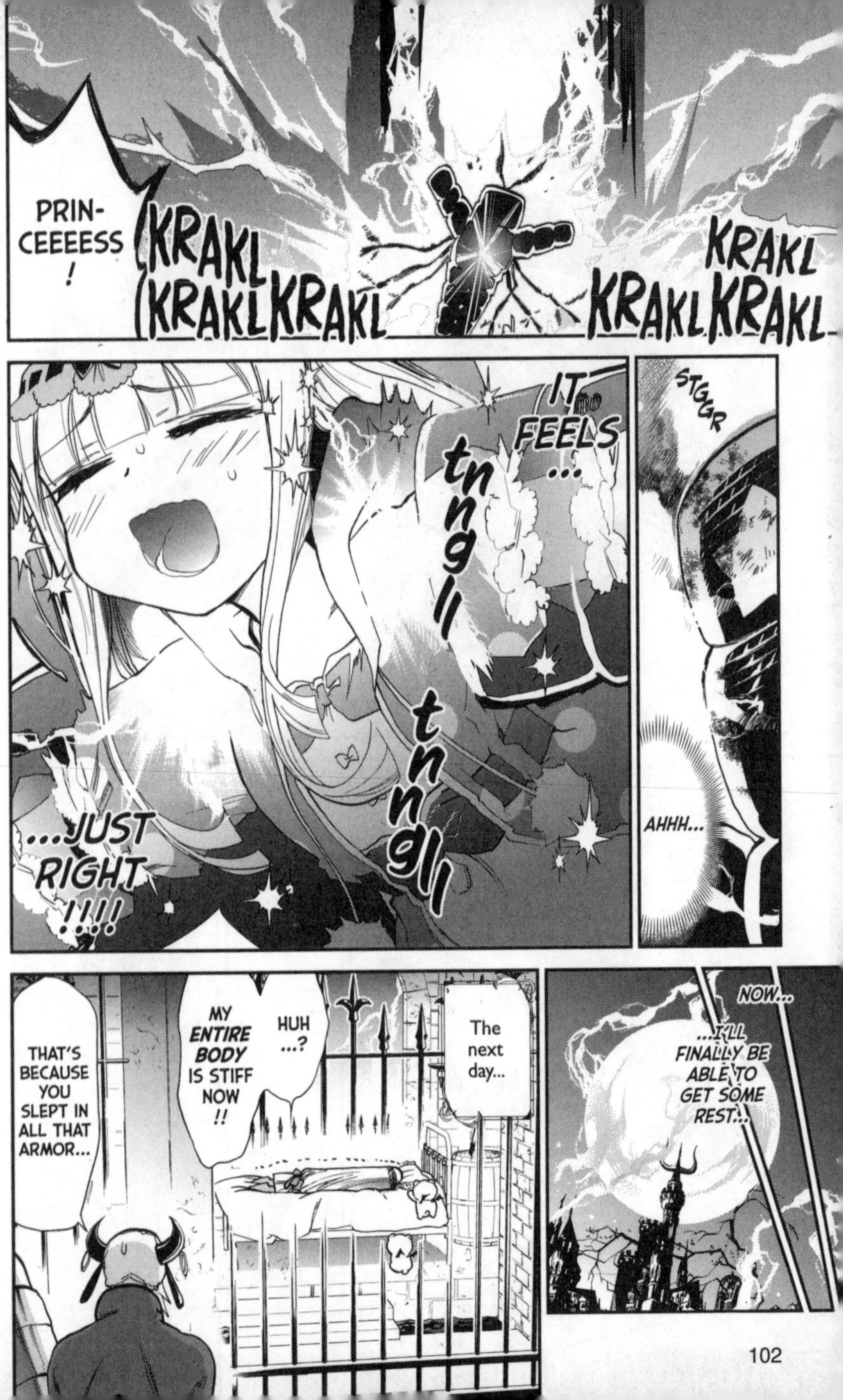
KRAKL
KRAKL KRAKL
PRIN-CEEEESS!
KRAKL
KRAKL KRAKL
STGGR
AHHH...
IT FEELS...
tnngll
tnngll
...JUST RIGHT!!!!
NOW...
...I'LL FINALLY BE ABLE TO GET SOME REST...
The next day...
HUH...?
MY ENTIRE BODY IS STIFF NOW!!
THAT'S BECAUSE YOU SLEPT IN ALL THAT ARMOR...

Tire Demon

The pride of three stars.

Sturdiness: ☆☆☆☆☆☆☆☆☆

Gourmet Taste: ★★★

A demon of the inspirited species.

A gaseous demon surrounded by tires, which provide it with a humanoid form. A large and slow moving demon with relatively high vitality and defense. Syalis was able to take over its body because it was essentially empty inside.

The tire demon was later revived at the Demon Temple.

However...

...because Syalis was using its body as armor at the time, the tire portion remained non-living; thus, only the gaseous demon was brought back to life.

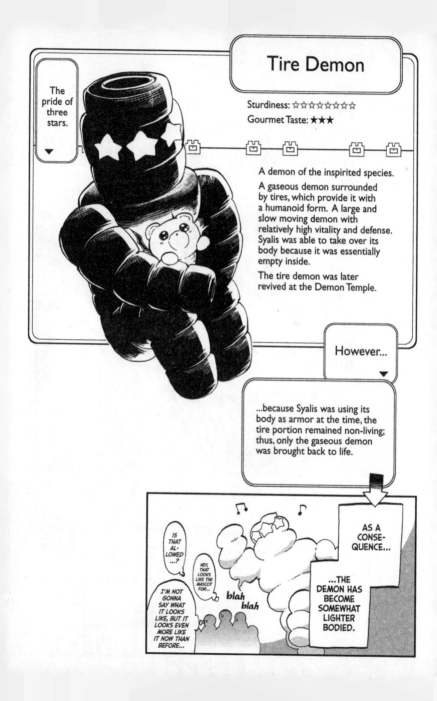

AS A CONSE-QUENCE...
...THE DEMON HAS BECOME SOMEWHAT LIGHTER BODIED.
blah blah
HEY, THAT LOOKS LIKE THE MASCOT FOR...
IS THAT AL-LOWED ...?
I'M NOT GONNA SAY WHAT IT LOOKS LIKE, BUT IT LOOKS EVEN MORE LIKE IT NOW THAN BEFORE...

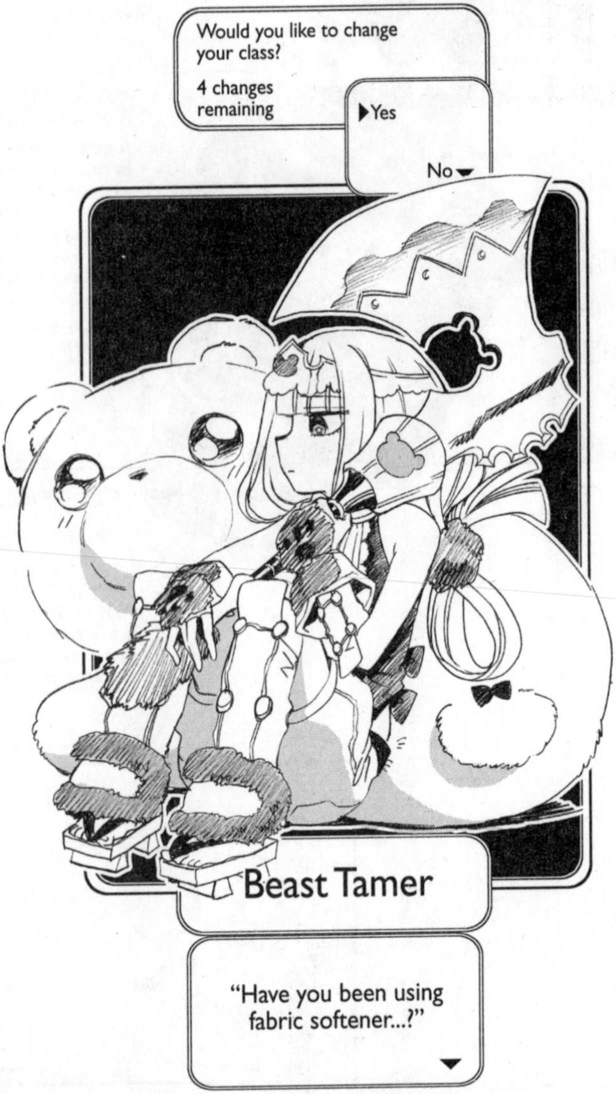
Would you like to change your class?
4 changes remaining
▶Yes
No
Beast Tamer
"Have you been using fabric softener...?"

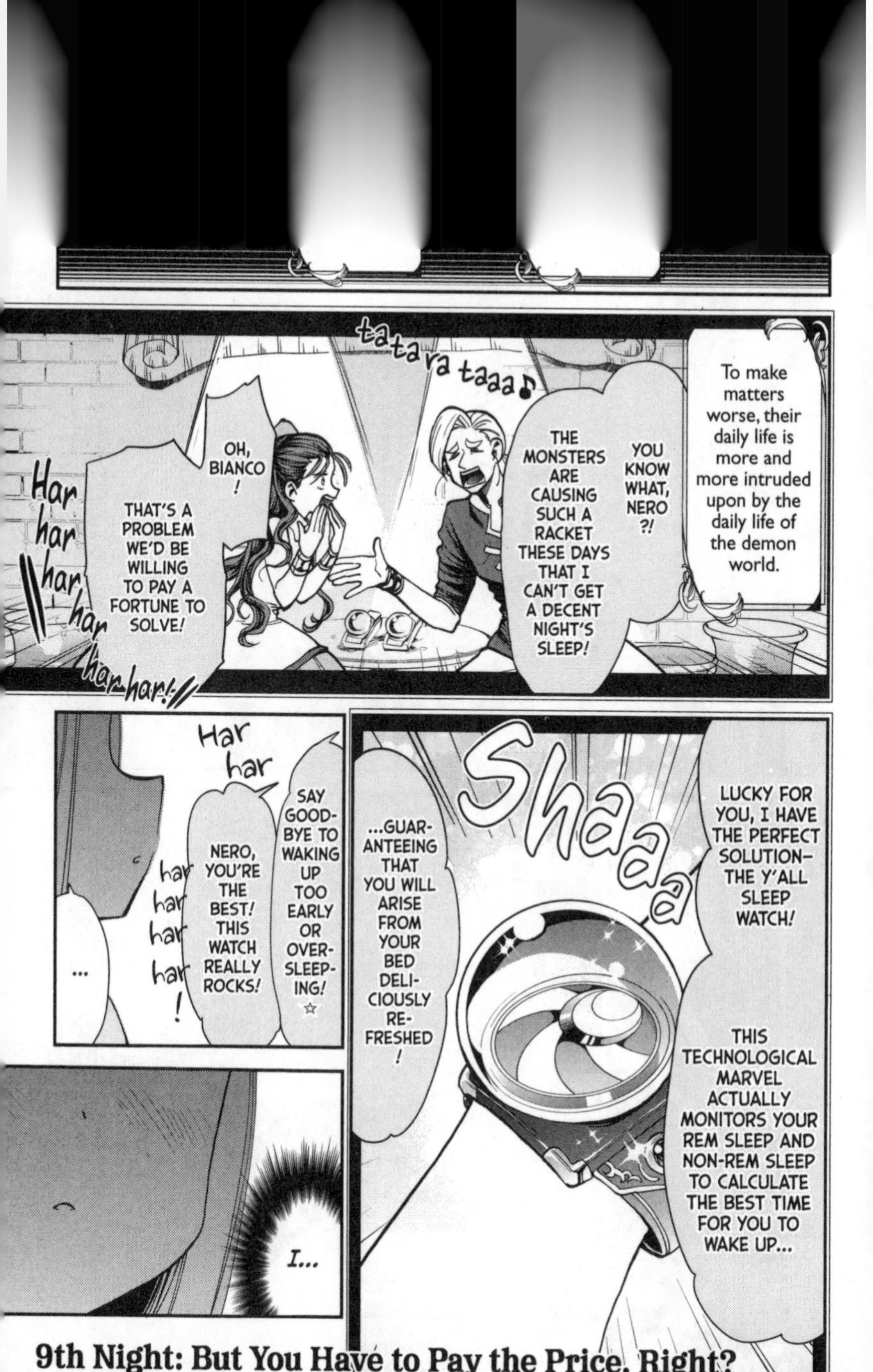
To make matters worse, their daily life is more and more intruded upon by the daily life of the demon world.
YOU KNOW WHAT, NERO?!
THE MONSTERS ARE CAUSING SUCH A RACKET THESE DAYS THAT I CAN'T GET A DECENT NIGHT'S SLEEP!
tatara taaa♪
OH, BIANCO!
THAT'S A PROBLEM WE'D BE WILLING TO PAY A FORTUNE TO SOLVE!
Har har har har har har!!
LUCKY FOR YOU, I HAVE THE PERFECT SOLUTION—THE Y'ALL SLEEP WATCH!
Shaaaa
THIS TECHNOLOGICAL MARVEL ACTUALLY MONITORS YOUR REM SLEEP AND NON-REM SLEEP TO CALCULATE THE BEST TIME FOR YOU TO WAKE UP...
...GUARANTEEING THAT YOU WILL ARISE FROM YOUR BED DELICIOUSLY REFRESHED!
SAY GOODBYE TO WAKING UP TOO EARLY OR OVERSLEEPING! ☆
NERO, YOU'RE THE BEST! THIS WATCH REALLY ROCKS!
Har har
har har har har!
...
I...

9th Night: But You Have to Pay the Price, Right?

9th Night: But You Have to Pay the Price, Right?

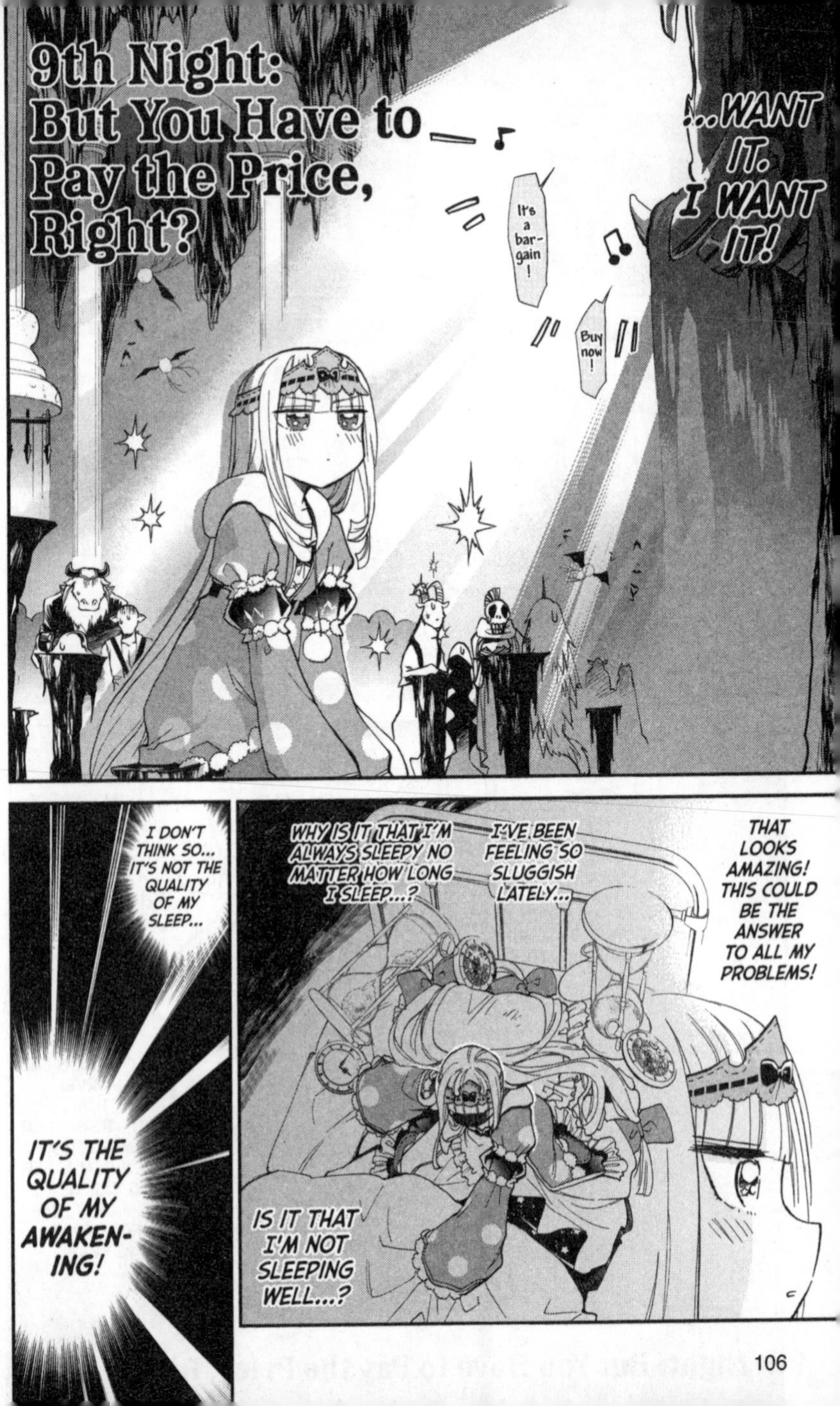
...WANT IT. I WANT IT!
It's a bargain!
Buy now!
THAT LOOKS AMAZING! THIS COULD BE THE ANSWER TO ALL MY PROBLEMS!
I'VE BEEN FEELING SO SLUGGISH LATELY...
WHY IS IT THAT I'M ALWAYS SLEEPY NO MATTER HOW LONG I SLEEP...?
IS IT THAT I'M NOT SLEEPING WELL...?
I DON'T THINK SO... IT'S NOT THE QUALITY OF MY SLEEP...
IT'S THE QUALITY OF MY AWAKENING!

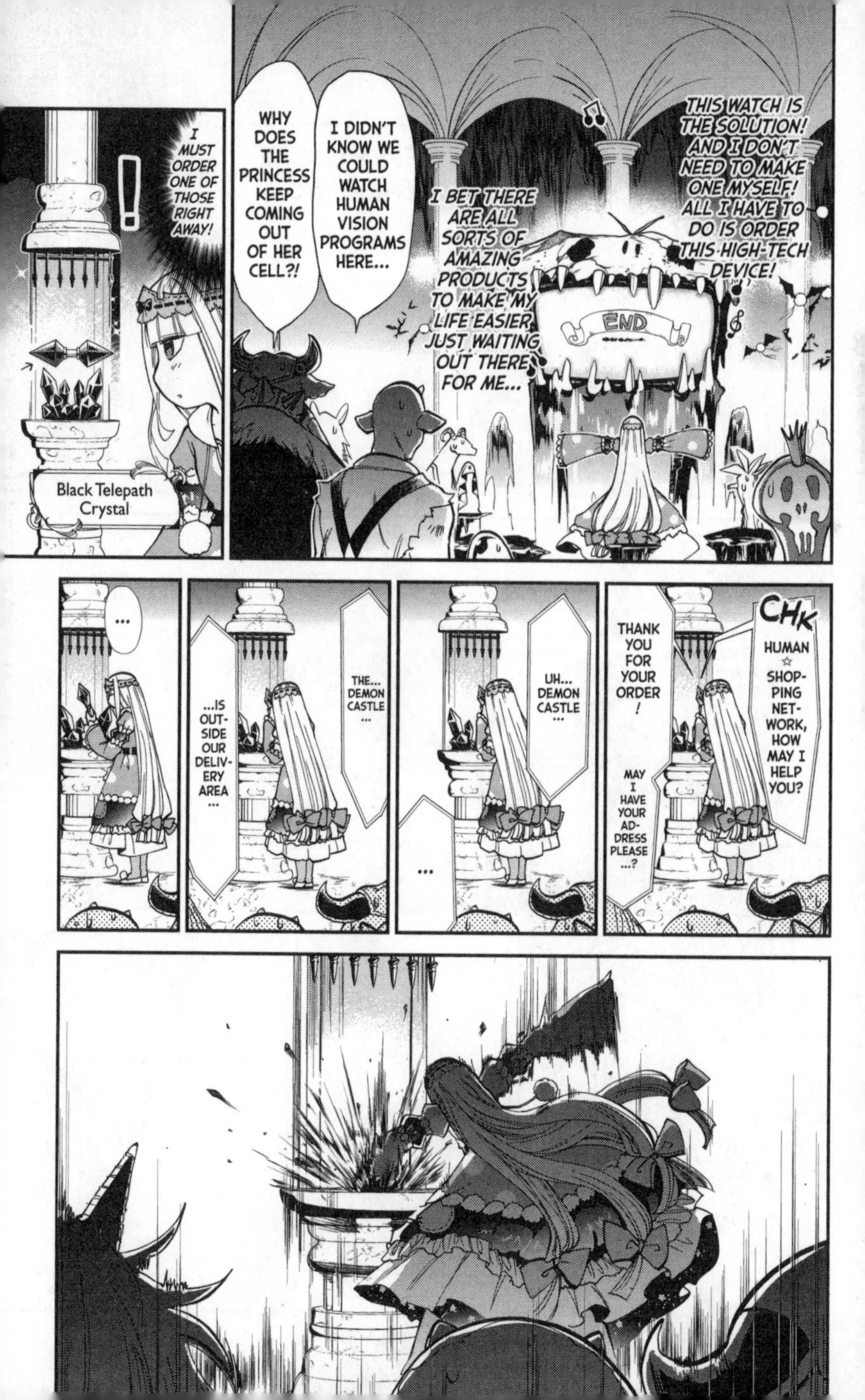

THIS WATCH IS THE SOLUTION! AND I DON'T NEED TO MAKE ONE MYSELF! ALL I HAVE TO DO IS ORDER THIS HIGH-TECH DEVICE!
I BET THERE ARE ALL SORTS OF AMAZING PRODUCTS TO MAKE MY LIFE EASIER JUST WAITING OUT THERE FOR ME...
END
I DIDN'T KNOW WE COULD WATCH HUMAN VISION PROGRAMS HERE...
WHY DOES THE PRINCESS KEEP COMING OUT OF HER CELL?!
I MUST ORDER ONE OF THOSE RIGHT AWAY!
!
Black Telepath Crystal
CHK
HUMAN ☆ SHOPPING NETWORK, HOW MAY I HELP YOU?
THANK YOU FOR YOUR ORDER!
MAY I HAVE YOUR ADDRESS PLEASE ...?
UH... DEMON CASTLE ...
...
THE... DEMON CASTLE ...
...IS OUTSIDE OUR DELIVERY AREA ...
...

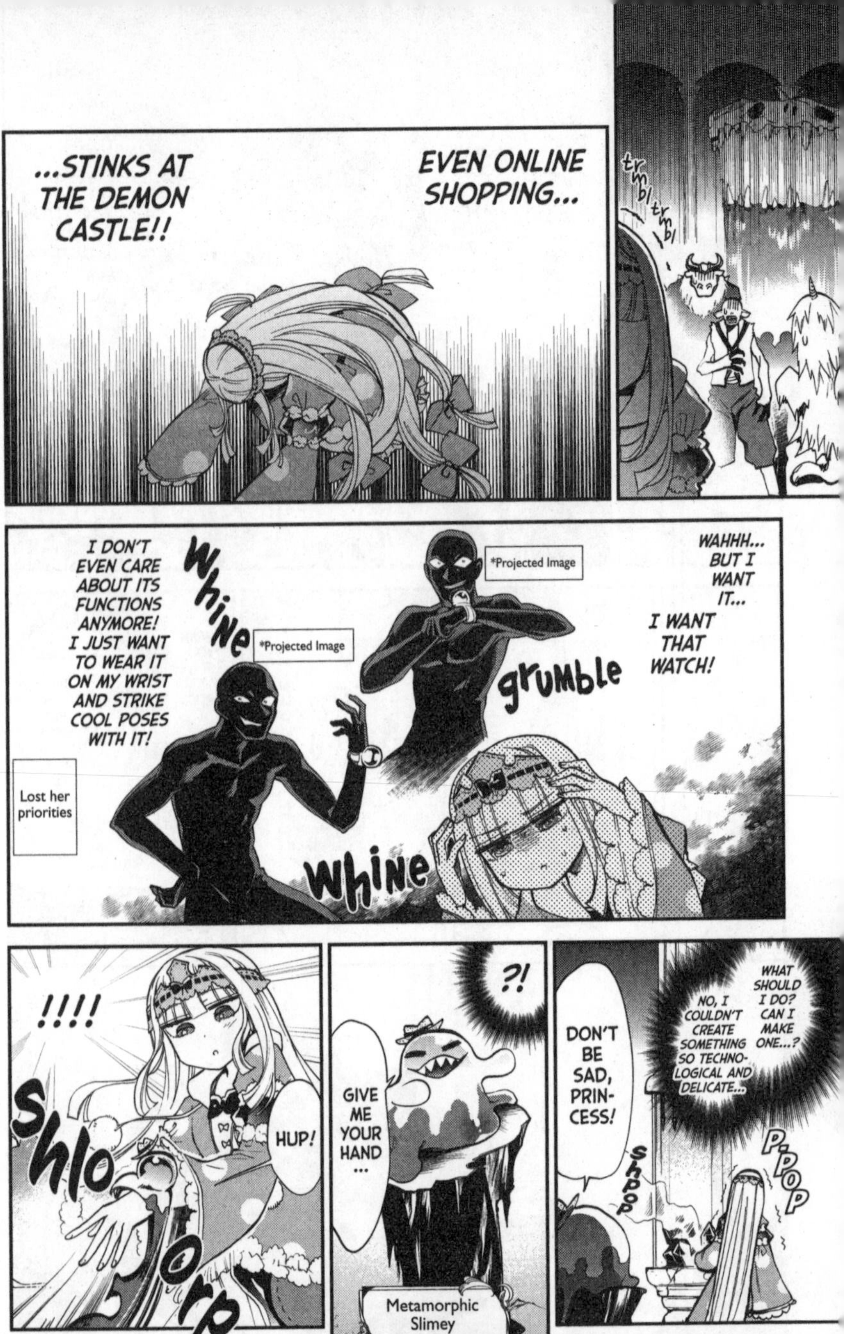
trmbl trmbl
EVEN ONLINE SHOPPING...
...STINKS AT THE DEMON CASTLE!!
WAHHH... BUT I WANT IT...
I WANT THAT WATCH!
*Projected Image
grumble
whine
I DON'T EVEN CARE ABOUT ITS FUNCTIONS ANYMORE! I JUST WANT TO WEAR IT ON MY WRIST AND STRIKE COOL POSES WITH IT!
*Projected Image
Lost her priorities
whine
WHAT SHOULD I DO? CAN I MAKE ONE...?
NO, I COULDN'T CREATE SOMETHING SO TECHNO-LOGICAL AND DELICATE...
DON'T BE SAD, PRIN-CESS!
SHPOP
P-POP
?!
GIVE ME YOUR HAND ...
Metamorphic Slimey
!!!!
HUP!
Shlorp

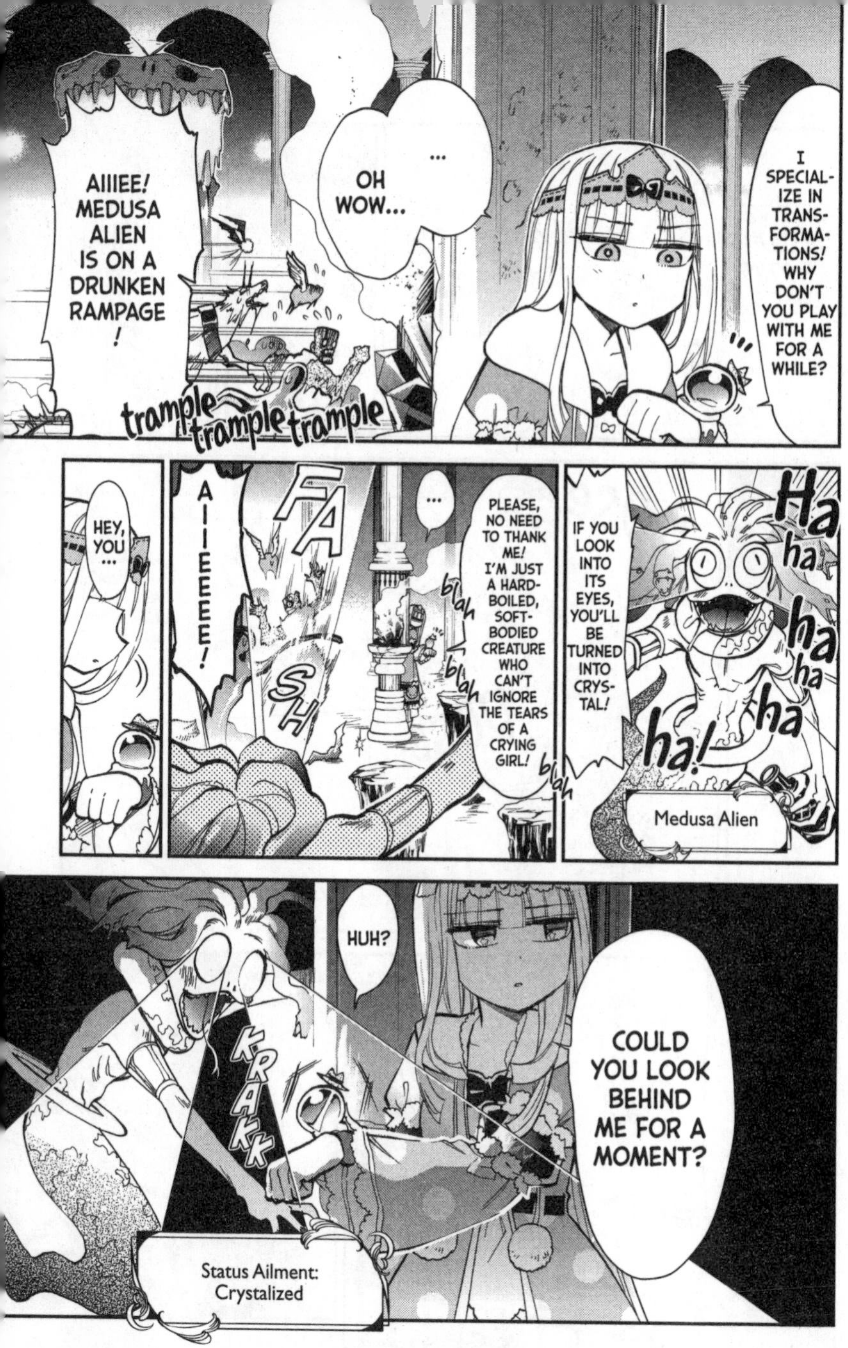
I SPECIALIZE IN TRANSFORMATIONS! WHY DON'T YOU PLAY WITH ME FOR A WHILE?
...
OH WOW...
AIIIEE! MEDUSA ALIEN IS ON A DRUNKEN RAMPAGE!
trample trample trample
Ha ha ha ha ha ha ha!
IF YOU LOOK INTO ITS EYES, YOU'LL BE TURNED INTO CRYSTAL!
Medusa Alien
PLEASE, NO NEED TO THANK ME! I'M JUST A HARD-BOILED, SOFT-BODIED CREATURE WHO CAN'T IGNORE THE TEARS OF A CRYING GIRL!
blah blah blah
...
FASH
AIIEEEEE!
HEY, YOU ...
COULD YOU LOOK BEHIND ME FOR A MOMENT?
HUH?
KRAKK
Status Ailment: Crystalized

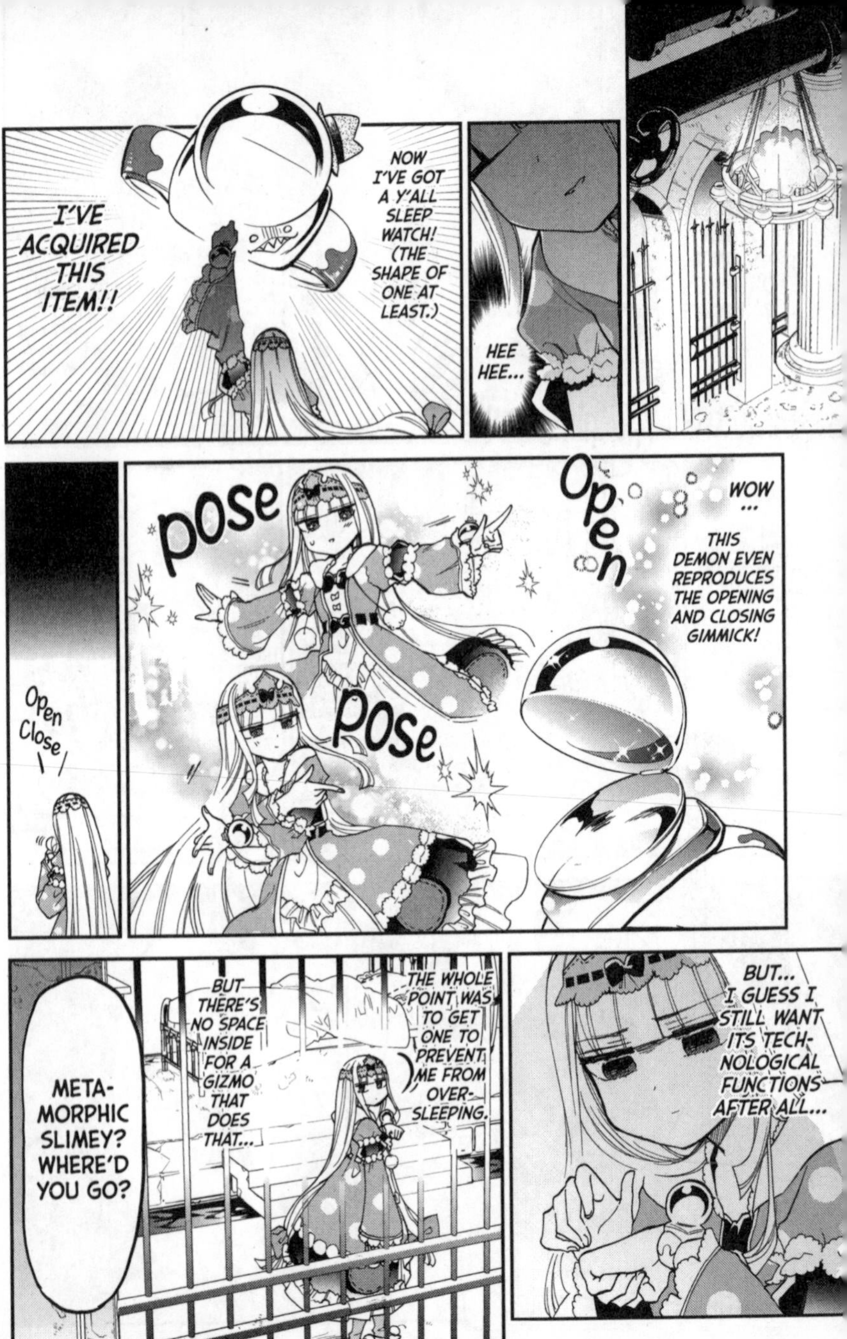
HEE HEE...
NOW I'VE GOT A Y'ALL SLEEP WATCH! (THE SHAPE OF ONE AT LEAST.)
I'VE ACQUIRED THIS ITEM!!
WOW...
THIS DEMON EVEN REPRODUCES THE OPENING AND CLOSING GIMMICK!
Open
pose
pose
Open Close
BUT... I GUESS I STILL WANT ITS TECH-NOLOGICAL FUNCTIONS AFTER ALL...
THE WHOLE POINT WAS TO GET ONE TO PREVENT ME FROM OVER-SLEEPING.
BUT THERE'S NO SPACE INSIDE FOR A GIZMO THAT DOES THAT...
META-MORPHIC SLIMEY? WHERE'D YOU GO?

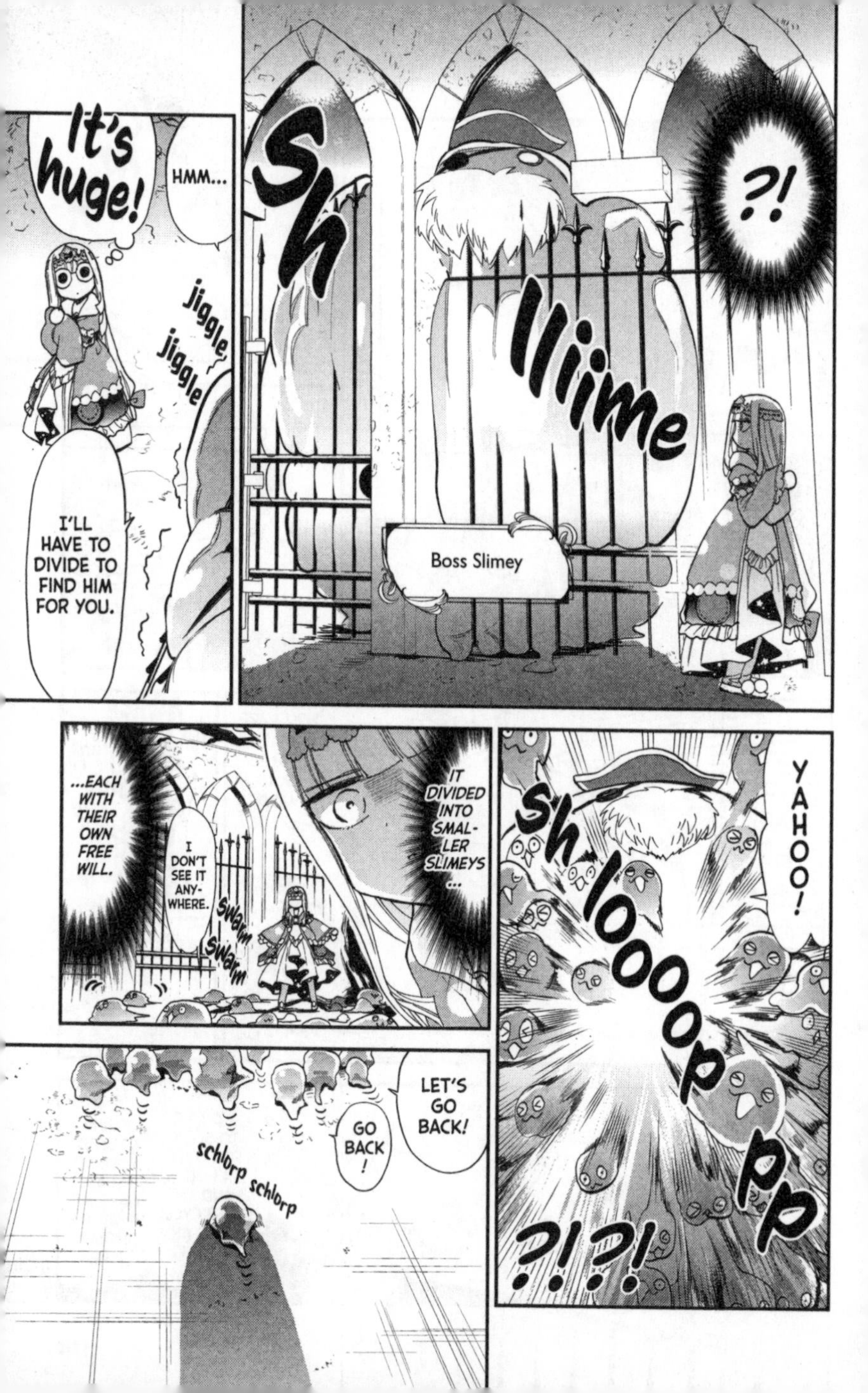
?!
Shlliime
Boss Slimey
HMM...
It's huge!
jiggle, jiggle, jiggle
I'LL HAVE TO DIVIDE TO FIND HIM FOR YOU.
YAHOO!
Shlooooopp
?!?!
IT DIVIDED INTO SMALLER SLIMEYS...
...EACH WITH THEIR OWN FREE WILL.
I DON'T SEE IT ANYWHERE.
swarm swarm
LET'S GO BACK!
GO BACK!
schlorp schlorp

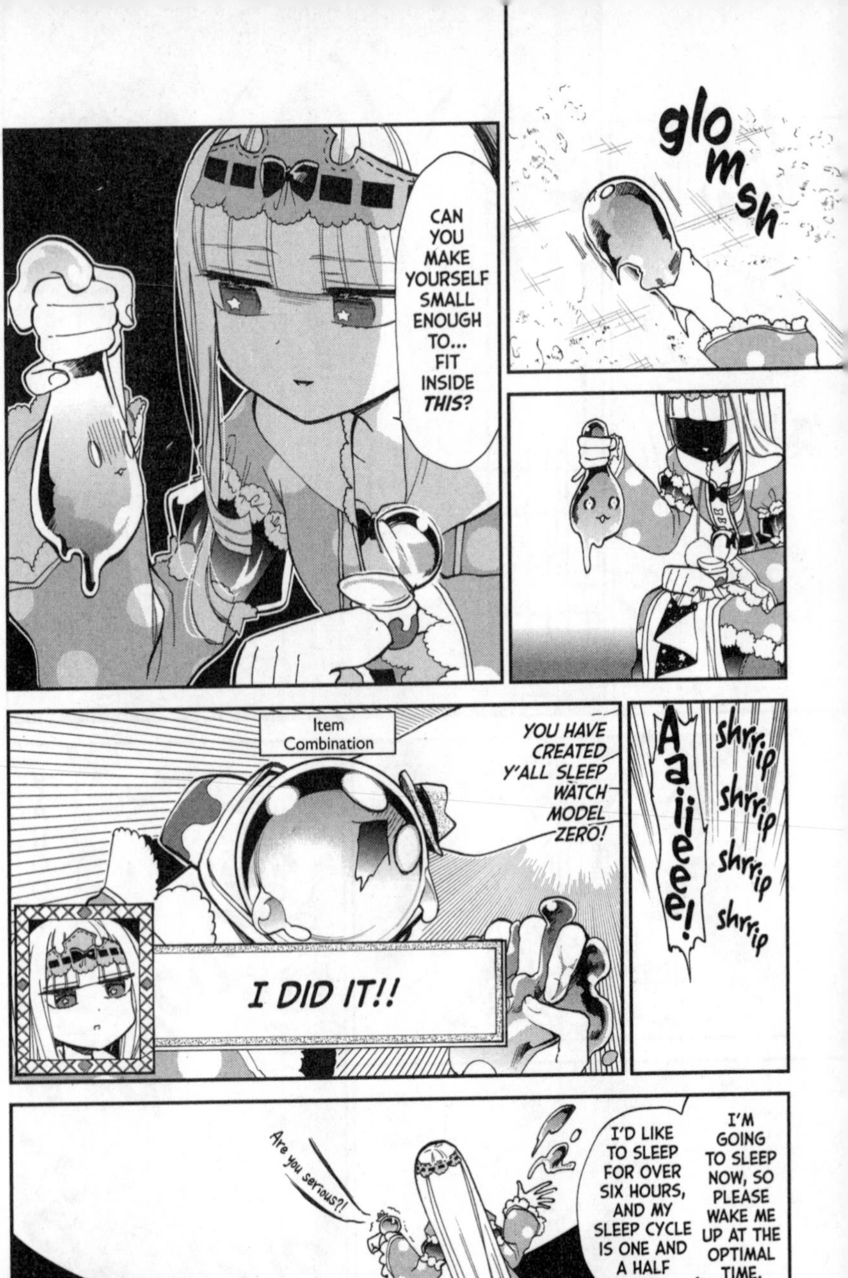
glomsh
CAN YOU MAKE YOURSELF SMALL ENOUGH TO... FIT INSIDE *THIS?*
Aaiieee!
shrrip
shrrip
shrrip
shrrip
YOU HAVE CREATED Y'ALL SLEEP WATCH MODEL ZERO!
Item Combination
I DID IT!!
I'M GOING TO SLEEP NOW, SO PLEASE WAKE ME UP AT THE OPTIMAL TIME.
I'D LIKE TO SLEEP FOR OVER SIX HOURS, AND MY SLEEP CYCLE IS ONE AND A HALF HOURS.
Are you serious?!

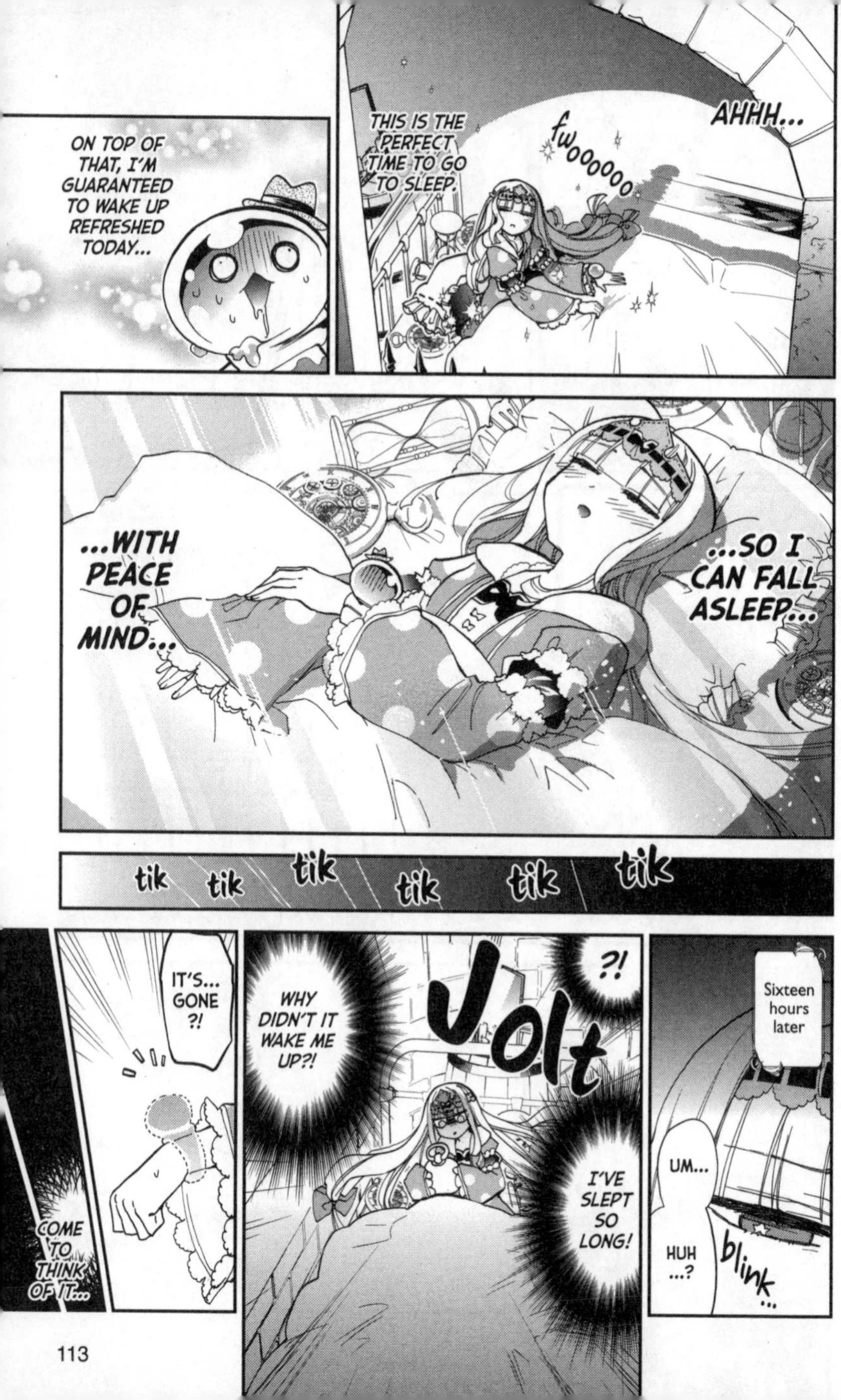

AHHH...
fwoooooo
THIS IS THE PERFECT TIME TO GO TO SLEEP.
ON TOP OF THAT, I'M GUARANTEED TO WAKE UP REFRESHED TODAY...
...SO I CAN FALL ASLEEP...
...WITH PEACE OF MIND...
tik
tik
tik
tik
tik
tik
Sixteen hours later
UM...
blink...
HUH ...?
?!
Jolt
WHY DIDN'T IT WAKE ME UP?!
I'VE SLEPT SO LONG!
IT'S... GONE ?!
COME TO THINK OF IT...

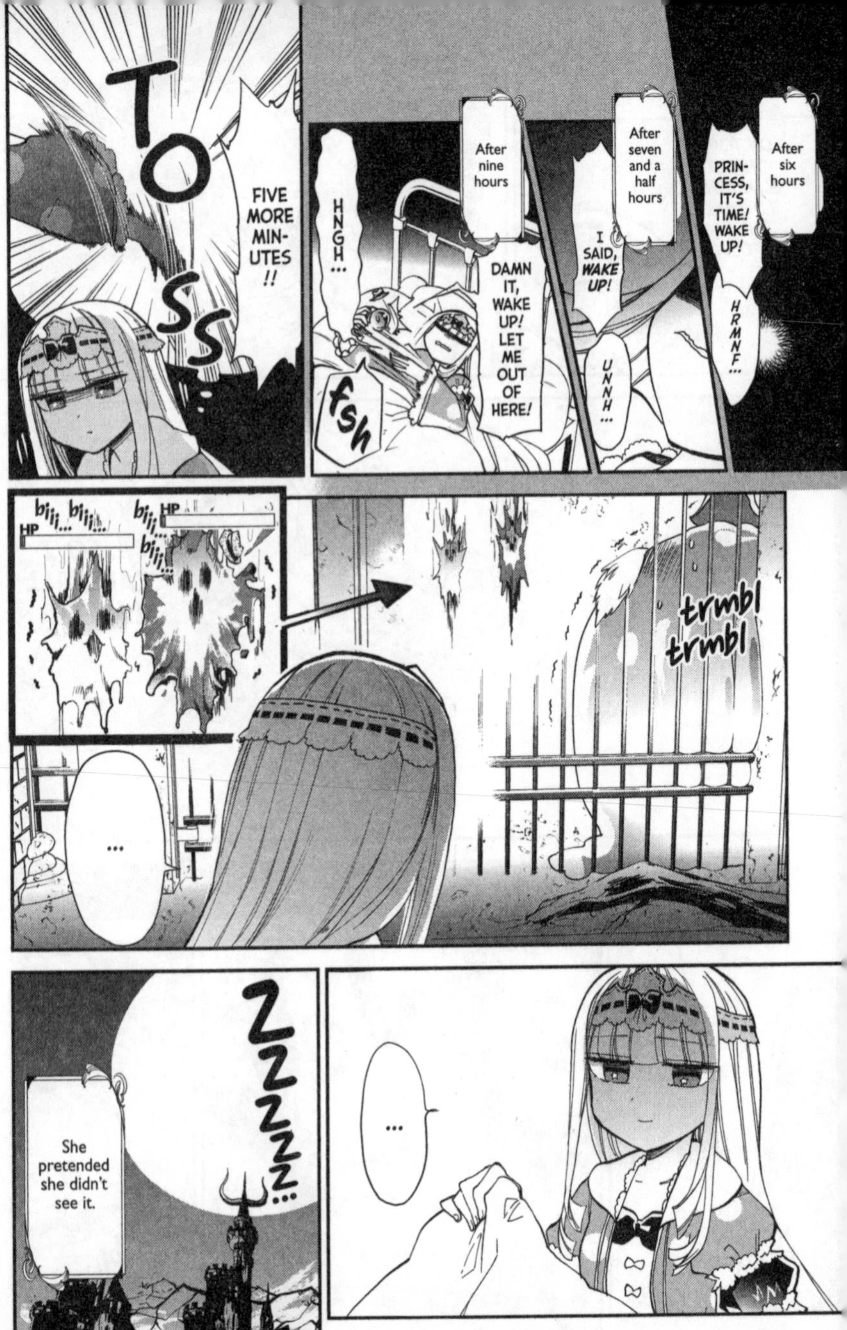
After six hours
PRINCESS, IT'S TIME! WAKE UP!
HRMNF...
After seven and a half hours
I SAID, WAKE UP!
UNNH...
After nine hours
DAMN IT, WAKE UP! LET ME OUT OF HERE!
HNGH...
fsh
FIVE MORE MIN-UTES!!
TOSS
trmbl trmbl
bjiii... bjiii...
bjiii... bjiii...
HP
HP
...
...
ZZZZZ...
She pretended she didn't see it.

Bianco & Nero

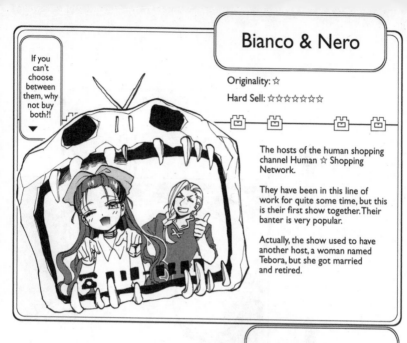

If you can't choose between them, why not buy both?!

Originality: ☆

Hard Sell: ☆☆☆☆☆☆☆☆

The hosts of the human shopping channel Human ☆ Shopping Network.

They have been in this line of work for quite some time, but this is their first show together. Their banter is very popular.

Actually, the show used to have another host, a woman named Tebora, but she got married and retired.

Current problems:
"Any problem can be solved by throwing some cash at it!"

"You're such a... Anyway, this product is amazing!"

I'M NOT SAYING...
...I'LL NEVER HELP A HUMAN AGAIN...
Nice guy
(Who actually strongly leans towards masochism.)

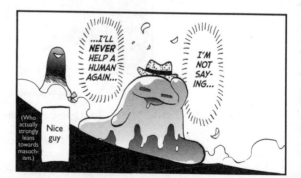

Would you like to change your class?
3 changes remaining
▶Yes
No
Tank
Lightning Repelling: ☆☆☆
"This is so cool!"

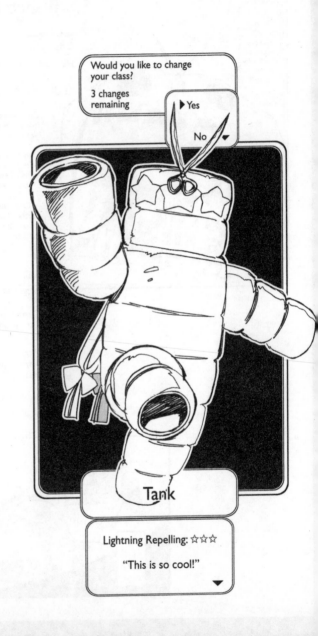

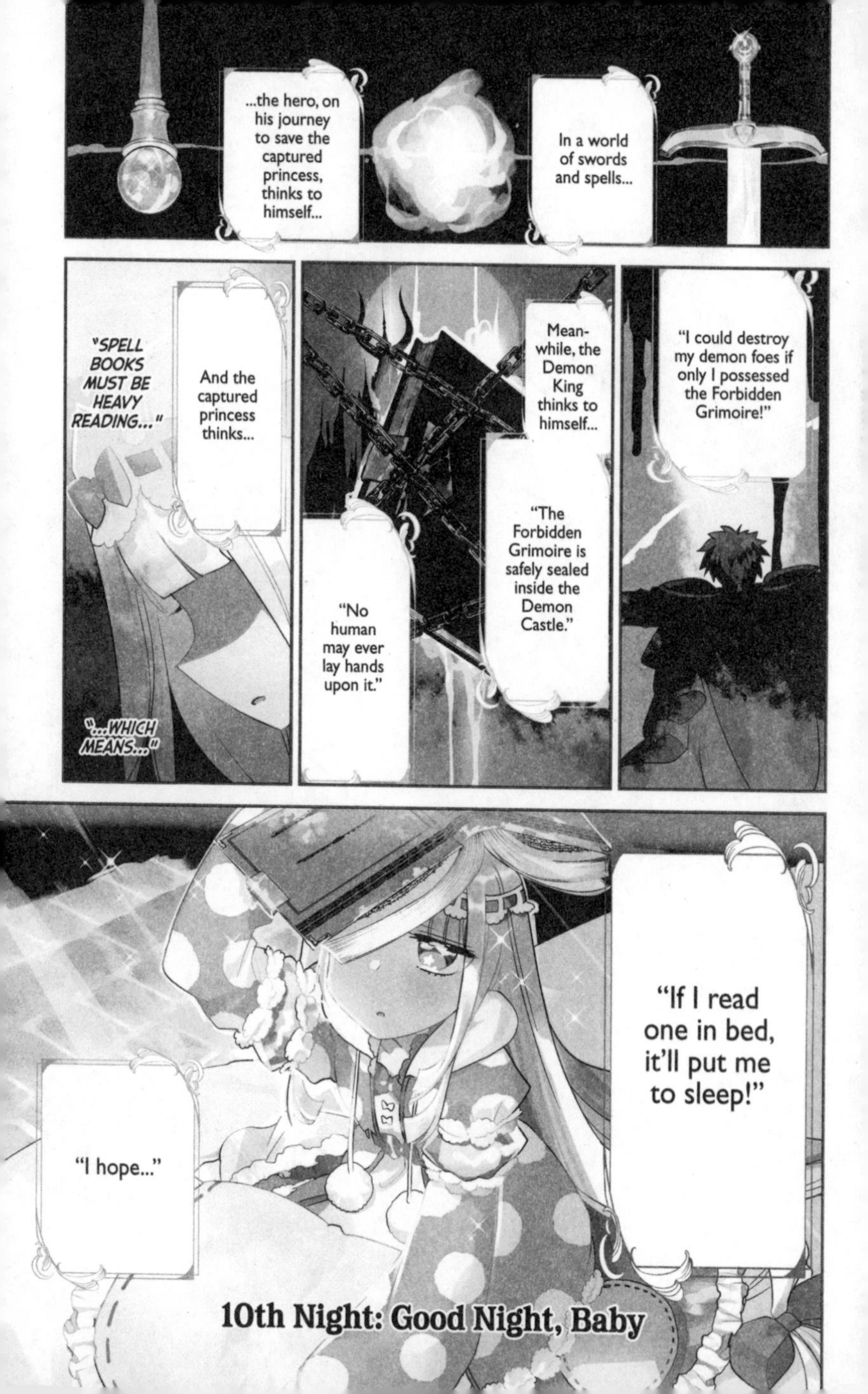
In a world of swords and spells...
...the hero, on his journey to save the captured princess, thinks to himself...
"I could destroy my demon foes if only I possessed the Forbidden Grimoire!"
Mean-while, the Demon King thinks to himself...
"The Forbidden Grimoire is safely sealed inside the Demon Castle."
"No human may ever lay hands upon it."
And the captured princess thinks...
"SPELL BOOKS MUST BE HEAVY READING..."
"...WHICH MEANS..."
"If I read one in bed, it'll put me to sleep!"
"I hope..."
10th Night: Good Night, Baby

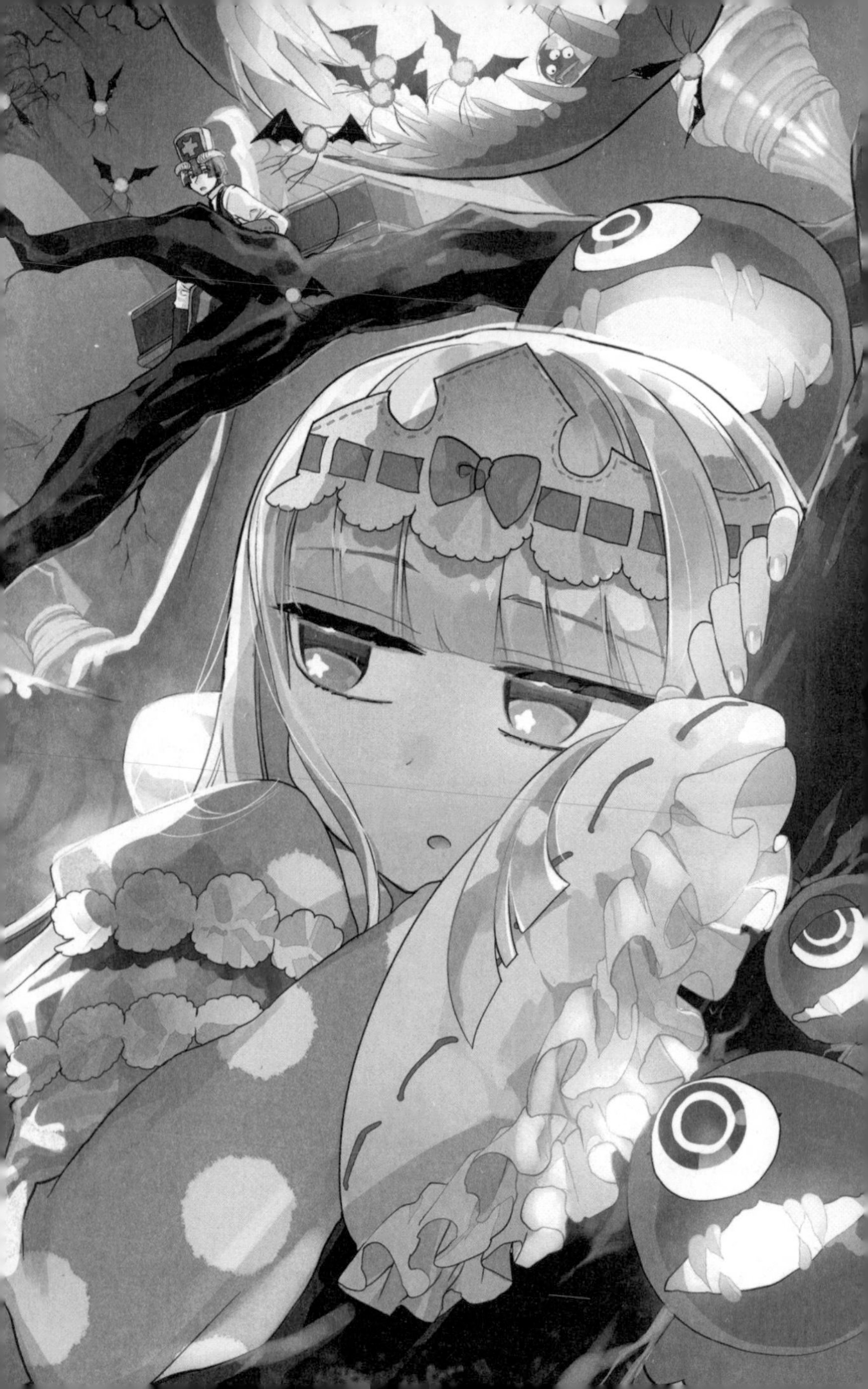

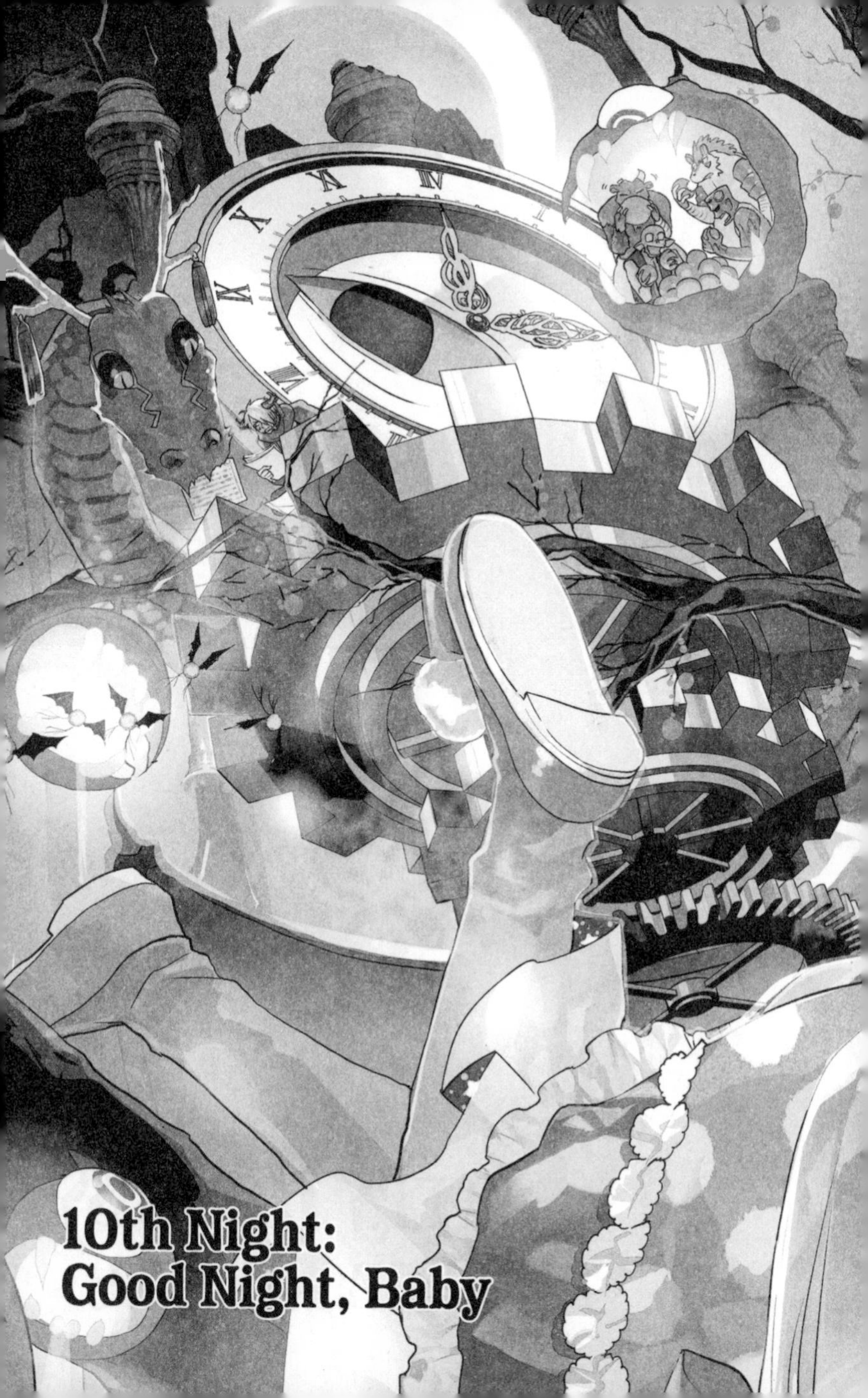
10th Night:
Good Night, Baby

SLEEPY PRINCESS
IN THE DEMON CASTLE

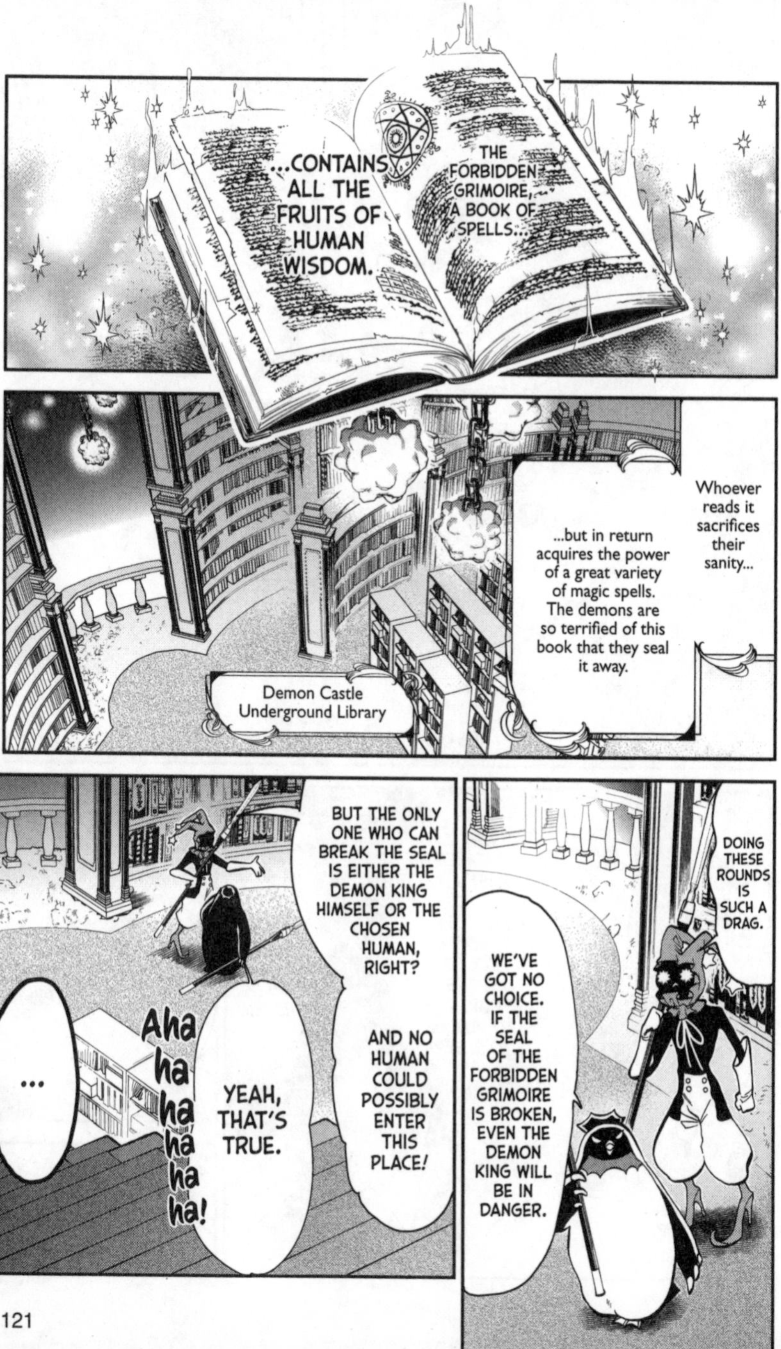
THE FORBIDDEN GRIMOIRE, A BOOK OF SPELLS...
...CONTAINS ALL THE FRUITS OF HUMAN WISDOM.
Whoever reads it sacrifices their sanity...
...but in return acquires the power of a great variety of magic spells. The demons are so terrified of this book that they seal it away.
Demon Castle Underground Library
DOING THESE ROUNDS IS SUCH A DRAG.
WE'VE GOT NO CHOICE. IF THE SEAL OF THE FORBIDDEN GRIMOIRE IS BROKEN, EVEN THE DEMON KING WILL BE IN DANGER.
BUT THE ONLY ONE WHO CAN BREAK THE SEAL IS EITHER THE DEMON KING HIMSELF OR THE CHOSEN HUMAN, RIGHT?
AND NO HUMAN COULD POSSIBLY ENTER THIS PLACE!
YEAH, THAT'S TRUE.
Ahahahahaha!
...

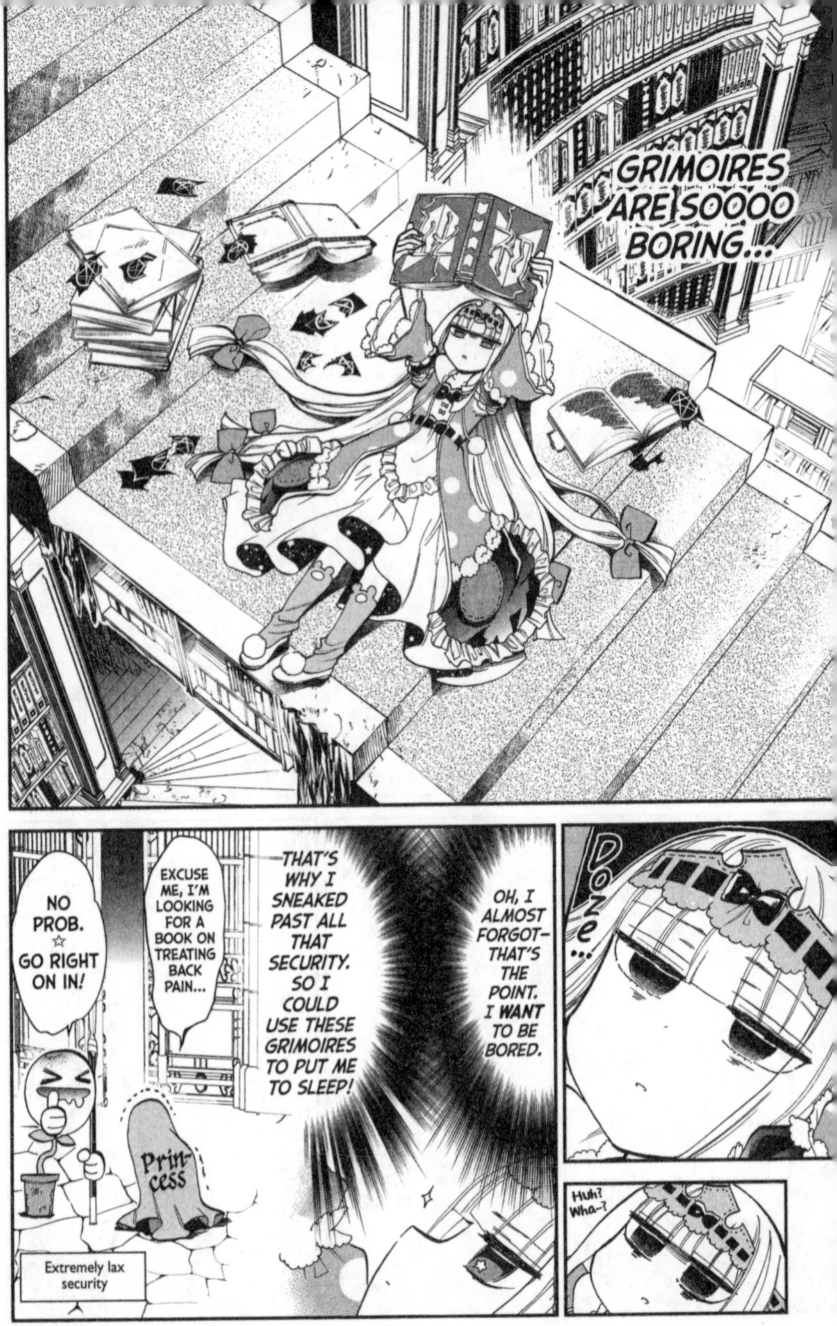
GRIMOIRES ARE SOOOO BORING...
Doze...
Huh? Wha-?
OH, I ALMOST FORGOT—THAT'S THE POINT. I WANT TO BE BORED.
—THAT'S WHY I SNEAKED PAST ALL THAT SECURITY. SO I COULD USE THESE GRIMOIRES TO PUT ME TO SLEEP!
EXCUSE ME, I'M LOOKING FOR A BOOK ON TREATING BACK PAIN...
NO PROB. ☆ GO RIGHT ON IN!
Prin-cess
Extremely lax security

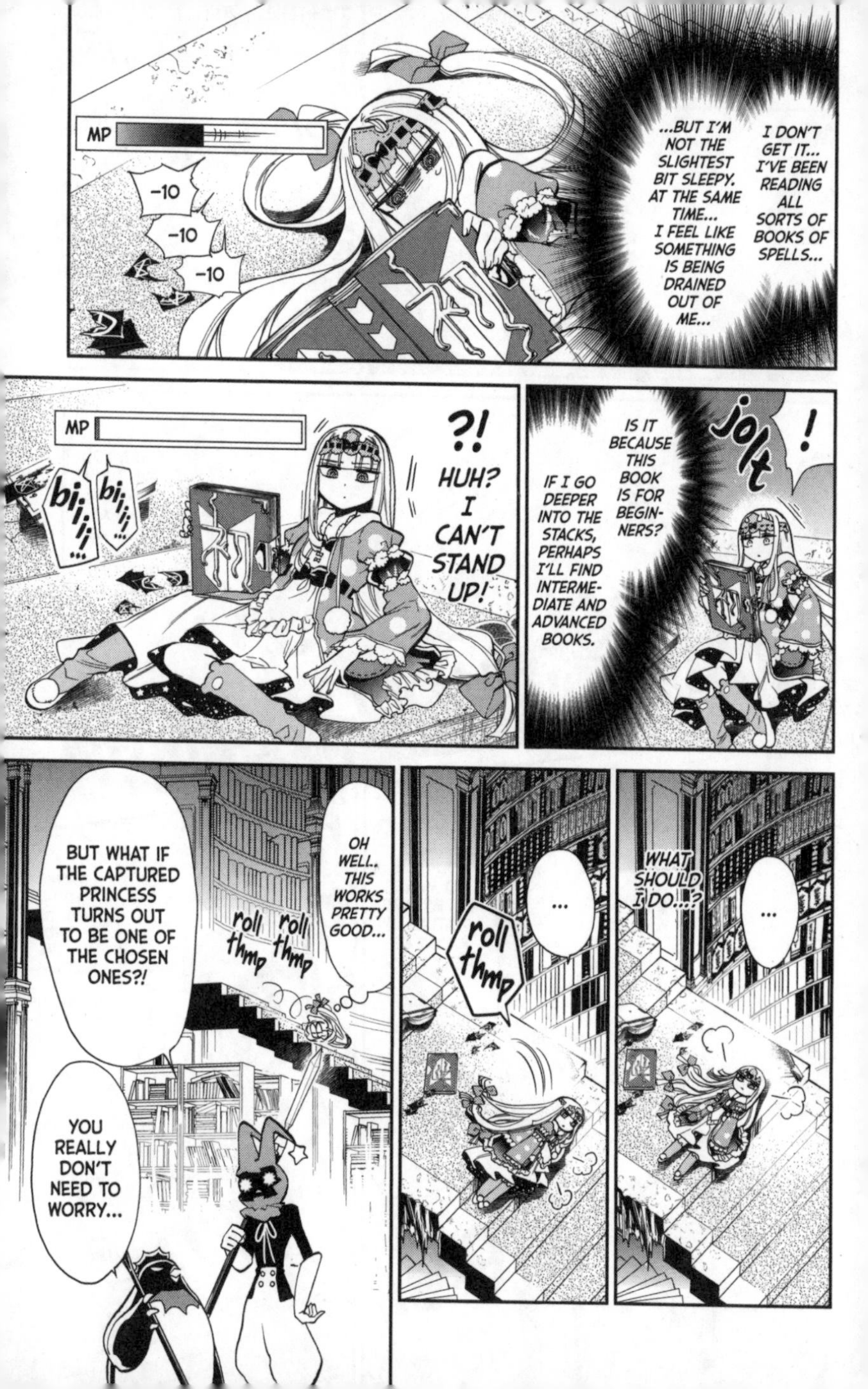
I DON'T GET IT... I'VE BEEN READING ALL SORTS OF BOOKS OF SPELLS...
...BUT I'M NOT THE SLIGHTEST BIT SLEEPY. AT THE SAME TIME... I FEEL LIKE SOMETHING IS BEING DRAINED OUT OF ME...
MP
-10
-10
-10
jolt
!
IS IT BECAUSE THIS BOOK IS FOR BEGINNERS?
IF I GO DEEPER INTO THE STACKS, PERHAPS I'LL FIND INTERMEDIATE AND ADVANCED BOOKS.
MP
?!
HUH? I CAN'T STAND UP!
bi...
bi...
WHAT SHOULD I DO...?
...
...
roll thmp
OH WELL.. THIS WORKS PRETTY GOOD...
roll thmp
roll thmp
BUT WHAT IF THE CAPTURED PRINCESS TURNS OUT TO BE ONE OF THE CHOSEN ONES?!
YOU REALLY DON'T NEED TO WORRY...

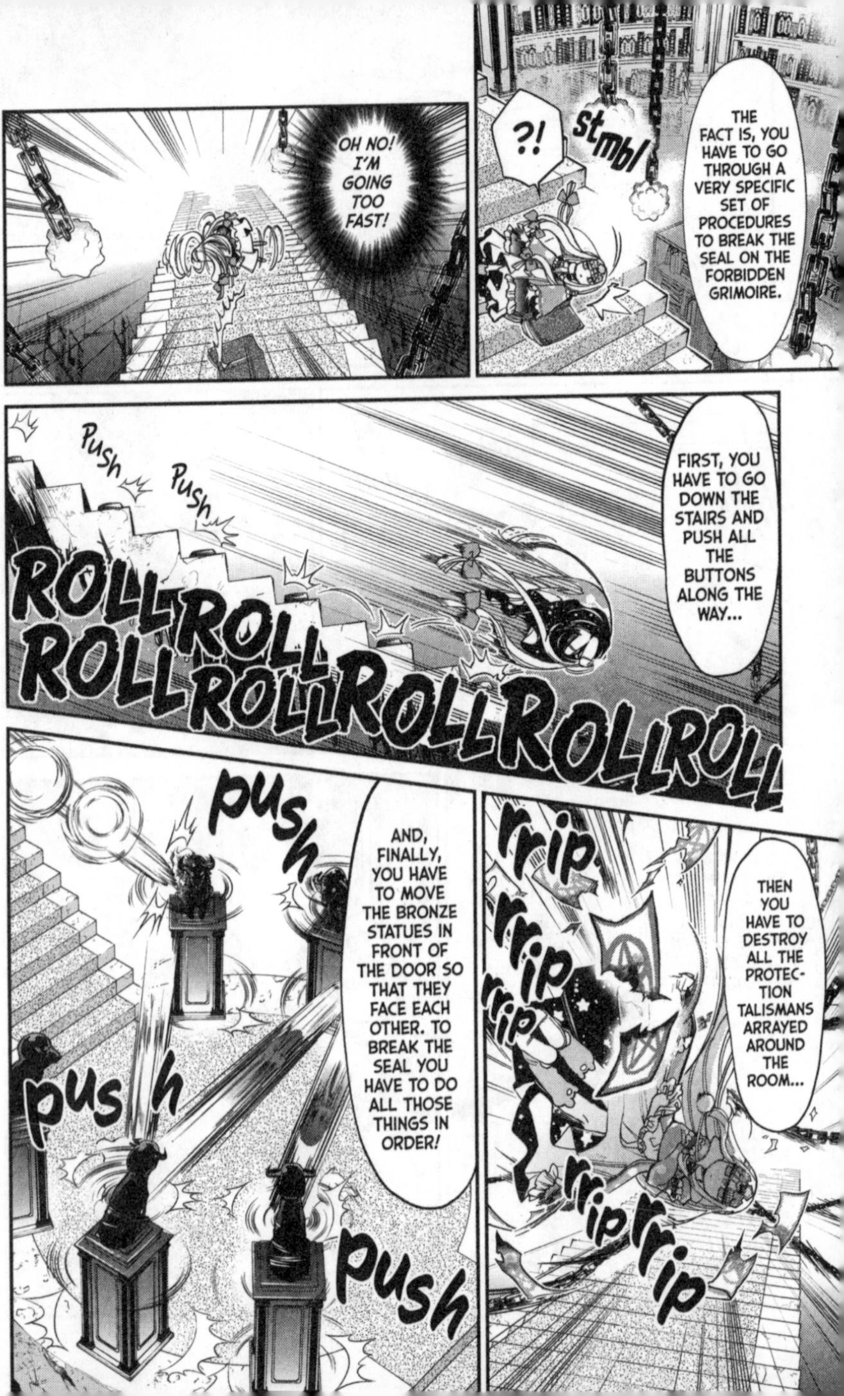
THE FACT IS, YOU HAVE TO GO THROUGH A VERY SPECIFIC SET OF PROCEDURES TO BREAK THE SEAL ON THE FORBIDDEN GRIMOIRE.
stmbl
?!
OH NO! I'M GOING TOO FAST!
FIRST, YOU HAVE TO GO DOWN THE STAIRS AND PUSH ALL THE BUTTONS ALONG THE WAY...
Push
Push
ROLL ROLL ROLL ROLL ROLL ROLL
THEN YOU HAVE TO DESTROY ALL THE PROTECTION TALISMANS ARRAYED AROUND THE ROOM...
rrip rrip rrip rrip rrip rrip rrip
AND, FINALLY, YOU HAVE TO MOVE THE BRONZE STATUES IN FRONT OF THE DOOR SO THAT THEY FACE EACH OTHER. TO BREAK THE SEAL YOU HAVE TO DO ALL THOSE THINGS IN ORDER!
push
push
push

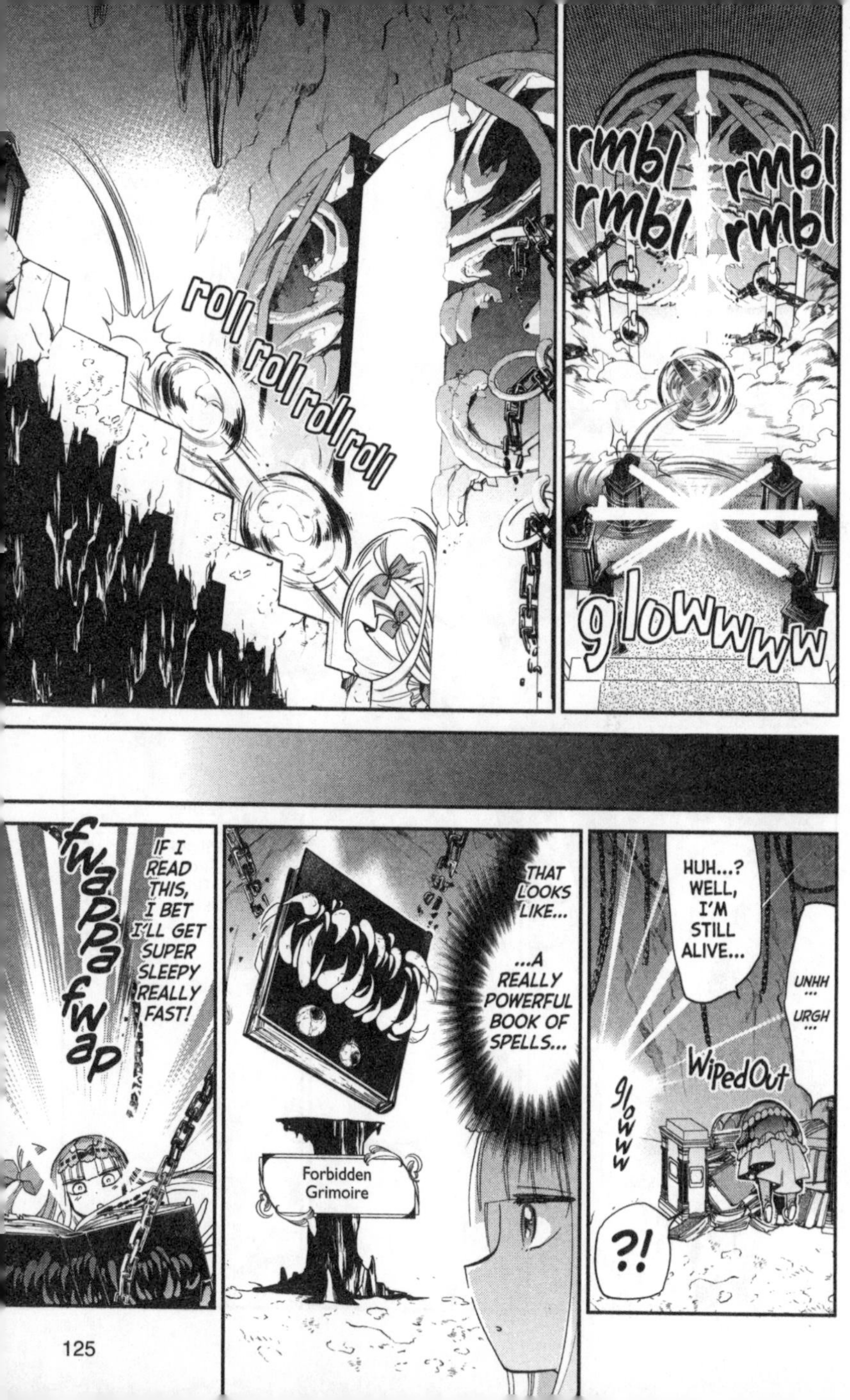
rmbl rmbl
rmbl rmbl
glowwww
roll roll roll roll
HUH...? WELL, I'M STILL ALIVE...
UNHH...
URGH...
Wiped Out
glowww
?!
THAT LOOKS LIKE...
...A REALLY POWERFUL BOOK OF SPELLS...
Forbidden Grimoire
fwappa fwap
IF I READ THIS, I BET I'LL GET SUPER SLEEPY REALLY FAST!

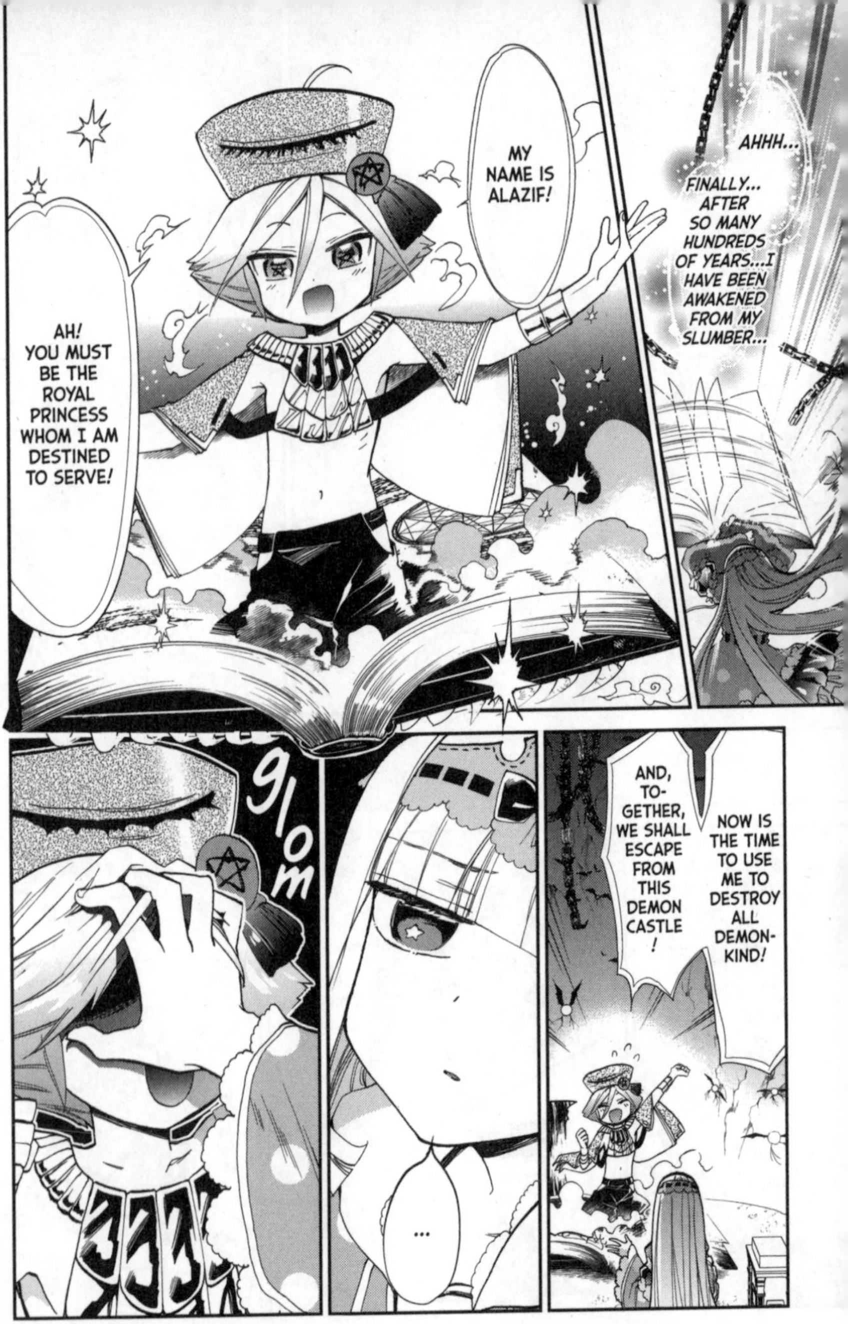
AHHH...
FINALLY... AFTER SO MANY HUNDREDS OF YEARS...I HAVE BEEN AWAKENED FROM MY SLUMBER...
MY NAME IS ALAZIF!
AH! YOU MUST BE THE ROYAL PRINCESS WHOM I AM DESTINED TO SERVE!
NOW IS THE TIME TO USE ME TO DESTROY ALL DEMON-KIND!
AND, TO-GETHER, WE SHALL ESCAPE FROM THIS DEMON CASTLE!
...
glom

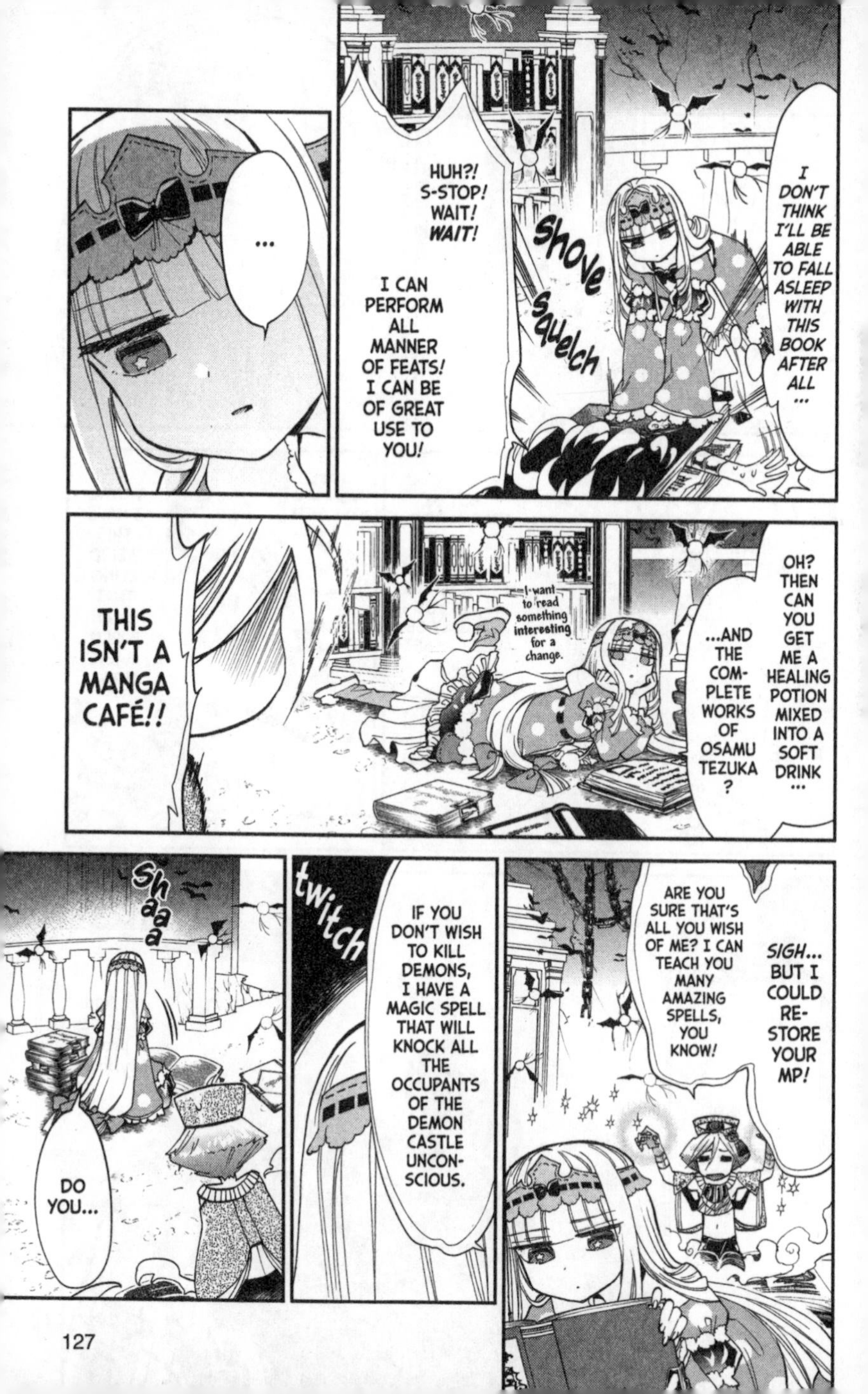
I DON'T THINK I'LL BE ABLE TO FALL ASLEEP WITH THIS BOOK AFTER ALL...
Shove
squelch
HUH?! S-STOP! WAIT! WAIT!
I CAN PERFORM ALL MANNER OF FEATS! I CAN BE OF GREAT USE TO YOU!
...
OH? THEN CAN YOU GET ME A HEALING POTION MIXED INTO A SOFT DRINK...
...AND THE COMPLETE WORKS OF OSAMU TEZUKA?
I want to read something interesting for a change.
THIS ISN'T A MANGA CAFÉ!!
SIGH... BUT I COULD RESTORE YOUR MP!
ARE YOU SURE THAT'S ALL YOU WISH OF ME? I CAN TEACH YOU MANY AMAZING SPELLS, YOU KNOW!
twitch
IF YOU DON'T WISH TO KILL DEMONS, I HAVE A MAGIC SPELL THAT WILL KNOCK ALL THE OCCUPANTS OF THE DEMON CASTLE UNCONSCIOUS.
Shaaa
DO YOU...

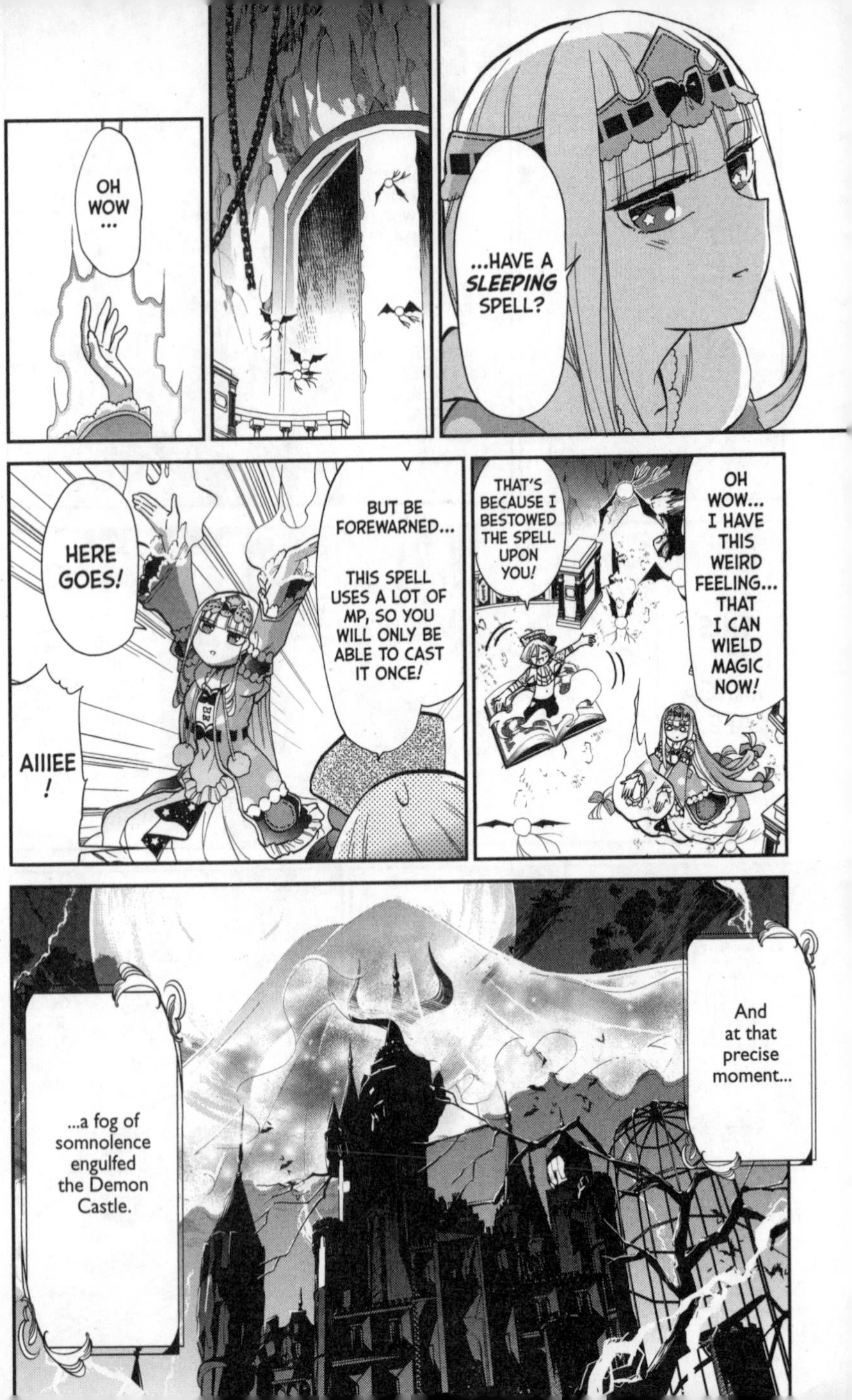
...HAVE A *SLEEPING* SPELL?
OH WOW ...
OH WOW... I HAVE THIS WEIRD FEELING... THAT I CAN WIELD MAGIC NOW!
THAT'S BECAUSE I BESTOWED THE SPELL UPON YOU!
BUT BE FOREWARNED...
THIS SPELL USES A LOT OF MP, SO YOU WILL ONLY BE ABLE TO CAST IT ONCE!
HERE GOES!
AIIIEE!
And at that precise moment...
...a fog of somnolence engulfed the Demon Castle.

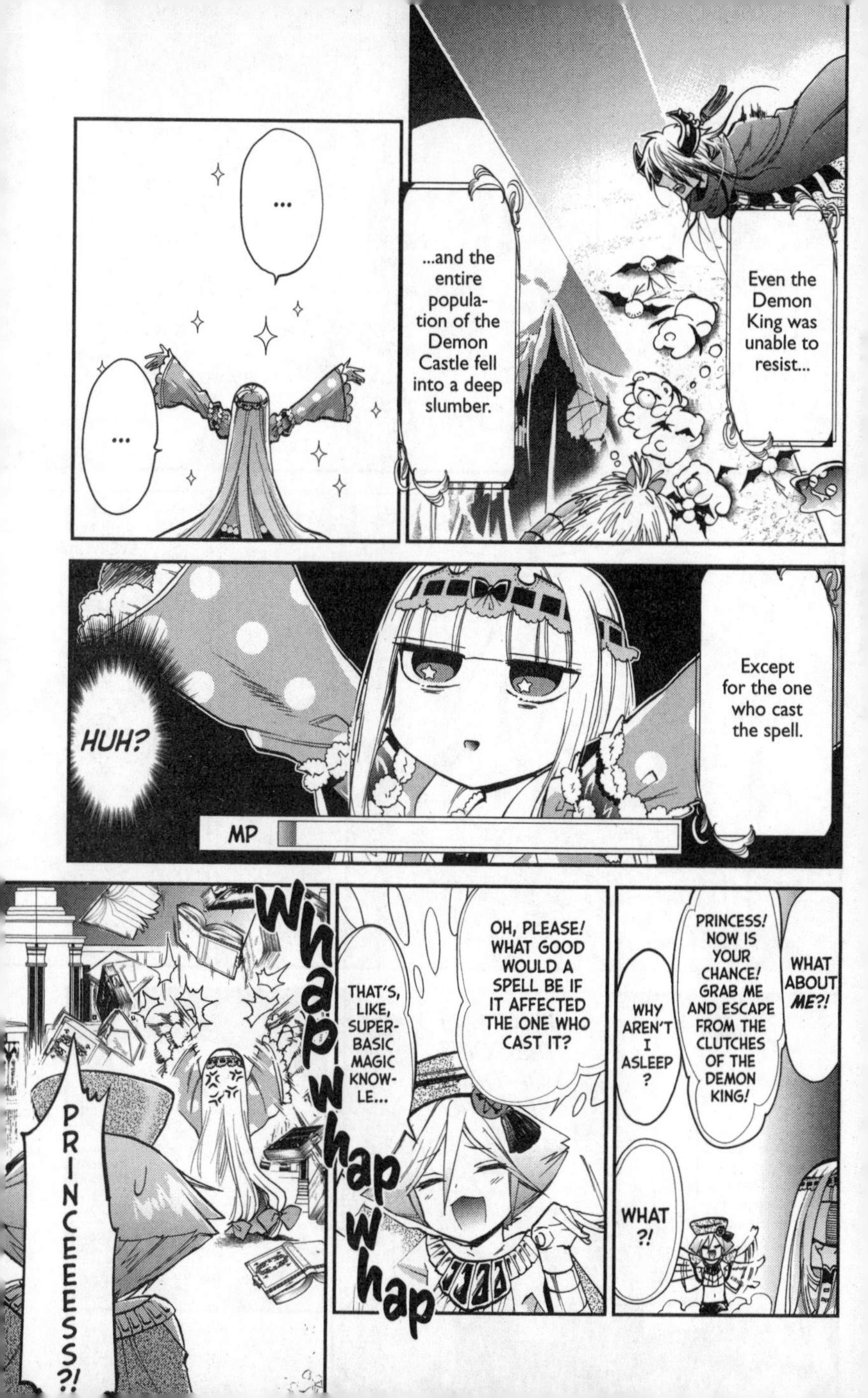
Even the Demon King was unable to resist...
...and the entire population of the Demon Castle fell into a deep slumber.
...
...
Except for the one who cast the spell.
HUH?
MP
WHAT ABOUT *ME*?!
PRINCESS! NOW IS YOUR CHANCE! GRAB ME AND ESCAPE FROM THE CLUTCHES OF THE DEMON KING!
WHY AREN'T I ASLEEP?
WHAT?!
OH, PLEASE! WHAT GOOD WOULD A SPELL BE IF IT AFFECTED THE ONE WHO CAST IT?
THAT'S, LIKE, SUPER-BASIC MAGIC KNOWLE-LE...
whap whap whap whap
PRINCEEESSS?!

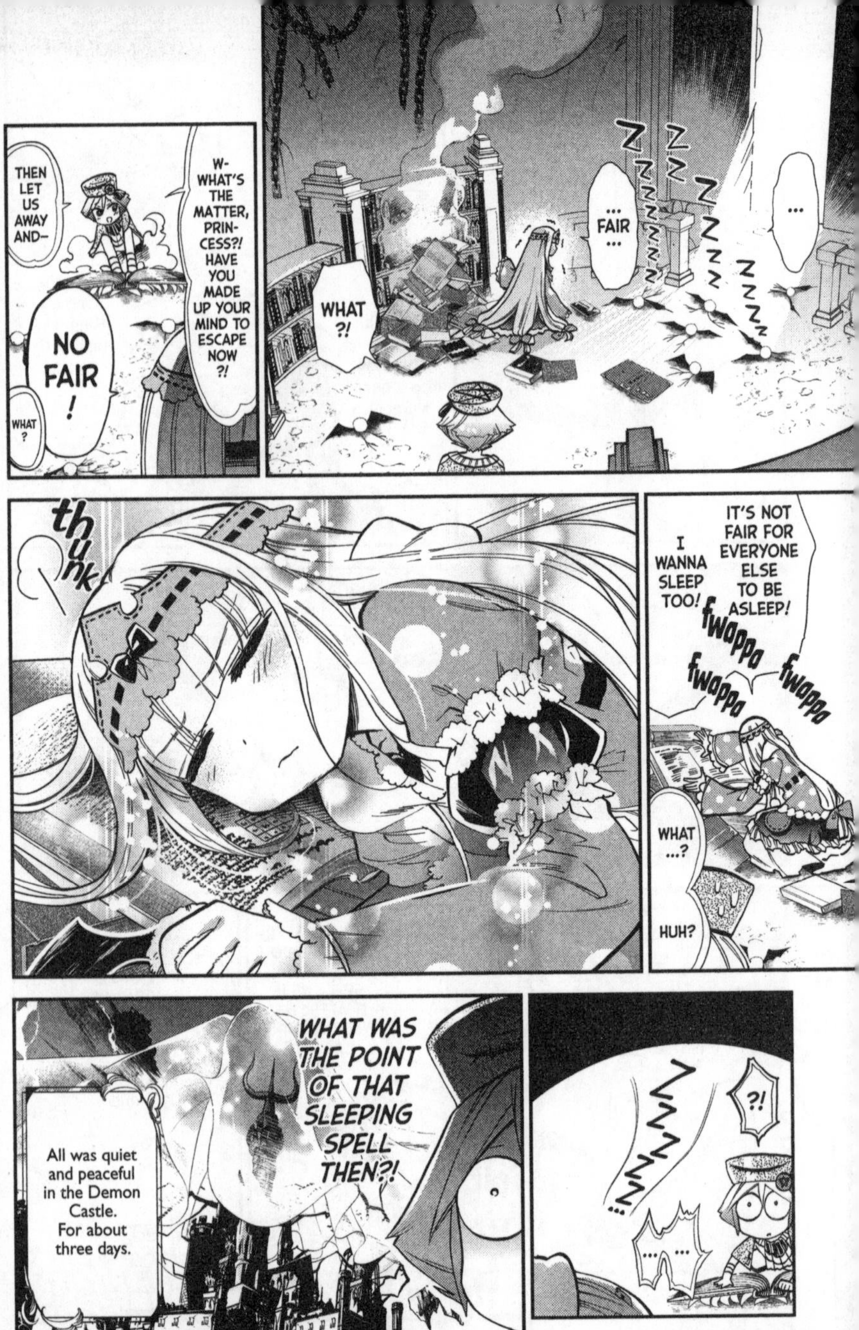
...
... FAIR ...
WHAT ?!
W- WHAT'S THE MATTER, PRINCESS?! HAVE YOU MADE UP YOUR MIND TO ESCAPE NOW?!
THEN LET US AWAY AND—
NO FAIR!
WHAT?
IT'S NOT FAIR FOR EVERYONE ELSE TO BE ASLEEP!
I WANNA SLEEP TOO!
fwappa
fwappa
fwappa
WHAT ...?
HUH?
thunk
?!
ZZZZZ...
... ...
WHAT WAS THE POINT OF THAT SLEEPING SPELL THEN?!
All was quiet and peaceful in the Demon Castle. For about three days.

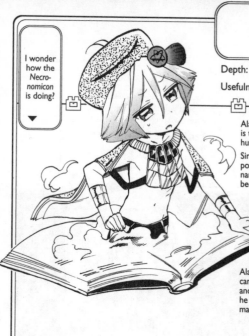

Alazif

I wonder how the *Necronomicon* is doing?

Depth: Immeasurable

Usefulness: ☆☆☆☆☆☆☆☆☆☆

Alazif, the spirit of the book of spells, is the embodiment of the dark fruit of human knowledge.

Since it contains a record of so many powerful spells, this compendium is named the Forbidden Grimoire and has been sealed away by demons.

His favorite food is steamed monster bird egg custard.

Alazif is ancient, but since he has been sleeping for most of his existence, his mental age is quite young. His raison d'être is to serve human royalty.

Alazif currently serves Syalis, but all he can do is imbue her with magical power and spells. Unable to wield his own power, he is now forced to expend his incredible magic on pointless things.

Problem it had for the past several hundred years:
"Demons must be destroyed."

Current problem:
"The princess."

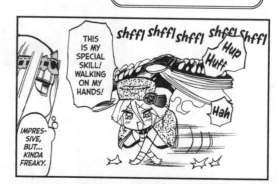

shffl shffl shffl shffl shffl
Hup
Huff
Hah
THIS IS MY SPECIAL SKILL! WALKING ON MY HANDS!
IMPRESSIVE, BUT... KINDA FREAKY.

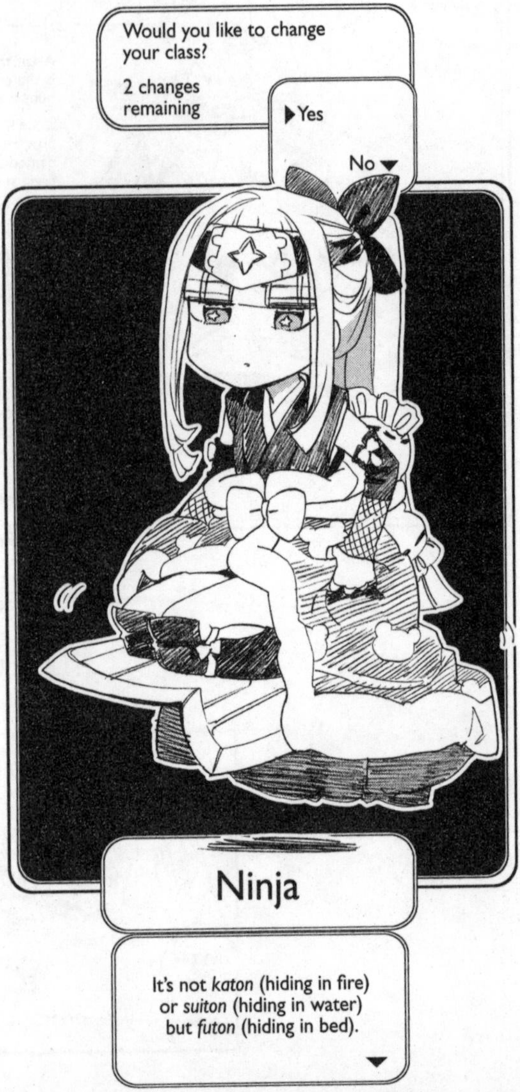
Would you like to change your class?
2 changes remaining
▶Yes
No
Ninja
It's not *katon* (hiding in fire) or *suiton* (hiding in water) but *futon* (hiding in bed).

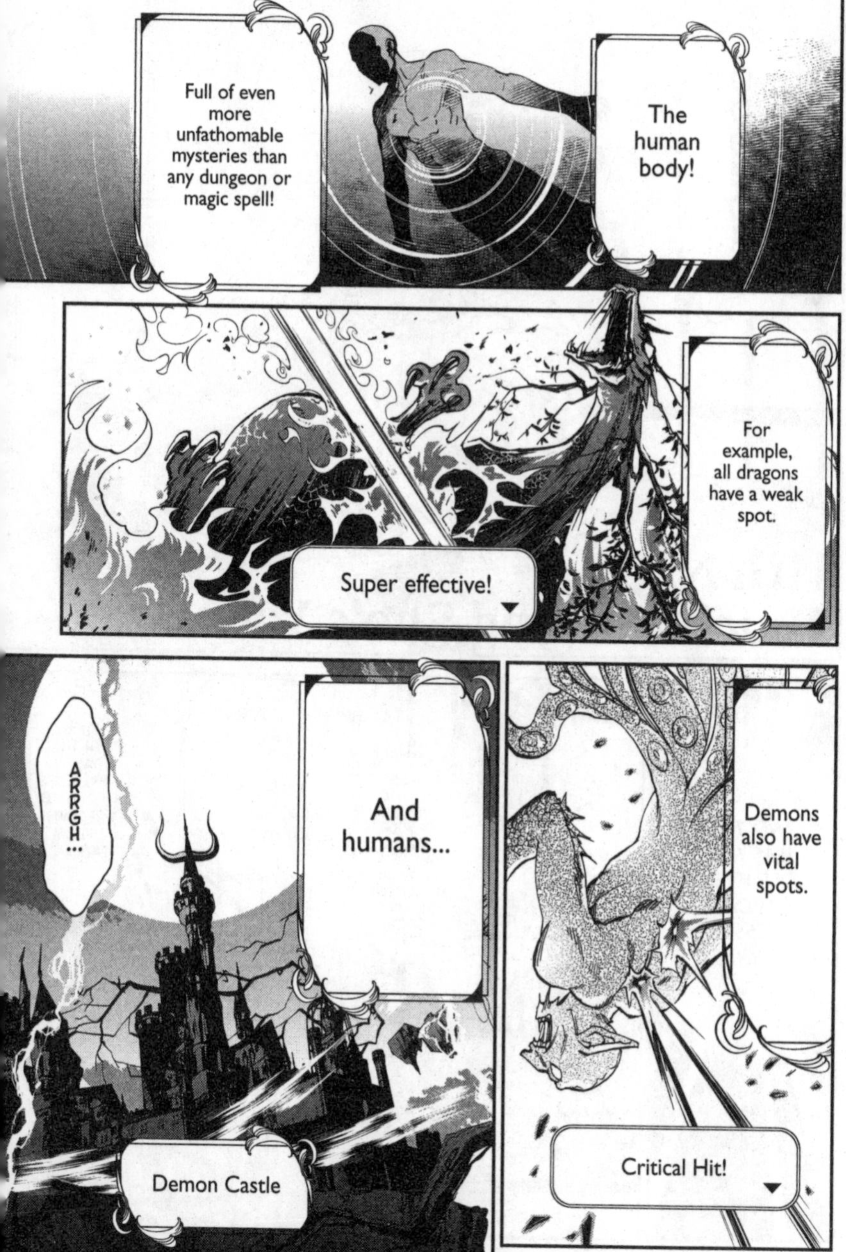
The human body!
Full of even more unfathomable mysteries than any dungeon or magic spell!
For example, all dragons have a weak spot.
Super effective!
Demons also have vital spots.
Critical Hit!
And humans...
ARRGH...
Demon Castle

11th Night: Touch Her and She's Yours

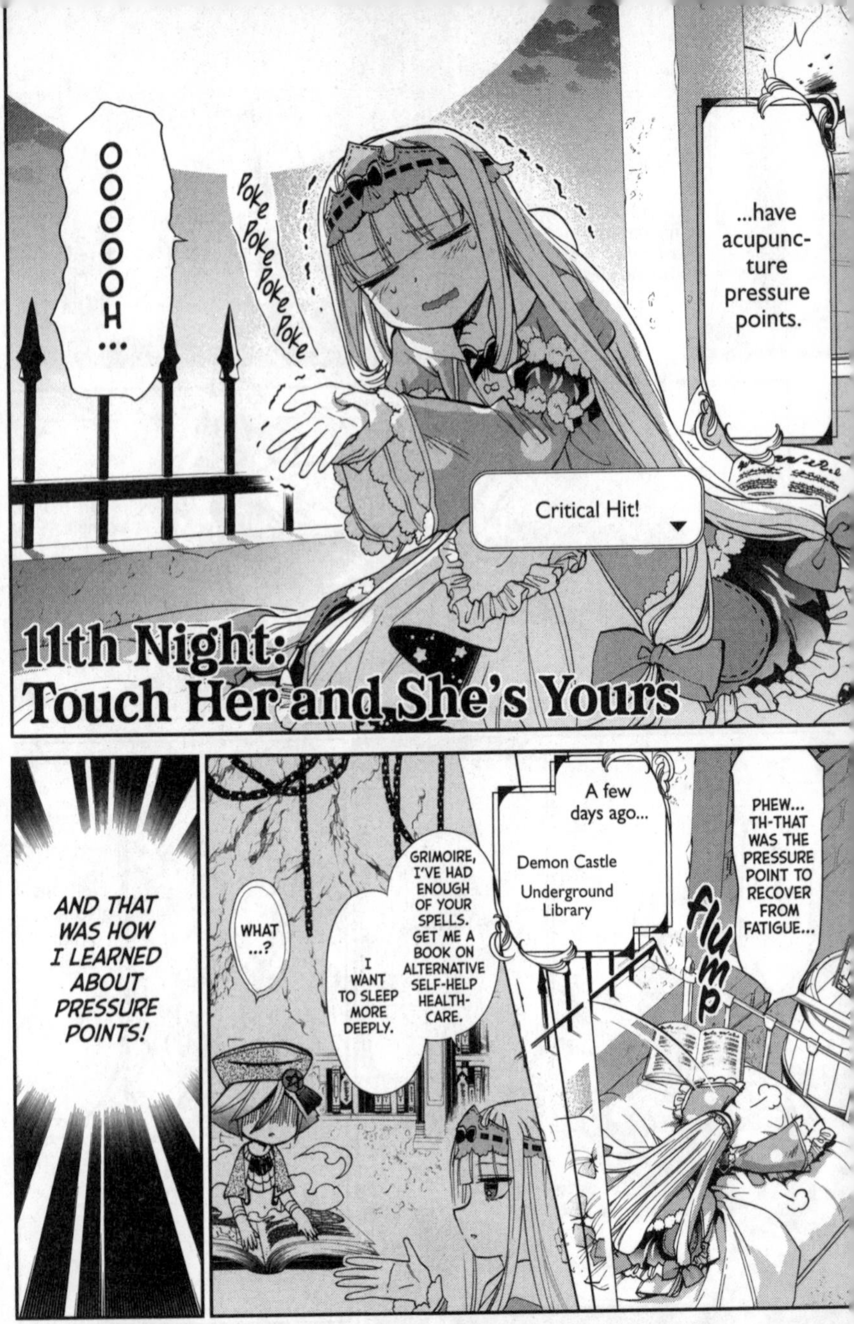
...have acupuncture pressure points.
Critical Hit!
Poke Poke Poke Poke
OOOOOOH...
11th Night: Touch Her and She's Yours
PHEW... TH-THAT WAS THE PRESSURE POINT TO RECOVER FROM FATIGUE...
flump
A few days ago...
Demon Castle Underground Library
GRIMOIRE, I'VE HAD ENOUGH OF YOUR SPELLS. GET ME A BOOK ON ALTERNATIVE SELF-HELP HEALTH-CARE.
I WANT TO SLEEP MORE DEEPLY.
WHAT ...?
AND THAT WAS HOW I LEARNED ABOUT PRESSURE POINTS!

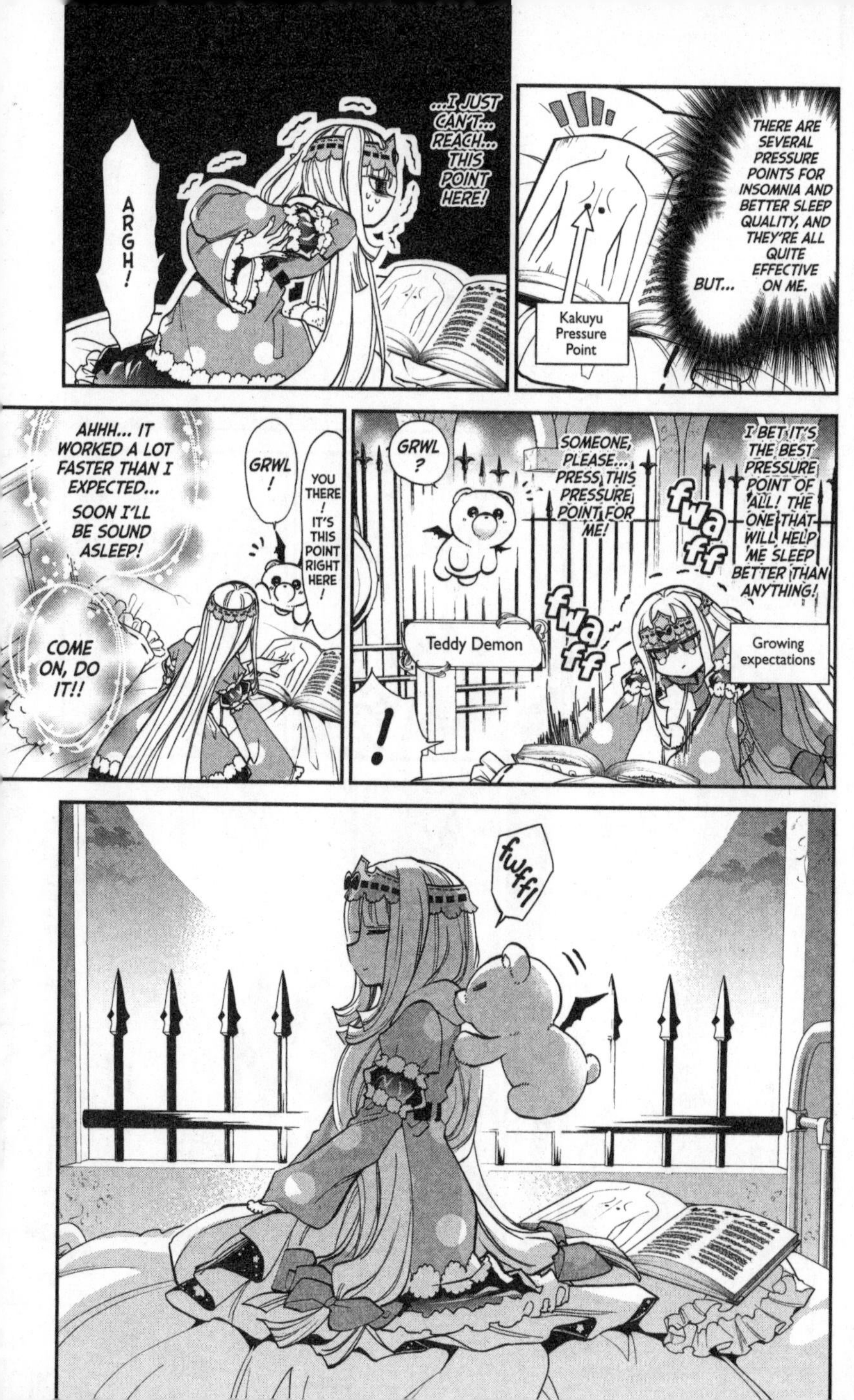

THERE ARE SEVERAL PRESSURE POINTS FOR INSOMNIA AND BETTER SLEEP QUALITY, AND THEY'RE ALL QUITE EFFECTIVE ON ME.
BUT...
Kakuyu Pressure Point
...I JUST CAN'T... REACH... THIS POINT HERE!
ARGH!
I BET IT'S THE BEST PRESSURE POINT OF ALL! THE ONE THAT WILL HELP ME SLEEP BETTER THAN ANYTHING!
fwaff
SOMEONE, PLEASE... PRESS THIS PRESSURE POINT FOR ME!
GRWL ?
fwaff
Growing expectations
Teddy Demon
!
YOU THERE! IT'S THIS POINT RIGHT HERE!
GRWL!
AHHH... IT WORKED A LOT FASTER THAN I EXPECTED...
SOON I'LL BE SOUND ASLEEP!
COME ON, DO IT!!
fwff!

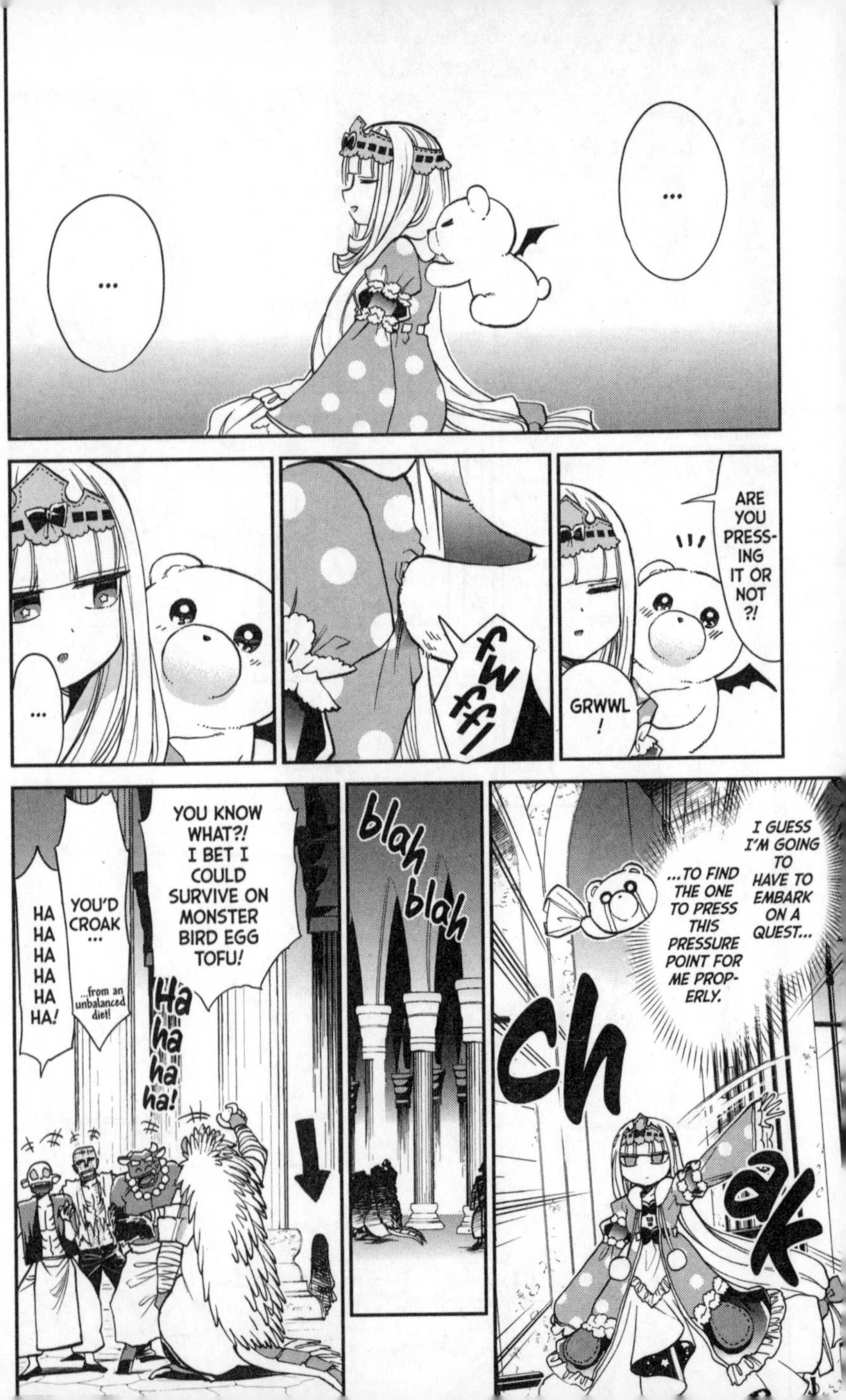
...
...
ARE YOU PRESS-ING IT OR NOT?!
GRWWL!
fwffl
...
I GUESS I'M GOING TO HAVE TO EMBARK ON A QUEST...
...TO FIND THE ONE TO PRESS THIS PRESSURE POINT FOR ME PROP-ERLY.
Ch ak
blah blah
YOU KNOW WHAT?! I BET I COULD SURVIVE ON MONSTER BIRD EGG TOFU!
Ha ha ha ha!
YOU'D CROAK...
...from an unbalanced diet!
HA HA HA HA HA HA!

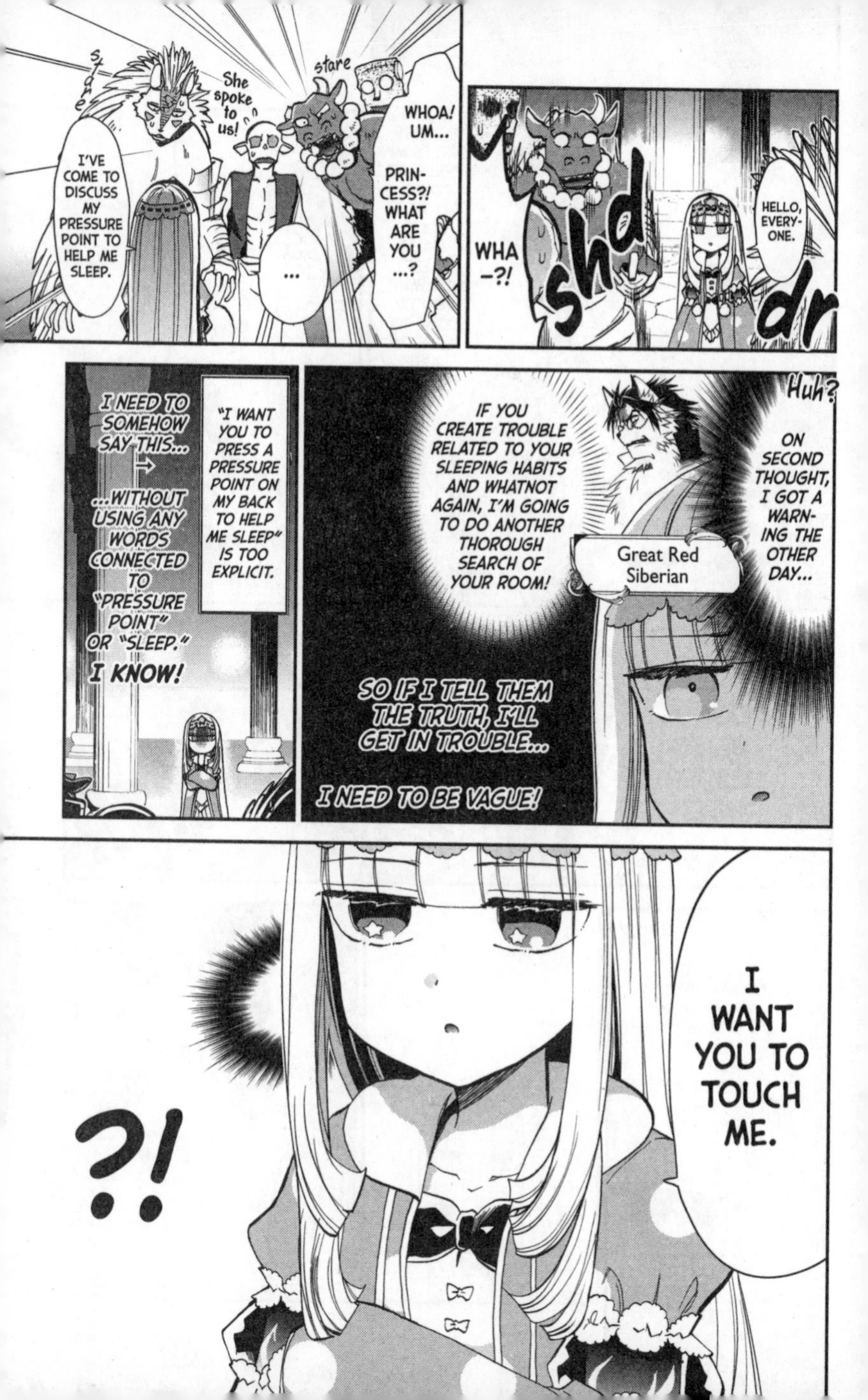
HELLO, EVERYONE.
dr
shd
WHA—?!
WHOA! UM...
PRINCESS?! WHAT ARE YOU ...?
stare
She spoke to us!
stare
...
I'VE COME TO DISCUSS MY PRESSURE POINT TO HELP ME SLEEP.
Huh?
ON SECOND THOUGHT, I GOT A WARNING THE OTHER DAY...
IF YOU CREATE TROUBLE RELATED TO YOUR SLEEPING HABITS AND WHATNOT AGAIN, I'M GOING TO DO ANOTHER THOROUGH SEARCH OF YOUR ROOM!
Great Red Siberian
SO IF I TELL THEM THE TRUTH, I'LL GET IN TROUBLE...
I NEED TO BE VAGUE!
"I WANT YOU TO PRESS A PRESSURE POINT ON MY BACK TO HELP ME SLEEP" IS TOO EXPLICIT.
I NEED TO SOMEHOW SAY THIS...
...WITHOUT USING ANY WORDS CONNECTED TO "PRESSURE POINT" OR "SLEEP."
I KNOW!
I WANT YOU TO TOUCH ME.
?!

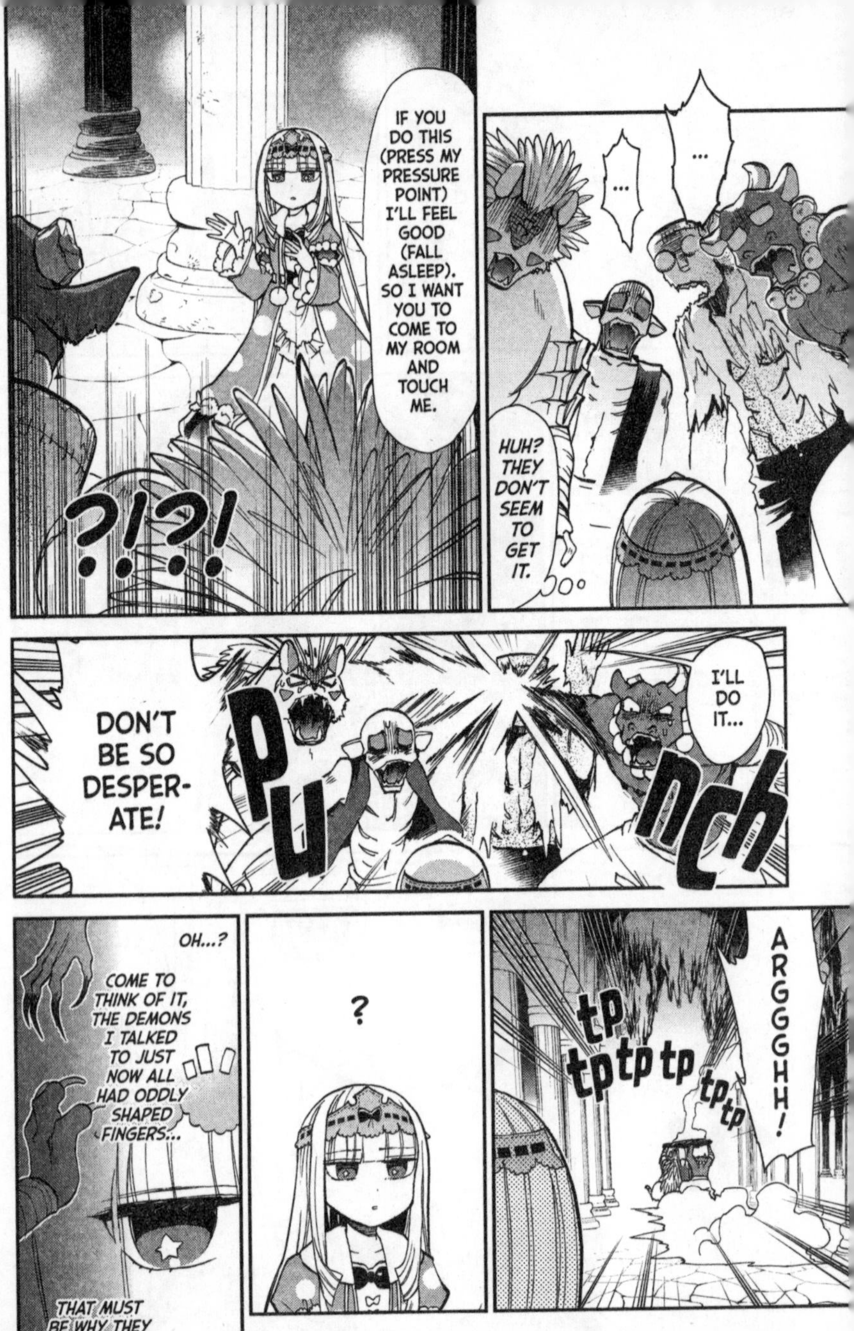
...
...
HUH? THEY DON'T SEEM TO GET IT.
IF YOU DO THIS (PRESS MY PRESSURE POINT) I'LL FEEL GOOD (FALL ASLEEP). SO I WANT YOU TO COME TO MY ROOM AND TOUCH ME.
?!?!
I'LL DO IT...
Punch
DON'T BE SO DESPER-ATE!
ARGGGH!
tp tp tp tp tp tp
?
OH...?
COME TO THINK OF IT, THE DEMONS I TALKED TO JUST NOW ALL HAD ODDLY SHAPED FINGERS...
THAT MUST BE WHY THEY HESITATED.

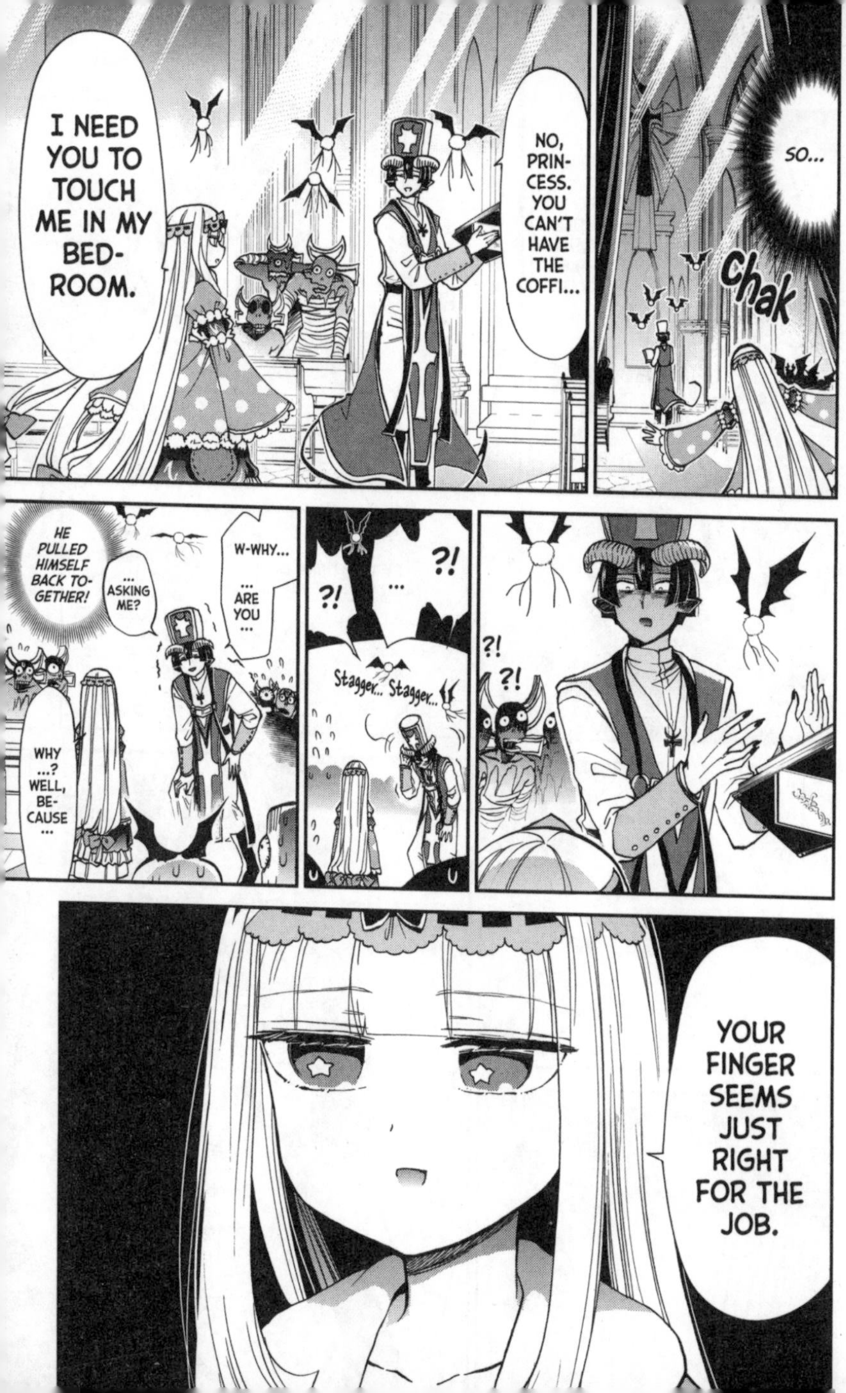
SO...
Chak
NO, PRINCESS. YOU CAN'T HAVE THE COFFI...
I NEED YOU TO TOUCH ME IN MY BEDROOM.
?!
?!
?!
?!
...
Stagger... Stagger...
W-WHY...
... ARE YOU ...
... ASKING ME?
HE PULLED HIMSELF BACK TOGETHER!
WHY ...? WELL, BECAUSE ...
YOUR FINGER SEEMS JUST RIGHT FOR THE JOB.

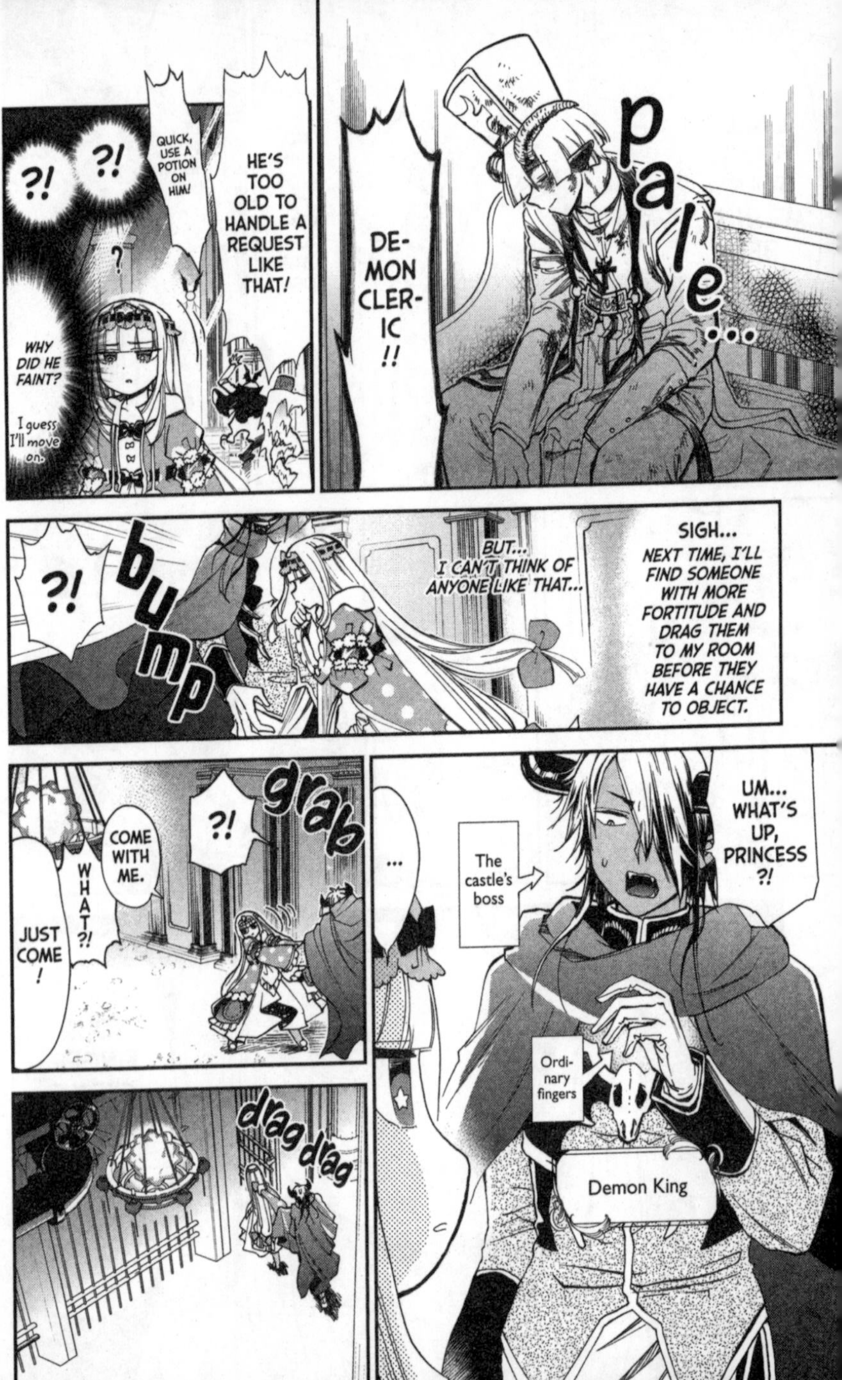
pale...
DE-MON CLER-IC!!
HE'S TOO OLD TO HANDLE A REQUEST LIKE THAT!
QUICK, USE A POTION ON HIM!
?!
?!
?
WHY DID HE FAINT?
I guess I'll move on.
SIGH... NEXT TIME, I'LL FIND SOMEONE WITH MORE FORTITUDE AND DRAG THEM TO MY ROOM BEFORE THEY HAVE A CHANCE TO OBJECT.
BUT... I CAN'T THINK OF ANYONE LIKE THAT...
bump
?!
UM... WHAT'S UP, PRINCESS?!
The castle's boss
...
Ordinary fingers
Demon King
grab
?!
COME WITH ME.
WHAT?!
JUST COME!
drag drag

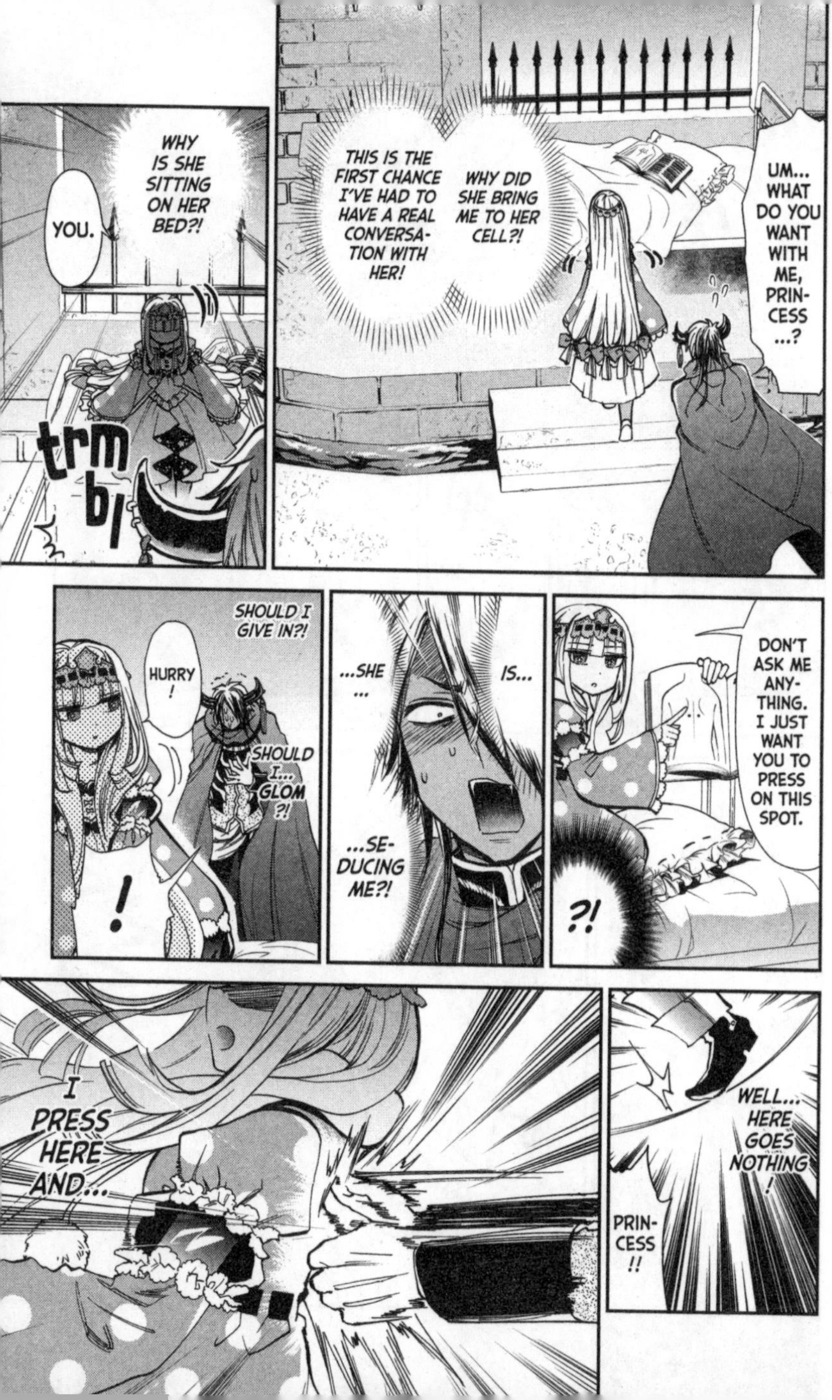
UM... WHAT DO YOU WANT WITH ME, PRINCESS...?
WHY DID SHE BRING ME TO HER CELL?!
THIS IS THE FIRST CHANCE I'VE HAD TO HAVE A REAL CONVERSATION WITH HER!
WHY IS SHE SITTING ON HER BED?!
YOU.
trm bl
DON'T ASK ME ANYTHING. I JUST WANT YOU TO PRESS ON THIS SPOT.
?!
IS...
...SHE ...
...SEDUCING ME?!
SHOULD I GIVE IN?!
HURRY!
SHOULD I... GLOM?!
!
WELL... HERE GOES NOTHING!
PRINCESS!!
I PRESS HERE AND...

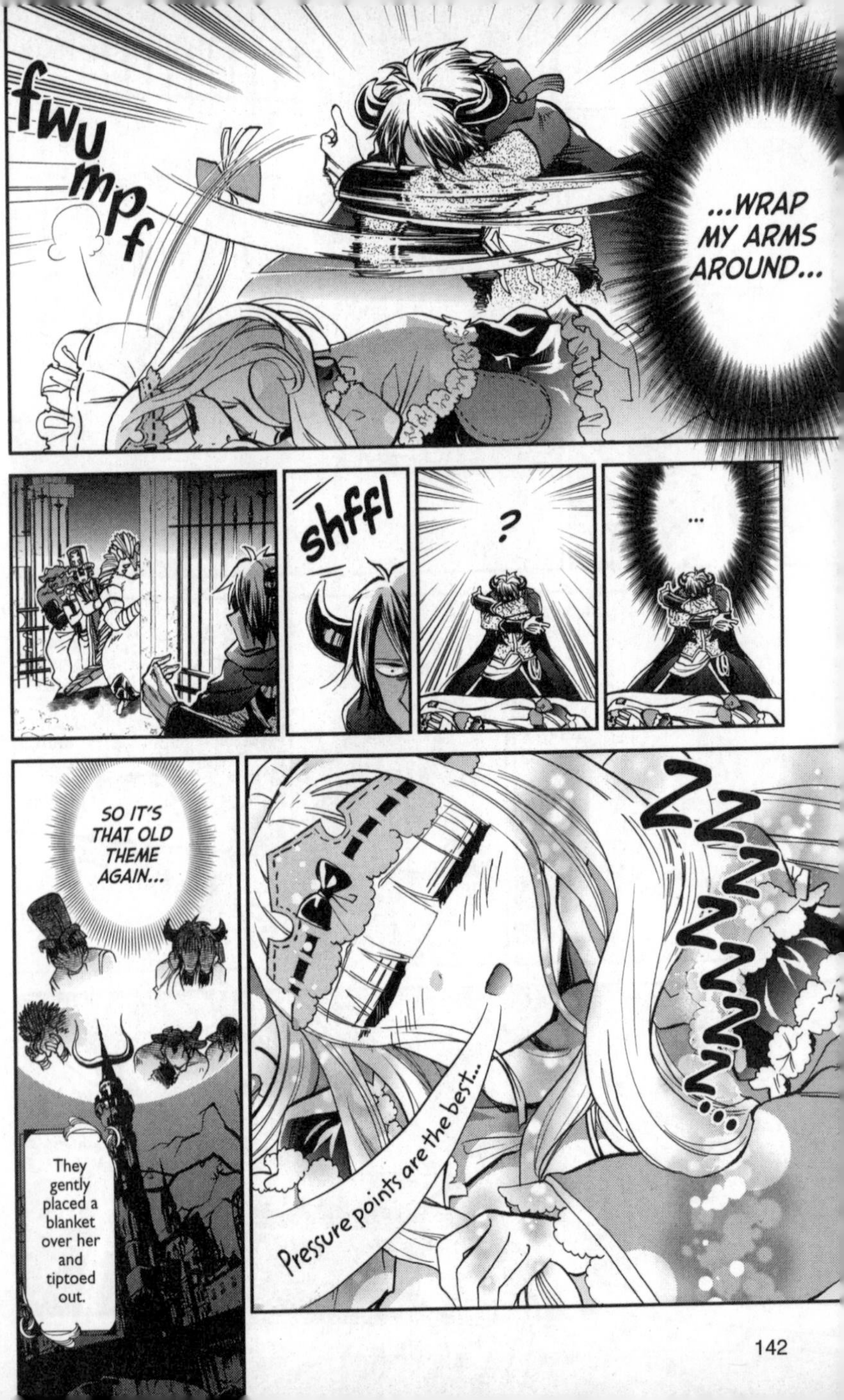
...WRAP MY ARMS AROUND...
fwumpf
...
?
shffl
ZZZZZZ...
Pressure points are the best...
SO IT'S THAT OLD THEME AGAIN...
They gently placed a blanket over her and tiptoed out.

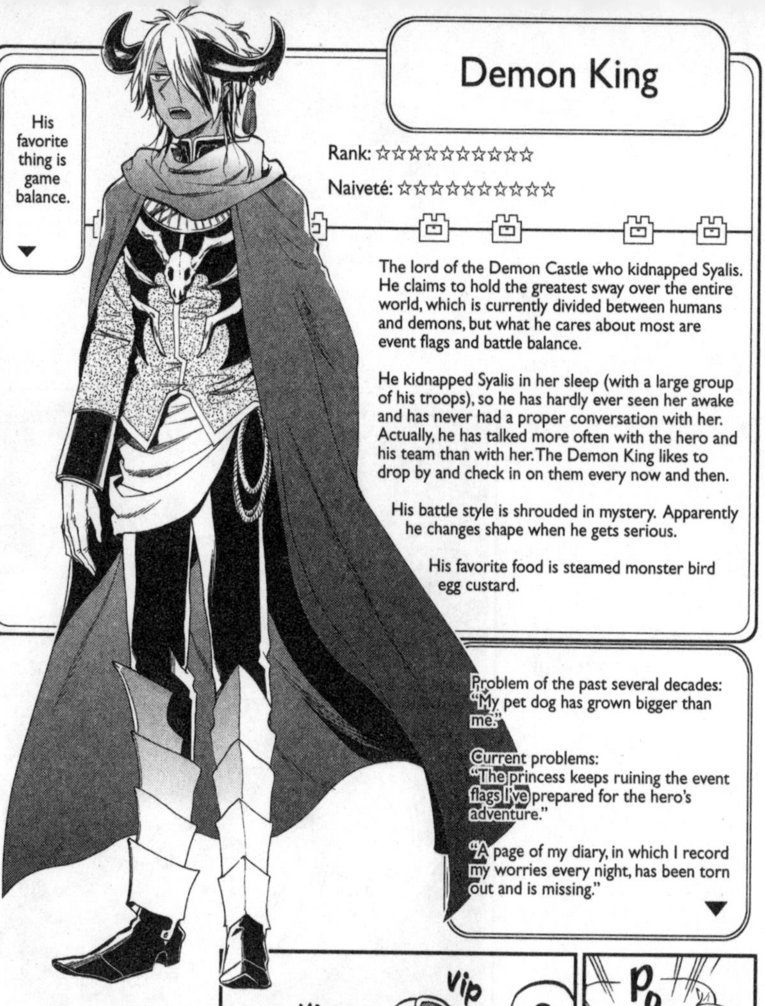

Demon King

His favorite thing is game balance.

Rank: ☆☆☆☆☆☆☆☆☆☆☆

Naiveté: ☆☆☆☆☆☆☆☆☆☆☆

The lord of the Demon Castle who kidnapped Syalis. He claims to hold the greatest sway over the entire world, which is currently divided between humans and demons, but what he cares about most are event flags and battle balance.

He kidnapped Syalis in her sleep (with a large group of his troops), so he has hardly ever seen her awake and has never had a proper conversation with her. Actually, he has talked more often with the hero and his team than with her. The Demon King likes to drop by and check in on them every now and then.

His battle style is shrouded in mystery. Apparently he changes shape when he gets serious.

His favorite food is steamed monster bird egg custard.

Problem of the past several decades:
"My pet dog has grown bigger than me."

Current problems:
"The princess keeps ruining the event flags I've prepared for the hero's adventure."

"A page of my diary, in which I record my worries every night, has been torn out and is missing."

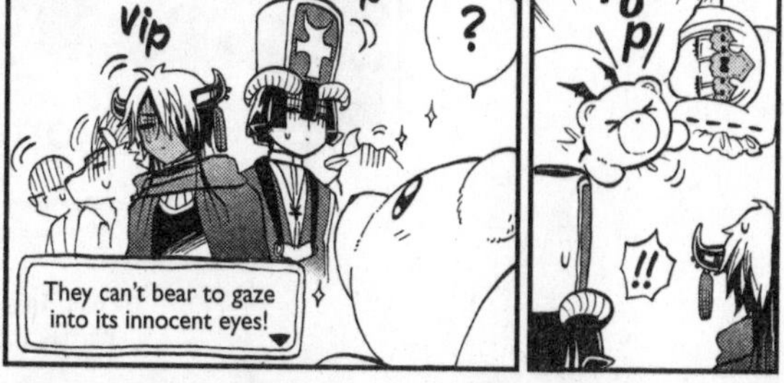
Pop
!!
vip
vip
?
They can't bear to gaze into its innocent eyes!

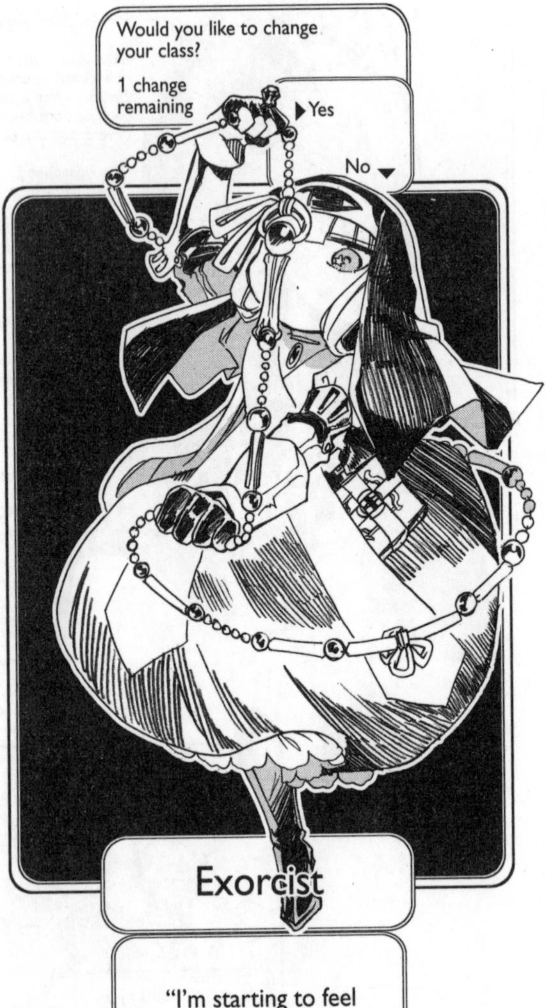
Would you like to change your class?
1 change remaining
▶Yes
No
Exorcist
"I'm starting to feel motivated."

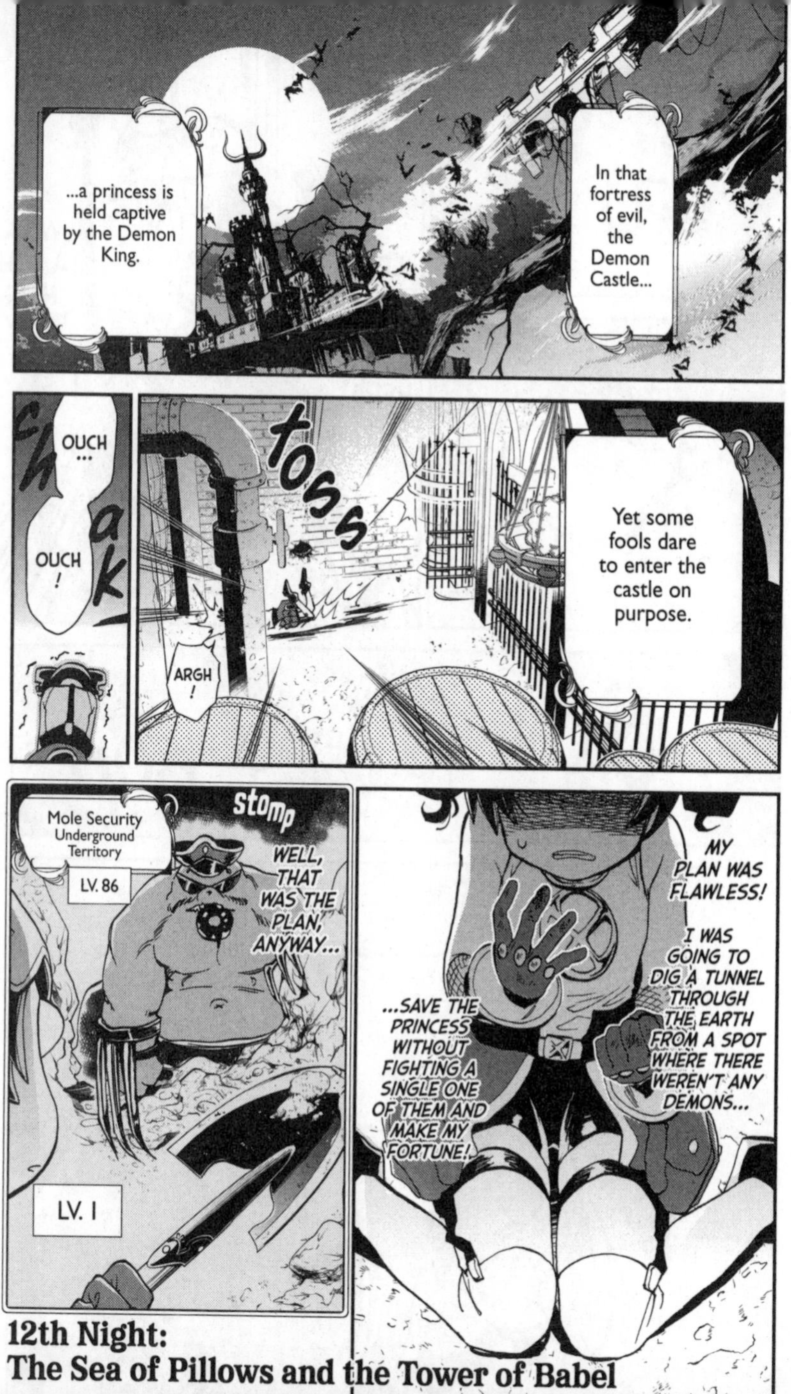
In that fortress of evil, the Demon Castle...
...a princess is held captive by the Demon King.
Yet some fools dare to enter the castle on purpose.
toss
ARGH!
chak
OUCH...
OUCH!
MY PLAN WAS FLAWLESS!
I WAS GOING TO DIG A TUNNEL THROUGH THE EARTH FROM A SPOT WHERE THERE WEREN'T ANY DEMONS...
...SAVE THE PRINCESS WITHOUT FIGHTING A SINGLE ONE OF THEM AND MAKE MY FORTUNE!
stomp
Mole Security Underground Territory
LV. 86
WELL, THAT WAS THE PLAN, ANYWAY...
LV. 1

12th Night: The Sea of Pillows and the Tower of Babel

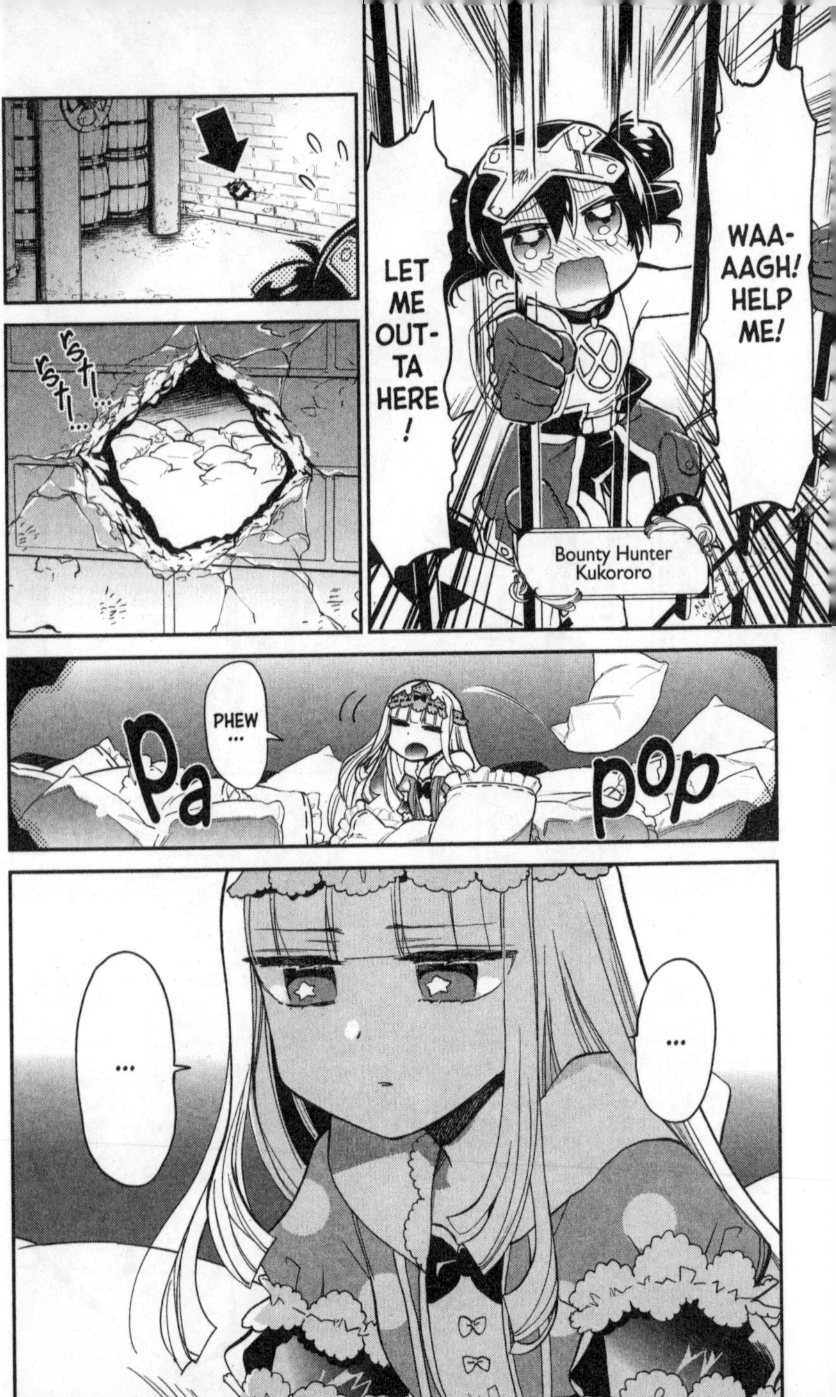
WAAAGH! HELP ME!
LET ME OUTTA HERE!
Bounty Hunter Kukororo
rstl... rstl...
PHEW...
Pa
pop
...
...

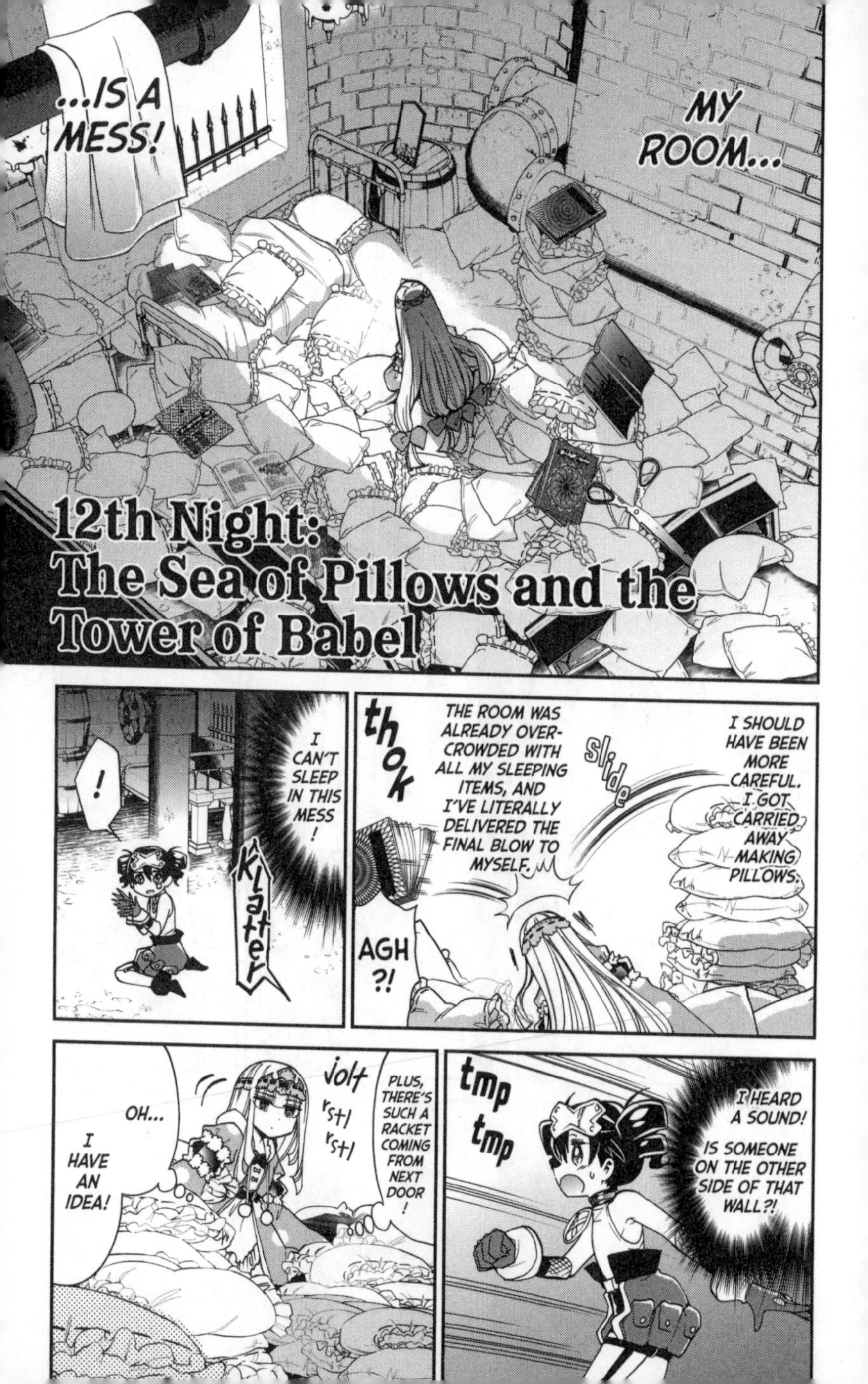
MY ROOM...
...IS A MESS!
12th Night: The Sea of Pillows and the Tower of Babel
I SHOULD HAVE BEEN MORE CAREFUL. I GOT CARRIED AWAY MAKING PILLOWS.
slide
THE ROOM WAS ALREADY OVER-CROWDED WITH ALL MY SLEEPING ITEMS, AND I'VE LITERALLY DELIVERED THE FINAL BLOW TO MYSELF.
thok
AGH ?!
I CAN'T SLEEP IN THIS MESS!
klatter
!
I HEARD A SOUND!
IS SOMEONE ON THE OTHER SIDE OF THAT WALL?!
tmp tmp
PLUS, THERE'S SUCH A RACKET COMING FROM NEXT DOOR!
jolt
rstl rstl
OH...
I HAVE AN IDEA!

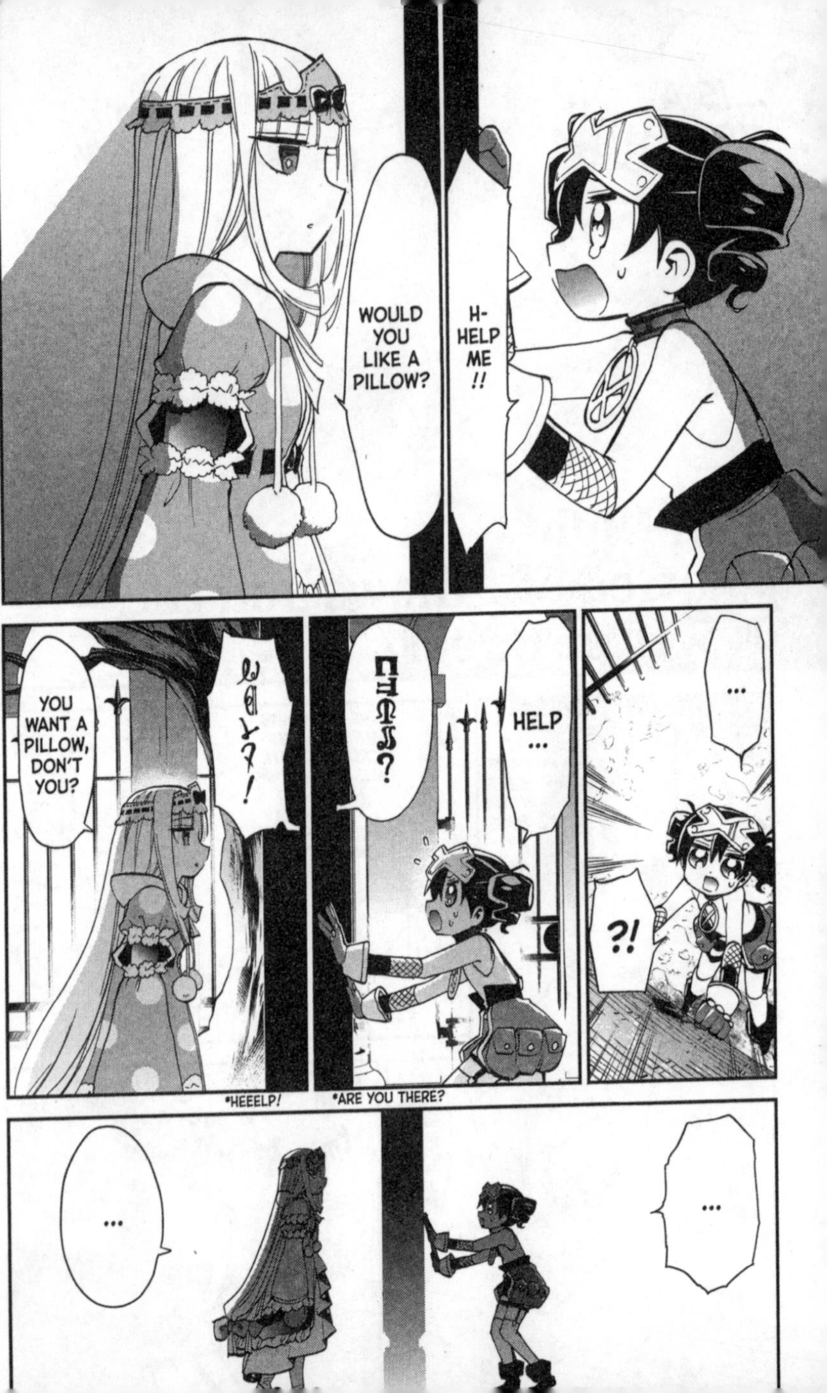
H- HELP ME !!
WOULD YOU LIKE A PILLOW?
...
?!
HELP ...
*ARE YOU THERE?
*HEEELP!
YOU WANT A PILLOW, DON'T YOU?
...
...

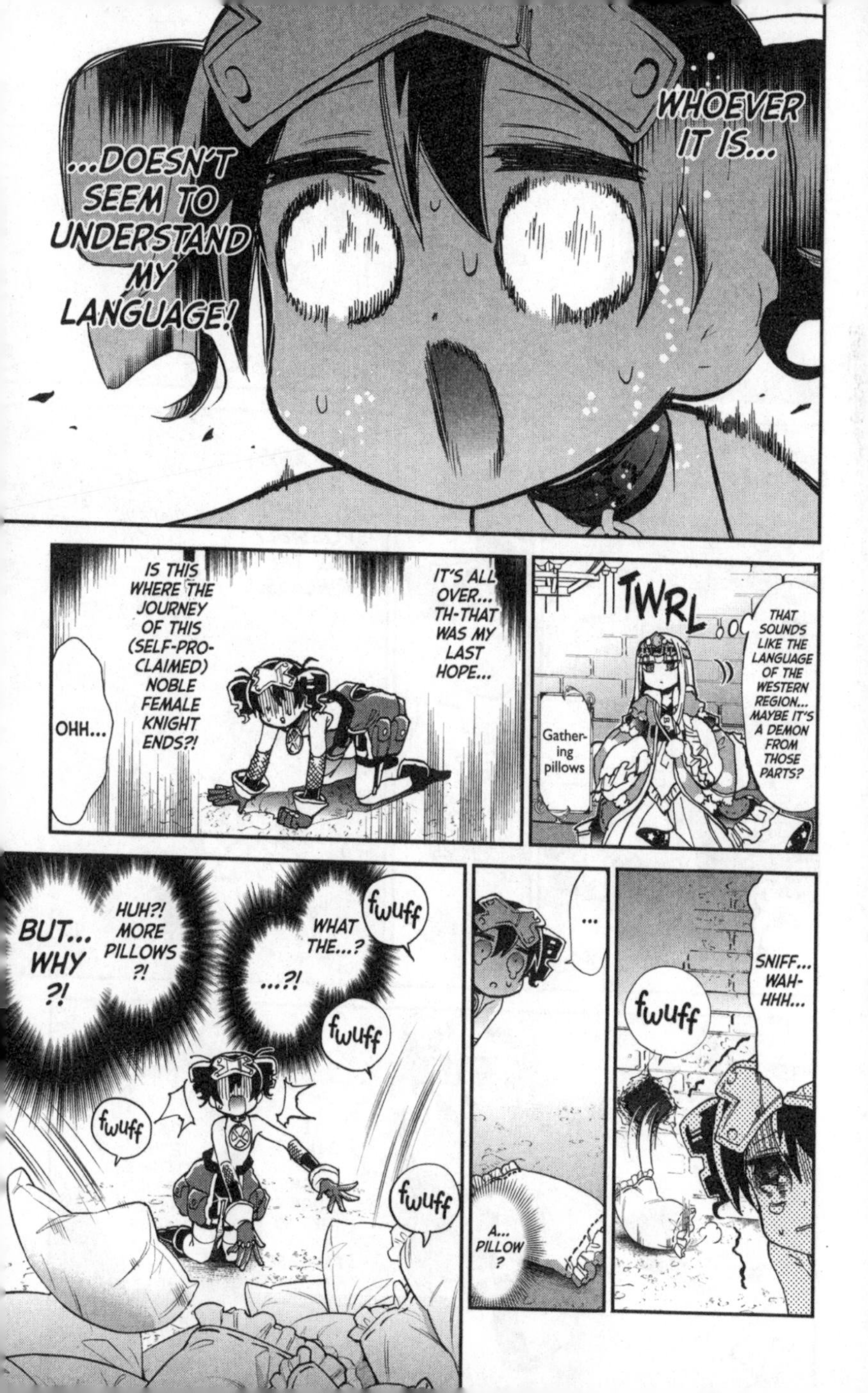
WHOEVER IT IS...
...DOESN'T SEEM TO UNDERSTAND MY LANGUAGE!
THAT SOUNDS LIKE THE LANGUAGE OF THE WESTERN REGION... MAYBE IT'S A DEMON FROM THOSE PARTS?
TWRL
Gathering pillows
IT'S ALL OVER... TH-THAT WAS MY LAST HOPE...
IS THIS WHERE THE JOURNEY OF THIS (SELF-PROCLAIMED) NOBLE FEMALE KNIGHT ENDS?!
OHH...
SNIFF... WAH-HHH...
fwuff
...
A... PILLOW?
fwuff
WHAT THE...?
HUH?! MORE PILLOWS?!
BUT... WHY?!
...?!
fwuff
fwuff
fwuff

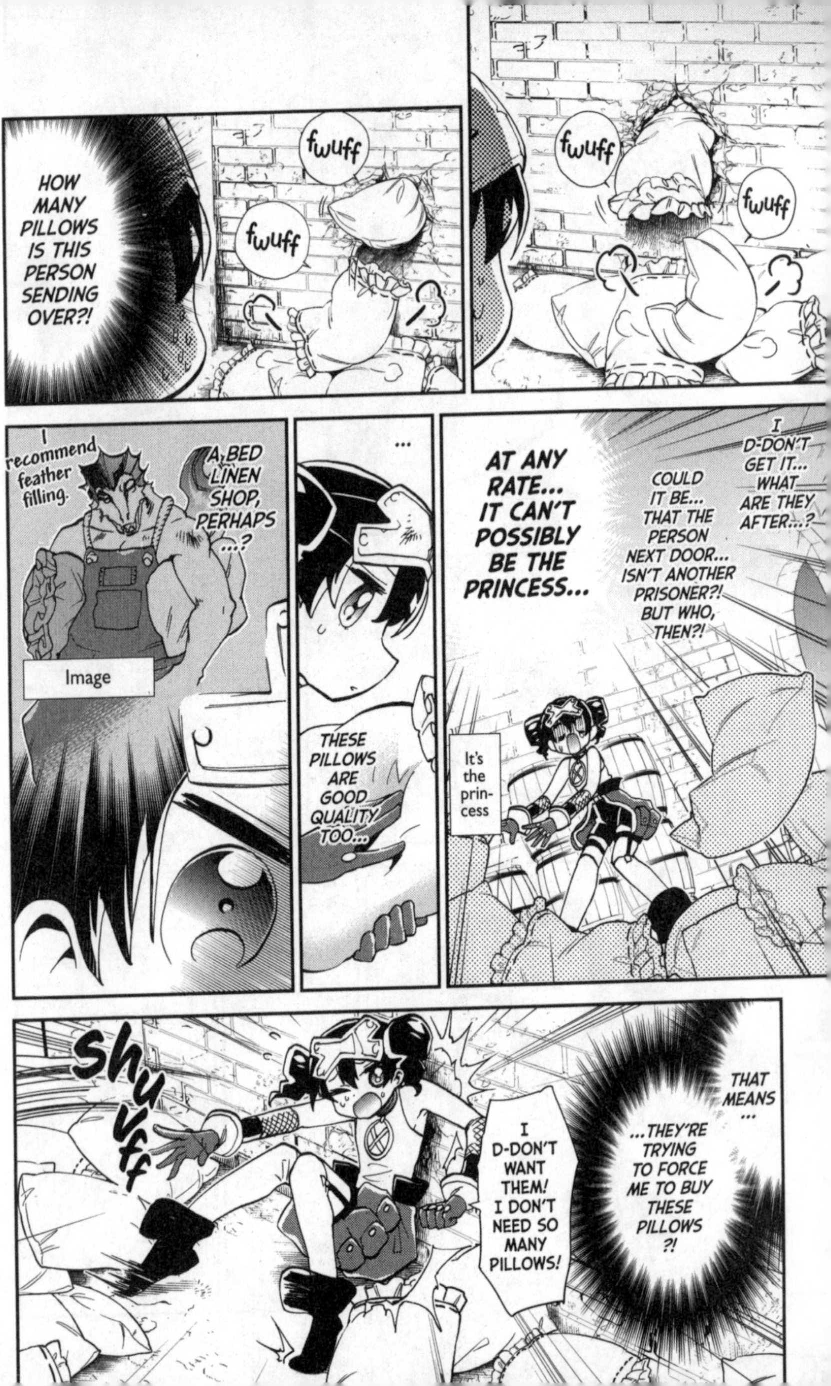
fwuff
fwuff
HOW MANY PILLOWS IS THIS PERSON SENDING OVER?!
fwuff
fwuff
I D-DON'T GET IT... WHAT ARE THEY AFTER...?
COULD IT BE... THAT THE PERSON NEXT DOOR... ISN'T ANOTHER PRISONER?! BUT WHO, THEN?!
AT ANY RATE... IT CAN'T POSSIBLY BE THE PRINCESS...
It's the prin-cess
...
THESE PILLOWS ARE GOOD QUALITY TOO...
A BED LINEN SHOP, PERHAPS...?
I recommend feather filling.
Image
THAT MEANS...
...THEY'RE TRYING TO FORCE ME TO BUY THESE PILLOWS?!
I D-DON'T WANT THEM! I DON'T NEED SO MANY PILLOWS!
Shuvff

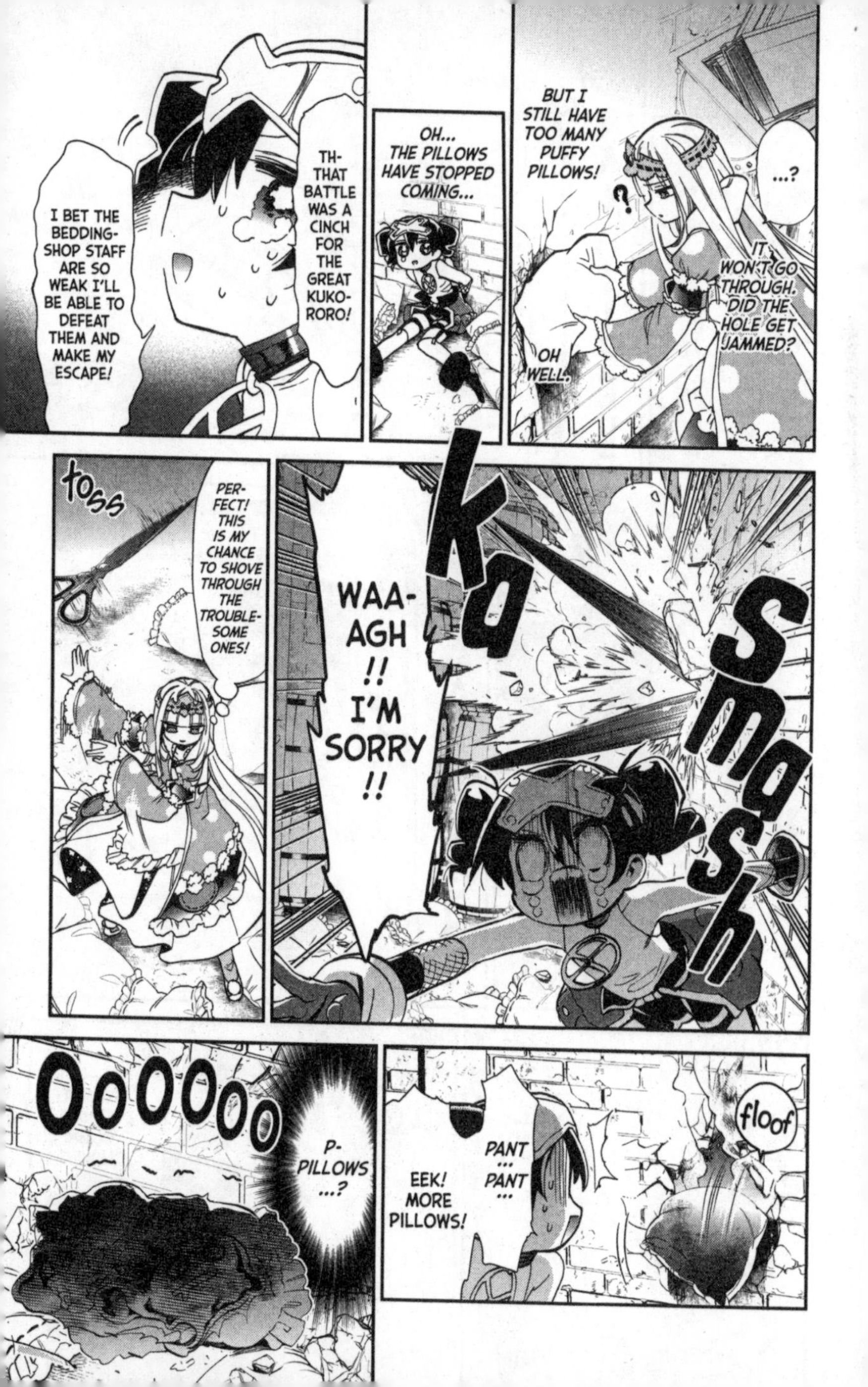
BUT I STILL HAVE TOO MANY PUFFY PILLOWS!
...?
?
IT WON'T GO THROUGH. DID THE HOLE GET JAMMED?
OH WELL.
OH... THE PILLOWS HAVE STOPPED COMING...
TH-THAT BATTLE WAS A CINCH FOR THE GREAT KUKORORO!
I BET THE BEDDING-SHOP STAFF ARE SO WEAK I'LL BE ABLE TO DEFEAT THEM AND MAKE MY ESCAPE!
ka
smash
WAA-AGH!! I'M SORRY!!
toss
PERFECT! THIS IS MY CHANCE TO SHOVE THROUGH THE TROUBLESOME ONES!
floof
PANT... PANT...
EEK! MORE PILLOWS!
P-PILLOWS...?
OOOOOO

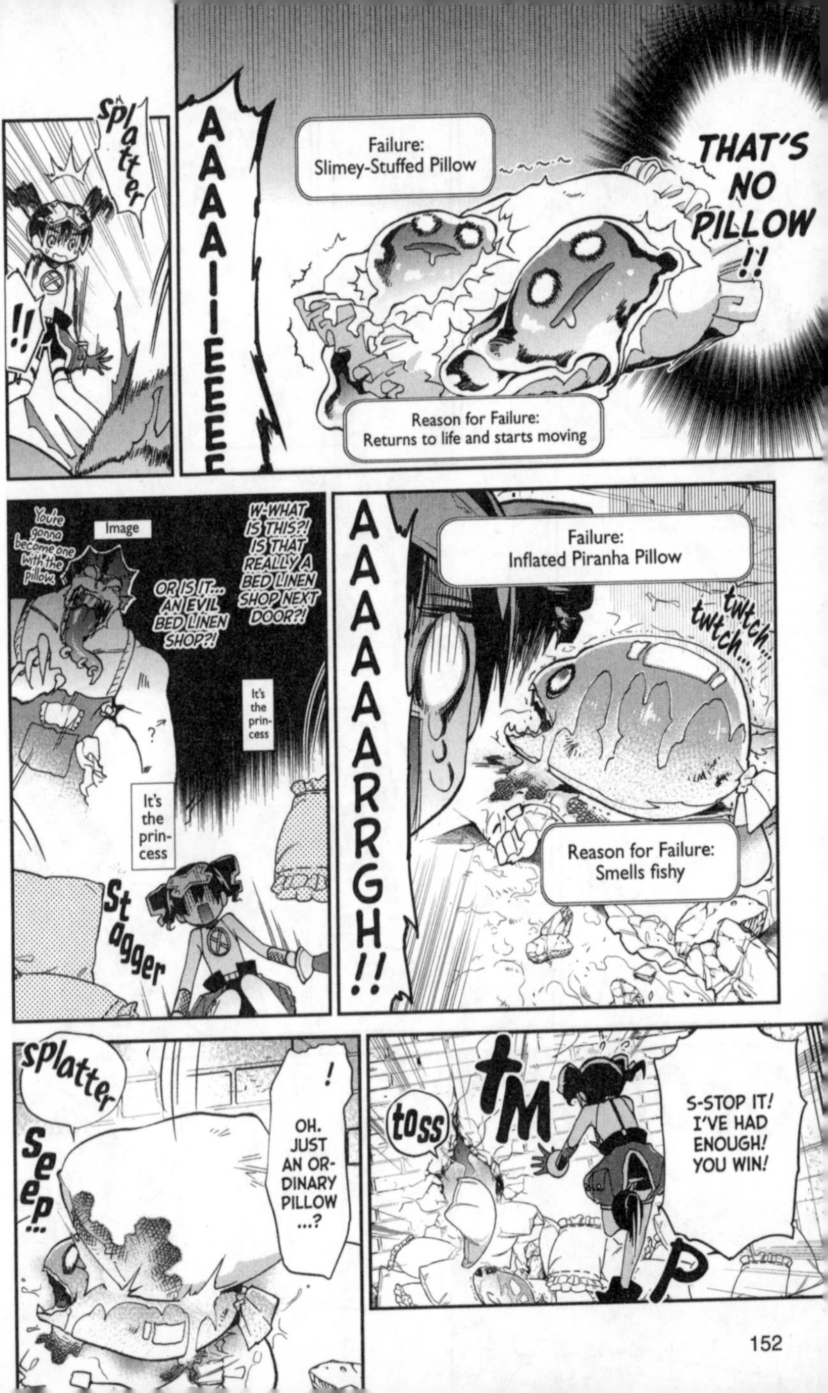
THAT'S NO PILLOW!!
Failure: Slimey-Stuffed Pillow
Reason for Failure: Returns to life and starts moving
AAAAIIEEEE
splatter
!!
Failure: Inflated Piranha Pillow
twtch... twtch...
AAAAAAAARRGH!!
Reason for Failure: Smells fishy
W-WHAT IS THIS?! IS THAT REALLY A BED LINEN SHOP NEXT DOOR?!
It's the prin-cess
OR IS IT... AN EVIL BED LINEN SHOP?!
Image
You're gonna become one with the pillow.
?
It's the prin-cess
Stagger
S-STOP IT! I'VE HAD ENOUGH! YOU WIN!
tMP
toss
!
OH. JUST AN OR-DINARY PILLOW ...?
splatter
seep...

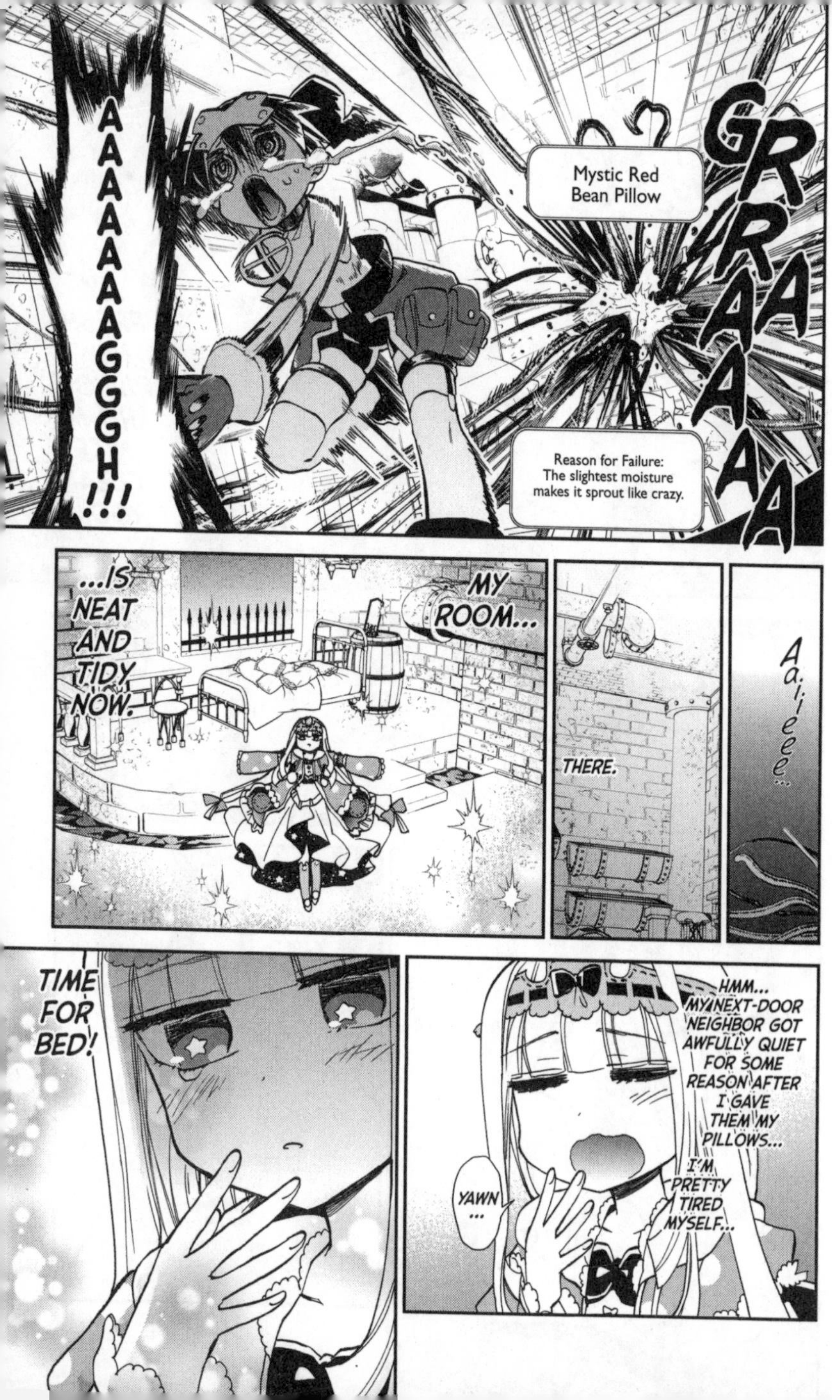
GRRAAAAA
Mystic Red Bean Pillow
Reason for Failure: The slightest moisture makes it sprout like crazy.
AAAAAAAAAGGGH!!!
Aaiieee...
THERE.
MY ROOM...
...IS NEAT AND TIDY NOW.
HMM... MY NEXT-DOOR NEIGHBOR GOT AWFULLY QUIET FOR SOME REASON AFTER I GAVE THEM MY PILLOWS...
I'M PRETTY TIRED MYSELF...
YAWN...
TIME FOR BED!

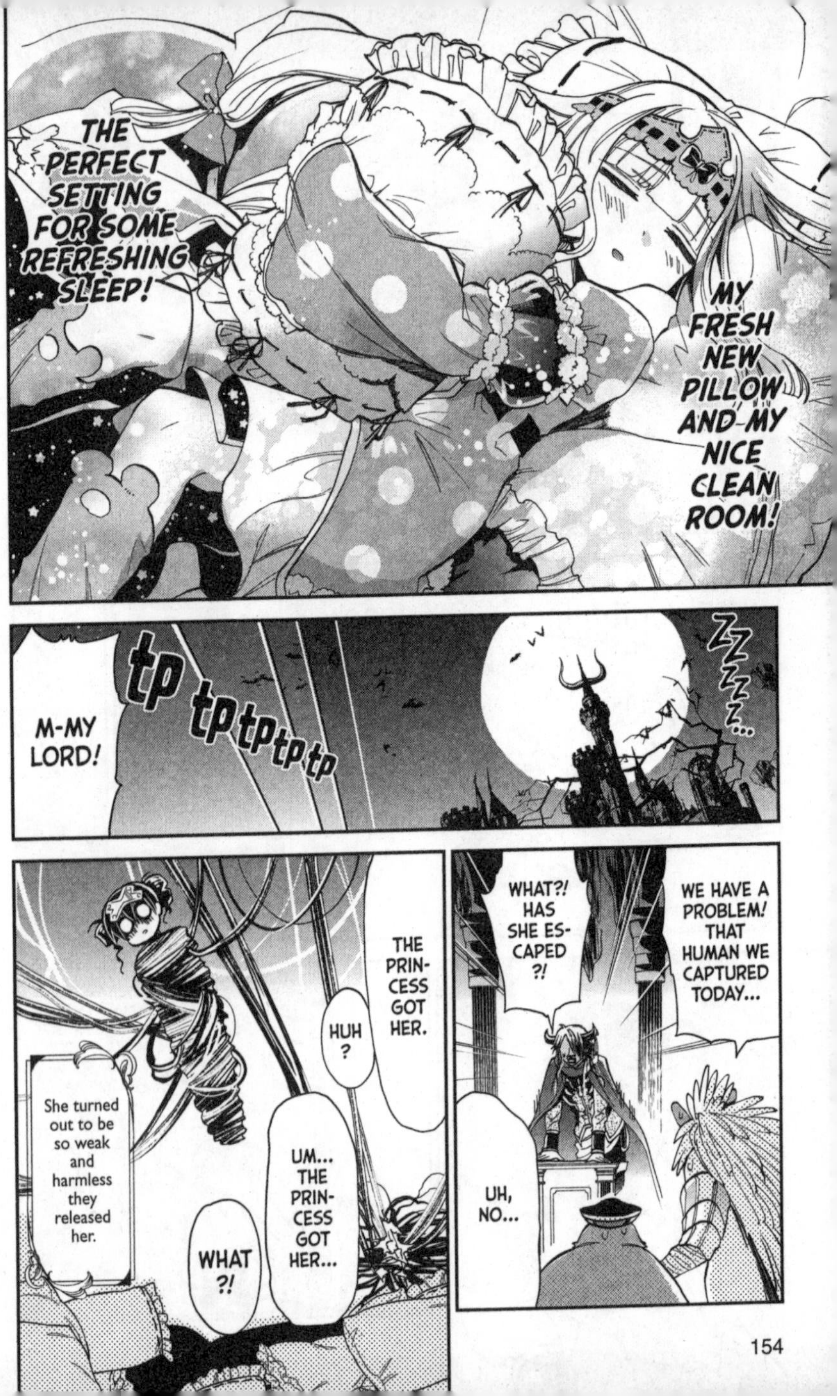
MY FRESH NEW PILLOW AND MY NICE CLEAN ROOM!
THE PERFECT SETTING FOR SOME REFRESHING SLEEP!
ZZZZZ...
tp tp tp tp tp
M-MY LORD!
WE HAVE A PROBLEM! THAT HUMAN WE CAPTURED TODAY...
WHAT?! HAS SHE ESCAPED?!
UH, NO...
THE PRINCESS GOT HER.
HUH?
UM... THE PRINCESS GOT HER...
WHAT?!
She turned out to be so weak and harmless they released her.

Kukororo Troisware

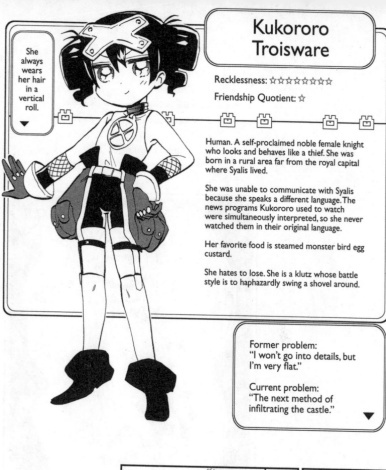

Recklessness: ☆☆☆☆☆☆☆☆☆

Friendship Quotient: ☆

She always wears her hair in a vertical roll.

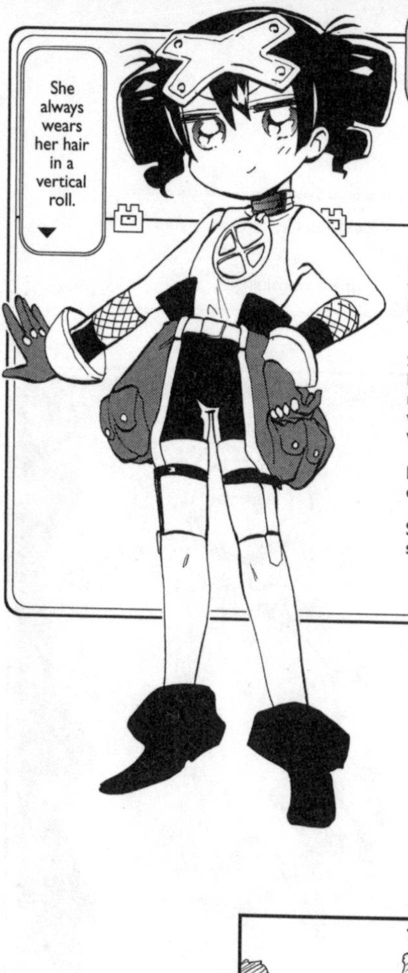

Human. A self-proclaimed noble female knight who looks and behaves like a thief. She was born in a rural area far from the royal capital where Syalis lived.

She was unable to communicate with Syalis because she speaks a different language. The news programs Kukororo used to watch were simultaneously interpreted, so she never watched them in their original language.

Her favorite food is steamed monster bird egg custard.

She hates to lose. She is a klutz whose battle style is to haphazardly swing a shovel around.

Former problem:
"I won't go into details, but I'm very flat."

Current problem:
"The next method of infiltrating the castle."

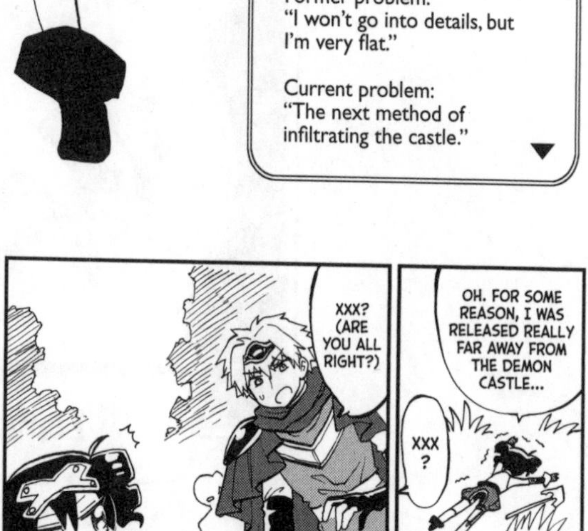
OH. FOR SOME REASON, I WAS RELEASED REALLY FAR AWAY FROM THE DEMON CASTLE...
XXX ?
HUH ?
XXX? (ARE YOU ALL RIGHT?)

Would you like to change your class?

0 changes remaining

Dancer

Dancer

" "
...

"Ha ha."

▼

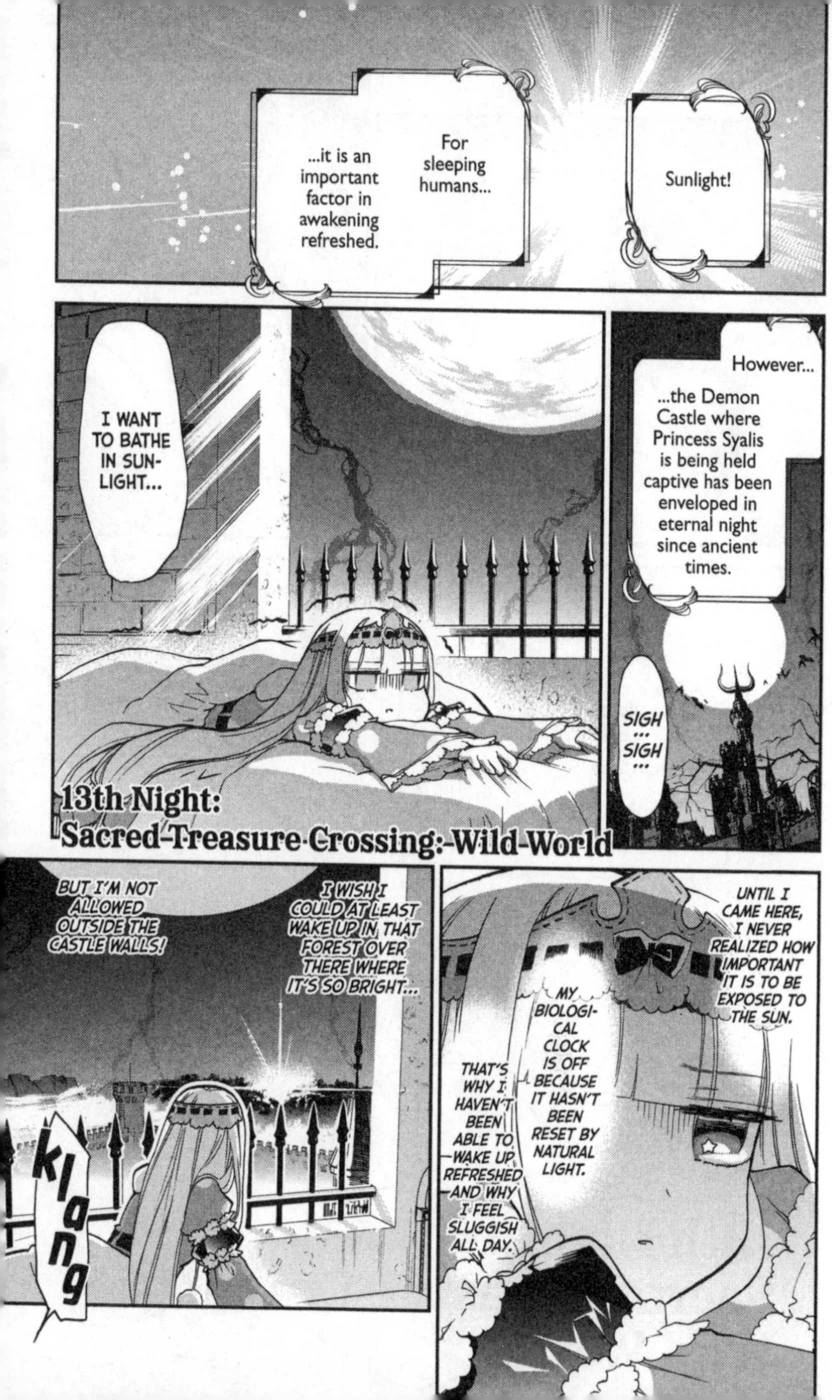
Sunlight!
For sleeping humans...
...it is an important factor in awakening refreshed.
However...
...the Demon Castle where Princess Syalis is being held captive has been enveloped in eternal night since ancient times.
SIGH... SIGH...
I WANT TO BATHE IN SUN-LIGHT...
13th Night: Sacred Treasure Crossing: Wild World
UNTIL I CAME HERE, I NEVER REALIZED HOW IMPORTANT IT IS TO BE EXPOSED TO THE SUN.
MY BIOLOGI-CAL CLOCK IS OFF BECAUSE IT HASN'T BEEN RESET BY NATURAL LIGHT.
THAT'S WHY I HAVEN'T BEEN ABLE TO WAKE UP REFRESHED AND WHY I FEEL SLUGGISH ALL DAY.
I WISH I COULD AT LEAST WAKE UP IN THAT FOREST OVER THERE WHERE IT'S SO BRIGHT...
BUT I'M NOT ALLOWED OUTSIDE THE CASTLE WALLS!
klang

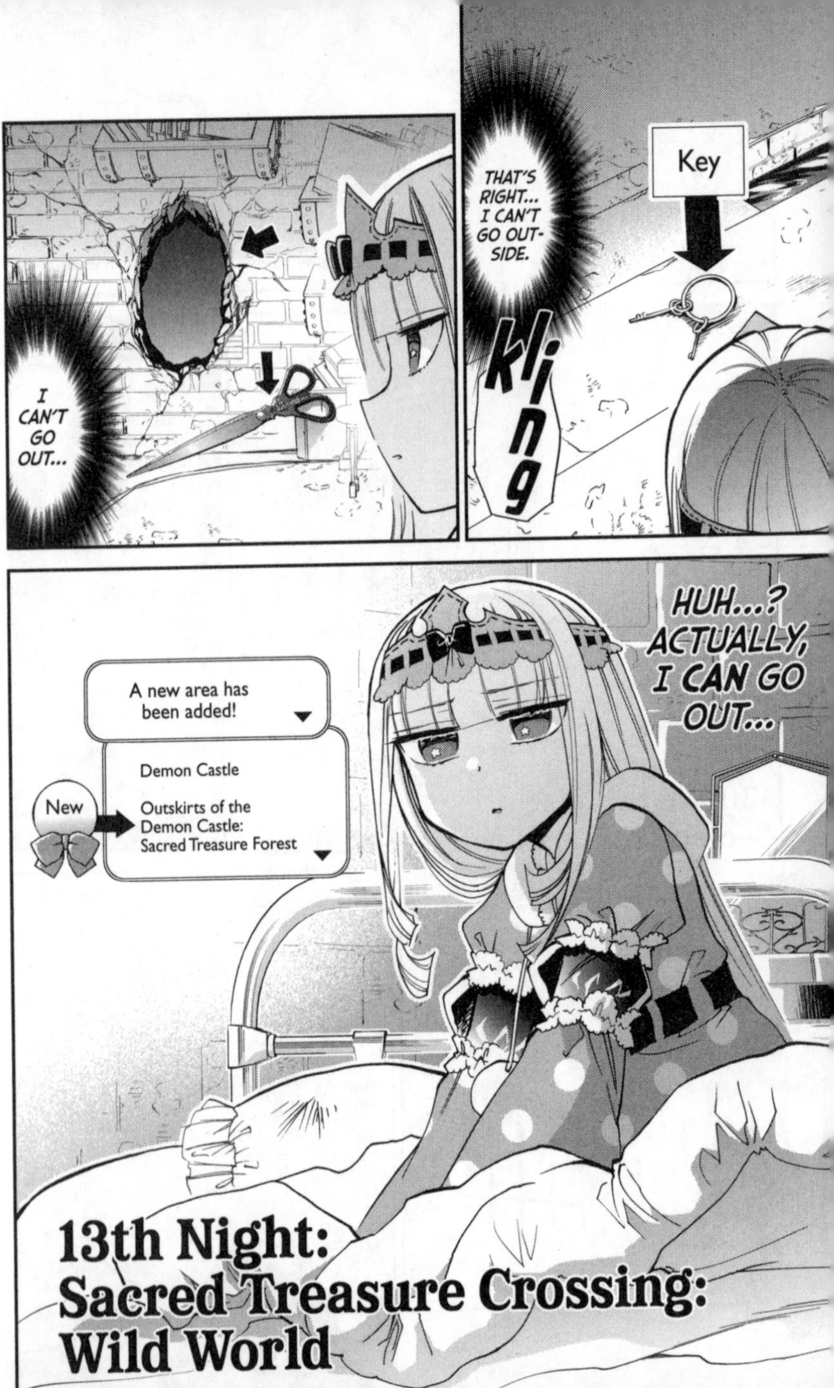
THAT'S RIGHT... I CAN'T GO OUT-SIDE.
Key
Kling
I CAN'T GO OUT...
HUH...? ACTUALLY, I CAN GO OUT...
A new area has been added!
Demon Castle
New
Outskirts of the Demon Castle: Sacred Treasure Forest

13th Night: Sacred Treasure Crossing: Wild World

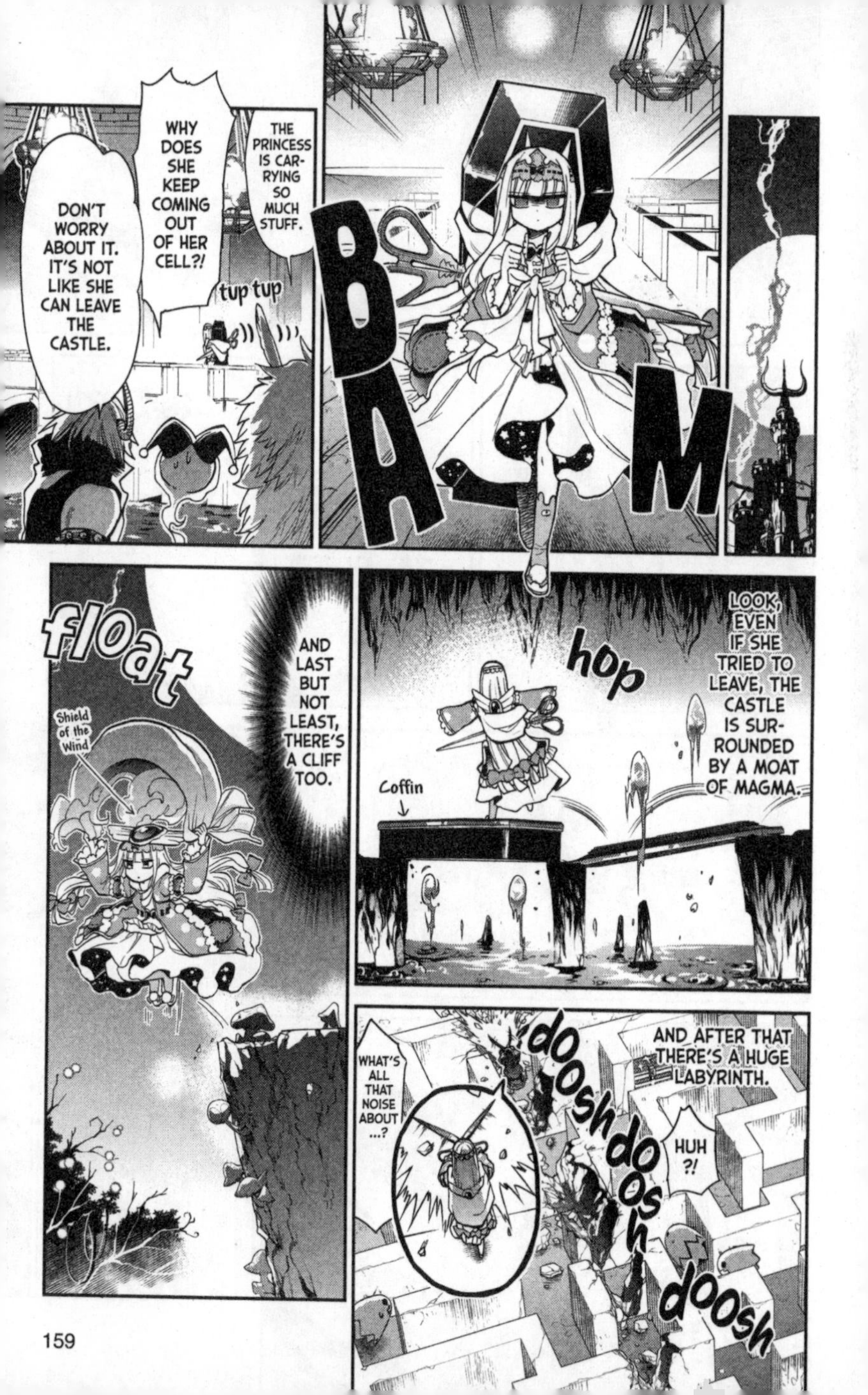
BAM
THE PRINCESS IS CARRYING SO MUCH STUFF.
WHY DOES SHE KEEP COMING OUT OF HER CELL?!
tup tup
DON'T WORRY ABOUT IT. IT'S NOT LIKE SHE CAN LEAVE THE CASTLE.
LOOK, EVEN IF SHE TRIED TO LEAVE, THE CASTLE IS SURROUNDED BY A MOAT OF MAGMA.
hop
Coffin
AND AFTER THAT THERE'S A HUGE LABYRINTH.
doosh doosh doosh doosh
HUH ?!
WHAT'S ALL THAT NOISE ABOUT ...?
float
AND LAST BUT NOT LEAST, THERE'S A CLIFF TOO.
Shield of the Wind

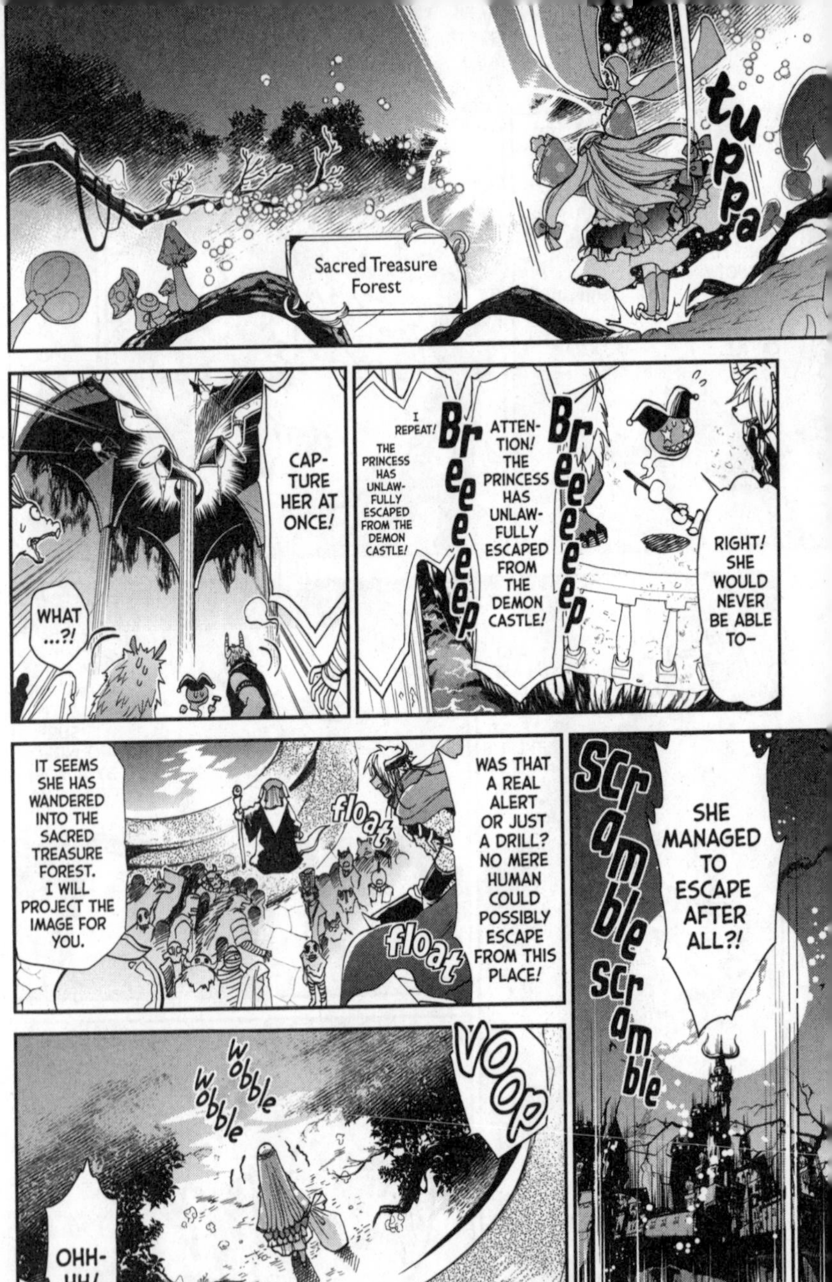
tuppa
Sacred Treasure Forest
RIGHT! SHE WOULD NEVER BE ABLE TO–
Breeeeep
ATTENTION! THE PRINCESS HAS UNLAWFULLY ESCAPED FROM THE DEMON CASTLE!
Breeeeep
I REPEAT! THE PRINCESS HAS UNLAWFULLY ESCAPED FROM THE DEMON CASTLE!
CAPTURE HER AT ONCE!
WHAT ...?!
SHE MANAGED TO ESCAPE AFTER ALL?!
scramble
scramble
WAS THAT A REAL ALERT OR JUST A DRILL? NO MERE HUMAN COULD POSSIBLY ESCAPE FROM THIS PLACE!
float
float
IT SEEMS SHE HAS WANDERED INTO THE SACRED TREASURE FOREST. I WILL PROJECT THE IMAGE FOR YOU.
VOOP
wobble
wobble
OHHHH!

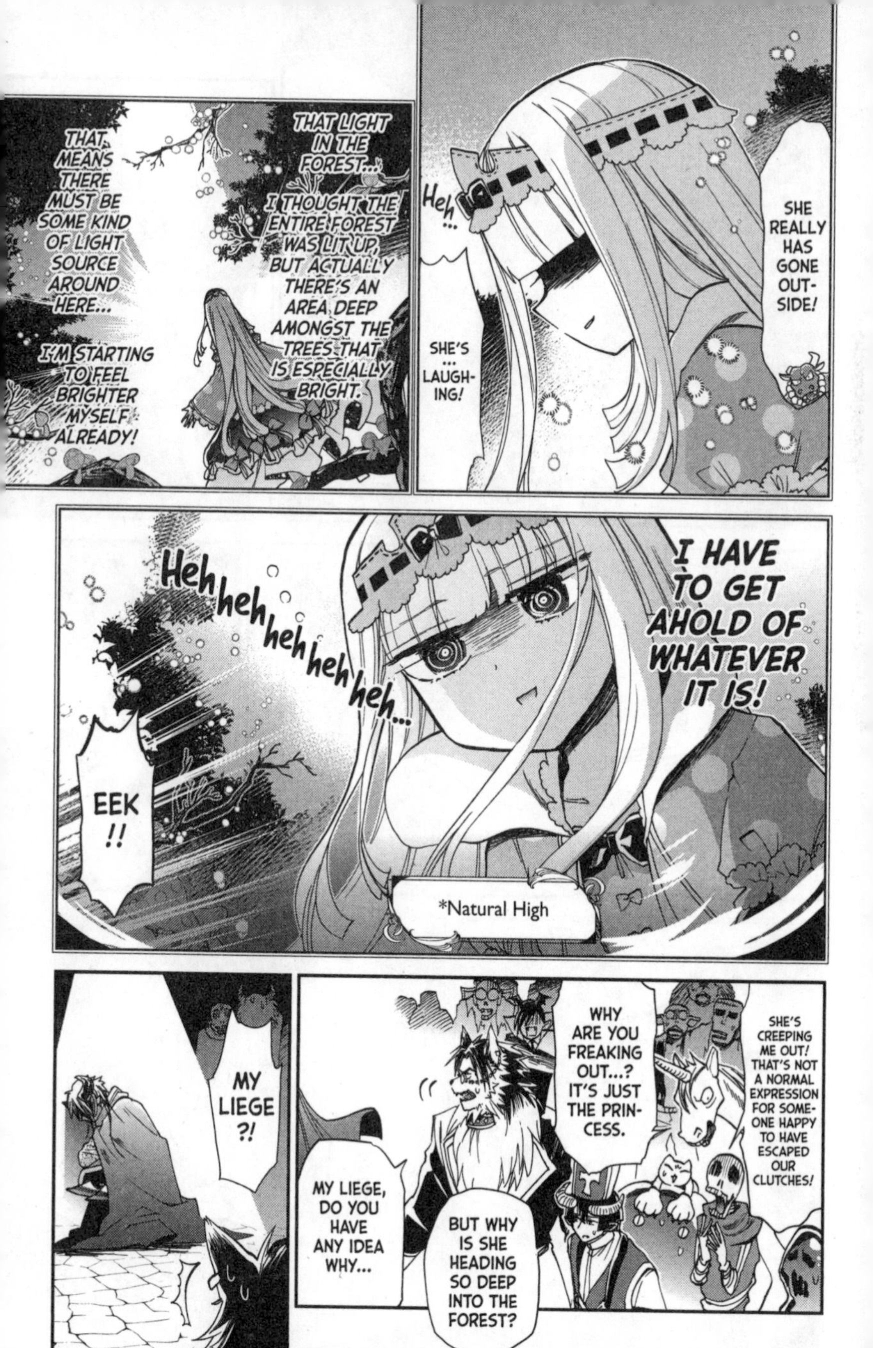
SHE REALLY HAS GONE OUT-SIDE!
Heh...
SHE'S ... LAUGH-ING!
THAT LIGHT IN THE FOREST...
I THOUGHT THE ENTIRE FOREST WAS LIT UP, BUT ACTUALLY THERE'S AN AREA DEEP AMONGST THE TREES THAT IS ESPECIALLY BRIGHT.
THAT MEANS THERE MUST BE SOME KIND OF LIGHT SOURCE AROUND HERE...
I'M STARTING TO FEEL BRIGHTER MYSELF ALREADY!
I HAVE TO GET AHOLD OF WHATEVER IT IS!
Heh heh heh heh heh...
EEK!!
*Natural High
SHE'S CREEPING ME OUT! THAT'S NOT A NORMAL EXPRESSION FOR SOME-ONE HAPPY TO HAVE ESCAPED OUR CLUTCHES!
WHY ARE YOU FREAKING OUT...? IT'S JUST THE PRIN-CESS.
BUT WHY IS SHE HEADING SO DEEP INTO THE FOREST?
MY LIEGE, DO YOU HAVE ANY IDEA WHY...
MY LIEGE?!

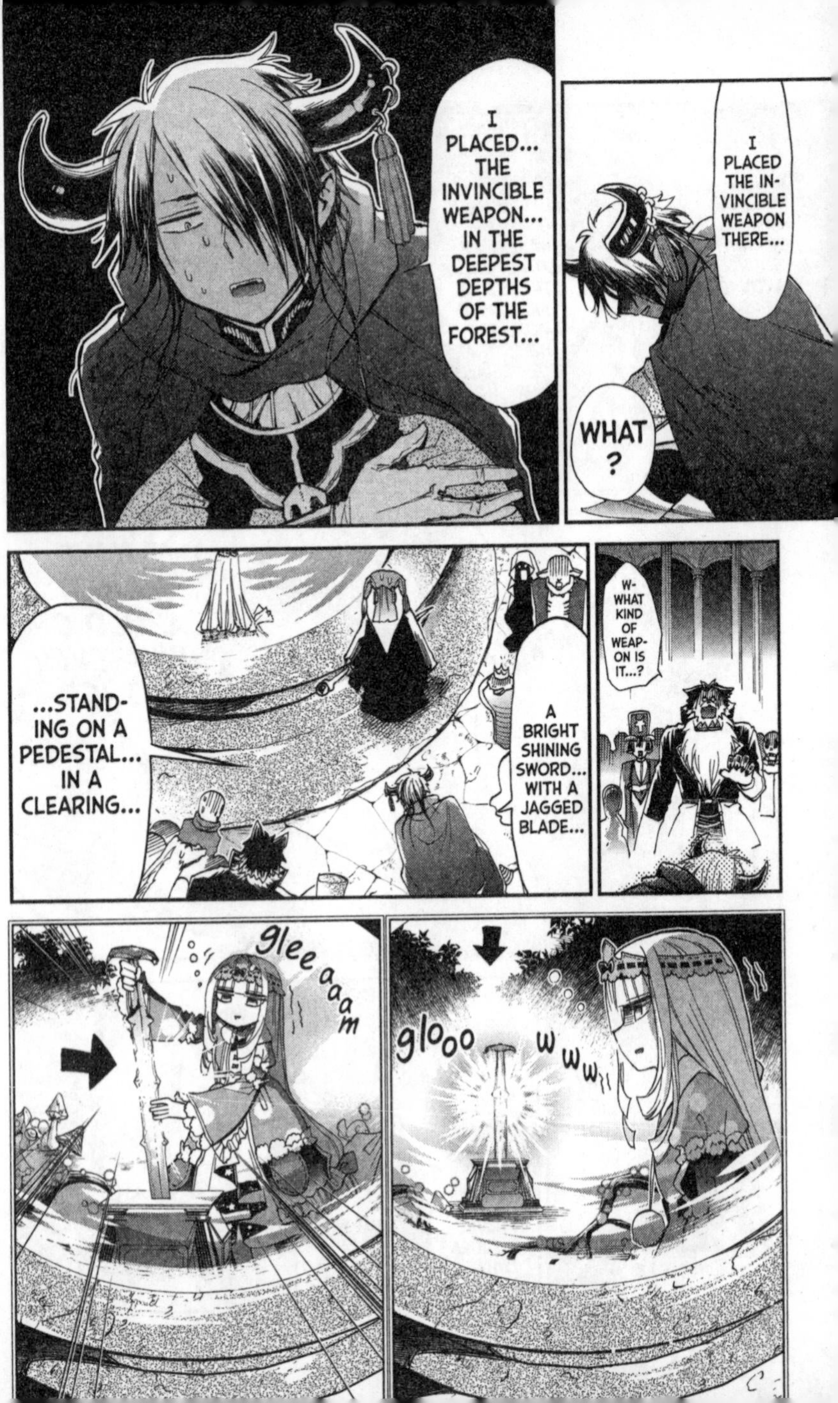
I PLACED THE IN-VINCIBLE WEAPON THERE...
WHAT?
I PLACED... THE INVINCIBLE WEAPON... IN THE DEEPEST DEPTHS OF THE FOREST...
W-WHAT KIND OF WEAP-ON IS IT...?
A BRIGHT SHINING SWORD... WITH A JAGGED BLADE...
...STAND-ING ON A PEDESTAL... IN A CLEARING...
glooowww
gleeaaam

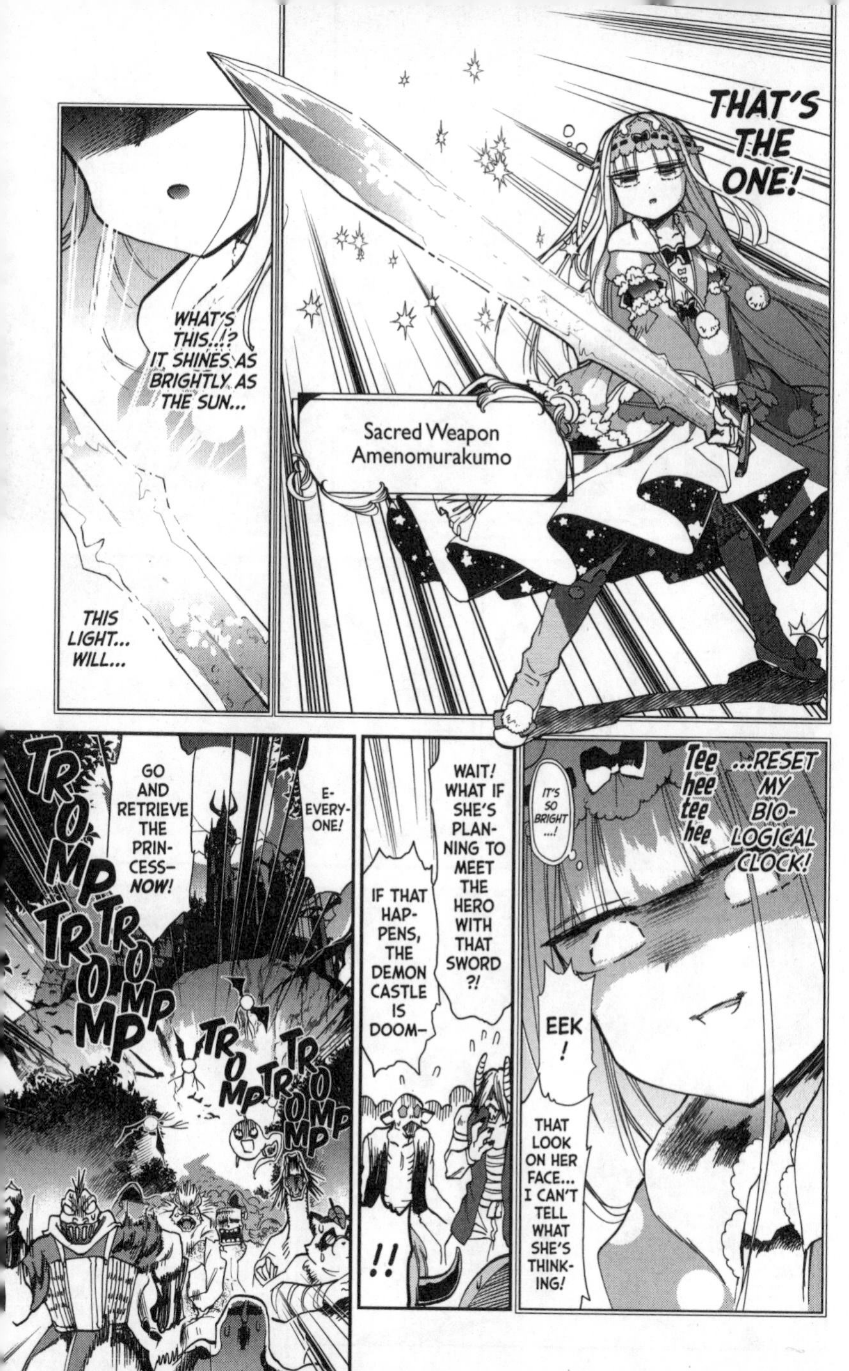

THAT'S THE ONE!
Sacred Weapon Amenomurakumo
WHAT'S THIS...!? IT SHINES AS BRIGHTLY AS THE SUN...
THIS LIGHT... WILL...
...RESET MY BIO-LOGICAL CLOCK!
Tee hee tee hee
IT'S SO BRIGHT...!
EEK!
THAT LOOK ON HER FACE... I CAN'T TELL WHAT SHE'S THINK-ING!
WAIT! WHAT IF SHE'S PLAN-NING TO MEET THE HERO WITH THAT SWORD?!
IF THAT HAP-PENS, THE DEMON CASTLE IS DOOM—
!!
E-EVERY-ONE!
GO AND RETRIEVE THE PRIN-CESS—NOW!
TROMP TROMP TROMP
TROMP TROMP TROMP

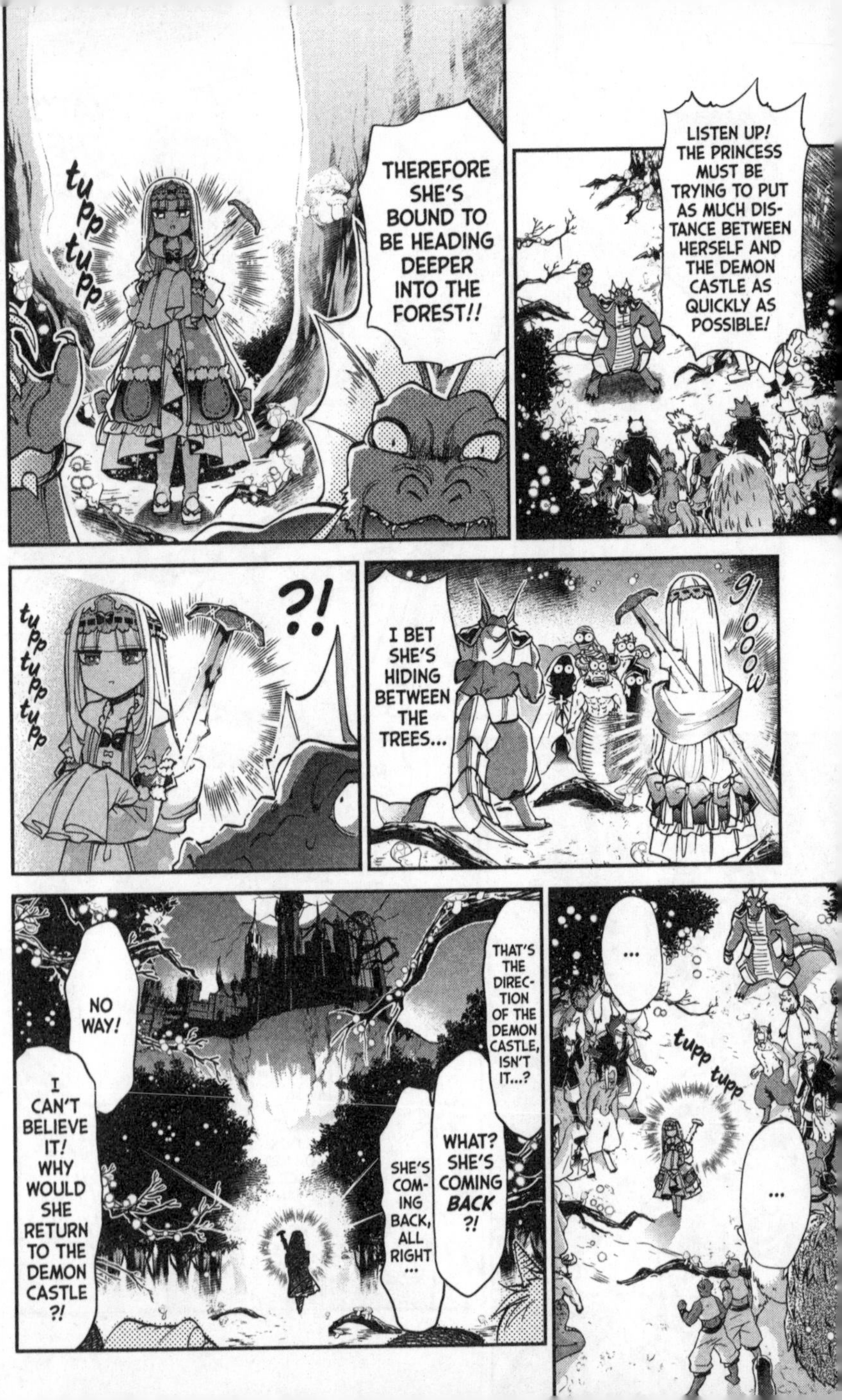
LISTEN UP! THE PRINCESS MUST BE TRYING TO PUT AS MUCH DIS-TANCE BETWEEN HERSELF AND THE DEMON CASTLE AS QUICKLY AS POSSIBLE!
THEREFORE SHE'S BOUND TO BE HEADING DEEPER INTO THE FOREST!!
tupp tupp
glooow
I BET SHE'S HIDING BETWEEN THE TREES...
?!
tupp tupp tupp
...
tupp tupp
...
THAT'S THE DIREC-TION OF THE DEMON CASTLE, ISN'T IT...?
WHAT? SHE'S COMING BACK?!
SHE'S COM-ING BACK, ALL RIGHT...
NO WAY!
I CAN'T BELIEVE IT! WHY WOULD SHE RETURN TO THE DEMON CASTLE?!

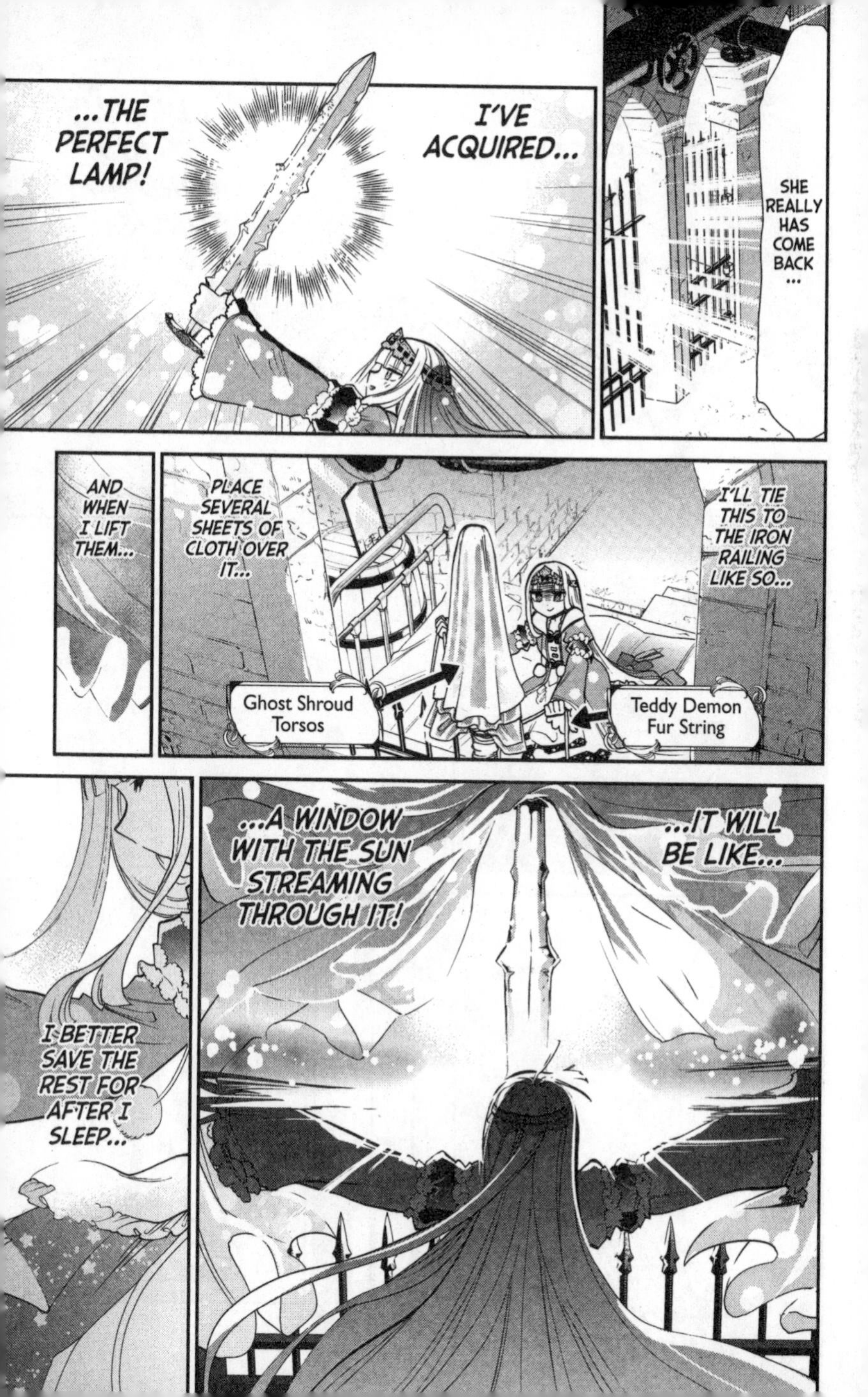
SHE REALLY HAS COME BACK...
I'VE ACQUIRED...
...THE PERFECT LAMP!
I'LL TIE THIS TO THE IRON RAILING LIKE SO...
Teddy Demon Fur String
PLACE SEVERAL SHEETS OF CLOTH OVER IT...
Ghost Shroud Torsos
AND WHEN I LIFT THEM...
...IT WILL BE LIKE...
...A WINDOW WITH THE SUN STREAMING THROUGH IT!
I BETTER SAVE THE REST FOR AFTER I SLEEP...

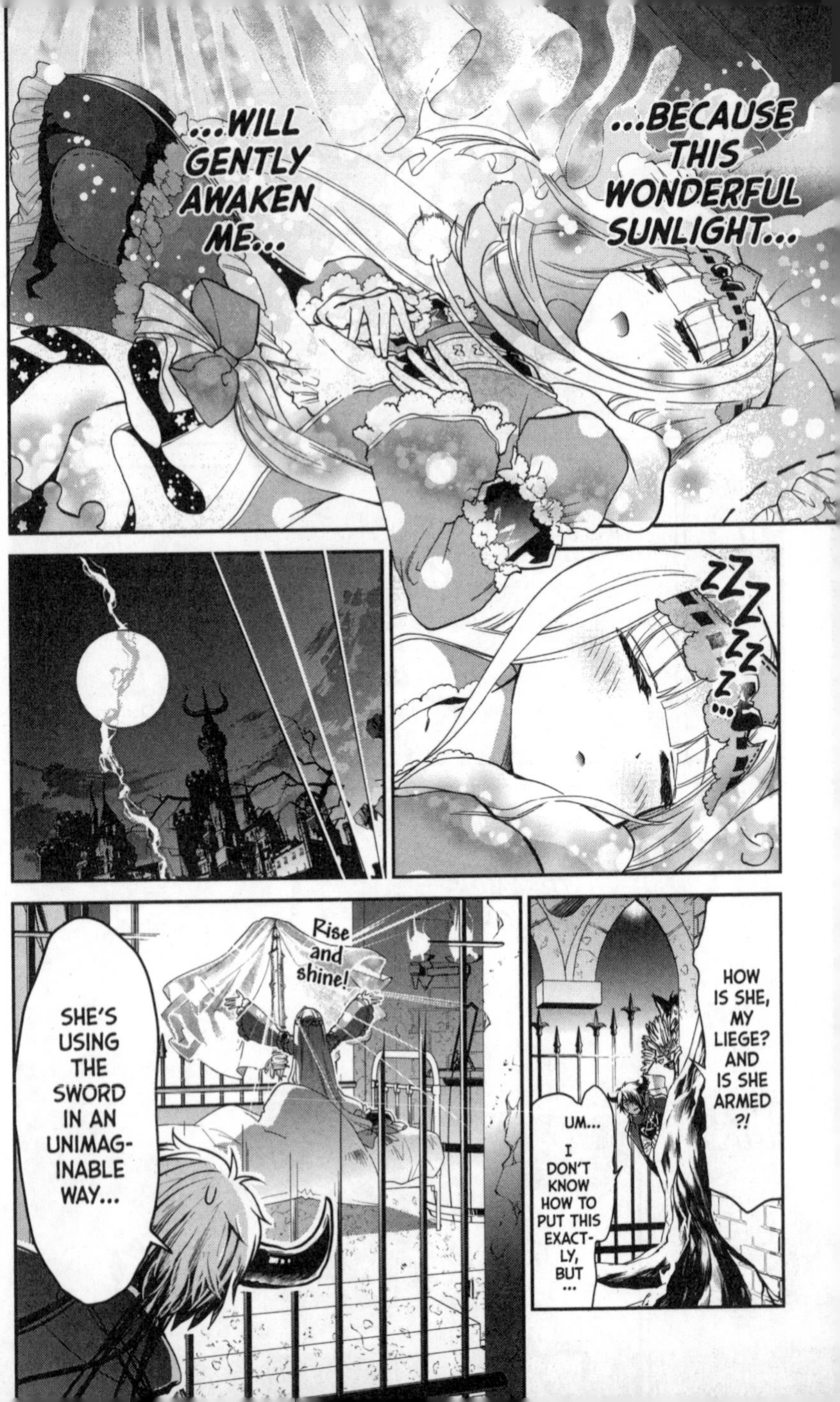
...BECAUSE THIS WONDERFUL SUNLIGHT...
...WILL GENTLY AWAKEN ME...
ZZZZZZ...
HOW IS SHE, MY LIEGE? AND IS SHE ARMED?!
UM... I DON'T KNOW HOW TO PUT THIS EXACTLY, BUT...
Rise and shine!
SHE'S USING THE SWORD IN AN UNIMAGINABLE WAY...

Demon King's Diary Entry

XXX9/XX98

The Sacred Treasure Forest is actually a secret dungeon and Amenomurakumo is a secret item, so they really have no direct impact on the hero's journey. I know that sounds like a rationalization, but...it's true.

As for the Shield of the Wind, I have no idea what happened with that either... I really do want the hero to beat that dungeon! Really!

I've created a different route for him, and the difficulty level is just right.

The princess is doing well. Too well, in my opinion... I really want to tell the hero that.

"That princess of yours is doing really, really well."

But I'm no quitter!

That's my strength!

My (THE PAGE IS TORN HERE, SO THE REST CAN'T BE READ.)

...?
ooo?
She found it on the floor.

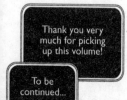

Thank you very much for picking up this volume!

To be continued...

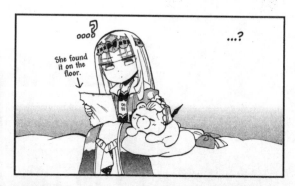

This is the first volume of *Sleepy Princess in the Demon Castle*. Thank you very much for reading it.

My pen name Kagiji Kumanomata reflects my lifestyle of hugging my beloved teddy bear every day. And my author photo is of that very teddy bear.

— KAGIJI KUMANOMATA

Luxury Bed Pillow

MATERIALS
Demon Castle Curtain
Teddy Demon Fur
Red Herb
Yellow Herb ▼

Those who lurk beneath the cover...

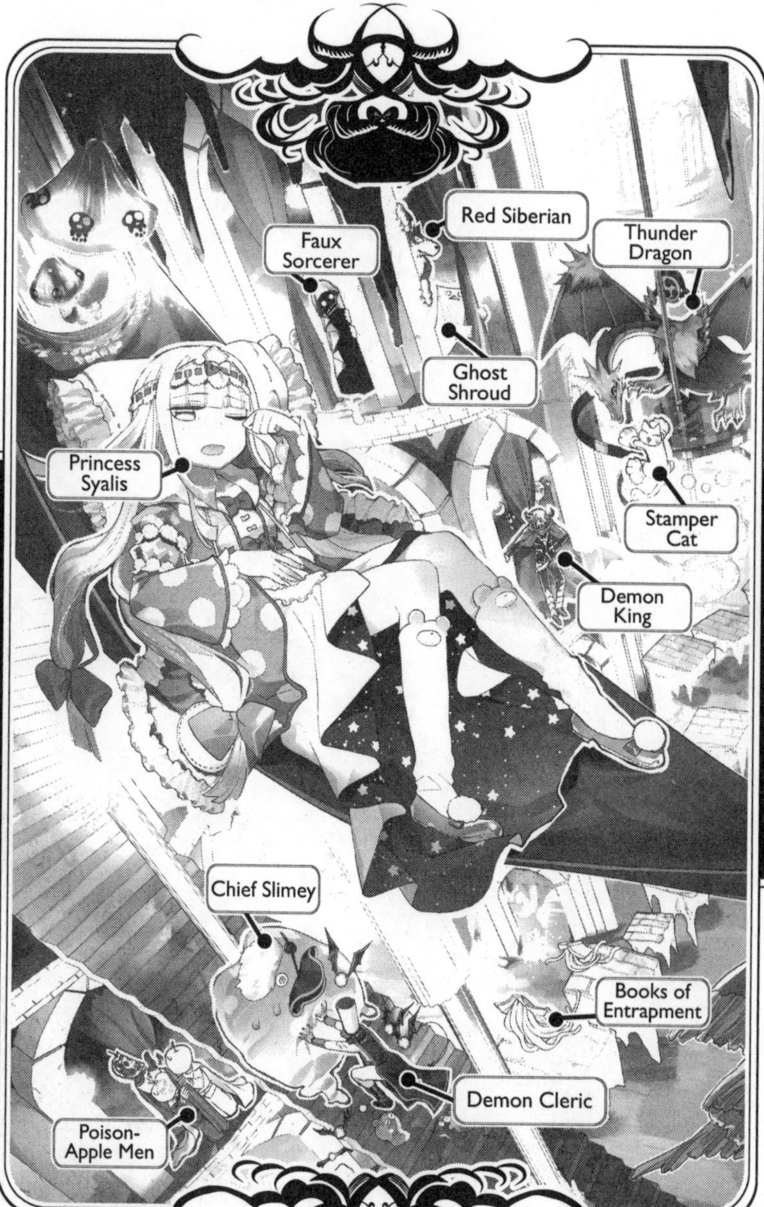

Red Siberian
Thunder Dragon
Faux Sorcerer
Ghost Shroud
Princess Syalis
Stamper Cat
Demon King
Chief Slimey
Books of Entrapment
Demon Cleric
Poison-Apple Men

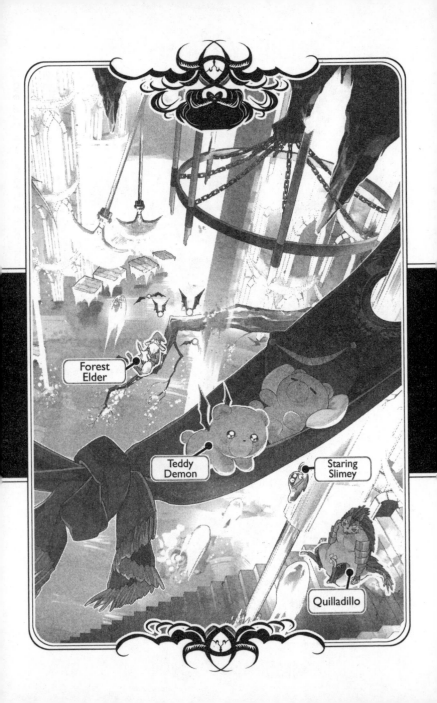

Forest Elder

Teddy Demon

Staring Slimey

Quilladillo

SLEEPY PRINCESS IN THE DEMON CASTLE

1

Shonen Sunday Edition

STORY AND ART BY

KAGIJI KUMANOMATA

MAOUJO DE OYASUMI Vol. 1
by Kagiji KUMANOMATA
© 2016 Kagiji KUMANOMATA
All rights reserved.
Original Japanese edition published by SHOGAKUKAN.
English translation rights in the United States of America, Canada,
the United Kingdom, Ireland, Australia and New Zealand arranged
with SHOGAKUKAN.

TRANSLATION **TETSUICHIRO MIYAKI**

ENGLISH ADAPTATION **ANNETTE ROMAN**

TOUCH-UP ART & LETTERING **SUSAN DAIGLE-LEACH**

COVER & INTERIOR DESIGN **ALICE LEWIS**

EDITOR **ANNETTE ROMAN**

Printed in Italy

Published by VIZ Media, LLC
P.O. Box 77010
San Francisco, CA 94107

10 9 8 7 6 5 4 3 2
First printing, June 2018
Second printing, April 2022

viz.com   shonensunday.com

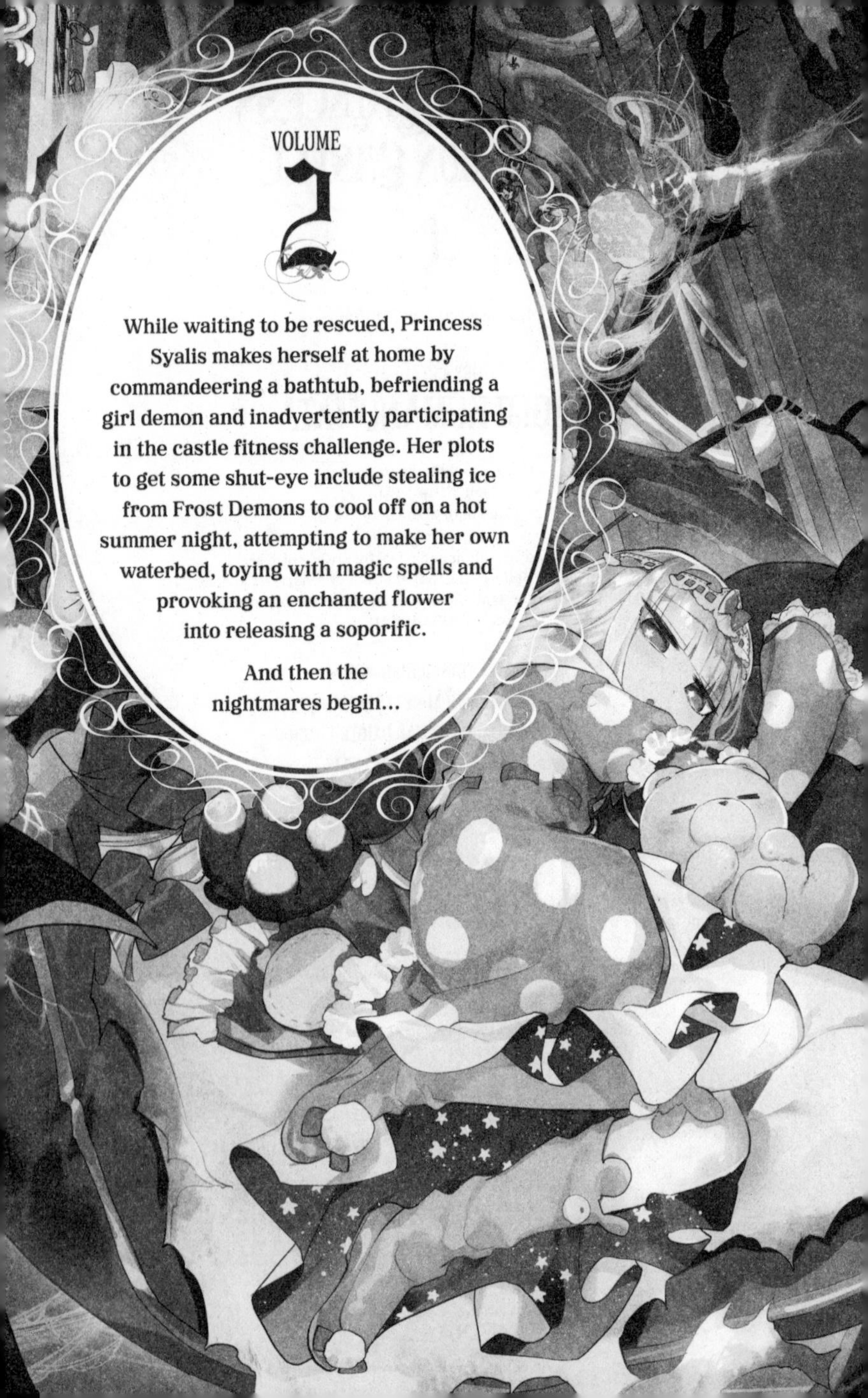
VOLUME
2
While waiting to be rescued, Princess Syalis makes herself at home by commandeering a bathtub, befriending a girl demon and inadvertently participating in the castle fitness challenge. Her plots to get some shut-eye include stealing ice from Frost Demons to cool off on a hot summer night, attempting to make her own waterbed, toying with magic spells and provoking an enchanted flower into releasing a soporific.
And then the nightmares begin...

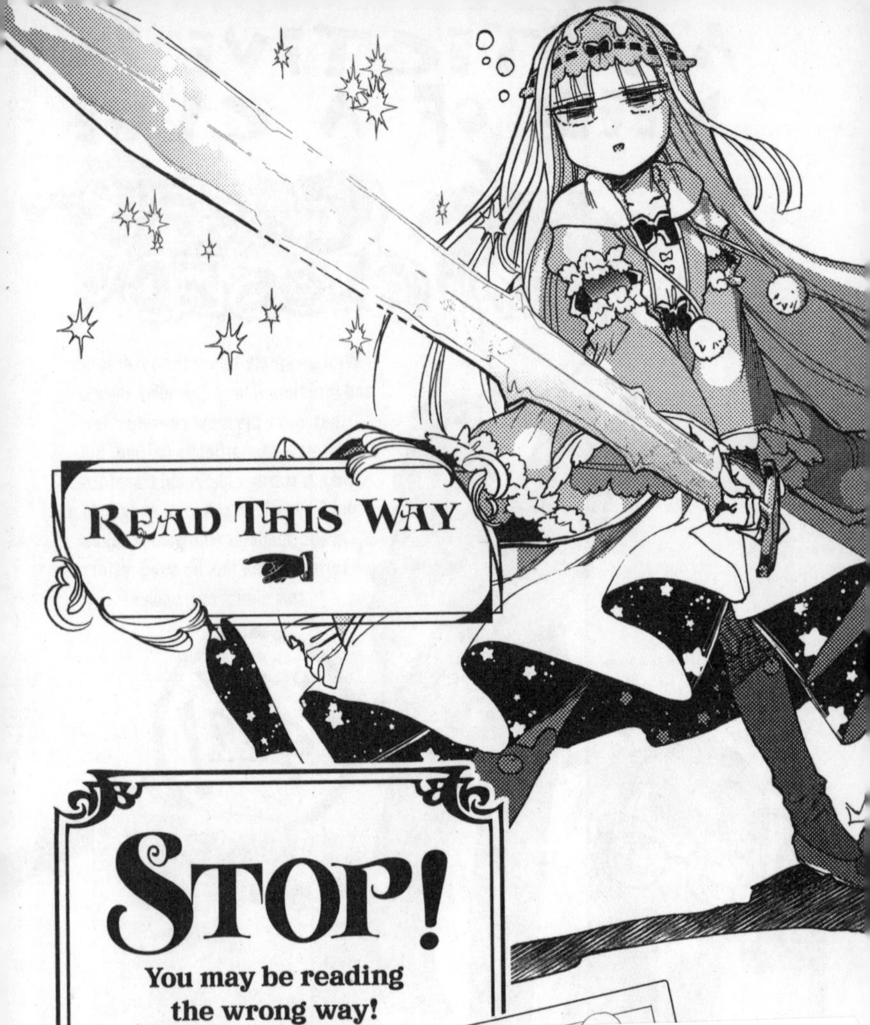
READ THIS WAY

STOP!

You may be reading the wrong way!

In keeping with the origi
Japanese comic format, this
reads from right to left—so a
sound effects and word ballo
completely reversed to prese
orientation of the original ar

Check out the diagram shown here to get the hang of things, and then turn to the other side of the book to get started!